GROW YOUR OWN VEGETABLES

JOY LARKCOM

ILLUSTRATIONS BY
ELIZABETH DOUGLASS

FRANCES LINCOLN LIMITED

To our dear granddaughter Jamila Celeste Aisla Rose

and with a special thank you to all my friends in the seed trade,
who have given me so much help in thirty years of garden writing

GROW YOUR OWN VEGETABLES

Frances Lincoln Limited
4 Torriano Mews
Torriano Avenue
London NW5 2RZ

Copyright © Frances Lincoln Limited 2002
Text copyright © Joy Larkcom 2002
Edited by Anne Askwith
Designed by Jane Havell
Illustrations by Elizabeth Douglass

First Frances Lincoln edition: 2002

First published in hardback as *Vegetables from Small Gardens*, Faber & Faber, 1976
Revised and reprinted as paperback 1986
Revised paperback edition *Vegetables for Small Gardens*,
Hamlyn/Reed Consumer Books, 1995

All rights reserved. No part of this publication may be reproduced, stored
in a retrieval system or transmitted, in any form, or by any means, electronic,
mechanical, photocopying, recording or otherwise, without either prior permission
in writing from the publishers or a licence permitting restricted copying. In the
United Kingdom such licences are issued by the Copyright Licensing Agency,
90 Tottenham Court Road, London W1P

ISBN 0 7112 1963 X

Printed in England

9 8 7 6

CONTENTS

Introduction   8
    Useful definitions and symbols   15

I   TOOLS AND EQUIPMENT   16

2   THE VEGETABLE GARDEN SITE   19

3   SOIL, MANURE AND COMPOST   26

4   DIGGING, MULCHING, WEEDING AND WATERING   66

5   SEED, SOWING AND PLANTING   81

6   PROTECTION   107

7   PESTS AND DISEASES   132

8   SPACE SAVING AND PRODUCTIVITY   152

9   PLANNING   175
    Feed the Family Plan   184
    Gourmet Plan   186
    Planning Information: annual vegetables   188

VEGETABLE DIRECTORY   190

Amaranthus, leaf   192
Artichoke, Chinese   193
Artichoke, globe   194
Artichoke, Jerusalem   195
Asparagus   196
Asparagus pea   198
Aubergine   199
Bean, broad   201
Beans, French   203
Bean, runner   205
Bean sprouts   208
Beetroot   210

Broccoli, Chinese	213
Broccolis, hybrid	214
Broccoli raab	215
Broccoli, sprouting	216
Brussels sprouts	217
Cabbage	219
Calabrese	225
Carrots	226
Cauliflower	231
Celeriac	234
Celery	235
Chenopodium giganteum 'Magentaspreen'	238
Chicory	239
Chinese cabbage	245
Choy sum group	246
Chrysanthemum greens	248
Corn salad	249
Courgettes	250
Cucumber	252
Endive	257
Florence fennel	259
Garlic	260
Hamburg parsley	263
Iceplant	263
Kales	264
Kohl rabi	268
Komatsuna	270
Land cress	271
Leeks	272
Lettuce	275
Marrows (squash, summer)	281
Mibuna greens	283
Mizuna greens	283
Mustard, salad rape, garden cress	284
Mustards, oriental	286
Onions	288
Orache	294
Oriental saladini	295
Pak choi	296

Parsnip   298
Peas   300
Pepper   305
Potatoes   307
Purslane, summer   314
Purslane, winter   315
Radish   316
Rhubarb   318
Rocket   320
Saladini   321
Salsify   322
Scorzonera   323
Senposai hybrids   324
Shallots   324
Spinach group   326
Squash, winter, and pumpkins   330
Swede   333
Sweet corn   334
Texsel greens   337
Tomato   339
Turnip   347

SEASONAL GUIDE TO MAIN GARDEN JOBS   350

APPENDIX
    Quick-maturing vegetables   358
    Cut-and-come-again seedlings chart   359
    Vegetables for successional sowing   360
    Vegetables in the ground all winter   360
    Fresh vegetables for the Vegetable Gap   362
    Vegetables suitable for freezing   362
    Vegetables for particular situations   362
    Vegetables for flower beds   364
    Vegetable groups for strip cropping with cloches   365
    Mind the Gap   367

Further reading   372
Seed suppliers   374
Acknowledgments   376
Index   378

INTRODUCTION

Little did I imagine when I started work on this book's forerunner, *Vegetables from Small Gardens*, on my old typewriter back in 1974 that I would be revising it for the third time on a laptop computer in the twenty-first century. Many things have changed beyond recognition in the intervening thirty years and, for most of us, the pace of life has accelerated. Perhaps this, coupled with increasing anxieties about the safety and quality of so much of our food, lies behind the current revival of interest in growing vegetables. Seed companies are reporting higher sales of vegetable seeds than for many years, in many cases outstripping the sales of flower seeds.

This is an interesting parallel with what was happening in the mid-1970s, when a new generation was discovering the delights and satisfaction of growing their own vegetables. It is always hard to pinpoint what lies behind a trend, but it seemed then that the limited choice and poor flavour of shop vegetables, coupled with growing wariness of the chemicals used by commercial vegetable growers, were underlying reasons. Today there is indisputably a far wider choice of vegetables in shops and markets, and far more interest in using both ordinary and exotic vegetables. At the same time the number of vegetarians has risen dramatically, with many people, for various reasons, cutting down on the amount of meat in their diets and eating more fruit and vegetables. And just as it is no longer considered odd to be vegetarian, it is no longer odd to garden organically. In the shadow of global warming, we are learning, perhaps belatedly, the importance of caring for our environment, and that there is no better place to start than in our own gardens.

The first extensive revision of the book was in 1986, in the wake of a great deal of research into commercial vegetable growing. Much of this had a bearing on home gardening, throwing new scientific light on traditional practices and 'hunch'. The new research told us precisely how spacing can be varied to get the size of vegetable we require, the stage in a plant's cycle when it most pays to water and so on. Much of this work was undertaken in the UK at what was then the National Vegetable Research Station (now part of Horticulture Research International), and the material was relayed to the gardening public in the two volumes of *Know and Grow Vegetables*, subsequently republished in one volume as *The Complete Know and Grow Vegetables*. This book is fascinating reading for anyone interested in vegetable growing and I made extensive use of it in revising *Vegetables from Small Gardens* in 1986.

Another reason for updating then, and again in 1995, lay in the rapid changes in vegetable varieties available to gardeners. (Strictly speaking we should refer to 'varieties' as 'cultivars' – the correct scientific term for varieties raised in cultivation – but the term 'varieties' lives on in popular parlance. In this book I use the terms synonymously.) Many excellent new cultivars were, and still are, being introduced by plant breeders but, at the same time, many old varieties were being withdrawn in Europe largely as a result of European Union legislation. While this has had some benefits, for example in clarifying the situation where one variety masqueraded under a dozen different names, it has meant that some old favourites, valued by home gardeners if not by commercial growers, have been withdrawn. And who knows what latent, potentially useful, genetic characteristics these old varieties may have. Fortunately organizations such as the Henry Doubleday Research Association in the UK and Seed Savers Exchange in the US have made it their business to collect and preserve old 'heritage' varieties in seed libraries, making seed available to their members. They deserve our full support. Heritage varieties are often interesting and rewarding to grow, but I would also urge gardeners to make the most of the undeniable merits of many of the new cultivars.

A third reason for the 1986 revision was much more personal. Not long after *Vegetables from Small Gardens* was published, our family – my husband Don Pollard and our children Brendan and Kirsten, then aged seven and five – set off for a year on what we called 'the Grand Vegetable Tour'. With a caravan as our home, we travelled around Europe in a southward arc from Holland to Hungary, visiting eight countries in all. Our purpose was to study traditional and modern methods of vegetable growing, and to collect the seed of old, local vegetable varieties which were in danger of dying out. We eventually sent over 100 samples to the national Vegetable Gene Bank at Wellesbourne, which was in the process of being established.

I learnt an enormous amount from that year of travel. Not only did we 'discover' many new plants, for example summer and winter purslane, iceplant, salad rocket and the many beautiful red and related chicories, but we saw at first hand the traditional intensive methods of vegetable growing used on the Continent, now widely known under the umbrella term 'cut-and-come-again'. These are explained fully later (see page 156), but in essence, they are used for growing wonderfully tasty salad seedlings which regenerate after the first, and sometimes after the second and third cutting. The same principle can be applied to mature crops, a fair number (including endives, oriental greens and cabbages) having the ability to regenerate even after the first main head has been harvested, so prolonging their useful life over many months. Combining these techniques with the traditional practice of spacing plants closely in narrow beds is a highly productive approach to gardening, and relevant to the modern gardener, for whom space is often at a premium.

When we returned from our tour we experimented with these new plants and methods in the small organic market garden we then established, finding much of what we had learnt particularly relevant to small gardens. These ideas were incorporated in the revised edition.

I should add here that while the earlier editions of this book were directed towards small gardens, in this edition the scope is broadened to make it useful for all gardeners. The emphasis is still on maximizing returns from whatever space is at your disposal – after all, even if you have a large garden, the smaller the area devoted to vegetables, the easier it will be to manage. But this edition includes some of the larger, slower-growing and space-consuming vegetables that were previously omitted, such as large cauliflowers, pumpkins and other squashes, maincrop potatoes, orache and the colourful giant spinach *Chenopodium giganteum* 'Magentaspreen'. It also includes the cultivation of cucumbers and tomatoes in unheated greenhouses, popular crops with gardeners in coolish climates. Perennial vegetables, such as asparagus, seakale and rhubarb, are covered in more detail than previously. The new title, *Grow Your Own Vegetables*, reflects the increased scope.

In much of the Western world today there is a bewildering range of vegetables in supermarkets and street markets, imported from all corners of the globe. Only a proportion can be grown satisfactorily in cool climates, although who knows what marginal crops will become mainstream if global warming brings significant changes in climate. For the moment, however, I have concentrated on crops that are guaranteed to succeed in the moderately cool climate of the British Isles.

Since our Grand Vegetable Tour my own excursions into foreign fields have focused on oriental vegetables. I was lured by the tempting names of unknown plants, many of which I originally spotted in Japanese seed catalogues. The quest for knowledge took me over the years to China, Japan, Taiwan, the US and Canada – and it is probably true to say that the whole character of our garden has changed as a result of these excursions. We now grow a wide range of oriental vegetables, concentrating on the many types of greens. As it happens, in our climate most of these are at their best from late summer to early spring. So they follow on naturally from our standard summer vegetables and offer variety during the leaner vegetable months. Almost all these oriental greens can be grown as cut-and-come-again crops, both as seedlings and at more mature stages, making them some of the most productive vegetables for temperate climates. The full story is told in my book *Oriental Vegetables*, but very many of them are included here. I strongly recommend them to gardeners with limited space and to gardening cooks longing for exotic variety, especially during the winter months. In common with other members of the brassica family, these oriental greens are a source of acknowledged agents which help prevent cancer.

To make space for the oriental newcomers, culinary herbs were squeezed out of the last edition, but I have covered their cultivation fully in the earlier companion volume *Salads from Small Gardens* and in the recently published *The Organic Salad Garden*. These two books also include a number of vegetables not covered in this edition, as do my earlier books *Oriental Vegetables* and *Creative Vegetable Gardening*. For details, see Further Reading, page 372.

Many of the oriental vegetables are beautiful to look at, which brings me to another aspect of vegetable growing close to my heart – the marriage of utility and beauty in the kitchen garden. While many owners of small gardens are content to devote the whole space to vegetable growing, others long for the colour and beauty associated with flowers. The answer, I feel, lies in the 'potager' approach – potager being shorthand for a decorative vegetable garden. On a grand scale this implies laying out the kitchen garden in a (usually symmetrical) pattern of designed beds, with trellises, arches and espalier fruit forming the background and linking the beds. The vegetables grown are selected, to some extent, for their decorative qualities, and are often planted in groups, rather than rows, to enhance the effect. Flowers, herbs and fruit can be grown among, beside or around the groups to create a beautiful, colourful vegetable garden.

I feel strongly that this approach can be applied on a much smaller, cottage garden scale, so that even a tiny vegetable plot can be as colourful as any conventional garden devoted to flowers and shrubs. Vegetables can also be incorporated into ordinary flower gardens. You can use arches and trellises for climbing beans and cucumbers; edge beds with herbs and the pretty Salad Bowl types of lettuce; sneak a few plants of the purple-leaved 'Bull's Blood' beet or ornamental kale into a flower bed; or include asparagus, a most beautiful fern-like plant, in a herbaceous border. This book is not about potagers, but where plants have decorative qualities which lend themselves to potager treatment, they will be pointed out. My book *Creative Vegetable Gardening* focuses on potagers.

Ever since returning from the Grand Vegetable Tour we have gardened organically. We no longer use any artificial fertilizers, chemical weedkillers or pesticides, other than the few approved by the organic standards authorities in this country, which rapidly break down into non-toxic compounds, doing minimal damage to other life forms.

Organic gardening undoubtedly involves a little more labour than chemically aided gardening. Building up soil fertility with manure and compost, keeping beds and paths mulched to control weeds and hand-picking pests all require physical effort – but the effort is repaid. The soil and the garden environment steadily improve, with an army of natural predators building up within the garden to help keep down pests. The joy of eating fresh produce untainted by chemicals far outweighs the unsightliness of the odd caterpillar-carved hole. Compared to nonorganically grown vegetables, those grown organically keep fresh longer after picking – greengrocers can confirm that – and most people find they are better flavoured. That, of course, is harder to prove. Certainly the quality of true freshness, from vegetables picked often less than an hour before they are eaten, is rarely found in shop-bought vegetables. It is a sad commentary on our times that some people have so little experience of eating 'real' vegetables that they complain about their 'strong' flavour! An optimistic sign is that the supermarkets, responding to consumer demand, are beginning to show an interest in flavour as opposed to appearance: tomatoes no longer have to be perfectly red and round to sell (though the skins still have to be tough enough to withstand transport).

The now widespread acceptance of the organic philosophy among gardeners has been accompanied by research into organic methods, some government-financed, focused mainly on pest and disease control and variety trials. Organic gardeners need varieties with resistance to pests and diseases, as well as natural vigour, enabling them to outstrip weeds and overcome adverse weather and soil conditions. Some of the research has been prompted by the fact that pests have built up resistance to the chemicals previously used to control them, so even commercial growers have been forced to resort to more benign methods, such as 'biological control', where a pest's natural enemy is introduced to control it. Although successful use of biological control agents requires some skill, they are a boon to organic gardeners. And the range of pests that can be controlled is continually being extended. Among recent developments, and I still have not tried them myself, is the control of leatherjackets (the grubs of the cranefly) and chafer grubs with parasitic nematodes.

And now a few words for the twenty-first-century gardener, especially to those for whom gardening is a new venture or who are growing vegetables for the first time. While classical books on vegetable growing assumed that the vegetable garden was in that ideal 'open site', many of today's gardeners are more likely to be struggling with a garden overshadowed by a neighbouring house, even a tower block, with the wind funnelling across the plot through the gap between their house and the next. Gardening books in the past tended to assume that your garden had reasonably fertile, well-drained soil, and advocated three- and four-year rotations to help maintain fertility, but it is not unusual for the modern gardener to be faced initially with a waterlogged patch of raw-looking clay, or little more than a pile of rubble the builders left behind – and you can't practise much rotation on a pocket handkerchief.

It's no good pretending that vegetables will grow anywhere. The old standbys of the kitchen garden – Brussels sprouts, cauliflowers, leeks and cabbages, for example – need good conditions and there is no getting away from that; the same holds true for the newer oriental greens. A lot of work has to be done to bring poor sites into a sufficiently fertile state to grow the more demanding vegetables. But it can be done, with even the most unpromising sites. Just be resigned to the fact that it may take a year or two: nature can be helped but not hurried. In the meantime you can make small areas fertile enough to grow less fussy or fast-growing crops such as radishes, turnips and salad seedlings; or you can make a start with tomatoes in pots, or lettuces and herbs in a window box, tub or growing bag.

Every family wants something different from their vegetable plot. It is obviously difficult to keep an average family fully supplied with vegetables from a very small plot but it is quite feasible in, say, a plot that is ten metres (roughly ten yards) square to have something worthwhile from the garden all year round. If you are prepared to put the whole garden down to small patches of cut-and-come-again seedlings, you could keep the family in greens and salads all year round.

The decision about what to grow is a very personal one. Some prefer to concentrate on vegetables that are difficult or expensive to buy locally. Others concentrate on those which lose most, in terms of quality and flavour, in the journey from field to shop to consumer – the flavour of freshly picked peas and sweet corn, for instance, or young carrots just pulled from the ground, is a world apart from anything you can buy. For others it is a question of maximum bulk. To this end, the descriptions of individual vegetables in the Vegetable Directory (pages 190–349) include a rough-and-ready 'value for space' rating for each vegetable.

The vegetable lover with a small garden is inevitably trying to get the proverbial quart out of a pint pot. The intensive cultivation methods which make this possible – catch cropping, intercropping and cut-and-come-again techniques – depend largely on soil fertility (see Chapter 3). Today's gardeners have other assets to draw on as well. Plant breeders have produced new cultivars that not only often have good disease resistance but are also compact, faster-maturing and higher-yielding. These can often be planted more closely than old-fashioned varieties and are much more productive. Then there are the new materials, from fleeces that offer protection from the cold and wind, to fine nets that exclude flying pests and polytunnels that can double any garden's capacity.

Newcomers to vegetable growing are sometimes at a loss as to how to start, and feel that they are bombarded with conflicting advice. This is hardly surprising: gardening is a very inexact science, and there are few wrong or right answers. What works one year may well fail the next; what is suitable for a mild coastal area would be most inappropriate in a hilly inland area. Each soil has its own characteristics. The real gardener is inevitably an experimenter, continually trying out different ideas until discovering what is best for their conditions and their requirements.

Then there is the weather. One of the first lessons we have to learn is the role played by our climate. A gardener is not quite his own boss: the 'master plan' is preordained by the seasons. Long ago a neighbouring farmer advised me to 'co-operate with the weather', and it was very sound advice. Even if your book tells you to sow parsnips in late winter, say February, there is no point in trying to sow them on sticky wet soil. Far better to wait until the soil has dried out. If there is a sunny spell in late summer when the onions are ready for harvesting, do not procrastinate for a moment. The weather might turn nasty on you, your onions will start to sprout or rot and your crop will be wasted.

It probably takes a newcomer to gardening three or four years to get the 'feel' of how the annual pattern of gardening operations fits into the overall pattern of the seasons. When the ground first becomes workable in spring, you can plant the shallots and onion sets; when the cold spring wind has dried out the surface, you can rake the soil to a tilth for the early sowings. When the danger of frosts is over you can plant out the tender crops such as tomatoes and cucumbers. When frost threatens again in the autumn, some crops will need harvesting, others protection. These are the indicators to which an experienced gardener reacts instinctively. Everything else fits neatly in between.

For new gardeners, or anyone new to an area, it is worth investigating what established gardeners in the locality are doing. What they grow, how and when, provides many a clue to success. It is always best to start with what does well naturally – you can tackle 'difficult' vegetables later.

I would advise anyone growing vegetables to keep records. It is always useful to know which cultivars proved successful in previous seasons, how many rows you found you needed and where there were gaps in the household supply that could be remedied. Records of sowing dates, quantities of seeds or plants needed, cultural details, pests encountered and what was planted where and before or after what are invaluable. You may be inundated with advice from experts, but your personal garden diary will be the only source of information about the unique conditions that constitute your garden.

Finally, a word of encouragement for beginners. I often come across people who, although they had never before grown anything, in their first season had results anyone would be proud of. They simply 'followed the instructions on the packet'. That could be beginners' luck, green fingers or plain common sense. Get a feel for the sort of conditions plants like and, from then on, gardening is very largely common sense. New gardeners who want to reinforce beginners' luck will find excellent advice in gardening magazines, on the radio, on television, on the Web and in seed catalogues (almost always free). Consider joining a local gardening club, where you will pick up hints from experienced gardeners, and from lectures and demonstrations. Many gardening societies are able to obtain seeds and gardening supplies at discounts for their members.

I hope this revised edition will prove useful to a new generation of gardeners. I am always interested in readers' experiences in different parts of the country, and in their comments on how this book could be improved. Letters sent care of the publishers will always be forwarded.

Joy Larkcom, March 2002

USEFUL DEFINITIONS

Annual Plant that germinates, flowers and dies within a year.

Biennial Plant grown from seed whose life cycle normally spans two years. It develops a leafy tuft or rosette the first year and flowers, seeds and dies in the second year.

Perennial Plant that lives for several years.

Tender Word used both to describe plants that a) are injured by frost or cold weather and b) can only be grown in a greenhouse or with protection in a given climate.

Hardy Describes a plant surviving outdoors in a given climate zone. Generally implies that it has some frost resistance.

Half-hardy Describes plants which survive only limited cold or very light frost unless in a protected site or situation.

SEASON AND MONTH CONVERSION CHART

General seasonal terms are widely used throughout the book to enable it to be used in different regions in both hemispheres. The months below relate to the British Isles in the northern hemisphere.

Mid-winter	January
Late winter	February
Early spring	March
Mid-spring	April
Late spring	May
Early summer	June
Mid-summer	July
Late summer	August
Early autumn	Sepember
Mid-autumn	October
Late autumn	November
Early winter	December

^ = Performed well in organic trials, so recommended for organic gardeners

I

TOOLS AND EQUIPMENT

Whatever the size of your garden, a set of basic tools is essential. Always buy the best you can afford: cheap tools are a false economy. Not only do they make the job harder, but they have a depressingly short life span. The best-quality tools are made of stainless steel with ash or fibreglass handles, and often carry a ten-year guarantee.

When buying tools try them out for weight, balance and size (particularly the handles), as it is most important that they feel comfortable. Specially adapted tools are available for disabled gardeners, while tools with extra long handles are an asset where bending is difficult.

The gardening market is flooded with gimmicky tools – most of which should be avoided. But occasionally someone with an inventive turn of mind produces an original, practical tool. My favourite example is a Taiwanese hoe, which has much the same dimensions as an onion hoe but is straight-handled. Made from an old saw blade, it has a toothed edge that serves as a rake, and the other straight edge of the blade serves as a hoe. I use it to make wide shallow drills for all my cut-and-come-again seedling sowings.

It is worth taking care of good tools so that they give long service. Scrape off the soil before putting them away and, ideally, wipe them clean with an oily rag. Needless to say, this does not always happen – even in the best gardening circles. Spades and hoes need occasional sharpening with a file or carborundum stone.

The following tools are almost essential: a spade, a digging fork, a rake, some kind of hoe, a hand fork and trowel, and a watering can. A spade is the traditional digging tool and the best for thorough digging on heavy soil, for breaking up clods and for work that involves moving soil. However, in a garden with reasonably well-worked soil, you could manage using only a fork. Various sizes of spade are sold, the smallest, the border or lady's spade, being the lightest to handle.

The standard garden fork has four or five prongs or tines. It is used for digging too and is preferable to a spade on stony soil. It is also used for breaking up soil that has already been turned with a spade, and for generally 'working' the soil. For ordinary garden use the round-pronged fork is the most popular, though some people prefer the flat-pronged fork, which is also used for lifting potatoes and other root vegetables as it does less damage to tubers. A 'lady's fork' is lighter in weight with shorter tines.

Useful long-handled garden tools. Left to right: spade, digging fork, rake, Dutch hoe, draw hoe.

Rakes are mainly used for levelling soil, removing stones and preparing the tilth on a seedbed. For general purposes an eight- or ten-tooth metal-headed rake is adequate. I am very attached to a handmade nail tooth rake (a wooden head fitted with iron teeth) which is perfectly balanced and easy to use (see above). This is worth getting if you come across one. A springbok rake comes in handy for raking up leaves and rubbish.

The Dutch hoe, the blade of which is pushed lightly through the soil, is for removing weeds and loosening relatively light soil. It can also be used for drawing a drill. When hoeing with a Dutch hoe, walk backwards as you work, so that you leave no footmarks on the soil. In small gardens, and gardens laid out in narrow beds, all hoeing can be done while standing on the path. Always hoe with gentle movements, as hoeing can quickly become surprisingly tiring.

The draw hoe is pulled towards you, rather than pushed. It can be used for hoeing on heavier soils, and for such jobs as earthing up and drawing a shallow flat-bottomed drill, typically for sowing peas.

The onion hoe is a small, swan-necked draw hoe on a short handle. It is invaluable for weeding, especially in confined spaces, for thinning, for drawing drills and even for earthing up. If I were restricted to one hoe in a small garden, this would be my choice (see below).

The Ibis hoe (also called a cultivator or plough) is a short-handled hand-forged steel tool of Asiatic origin, with a subtly curved triangular blade tapering to a point. This is another very versatile tool, and is used for weeding, planting, thinning and making a drill.

Some useful small hand tools. Left to right: onion hoe, hand trowel, hand fork, Ibis hoe.

Triangular, serrated edge, oscillating and double-edged hoes are very useful. It is really a question of finding what personally suits you.

The cultivator is a tool with three to five, occasionally more, claw-like prongs, which can be very useful for breaking up ground and for weeding between plants.

A hand trowel is primarily used for planting and must be sturdy. The strongest models have a concave steel blade and an angled or curved, rather than straight, shank. Its natural partner, a small hand fork, is useful for weeding near plants and loosening the soil in small areas.

A dibber is a pointed metal or wood tool, generally used to make holes for planting. Many a dibber has been whittled from a broken fork handle. A dibber is ideal for making a straight 20cm/8in-deep hole into which transplants are dropped (see page 94). It can also be used to make shallower holes for sowing large seeds such as broad beans; make sure that the seeds lie on the bottom of the hole and are not suspended in mid-air.

Garden lines, to ensure sowing or planting in straight rows, can be purchased or made by attaching twine to a pair of skewers or metal tent pegs. If your garden beds are a constant width, make the line the same width: that will save hours of ravelling and unravelling.

Watering cans should be robust and, for general watering, have a capacity of 7–9 litres/1½–2 gallons. Detachable coarse and fine roses which are fitted to the spout allow you to moderate the force of the water according to the size of plant. Small cans of 1.5 litres/2½ pints capacity with very narrow spouts are handy for watering seedlings, but are easily blocked if there is debris in the water supply.

Other useful items of equipment include a wheelbarrow and a small hand syringe or hand sprayer for applying pesticides. A capacity of ½ litre/1 pint is probably sufficient for most organic gardeners. For irrigation equipment see page 80; for plant-raising equipment see page 97. In large gardens there may be a case for using a mechanical cultivator; if you require machinery only occasionally, it is useful to hire it.

2

THE VEGETABLE GARDEN SITE

Vegetables need as much sunshine as possible, so the ideal site for vegetable growing in a temperate climate is 'open', in the sense that it is in full sunshine for most of the day and (in the northern hemisphere) is not facing due north. Shelter from strong winds is another key element in creating optimum conditions for vegetable growing. It goes without saying that a flat site, provided it is well drained, is far easier to work than a sloping site. So where there is a choice avoid deeply shaded, exposed and steep sites.

Shade is frequently cast by large trees or tall buildings and only a handful of vegetables will thrive in these conditions. Moreover, the drips from overhanging trees tend to damage plants beneath. In essentially shady gardens utilize any sunny spots, and consider growing vegetables in containers that can be moved around to catch the sun.

Exposure is more easily remedied (see Shelter, below).

One of the main problems with steep slopes is soil erosion, so working to the contours, that is laying out beds and paths to run across, rather than down, the slope, is recommended. In extreme situations a slope can be terraced.

Sites that are known frost pockets should be avoided. Frost pockets are liable to occur at the lowest points in a sloping garden, and can be remedied by making a gap in a hedge or fence at that point, so allowing the cold air to drain away.

Fertile soil, good drainage and an adequate supply of water are important, interrelated elements in any site intended for vegetable growing. They are covered in Chapters 3 and 4.

On the question of having a garden of appropriate size, let me quote my fellow garden writer Leonard Meager, writing in *The New Art of Gardening* over 300 years ago:

> As for the quantity of Plot of ground to make a Suitable Garden . . . let me caution all, not to undertake more than can be well looked after with hands enough for the well management of things in their proper season; for a small Plot of ground well ordered, turns to greater advantage than a large one neglected . . . for if the weeds get the mastery for want of hands to rid them, it will not be easy to root them out . . . Also watering a large garden in droughty weather requires much Time and Pains.

SHELTER

The benefits of shelter cannot be exaggerated. Research has shown that sheltering vegetables from even light winds can increase their yields by up to 30 per cent – which is equivalent to the increase in returns from optimum irrigation or optimum fertilizer use. The benefits of sheltering plants from severe winds are considerably higher. In coastal areas windbreaks also give protection from wind-borne salt spray.

The mechanics of windbreaks

The most effective windbreaks are about 50 per cent permeable, allowing the wind to filter through to the other side. A completely solid windbreak, such as a wall or fence, can create a destructive area of turbulence on the leeward side. A well-grown hedge, lath fences, wattle hurdles and windbreak netting battened to posts are examples of good windbreaks.

As a general rule, windbreaks should have a gradually diminishing sheltering effect for up to at least six times their height. So a large exposed garden would benefit from several windbreaks sited across it. For maximum effect windbreaks 1.5m/5ft high, for example, should be spaced roughly 9m/30ft apart. As far as possible they should be erected across the path of the prevailing wind.

Exposed gardens benefit enormously from protection with some kind of windbreak. A choice has to be made between living windbreaks, such as trees or hedges, and artificial windbreaks.

Living windbreaks

The disadvantages of living windbreaks are that they compete with vegetable crops for nutrients, light and moisture, and normally require some pruning to keep them in check. With young trees and hedges it may be necessary to erect temporary artificial windbreaks until they have reached a reasonable size; indeed they may require protection themselves in the early stages of growth. Within the confines of a garden, robust tall annual crops can offer protection to lower-growing vegetables. Jerusalem artichokes and sunflowers are used in temperate climates, sweet corn or maize in warmer climates. They can be planted in rows two to three deep to make a sheltering enclosure for more tender vegetables.

Artificial windbreaks

A wooden lath fence makes an efficient artificial windbreak. To get the 50 per cent permeability, nail horizontal lath strips about 2.5cm/1in apart on to a lath framework.

Manufactured web and net windbreaks are another option. There's no pretending that they are aesthetically pleasing and they are not cheap, but if erected around an exposed garden they transform the environment within it. They can be up to 2m/6½ft high. They take an enormous strain in high winds, so posts must be rot-proof and exceptionally strong

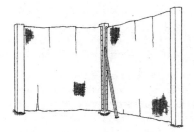

Our exposed garden is surrounded by a net windbreak, battened to strong posts with corner posts reinforced by a short bracing post.

Low strips of hessian sacking attached to short poles or canes serve as a windbreak between rows of vegetables.

(at least 5–7.5cm/2–3in diameter), spaced about 1.8m/6ft apart. Corner posts should be reinforced with short bracing posts at a 45-degree angle (see above, left). Good modern windbreak materials last for many years.

Where high surrounding windbreaks are not feasible or too costly, you can increase shelter within the garden with strips of low windbreak 30–60cm/1–2ft high. Nylon, hessian sacking, the fine mesh nets used to protect against insects, even heavy-duty polythene film can be stapled or battened to canes or short posts and placed between rows of vegetables (above right). Even ordinary 13mm/½in-mesh wire netting has some effect in breaking the force of the wind.

Wind funnels

Some gardens suffer from wind funnelling through gaps between nearby buildings. If you erect artificial windbreaks across the gap, make sure that they extend at least 60cm/2ft on either side of the gap. Gusting winds have nasty sneaky habits!

All the devices used to protect crops, from fleece films to cloches to walk-in polythene tunnels are in effect forms of shelter (see Chapter 6).

Too much shelter

Although shelter is of overwhelming importance, there is a reverse side to the coin. Conditions that are so sheltered as to be claustrophobic encourage the build-up of pests and diseases. It is a question of applying common sense to find a happy medium.

Walled gardens

Traditionally many vegetable gardens were made within a walled site. In such gardens the walls themselves are put to excellent use for trained fruit, though, unless the dimensions are very carefully designed, wind turbulence within the garden can cause problems. A feature of walled gardens is the microclimate at the foot of the walls – particularly of a south-facing wall. Early in the year this is an excellent spot for early salads; in summer it is ideal for warmth-loving crops such as tomatoes, peppers and aubergines. The soil at the foot of a wall is often protected from rainfall and is liable to dry out so it must be kept fertile and well watered.

THE NARROW BED SYSTEM

The layout of the vegetable garden is largely determined by the size, shape and nature of the beds. For much of the twentieth century a typical vegetable garden consisted of large rectangular beds – often 3–6m/ 10–20ft wide – in which the vegetables were grown in widely spaced rows. More recently gardeners have returned to the traditional system, adopted by market gardeners the world over, of growing vegetables in small, permanent 'narrow' beds, separated by permanent paths. The beds are cultivated from the paths and, in most cases, plants are spaced evenly along the beds rather than in rows. This system is widely used by organic gardeners and I highly recommend it.

The advantages of narrow over wide beds are:

- All cultivation and harvesting is done from the path, so there is no need to tread on the soil. This conserves the soil structure, and hence its fertility (see Chapter 3).
- All manure and compost is concentrated precisely where the plants will grow, rather than on ground between rows that in large beds effectively becomes trodden into a pathway. The beds gradually become more fertile than would otherwise be the case.
- Increased soil fertility allows plant roots to penetrate more deeply, increasing the plants' resistance to drought.
- Narrow beds lend themselves to intensive planting and equidistant spacing (see Chapter 5). This minimizes competition between plants for light, moisture and nutrients, resulting in even growth and high yields.
- When mature the leaves of adjacent plants touch, making a dense canopy over the soil. This virtually prevents weed seeds from germinating and subsequent weed growth. (An exception is narrow-leaved plants like onions, which cast little shade.) Mulching between plants is all that is necessary to keep weeds down completely.
- Being so accessible, the beds are easy to ridge up in winter (see page 69).
- The beds are similarly easy to cover with low tunnels, supporting either insect-proof netting or polythene films.
- It is easier to work out a flexible rotation system for several narrow beds rather than one large plot.
- Well-trodden paths between beds encourage earthworm activity, while paved or brick paths prevent mud splashing up on to plants.

Bed width

The recommended width for narrow beds is 90–150cm/3–5ft wide. Opt for a width that suits you and the dimensions of your garden. I eventually settled for 1.2m/4ft wide beds – which for me is a comfortable stretch from the path to the centre. Bear in mind that the narrower the beds, the higher the overall ratio of path to bed in the garden. Also consider any equipment you are likely to use. For example, it is a great help if the beds are the same width as the hoops you use for low tunnels.

Narrow beds can be of any length, but in practice if they are too long people inevitably take short cuts across them, defeating the object of not treading on the soil. I have occasionally put stepping stones of old tiles or pavers across beds which seem to pose a particular 'short cut' temptation.

Bed shape

The standard narrow bed is straight-sided and rectangular in shape, but there is no reason why it shouldn't be gently curved or sinuous, especially if this helps to make the most of available space. Square beds are functional, but if the sides are much more than about 1.3m/4½ft long it becomes awkward to reach the centre from the path. Vegetables can of course be planted in circular, crescent-shaped or irregularly shaped beds. Indeed much of the art of the potager (see page 11) lies in designing beds of various shapes, co-ordinated into patterns. Don't be afraid to throw convention to the winds when planning your vegetable garden! Gardening operations may be more complicated in an unorthodox garden, but the overall effect can be beautiful.

Bed height

Beds can be either at ground level or raised off the ground to varying heights. Narrow beds at ground level tend to become slightly raised over time, the natural result of being continually manured and not being trodden. If the soil is spilling out on to the path, they may need to be edged (see below).

The height of raised beds can be anything from 10cm/4in to about 60cm/2ft, a height considered practical for disabled or wheelchair-bound gardeners. Raised beds can be free-standing, or permanently edged, boarded edges being the most popular.

As raised beds can be built up with imported soil, they offer a means of overcoming fundamental problems such as chronically bad drainage, contaminated or very poor soil. They can be made in a garden where there is no soil, only concrete. On steep slopes they can serve as a levelling device, if you make them lower at the back than the front. Raised beds have good drainage and warm up quickly in spring. However, the sides are exposed to sun and wind and dry out rapidly – a factor to consider in areas of low rainfall.

Left: a raised bed mulched with manure, making a rounded surface and (right) a flat bed. Paths between the beds are mulched with weed-suppressing permeable black woven films.

Free-standing raised beds A free-standing raised bed is rarely more than about 30cm/12in high, and is generally wider at the base than the top: a 1.2m/4ft base and 90cm/3ft top are practical dimensions. The top of the bed can be level or rounded. (Flat-topped beds are more often edged with boards as soil is liable to erode off the sides on to the paths.) Rounded beds have the theoretical advantage of increasing the potential surface area for cultivation. Moreover, in northern latitudes, if the beds are orientated in an east–west direction, the south-facing side and top benefit from increased exposure to sunlight and radiation. Research in California has shown that the benefits of a 5-degree slope are equivalent to moving 50 km/30 miles to the south. As digging is awkward and tends to distort the shape of raised beds, fertility is normally maintained by keeping the surface heavily mulched. This also helps prevent the sides being eroded. (To make a free-standing raised bed, see page 69.)

Built-up raised beds To eliminate the need to bend or to overcome soil problems, beds about 60cm/2ft high can be constructed within a con-crete or brick frame. Fill the lower 30cm/12in with rubble to ensure good drainage, then cover it with 30cm/12in of good soil.

Bed edgings
Beds can be edged with a wide range of materials including stone, tiles, weatherproof bricks and timber boards (see illustration opposite). Timbers should be pressure-treated and at least 2–4cm/¾–1½in thick. Provided they are nailed together securely, they can rest on the ground without being embedded. However, for extra strength, and to provide more resistance to the weight of the soil, which tends to push outwards, they can be nailed to 5cm/2in wide wooden pegs, set either outside or within the confines of the bed. Raised beds are sometimes edged with railway sleepers. Sleepers can be piled two high on one side, but laid singly on the other, to make a sloping bed easily converted into a garden frame (see page 121).

Beds edged with timber (above) and bricks (above right).

Ground-level beds can be edged in all sorts of ways – with stones, bricks laid flat or upended and set at an angle to get a dog-tooth effect, terracotta tiles or timber. Or they can be edged with plants; among my favourites for this purpose are alpine strawberries and Chinese chives.

Bed direction

To make maximum use of sunshine, in the northern hemisphere beds should theoretically be oriented in a north–south direction for summer crops, and east–west for winter crops. This is not always easy to carry out in practice. Of more immediate relevance is ensuring that tall plants such as climbing beans and sweet corn will not shade low-growing plants.

Paths

Paths must be firm, clean so that plants don't become soiled, well drained and easily maintained. A minimum practical width is 38cm/15in but as growing vegetables inevitably spill over on to paths, where there is space make them up to 60cm/2ft wide. Make at least one main path 90cm/3ft wide so that you can manoeuvre laden wheelbarrows comfortably.

The cheapest paths are bare soil, but these will require weeding. Very serviceable paths can be made by covering bare soil with heavy-duty, permeable, polypropylene black fabric. This suppresses weeds and allows drainage. It is usually manufactured with rather garish planting lines marked on the surface, but these can be easily disguised with a layer of bark chippings, which makes a very pleasant surface. Bare paths can also be mulched with straw, which both looks nice and encourages earthworm activity. Old carpets are popular with organic gardeners and can work. However, they become slippery, provide no drainage and eventually become colonized with weeds.

Mown grass paths look very attractive, but must be able to withstand the wear and tear inevitable in a vegetable garden. They are unsuitable in areas of high rainfall. Make sure that the paths are a suitable width for the lawn mower.

Permanent paths can be made by laying bricks, gravel, stone or paving slabs. Decide on the layout of the beds in the garden before laying the paths: they are not easily changed. Durable but movable wood duckboard paths can be made from pressure-treated gravel boards. (For further reading, see *Creative Vegetable Gardening*.)

3

SOIL, MANURE AND COMPOST

SOIL FERTILITY

Soil fertility is the key to growing vegetables successfully. Some soils are naturally fertile but in most cases steps have to be taken to increase, and then maintain, soil fertility. Once the soil is fertile, crops grow fast and vigorously, they stand a better chance of overcoming pests and disease, and they yield heavily – your garden, whatever its size, will have an aura of abundant productivity.

What is soil fertility? To answer that question it is worth taking a look at what soil is, how it functions and what it does for the plant.

THE NATURE OF SOIL

Although soil looks solid, in an average garden slightly less than half of the soil consists of solid matter. This is mainly made up of mineral particles of sand, silt and clay which have been formed over the centuries by the breakdown of rocks. About 5 per cent of the soil, an extremely important 5 per cent, is organic matter. This is a mixture of the remains of plants and animals, decomposing vegetation and humus, and tiny creatures living in the soil known as micro-organisms, many of which play a vital role in breaking down all this material. The rest of what we call the soil, about half of it, consists of air and water, which fill the spaces or pores between the crumbs of soil.

What does soil do for plants? It supplies anchorage, and a medium through which the roots can breathe. It supplies water, essential for all living things, which is absorbed through the roots. It also supplies most of the nutrients, or foods, required by plants.

Sources of nutrients

A plant gets its nutrients from two sources. Through its leaves it takes in carbon dioxide from the air which, together with water absorbed through the roots, is converted in the presence of light into sugars and starches. This takes place in the 'factories' of the leaves during the process known as photosynthesis. The rest of the nutrients necessary for healthy plant growth are obtained from the soil and absorbed into the plant's system in dilute solution through the roots. Of these nutrients the plant requires nitrogen, phosphorus and potassium (usually called potash) in large quantities; calcium, sulphur and magnesium in more moderate quantities; and in really minute quantities the so-called 'trace elements', such as iron, manganese, zinc, boron, copper, molybdenum and several others.

Nitrogen is the most important nutrient for plants. Its principal source is decaying organic matter in the soil, but it also comes from atmospheric nitrogen in the soil. This is 'fixed' and converted into forms plants can use by bacteria in the soil organic matter, and by nitrogen-fixing bacteria on the root nodules of leguminous plants (members of the pea and bean family). Nitrogen is easily washed or leached out of the soil, especially during the rainy winter months. Generally speaking, plant growth is seriously inhibited by a shortage of nitrogen. Of the other nutrients, some are found in the mineral particles of the soil, particularly in clays. But they occur mainly, in highly complex forms, in the organic matter in the soil.

So it follows that the most important process at work in the soil is the breaking down of organic matter by minute micro-organisms, mainly types of bacteria, to release nutrients in simple forms which can be taken up by plants or – as the jargon has it – making the plant nutrients 'available'. This can only take place if conditions are right for the micro-organisms. Their requirements are oxygen and moisture, soil that is neither too acid nor too alkaline for them and, above all, an adequate supply of organic matter to work on.

Fertility can be summed up as the best conditions for soil micro-organisms to go about their work of breaking down organic matter into humus. Humus is organic matter in a very advanced state of decay, and it is from humus that plant nutrients are released. Good soil structure is an important factor in creating these conditions.

SOIL STRUCTURE

Soil structure is determined by what are known as 'soil crumbs'. In all except very sandy or silty soils, the mineral and organic particles in the soil join together to form small lumps, or crumbs, of varying sizes. You can easily see the crumbs if you crush a small clod of garden soil in your hand. You can break it down so far, but after that only the resistant crumbs are left, and to break them down into dust-size fragments is a much harder business.

In a good soil the crumbs vary in size and are very stable, and around them and between them a network of spaces or pores is built up. It is this combination of crumbs and spaces that makes up the soil structure. The channels made by the spaces between the crumbs form the aeration and drainage system of the soil. When rain falls the surplus water drains off through the channels, which prevents the soil from becoming water-logged. However, water remains in the smallest pores, forming a moisture reservoir for plant roots and soil organisms. The large spaces are filled with air, supplying the oxygen which is necessary for the plant roots and the various living organisms in the soil. A soil with a good structure is one in which the crumbs remain stable even when wet, allowing the effective drainage and aeration that is essential for plants to thrive. The innate soil structure is determined by the underlying type of soil. A crucial difference between the basic types of soil lies in their ability to form crumbs.

Types of soil

The mineral element in soils is made up of particles of varying size, which are classified, according to their size, as sands, silts and clays. The particles of sand are the largest: the individual grains are visible to the naked eye. Next come silt particles, which are infinitely smaller and which cannot be distinguished by the naked eye. The smallest of all are clay particles.

Most soils in the British Isles are loams, a mixture of one or more types. But because sands and clays, to take the extreme types, have very different characteristics, the proportion of these predominating in any particular soil largely determines its structure and how rich it is in nutrients.

The large particles of a sandy soil are the most reluctant to stick together naturally to form crumbs. The spaces between the particles are also large, so water drains away easily and the soil contains plenty of air. Sandy soils warm up quickly in spring, but dry out in summer. They are usually poor in nutrients, because nutrients are easily washed out of the soil in the drainage water. Sandy loams, however, are richer in nutrients than pure sands and hold water better.

A clay soil, on the contrary, consists of microscopic particles which have a great tendency, because of their chemical nature, to stick together. A pure clay is extremely sticky, there are few spaces for air, and water cannot drain through it easily. When it does dry it is apt to dry into hard, impenetrable lumps. A clay soil, however, is very rich in nutrients and, when organic matter is worked into it, can develop an excellent crumb structure and become a very fertile soil.

Silts have intermediate characteristics, although in practice they behave more like clays than sands. Like clay, they retain moisture well but can dry into hard clods. They are often very fertile and, again like clay, respond well to the incorporation of organic matter.

Sandy soils are generally considered 'light', clay soils 'heavy' and silts intermediate.

Other distinct types of soil are peats and chalk soils (see page 37).

The ideal soil, the loam that gardeners dream about, is a balanced mixture of sand, silt and clay. The sandy elements make for good drainage and aeration, the clay elements for richness, retention of water in summer and the cohesiveness which is essential for the formation of crumbs. Even soils such as these are dependent on fresh organic matter being added continually so that they retain a good crumb structure.

Topsoil and subsoil

When considering soil fertility, the gardener is usually concerned with the dark layer of soil we cultivate known as the 'topsoil'. This varies in depth from only a few centimetres to several metres thick, and generally lies over a lighter coloured, poorer layer of 'subsoil'. The main difference between the two layers is that the topsoil contains organic matter, which has given it a relatively good structure, while the subsoil, with no organic matter, is solid, lifeless, of poor structure and often badly drained as a result, and roots cannot penetrate it easily.

From a gardener's point of view, the deeper the topsoil the better. (For the various ways of increasing its depth, see page 67.) On the whole, subsoil is best left alone and should never be brought to the surface. Over the years cultivation of the topsoil will gradually lead to an improvement in the subsoil, largely through the infiltration of roots and worms from the topsoil.

The one exception to the general rule of not disturbing the subsoil is where the topsoil is very thin, say only a finger length deep. In this case it is worth double digging the soil, which means penetrating the subsoil, working a layer of organic matter into it and then replacing the topsoil (see page 67). This will improve the fertility of the subsoil, which will gradually assume the character of topsoil.

Assessing your soil type

You can get some indication of the type of soil you have by what is called 'finger analysis'. Hold some soil in the palm of your hand, and then rub a little between your fingers. If the predominant feeling is of grittiness, it is basically a sandy soil. If it feels silky, it is a silty soil; if it feels sticky and can almost be 'polished' under pressure from the fingers, it is a clay soil. If it doesn't really feel either gritty, silky or sticky, it is a loam.

Even within a small area, soil can be very variable. After cultivating a soil for a few years, you acquire a feel for the type of soil you have and how to cater for its particular characteristics.

The part humus plays in soil structure

The crumbs of a well-structured soil are formed by contrasting actions: by particles of sand and silt being bound together and by clods of clay being broken apart. In both cases the main agent is humus. Certain elements in humus have the ability to coat particles of sand and silt so that they cohere. Humus plays an important intermediary role in the breakdown of large clay clods, initially into small clods and finally into crumbs.

Humus also has great water-holding capacity. This is particularly important in sandy and chalk soils, making them more resistant to drought and preventing nutrients from being washed out.

The part earthworms play in soil structure

Earthworms, especially the burrowing and casting species, play a very important part in creating a good soil structure. Their burrows, some of which are permanent with 'cemented' sides, open up the soil and create aeration and drainage channels. They work and plough through enormous quantities of earth, literally eating their way through the soil. They take in soil and organic matter, mix it intimately together and treat it with gums and lime as it passes through their stomach. This is the crucial first stage in the breakdown of organic matter. With several types of worm the result is the familiar coil-like casts which are deposited both on the surface and within the soil.

Worm casts are extraordinarily beneficial. They contain more microorganisms, more inorganic minerals and more organic matter than the soil from which they were derived; moreover the nutrients present in them are converted into forms plants can use immediately. Of equal importance, the casts are remarkably stable even when wet, and perform a key role in the formation of stable crumbs in the soil. Over the course of time worm casts deposited on the surface build up a stone-free layer of soil. In soils with many worms, this could be the equivalent of a 5cm/2in-deep layer in a year. The surface casts also contain enzymes which break down organic matter on the soil surface.

Yet another virtue is that worms help to control some plant diseases by removing the surface debris on which the disease spores overwinter.

Worms feed on fresh organic matter. Their preference is for animal manure; semi-rotted compost is second choice. The fastest way of increasing the worm population is to add organic matter to the surface of the soil. A traditional method of improving soil structure was the use of grass leys – grassing down land for several years. (Soil structure in old pasture land is excellent.) It is now thought that this is effective primarily because the decaying grass roots provide a constant source of food for worms. Subsequently the grass roots reinforce the casts, so making stable aggregates of soil crumbs.

There is a temptation to import earthworms into a poor soil to increase the population. In practice they rarely adapt to being transferred bodily: they tend to die or their numbers build up only very slowly. The most successful method is to dig up grass turves in worm-rich pastures and relocate these in a garden.

When worms die their protein-rich bodies decay and return nitrogen to the soil. In a typical soil this could amount to the equivalent of nitrogen fertilizer applied at the rate of 100kg per ha/89lb per acre per annum.

SOIL ACIDITY AND ALKALINITY

Another cause of soil infertility can be that the soil is too acid or too alkaline. Soil acidity is measured on the pH scale, which broadly speaking reflects the amount of calcium, that is chalk or lime, in the soil. The scale ranges from 0 to 14. A neutral soil has a pH value of 7.0, an acid soil a pH below 7.0 and an alkaline soil one above 7.0. The change from one pH level to the next indicates a soil that is ten times as acid (or alkaline) as the one above (or below) it.

In a humid climate, rainwater regularly washes calcium out of the soil, so there is a tendency for soil to become more acid all the time. This process is most marked in areas with very high rainfall, in cities and industrialized areas where acids in the atmosphere wash the calcium out even faster, and on free-draining light sandy soils. Heavy soils such as clays are less likely to become seriously acid, and may have enough reserves of calcium to last for many years. Most soils in the British Isles tend to be slightly acid.

Why does pH matter?
Firstly, pH matters because plants only grow well within a certain pH range, which varies from plant to plant. Most vegetables do best on a slightly acid soil with a pH of about 6.5. This is mainly because the pH value affects the availability of the soil nutrients which plants need. At pH 5.0 most nutrients are available. However, phosphate, one of the key nutrients, becomes 'locked up' if the soil becomes too acid and the pH falls below 5.0. Calcium, potassium and magnesium may be washed out of the soil altogether under very acid conditions. At a low pH other nutrients may be present in such large quantities that they become phytotoxic – that is, poisonous to the plant. When the pH rises above 7.5 – that is, if the soil becomes too alkaline – most of the trace elements that are essential for healthy plant growth become locked up and unavailable to plants. In other words, if the pH is seriously wrong, plants will be starved or poisoned.

Secondly, pH matters because micro-organisms such as bacteria, which break down the organic matter into humus, become progressively less active as the soil becomes more acid. When the pH falls to 4.5 they cease to function altogether. This means that not only are no more nutrients released into the soil, but the soil structure starts to deteriorate through lack of humus.

Earthworms prefer slightly acid soil with a pH between 5 and 6. They quickly migrate out of very acid soils, which should be limed (see below) as the first step towards encouraging their return.

Finally, certain plant diseases are worse in notably acid or alkaline conditions. Clubroot in cabbage is most serious in acid soils, potato scab in alkaline soils.

Note that on peaty soils (technically known as 'organic' soils – see page 37) vegetables will tolerate a lower pH, of about 5.5–6, than on standard 'mineral' soils.

Correcting high acidity

The most common pH problem in the British Isles is over-acidity, which is corrected by liming. However, over-liming can be harmful and suppress the availability of minor nutrients, so only lime your soil if it is really necessary. If plants seem to be doing well and there is a large worm population (particularly if your soil is on the heavy side), assume that everything is all right.

Indications that a soil is too acid and needs liming are a 'sour look', typified by moss growing on the surface, certain weeds such as sorrel and docks, and vegetation on the surface that is not rotting.

A chemical test is the only certain way of finding out what the pH is and if lime is needed. Soil-testing kits are available for the amateur, or tests can be carried out by advisory services. The kits give an accurate indication of the acidity of the soil, but they cannot tell you precisely how much lime you require, as this varies with the type of soil. Lighter dressings of lime will be required for a sandy soil, heavier for a silt or loam soil and the heaviest of all for a clay. Consult an expert; otherwise, if in doubt, err on the light side. Sandy soils in particular are easily over-limed. Soil pH can only be raised gradually, preferably by about 0.5 a year. Aim to raise it to a pH of 6.5 over several years if necessary.

Organic gardeners are advised to use slow-acting ground limestone rather than the fast-acting 'gardener's' slaked or hydrated lime. Other alternatives to liming are dolomite (which is a source of magnesium as well as calcium) and calcified seaweed, which contains calcium and trace elements. The quantity applied depends on the soil type. The following guidelines on levels of ground limestone applications are from the National Centre for Organic Gardening.

Soil type	g per sq. metre	oz per sq. yd
Sand	146	4¼
Loam	187	5½
Clay or peat	238	7

Dolomite can be applied where a magnesium deficiency has been identified, at a slightly higher rate of up to 270g per sq. m/8oz per sq. yd, and calcified seaweed at 70g per sq. m/2oz per sq. yd. The lime content of the soil can also be increased by using mushroom compost, which contains chalk. Ground limestone and mushroom compost can be worked into a compost heap in small quantities, as an indirect means of adding lime to the soil.

As a general rule, if you have a soil that tends to become too acid, apply lime dressings every third or fourth year at the most. Lime needs a while to take effect, but further dressings can be made later if necessary. Liming is best done in the autumn, ideally before a lime-loving crop such as one of the brassicas is planted. Although lime is traditionally spread on the surface of the soil, with medium and heavy soils it is far better to work it thoroughly into the top spit of soil when digging.

Never apply lime at the same time as fertilizers, farmyard manure or composts, as undesirable chemical reactions occur. Allow about a month to elapse between applications of any of these materials and liming. As far as possible, lime six months before sowing or planting.

Correcting high alkalinity

The problem of soils that are too alkaline for vegetable growing – as they have too much chalk in them – is much less common, which is just as well, as correcting over-alkalinity is more difficult. Working in organic matter will always help; working in composted pine needles is suggested in organic circles. In practice the quickest method of correcting deficiencies which occur in plants growing in alkaline soils is to use seaweed-based foliar sprays. In extreme cases there may be no alternative but to avoid crops such as potatoes or rhubarb, which require acid conditions, or to grow them in containers or raised beds in imported soil.

DRAINAGE

Poor drainage is another likely cause of soil infertility. A waterlogged soil is one in which surplus water cannot drain away. Consequently all the spaces between the soil crumbs are filled with water and air is driven out. Roots are unable to breathe and bacteria cease to function, with the result that the level of nutrients in the soil falls and its structure deteriorates. A waterlogged soil can therefore never be fertile. A badly drained soil is also a cold soil, and plants never thrive in such soils. The best way to remedy a waterlogged soil is by drainage.

Often it is obvious that a soil needs drainage. If water lies on the surface for several days after a heavy rain, or if you encounter water when digging 30cm/12in or so deep (this is what is meant by a high water table) drainage is necessary. Less obvious indications of a badly drained soil are poor vegetation, plants with a mass of small shallow roots rather than deep roots, lack of worms and soil that is grey, bluish, black or mottled rather than brown.

Causes of poor drainage

Bad drainage may be caused by the nature of the topsoil. This is the case with a heavy clay soil with little organic matter in it. It can also arise where the topsoil lies over a non-porous layer of subsoil or rock, such as clay or granite, which does not allow water to drain away. Where the underlying layer is porous, such as gravel or sand, there will be no problem.

Drainage is sometimes impeded by an extremely hard layer, known as a hard pan. You may suspect the presence of a hard pan when digging. At a certain depth the fork or spade seems to encounter far greater resistance. A hard pan can be caused by a layer of mineral salts, possibly 30cm/12in or so down, or it may be the result of extreme compaction caused by heavy machinery working on the soil. This situation may arise on new housing estates. A hard pan can be so impenetrable that it prevents all natural drainage, thus making the topsoil waterlogged.

Improving drainage
The method for improving drainage depends on the cause and severity of the problem.

Improving the topsoil If poor drainage seems to stem from the nature of the topsoil, digging in plenty of organic matter, which encourages worm activity (see page 30), goes a long way towards putting the matter right. This has certainly been the case with our Suffolk garden. During the winter we moved in, over thirty years ago, half the kitchen garden was semi-permanently under water and the rest waterlogged, making it quite unworkable until early the following summer – and hard work then. By digging in vast quantities of spent mushroom compost over the next few years we created a fertile, reasonably well-drained soil.

Breaking up a hard pan A hard pan has to be broken up by physical means. A spade will usually do the job; or plunge the tines of a fork in at an angle and move them about. Failing that, use a pickaxe.

Simple trench drains Where the drainage problem is caused by the nature of the subsoil, the addition of some form of artificial drainage will be necessary. In a small garden drainage can often be improved sufficiently by making a few trench drains. This is done by taking out a trench about 30cm/12in wide and 60–90cm/2–3ft deep, and filling the bottom 30cm/12in with a layer of large clinkers, stones, broken bricks and similar material before replacing the soil (see below). A trench like this could be made across the lower end of a slope, or at both ends of a

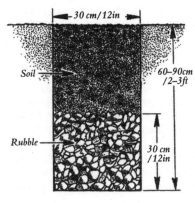

A simple trench drain partly filled with rubble before the soil is replaced. Clay or plastic pipes can be laid at the bottom of the trench to remedy more serious drainage problems.

level site. Or it could be incorporated into a path; a gently meandering path through a small garden could easily conceal an effective drain as well as provide a decorative feature. In the past reasonably efficient drains were made simply by filling trenches with brushwood.

Drainage network In a persistently wet garden, the only solution may be to lay a network of drains, draining into a ditch, artificial soakaway or sump. Clay or plastic pipes can be laid in the drains. Both are satisfactory, but for the amateur modern plastic pipes, 4–5cm/1½–2in diameter, are easier to handle and lay. It is common practice to lay the pipes at the bottom of the trench and cover them with 30cm/12in or so of drainage material such as clinker or rubble. Laying drains is a skilled job, so, if it is necessary, it would be well worth seeking expert advice on the sort of drains to use, their depth, spacing and gradient, and the most suitable layout for your particular plot.

Growing in raised beds (see page 23) often provides a satisfactory solution to a poor drainage problem.

IMPROVING AND MAINTAINING SOIL FERTILITY

Gardeners are continually working to improve their soil, to increase the depth of the topsoil and to maintain the soil's fertility. Since good soil structure is an important factor in a soil's fertility, improving fertility means improving soil structure. If your soil is essentially a loam soil, not an extreme soil type, a simple test will show if it has a good, stable, crumb structure – an indicator of high fertility – and, what is very useful to know, how fertility varies in different parts of the garden.

Take samples from different parts of the garden, ideally from different depths, anything down to 45cm/18in deep. For each sample take half a trowel of soil, dry it overnight on a saucer, then sieve it through a house-hold sieve to remove all the very light material. Then take a teaspoon of the soil, put it in a glass, cover it with water and shake. Poor soil disintegrates rapidly, making the water cloudy, but the crumbs of a well-structured soil will remain intact however long you shake the glass. Soils of intermediate quality come between these extremes. You'll find that the best samples come from ground that has been mulched, or from soil beneath a compost heap, or from worm casts. Aim to bring your poorer soils up to the quality of these by any of the following methods.

Adding organic matter In practice, the structure of almost any soil can be improved by adding organic matter, which will eventually be converted into humus. Organic matter is anything with animal or vegetable origins: manure, compost, straw or seaweed are typical examples (see page 43). Either spread organic matter on the surface as a mulch (see page 45), allowing the worms to work it in, or work it into the soil when digging in autumn or spring. The fertility of the soil depends chiefly on the rate at which organic matter is added. The supply must be continually replenished – not least because vegetables remove considerable quantities of nutrients from the soil. The job is never done!

Cultivation With heavy soils, simply cultivating the ground and letting in air enables earthworms, bacteria and other micro-organisms to get to work, so kickstarting the process of improving the soil structure. Growing plants carry the process further, as plant roots penetrate the soil and build up organic matter.

Exposure to frost Also with heavy soils, it is remarkable how the action of frost, alternately freezing and thawing the soil, breaks down the clods of a clay soil to produce a crumb structure. This is why clay soils should be dug over 'rough' in autumn, generally by the end of November, exposing the clods to the frost. The practice of ridging up the beds in autumn increases exposure to frost action, at the same time ensuring good drainage (see page 69).

Mulching the soil Soil structure is a fragile quality, easily destroyed by heavy rain on the bare surface or by walking on the bare soil more than is necessary. The practice of keeping the surface continually mulched – that is, covered with a layer of compost or other form of organic matter – goes a long way towards improving and conserving the soil structure. The structure of light sandy soils is the most vulnerable, and therefore cultivation is best delayed until the spring, but the soil can be mulched in autumn with, say, straw, bracken or compost, or even left weedy, to protect the surface from the elements.

Over the years I have become such a mulching addict that the sight of bare soil in the kitchen garden now makes me distinctly uneasy! (For mulching, see page 70.)

Green manuring Green manuring is the practice of growing a crop that is dug into the soil to enrich it rather than removed for consumption. It is a time-honoured method of maintaining and improving fertility and, when hardy autumn-sown crops are used, keeps the soil surface protected during the winter months. (For the benefits and use of green manures, see page 60.)

The narrow bed system Laying out a vegetable garden in narrow beds (see page 22) enables you to do all cultivation from the paths, so there is no need to tread on the soil. This goes a long way towards conserving the soil structure. The soil structure is also likely to be damaged, especially on fragile sandy soil, by cultivating when the soil is very wet or very dry.

Soil conditioners These, including biostimulants and bacterial innoculants, appear on the market from time to time. They claim to improve soil fertility by helping the formation of crumbs or tilth on sandy or clay soils. They are generally raked into the surface. The extravagant claims made for these products should be taken with a pinch of salt, though they could be beneficial in extreme conditions, for example where most of the topsoil has been removed in building operations. As they are expensive, if cost is a limiting factor, confine their use to special areas such as a seedbed. It seems that some of the seaweed-based products are among the most effective. Calcified seaweed can be considered a natural soil conditioner. It is doubtful whether the benefits of soil conditioners outweigh the application of organic matter in the course of good garden husbandry.

Inert additives Sharp sand, coarse grit or weathered ashes can be worked into the surface of a heavy soil to improve drainage and help it to warm up in spring.

Peat In the past peat was fairly widely used to improve soil structure, particularly in clay and chalk soils, though it has very little nutrient value. With current anxiety about destruction of peat bogs and depletion of the natural reserves of peat, I do not recommend its use.

DISTINCTIVE SOIL TYPES

Peat soils
The high, boggy moorland peats are usually too acid to grow vegetables. However, the peat soils derived from the drainage of peat bogs, such as the Fenland peats in East Anglia, are exceptionally high in organic matter. Once drained they are very moisture-retentive, easily worked and fertile. Mineral deficiency problems may occur, caused by their high acidity, which is more difficult to correct by liming than with standard mineral soils. Peat soils are also prone to wind erosion when dry, so it is advisable to keep something growing continually to avoid exposing bare soil. Peat soils are the one case where adding organic matter is unproductive.

Chalk soils
Chalk soils occur in areas with underlying chalk or limestone, and vary from deep chalky soils, where most vegetables can be grown successfully, to a more problematic thin layer of topsoil overlying chalk. Chalk soils tend to be light, warm and easily drained, with varying levels of fertility, though some become sticky when wet and dry into steely lumps, which leads to a shortage of water for plants. Mineral deficiency problems may occur because of the high pH. To improve fertility, increase the depth of the topsoil by frequently adding well-rotted organic matter, which decomposes rapidly on chalk soils; break up the underlying chalk where feasible, and avoid working the soil when it is wet.

Contaminated soils

It is a reflection of our times that in both rural and urban situations, soils can be seriously contaminated. Common causes are previous industrial use and waste dumping. If you suspect or encounter problems, you will need to have the soil analysed by a professional laboratory. In the first instance seek advice from agencies such as the environmental health department. The solution may lie in building raised beds well clear of the ground.

The neglected garden

Neglected gardens create special problems. They can be excessively weedy and have a low level of fertility, and the soil is often intractable and difficult to work. A suggested line of approach is as follows (see also Pockets of fertility, page 40):

1 Cut down and clear away all surface vegetation.
2 Dig over the ground, removing the roots of all perennial weeds by hand. Ideally complete this by the autumn. If the weed problem is severe it may be necessary to mulch with heavy carpeting or black polythene for several months before proceeding any further. (For more on perennial weeds and weed-suppressing mulches, see Chapter 4.)
3 If the soil is compacted, try to at least fork over the soil surface to help air and rain to penetrate. Then spread a thick layer of bulky manure, compost, straw, sewage sludge, spent mushroom compost, seaweed or any other kind of organic matter over the ground. It can easily be as much as 15cm/6in deep. If it is reasonably well rotted it can be dug in; if it is very fresh, or digging proves very difficult, leave it in place over the winter, allowing worms to work it into the soil. It is extraordinary how they appear from nowhere and undertake the work you found daunting!
4 In spring, dig in the residue of the organic matter and rake down the surface of the soil.
5 There is bound to be a huge reserve of weed seed in the soil, so before attempting to sow or plant anything allow the first flush of weed seeds to germinate. Hoe off these weeds before sowing or planting. Don't try to sow too early. If the garden is still very weedy, don't sow directly into the ground during the first season, but raise plants in pots, planting them out when they are a reasonable size (see Chapter 5). Alternatively plant through weed-suppressing mulching films or similar materials (see page 72).
6 In the first year concentrate on vegetables that are naturally vigorous and cover the ground well, such as potatoes and Jerusalem artichokes (both excellent crops for breaking in neglected soil), broad beans,

Swiss chard, New Zealand spinach, turnips and Chinese artichokes. These all keep weeds down well once established. Another option is to make frequent sowings of cut-and-come-again seedling crops (see page 157) which will grow in shallow soil. Suggestions are garden cress, salad rape, salad mustard and salad rocket. Feed regularly with organic liquid feeds to stimulate growth.

7 Mulch as much as you can to prevent weeds from germinating and to control perennial weeds. After two years or so of cultivation, weeds become less of a problem.

Do not expect marvellous crops the first year. However, by growing something and working the soil, you will see it start to improve. If crops do not seem to be doing better in the second year, it may be worth having a professional soil analysis to check on the pH and to see if there are any serious nutrient deficiencies. This can, of course, always be done at the outset.

The rubble the builders left behind

Owners of new houses are often faced with the prospect of converting a pile of rubble or raw clay into a vegetable garden. The topsoil has been removed, and the soil that remains looks impossible. Don't despair. It can be converted into a garden.

A common practice is to import topsoil but this is very expensive and, if the soil has been stacked in a heap more than 1m/3ft high, it will be devoid of worms. The cheaper and most effective method is to import large quantities of organic matter.

Here is one way to tackle the problem:

1 Remove the largest stones, bricks and similar rubbish. Don't worry about removing every stone over the whole area. The main drawback of stones is that they make it difficult to grow root crops like carrots and parsnips; it may be easier to prepare a special area for these crops, or grow them initially in deep boxes.
2 Fork over the soil as far as possible.
3 In the autumn cover the soil with a thick layer of organic matter as suggested above for the neglected garden. Make no attempt to dig it but leave it undisturbed during the winter.
4 Proceed as for the neglected garden.

Digging up lawns and rough grass

Tackle this job in the autumn. It is best to double dig (see page 67) the area that is being converted into a vegetable plot. Slice off the top 5cm/2in of turf, and bury it grass side down in the first trench. Chop it up before covering with soil from the next trench.

If the soil in the lawn is acid, it will probably be necessary to lime it after the autumn digging.

POCKETS OF FERTILITY

In the early days of a raw garden, it may be expedient to concentrate resources. Use any spare compost or manure in one area, dig it in, and plant or sow there initially. You can create fertile 'pockets' by making small trenches up to 15cm/6in deep, filling them with commercial potting compost topped with a couple of centimetres/an inch or so of soil. Lettuce, spring onions, radishes, early carrots, dwarf beans, seedling salads and so on could be sown in these pockets. As mentioned before, simply getting things growing stimulates the process of building soil fertility.

SOIL FERTILITY: A SUMMARY

A fertile soil is well drained, probably slightly acid or neutral, has a good crumbly structure and is rich in nutrients which are available to the plants.

If things are growing well in your garden, assume that it is fertile. A vigorous crop of weeds in a neglected garden can be taken as a sign of fertility, even if it does mean a lot of work before you produce an equally vigorous crop of vegetables. But if either cultivated plants or weeds seem poor and sickly, something is wrong. In this case, the steps to take in restoring fertility are:

- ∞ Improve drainage if it is faulty. This often brings dramatic results.
- ∞ Check acidity. Faulty pH is often at the root of failure, especially in city gardens. It can be corrected by liming.
- ∞ Work in bulky organic matter such as manure, compost, seaweed, sludge or whatever is available. This will improve the soil structure and provide nutrients, and of course encourage earthworm activity. It may also be necessary in the early stages to increase the supply of nutrients with regular organic feeds, for example of liquid seaweed or comfrey liquid (see page 56).

MANURES AND FERTILIZERS

The term 'manure' usually refers to a bulky product derived from animals, and 'fertilizer' to a concentrated powder, granules or liquid, in most cases man-made or 'artificial'. But there is no hard and fast rule, and in practice the terms are very loosely interchanged. Both manures and fertilizers can be either organic or inorganic in origin.

Essentially manures improve the soil, as described above. They are also a source of plant foods or nutrients, which are released slowly when they are broken down by soil micro-organisms; in addition they are a source of food for earthworms. Artificial fertilizers have a minimal effect on the soil and supply no food for earthworms, but they are a quick source of plant foods.

Organic versus non-organic

Modern gardeners tend to be divided into two camps – those who are happy to use chemical products such as artificial fertilizers, weedkillers and chemical sprays for pest and disease control, and the 'organic' or 'biological' school, who avoid the use of chemicals.

In relation to manures and fertilizers, organic gardeners use only those which are derived from animal or vegetable material, ruling out manufactured artificial fertilizers and most of those that have been extracted from rocks (unless they are subsequently broken down in the soil by natural processes). The basic philosophy of organic gardening is 'feed the soil, not the plant'. Bulky organic manures primarily feed the soil; artificial fertilizers are directed at feeding the plant.

There are other practical reasons for not using artificial fertilizers:

✺ Artificial fertilizers are, in the main, water soluble and very fast-acting. Plants respond quickly, but the resultant soft, sappy growth is more susceptible to pest and disease attack. These 'soft' plants are also less able to withstand the adverse effects of poor weather.

✺ The nutrients in artificial fertilizers are immediately available to plants but have only a short-term effect. The nutrients in organic fertilizers, released by the action of soil bacteria, become available slowly but over a much longer period. Plant growth is therefore steadier and sturdier.

✺ Artificial fertilizers supply only a limited range of the key elements such as nitrogen, phosphorus and potash. Most organic fertilizers also supply minor elements, trace elements and other growth-promoting substances.

✺ The dosage of artificial fertilizers is critical; it is easy to apply too much and damage the plant or, through chemical reactions, to bring about deficiencies in other key nutrients. This effect is unlikely with the gentler action of organic fertilizers.

✺ Artificial fertilizers can easily pollute the environment. The high level of nitrates in the water supply in farming areas is an example of this. There is far less risk of pollution with the use of organic manures and fertilizers, though where fresh manure is used the risk is not negligible.

Aim of the manuring programme

In organic gardens the main aim of the manuring programme is to be constantly improving soil fertility by the addition of as much bulky organic matter, preferably manure, as possible. Where bulky manures are in short supply, home-made compost and green manuring can be used to make up the shortfall (see pages 49–62). Once a garden is brought to a high level of fertility, and maintained at that level, little supplementary feeding with concentrated organic fertilizers is required. But reaching this level may take a few years, and organic fertilizers can play a useful role in bridging the gap.

Generally speaking, nitrogen, which is essential for all plant growth but needed in greatest quantities by bulky leafy plants, is the nutrient most likely to be in short supply. Nitrogen is washed out of the soil in winter, and the natural supplies are not replenished until soil temperatures are warm enough in spring for the soil organisms to start breaking down organic matter. This is when non-organic gardeners apply a nitrogenous fertilizer to stimulate plant growth. Organic gardeners either have to be patient, or they can use slower-working concentrated organic fertilizers, such as forms of seaweed.

Most gardens have considerable reserves of the two other main elements, phosphorus and potash, and in gardens where all plant wastes are returned to the soil as compost, overall losses are low. The average garden's requirements for phosphorus and potash should be met with annual applications of manure of about 5.5kg per sq. m/10lb per sq. yd, or at least 2kg per sq. m/5lb per sq. yd of good compost.

Potash deficiency is most likely in chalk and light sandy soils; phosphorus deficiency in heavy soils and peat soils. Amateur soil-testing kits give some indication of major nutrient deficiencies but, if growth is consistently poor and you suspect a soil problem, it is advisable to have a professional soil analysis carried out. Serious deficiencies of phosphorus or potash can be corrected organically in the long term by the use of rock phosphate and rock potash. They will also be gradually corrected by the addition of organic matter.

Trace elements

Most soils contain sufficient quantities of the trace elements required by plants but occasionally deficiencies occur, usually in fairly extreme soil types. Typical deficiency symptoms are stunted growth and pale, often yellowing leaves. Boron, manganese and copper deficiencies are the most likely to show up in vegetables. Once diagnosed (professional help may be needed for this), they can be corrected by applying specific foliar feeds: borax, for example, to correct boron deficiency. Seaweed foliar feeds also appear to help correct trace element deficiencies. Indeed some crops respond surprisingly well to treatment with fertilizers such as seaweed extracts, which contain trace elements, even though no deficiencies are apparent.

In the long term the best remedy for trace element deficiencies is adding organic matter and correcting the soil pH (see pages 32–3). One of the many benefits of organic systems is that soil deficiencies are far less likely to arise.

BULKY ORGANIC MANURES

It is no longer easy to find supplies of the traditional bulky animal manures – horse, cow and pig manure. Indeed tracking down any source of organic matter in the twenty-first century calls for initiative, particularly in urban areas. But it can be done. I have friends in London who get free horse manure from police stables, sacks of vegetable waste from markets and greengrocers, and packing straw for composting from shops. Those great piles of leaves which are swept up in city parks and streets, and are so often burnt, rot down beautifully (see page 55). The popularity of horse riding means that there is a lot of very useful muck somewhere for the asking. If you have a supply, make the most of it. If not, concentrate your efforts on making your own compost and green manuring.

Sources of bulky manure

Farmyard manure Much of the value of farmyard (and other animal manures) is in the bedding, which is soaked with nitrogen-rich urine. So the more straw in the manure the better. Fresh manure may scorch plants, because of the release of ammonia, and is liable to contain pests and weed seeds. Moreover when fresh manure is dug in there is initially a loss of nitrogen in the soil, as the bacteria in the soil start to break the manure down. For these reasons it is advisable to compost fresh manure for three to six months before use. Preferably stack it on a concrete base (to minimize the loss of nutrients), and cover it with black plastic, tarpaulin or old carpeting to protect it from the rain and keep out light, so preventing weed growth on the surface. Where wood shavings or sawdust have been used as litter, stack the manure in a heap for twelve to eighteen months to break it down. Otherwise nitrogen will be 'robbed' from the soil in the early stages of decomposition.

Poultry, pigeon, other bird manures and rabbit manures These are very concentrated, and are therefore best added to the compost heap in small quantities as an activator (see Making compost, page 49).

Spent mushroom compost This is widely available in rural areas. In the past mushroom compost was made from farm or stable manure, but today it is often made from composted straw. All forms are excellent for improving soil structure and drainage. Mushroom compost is normally sterilized, so it is free of disease and weed seeds. It has a high chalk (lime) content, and its use gradually raises the pH of the soil. It is therefore not suitable for alkaline soils. The lime content is an asset on acid and heavy clay soils as it helps to break them down. However, to avoid a build-up of lime in the soil and the possible development of mineral deficiencies it is advisable to rotate the use of mushroom compost around the garden, rather than using it continually in any one area. Mineral deficiencies are most likely to affect fruit crops.

Straw This is an excellent source of organic matter. Unless it is already partially or well rotted, it is advisable to compost it for several months before use. Either simply cover it as suggested for farmyard manure above or, for a superior product, build up a heap in layers. Make the layers about 15cm/6in thick, water each layer until thoroughly moist, then sprinkle with a thin layer of poultry manure, lawn mowings, seaweed meal, blood, fish and bonemeal, even a double layer of comfrey leaves, as a source of nitrogen and to hasten decomposition. Try to turn in dry material on the outside and bury it in the heap. The heap, which can be up to 1.8m/6ft high, should be ready in a few months. It can be kept covered. In my experience mulching with rotted straw leads to a huge increase in earthworm activity in the soil beneath. We regularly mulch the paths in our polytunnel with straw, prior to turning it in and converting the paths into beds for the next crop. The soil, which would otherwise have been baked solid, is in a beautiful condition when it comes to planting time.

Hay This is less bulky than straw, but can also be a useful bulky manure. It is essential to cover it for up to about six months to kill grass and other weed seeds. Lawn mowings are best incorporated into the compost heap after being partially dried (see Making compost, page 49).

Seaweed Seaweed is a valuable manure, containing roughly the same amount of organic matter and nitrogen as farmyard manure, as well as numerous trace elements. It can be used fresh, dried or composted and mixed with other wastes. Fresh seaweed can be spread on the soil as a surface mulch, but may pass through a rather glutinous phase before decomposing, attracting flies and smelling unpleasant. You can counteract this by sprinkling soil over the seaweed. If you are digging it into the soil it is advisable to incorporate it fresh, before it has dried out, at the rate of at least 5.5kg per sq. m/10lb per sq. yd.

Treated sewage sludge and municipal waste These are potentially useful products. Just make sure that they are guaranteed free of heavy metals.

Pond mud Although not strictly speaking a bulky manure, the layers of mud that accumulate at the bottom of ponds are very fertile. Pond mud was traditionally used to build fertility in Chinese agriculture, and we noticed a distinct improvement in fertility in beds we mulched with our pond mud several years ago. Where feasible, dredge it up and spread it on the top of the beds.

Applying bulky manures
How much bulky manure should you put on a garden? The answer in the majority of gardens is as much as possible, and the poorer the soil, the faster it will improve with applications of bulky manure. The organic matter in bulky manures is literally food for earthworms. An abundant supply is said to lead to a tenfold increase in their population within three years. It breaks down and disappears fairly fast, especially in hot

weather and areas of high rainfall, so it is reasonable to aim to work some organic matter into a piece of ground every year. On poor soils aim to apply at least 5.5kg per sq. m/10lb per sq. yd annually; in other soils about 2.75kg per sq. m/5lb per sq. yd should be sufficient.

Either work bulky manures into the soil when digging in autumn, winter or spring, or spread them on the surface as a mulch.

Digging in When digging in manure, distribute it as deeply and evenly throughout the soil as possible, rather than adopting the traditional method of putting it in a layer at the bottom of a trench. Spreading it throughout the soil encourages deep rooting, which enables plant roots to draw on nutrients and moisture from deeper levels in the soil – the first line of defence against drought. Plant roots can penetrate surprisingly deep: Brussels sprouts to a depth of 60–90cm/2–3ft, for example. On heavy soils digging and incorporating bulky manure is generally done in autumn; on light soils it is done in spring (see also Digging, page 66).

Mulching Mulching with bulky manures requires less physical effort than digging them in: the worms do the heavy work. Indeed if a ground is manured in the autumn, the bulk of the organic matter will have disappeared from the surface into the upper layers by spring. Any residue is then easily forked in. Mulching is especially recommended on light soils, as it physically protects the bare soil surface from winter rains that both destroy its structure and wash out nutrients. Manures can be spread on the surface in a layer 7.5–10cm/3–4in deep, or more. However, rather than applying in one heavy layer, it is probably more effective if it can be applied in a couple of thinner layers, allowing the first to be more or less worked in before the next is applied. When mulching with fresh animal manures in the winter months there is a risk of nitrogen being washed out of the soil and causing nitrate pollution. (In the growing season the nitrogen is taken up by plants so there is no problem.) For this reason I recommend only applying well-rotted manure in the autumn, and delaying mulching with fresh or partially rotted manure until late winter or early spring. Never put fresh animal manure on to growing vegetables, as foliage may be scorched by the release of ammonia.

There are no hard and fast rules about manuring. The nature of the soil, the severity of winter and the amount of winter rainfall are all factors to consider. For example, in areas where rainfall is high in spring, a heavy layer of manure on the soil in spring will prevent it from drying out and would therefore be counter-productive. Experiment with different systems until you find what seems to work best in your conditions. As mentioned earlier, on my heavy clay soil in an area of low rainfall, I opted for ridging up the beds in autumn (see illustration on page 24) and covering them with manure or mushroom compost, forking in any residues in spring.

Don't worry too much about the dos and don'ts. The important thing is to be working something organic into your soil somehow!

CONCENTRATED ORGANIC FERTILIZERS

If you keep the soil fertile with regular applications of bulky manure and/or compost, there should be little need for the use of concentrated organic fertilizers. However, there are circumstances where their use helps to raise soil fertility:

~ To raise nutrient levels in the interim period before a poor soil has been brought up to a reasonable level of fertility; nitrogen is most likely to be in short supply.

~ To obtain higher yields, notably of 'hungry' crops such as potatoes and brassicas. Tomatoes, to take another example, will respond well to extra potash once they are flowering and fruiting.

~ Where soil deficiencies need to be corrected.

~ In containers, where the soil nutrients are quickly exhausted.

Forms of concentrated fertilizers

Organic fertilizers are available in solid forms, generally powders, pellets or granules, or as concentrated liquid solutions.

The dried forms are spread evenly on the surface and raked or hoed into the soil. If the ground is dry, water it afterwards to wash the fertilizers in.

Liquid forms are diluted and are usually watered on the ground around the plants with a watering can. The soil should be moist before applying fertilizer, so water beforehand if necessary. They can sometimes be applied as a foliar feed (see below).

Applying fertilizers

Fertilizers are applied as a base dressing before sowing or planting, or as a top dressing or foliar feed during growth. In non-organic gardening a base dressing is generally worked into the soil two to three weeks before sowing or planting in the spring, to meet the plant's requirements for nitrogen and, to a lesser extent, phosphorus in the early stages of growth. Top dressings are applied during growth as a booster. For example, crops that have overwintered in the soil, such as spring cabbage and autumn-sown or autumn-planted onions, can benefit from a nitrogen-rich top dressing in spring. Top dressings can also be applied as a foliar feed.

With the slower-acting organic fertilizers the feeding system is more flexible. Slow-acting general-purpose fertilizers like seaweed meal can be applied to the soil several months before sowing or planting. During growth, comfrey, seaweed and other general-purpose organic fertilizers or liquid feeds can be used as a top dressing.

Foliar feeds Plants – other than those with waxy leaves – can take in limited amounts of nutrients directly through their leaves. These feeds are applied with an ordinary watering can with a fine rose, or with standard spraying equipment. Foliar feeding is a useful means of overcoming trace element deficiencies quickly, using appropriate feeds. Foliar feeding with seaweed extracts can be used as a tonic for plants that are below par. The leaves often turn a deep, healthy-looking green soon afterwards: no one is quite sure why. Foliar feeding is sometimes used in dry weather, obviating the need to water the soil before or after applying a fertilizer. It is best done in the evening or in dull weather, watering or spraying so that the leaves are evenly covered. Foliar feeding should always be considered a supplementary method of feeding, never the sole source.

Organic fertilizers

Below are examples of organic fertilizers that can be purchased. It has to be said that on the whole they are a fairly expensive way to buy nutrients, and are relatively slow-acting. As their composition can vary considerably the application rates given are for general guidance only. Use gloves when handling any products derived from meat or bone. Fertilizers should be stored in cool, dry, conditions out of direct sunlight.

Hoof and horn Primarily a source of nitrogen, which is released within a few weeks of application. Use it as a top dressing on leafy crops such as overwintered greens, in spring or early summer, or when preparing new ground. Apply at roughly 135g per sq. m/4oz per sq. yd.

Blood, fish and bonemeal A source of nitrogen and phosphorus. Use as a base dressing for vegetables two to three weeks before sowing or planting, or as a top dressing during growth. Apply at 65–200g per sq. m/ 2–6oz per sq. yd.

Bonemeal A source of phosphorus, which promotes strong root growth. It is used mainly as a base dressing when planting perennial shrubs, trees and fruit, but can be used as a source of phosphate for vegetables grown on light land. Only use steamed or sterilized bonemeal, as anthrax can be contracted from raw bonemeal. Apply at 100–135g per sq. m/3–4oz per sq. yd.

Seaweed meal Contains potash, nitrogen and trace elements, and various compounds that stimulate plant growth. Now classified as a 'plant stimulant' rather than a fertilizer, it essentially acts as a soil conditioner and is beneficial on poor soils. Apply it in the autumn as a base dressing several months before sowing or planting. Hoe or dig it into the ground or it may 'gel' on the surface. Apply at the rate of 135–200g per sq. m/4–6oz per sq. yd.

Rock phosphate A source of phosphorus, this pure ground rock is used in the long-term improvement of soils deficient in phosphorus – though its effectiveness is not guaranteed. Apply at the rate of 200–275g per sq. m/6–8oz per sq. yd.

Proprietary concentrated organic composts Various products appear on the market, made from chicken manure, fish wastes, worm-worked wastes, cow slurry, farmyard manure and other sources. Their precise value varies from product to product. Some are available only in liquid form. Use them as general-purpose fertilizers, according to the manufacturer's instructions. Although these are derived from organic wastes, remember that these concentrated products are no substitute for bulky organic manures. Check that they are approved by the organic standards authority. In the UK this is the United Kingdom Register of Organic Food Standards.

Seaweed extracts Various products derived from seaweed extracts are also officially classified as plant stimulants rather than fertilizers. They are available in liquid form, the highly concentrated forms being very economic. They contain plant nutrients, minerals and trace elements in complex forms. Dilute and use according to the manufacturer's instructions. Treat them essentially as plant tonics to stimulate growth and general healthiness. Maxicrop and SM3 are two well-known brand names.

Liquid comfrey concentrate This is a liquid feed containing reasonable levels of nitrogen and phosphate and high levels of potash, hence its wide use on potash-loving fruiting vegetables such as tomatoes, peppers and aubergines. It is also used as a general-purpose fertilizer. Dilute and use according to the manufacturer's instructions. (For more on comfrey and making your own liquid comfrey, see page 56.)

A note on dried blood

Dried blood is a very rich source of nitrogen, and widely used to stimulate growth in leafy vegetables from early spring to mid-summer. Unlike other organic fertilizers it is soluble and very fast-acting, effectively behaving like a chemical fertilizer. Therefore its use is not permitted in strictly organic systems.

Domestic organic fertilizers

Soot No longer widely available as coal fires become rarer, soot contains nitrogen, and is a good general stimulant. Don't use it fresh, as the sulphur released can damage plants. Store it somewhere dry for about three months, then apply it as a top dressing on young plants. It also improves the texture of clay soil and, because of its dark colour, helps to warm soils through absorption of heat. It is said to deter pests such as pea weevil, celery fly, carrot fly and slugs.

Ash Ash from wood fires and bonfires contains potash. Slow-burning hardwoods are particularly rich in potash. Potash is very soluble and is rapidly washed out in rain, so either work fresh ash into the compost heap or store it in a dry place and apply to growing crops in spring.

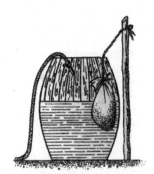

A 'Black Jack' tub: a sack filled with rotted animal manure, soot and grass cuttings, is suspended in a barrel of water to make a liquid manure.

Liquid manure or 'Black Jack' Almost the first thing I learnt when a gardening student with a wonderful 'old school' head gardener was how to make the general-purpose fertilizer 'Black Jack'. Simply suspend a sack of well-rotted animal manure in a barrel of rainwater (see above). Leave it for about ten days before using, stir it before use and dilute it to the colour of weak tea before watering plants with it. The manure is often mixed with soot or lawn mowings.

Liquid feeds made from comfrey and nettles See pages 56 and 57.

MAKING COMPOST

Bulky manure costs money and is not always easy to obtain. Home-made compost costs nothing and is also an invaluable source of humus. So however small your garden, if you are growing vegetables make space for a compost heap or bin. You can never have too much compost. It is extraordinary how a huge heap settles into an insignificant pile.

A compost heap is essentially a pile of vegetable waste, which generates heat and decomposes naturally with the aid of bacteria. When the waste is fully decomposed the resulting compost is blackish brown in colour, moist, crumbly and uniform in texture, with no half-decayed stalks or vegetation that is still recognizable as such. However, even partially decomposed compost benefits the soil – in fact it will provide more food for earthworms than fully decomposed material. It is just a little more awkward to handle. Recent research has indicated that good compost made from green wastes can actually help suppress some common plant diseases.

Composting processes

There are many theories about the best way to make compost, with even the experts often failing to agree – at least over details. You can use either of two processes: aerobic composting, where the presence of air accelerates the decomposition, or the much slower anaerobic process, with the virtual exclusion of air.

Aerobic composting offers several advantages:

- In temperate climates the compost is normally ready within two to six months, depending on the season.
- High temperatures are reached, so most disease organisms, weed seeds and roots of most perennial weeds are killed.
- Almost any organic material can be included and will decompose.
- It is virtually odourless and flies are not attracted to it.
- The resulting compost is an acceptable pH and will not require liming.

But it has its drawbacks:

- Reasonable quantities of waste are required. Unless there is a volume of at least 1 cub. m/1 cub. yd, high temperatures cannot be generated.
- The material must be held in some kind of box or container to retain the heat.
- There must be a balance between woody, carbon-rich material and lush, leafy, nitrogen-rich material. This is known as the carbon/nitrogen ratio (see below).
- The compost may need turning and the use of activators to accelerate the process.

Anaerobic composting differs in that:

- It requires little preparation, attention or turning.
- The heap can be any size: even small quantities can be composted.
- The carbon/nitrogen ratio is unimportant.

Its drawbacks are:

- In temperate climates it may take up to a year to produce good compost.
- Weed seeds, disease organisms and perennial weeds may not be killed.
- Tough material will not be broken down.
- The resulting compost may be cold, heavy and acid, and may require liming.
- Unless well covered the heap may produce odours and attract flies.

From this it is evident that, where possible, it is worth going to the extra trouble of making aerobic compost. However, in small households where little waste is generated, or if you do not have the time or space to make a compost heap, it is still worth making anaerobic compost. It will take longer and be less efficient than a 'proper' heap, but eventually organic matter is returned to the soil – and that is what matters.

Simple anaerobic composting

Either make the heap by piling up waste as it accumulates or, preferably, collect together enough material to build it up a layer at a time. The more diverse the material, the better. The layers can be about 15cm/6in thick. When the heap is about 90–120cm/3–4ft high, cover it with 2.5cm/1in of soil, then cover it completely with an old carpet, hessian or heavy-duty plastic, and leave it to rot. This could take about a year. Any large pieces of undecomposed material can be put into the next heap.

As an alternative, you can put small quantities of household or garden waste into black plastic rubbish bags, tied at the neck, and leave them to decompose slowly.

Standard aerobic compost heap (see overleaf)

The purpose of a compost heap is to bring about rapid decomposition. To do so the numerous bacteria involved need moisture, air, warmth and a source of nitrogen, normally leafy vegetation. The key to making good compost is providing these conditions.

The site Although compost bins can be moved around the garden (they enrich the soil on which they stand), an area set aside for composting is more manageable. Shaded sites might be appropriate in hot climates, but in temperate climates preferably choose a reasonably open sunny site. Make the heap on a soil base so that worms can move in and out of it.

Purpose-made bins Where there is space, erect two semi-permanent bins side by side, or a single bin with two or even three compartments. These enable you to use compost from one bin while the second is still being built up. Individual bins or compartments must be at least 90–120cm/3–4ft high and the same width – the larger the better; otherwise the necessary heat will not be generated. There must, of course, be enough compost to fill that capacity. A long narrow bin might prove feasible in some gardens, tucked alongside a fence or hedge. Bins must be of robust construction. Three sides should be made of material with good insulation properties, such as timber, bricks, breeze blocks or even hay or straw bales. Where timber is used, cornerposts should be 5 × 10cm/2 × 4in thick, with side panels 1–3cm/½–1¼in thick. It is much easier both to put in raw materials and, later, to remove the rotted compost if the front wall is made of loose boards or panels, which can be slid in behind upright posts. Alternatively you can put pairs of upright metal pipes at the corners, and slip the boards between them. A simple, more temporary bin can be made from strong wire mesh, lined with carpet or cardboard as a form of insulation (see illustration, page 55).

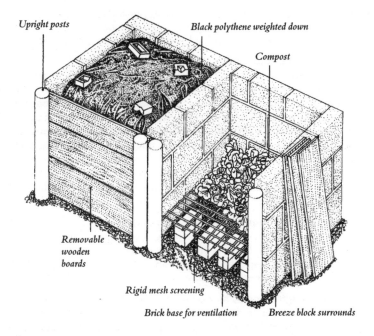

Upright posts

Black polythene weighted down

Compost

Removable wooden boards

Rigid mesh screening

Brick base for ventilation

Breeze block surrounds

A pair of purpose-built compost bins. Three sides are made of breeze blocks and the front of removable wooden boards, slipped behind upright posts. The left-hand bin is full, and covered with black polythene sheeting punctured with ventilation holes. The right-hand bin is being built up on rigid mesh, laid on a brick base, to ensure good ventilation.

Patented bins Provided they are reasonably strong, some of the patented bins on the market can be useful. The larger they are, the better. Make sure that it is easy to put in waste and remove the compost.

Foundations When you start to build the heap, fork the soil underneath. This improves drainage and helps worms to move in later on. On heavy or poorly drained soil aeration and drainage will be further improved if the base layer is made of an 8–10cm/3–4in layer of tree prunings, brushwood or even loose rubble. Another option is to start with a layer of clay land-drain pipes or rows of bricks with small gaps between them. Rigid mesh concrete reinforcement wire can be laid over the bricks to support the heap. These steps are unnecessary on light and well-drained soil.

What to use You can use almost any material of vegetable origin, mixed together in the heap:

∽ household waste and kitchen waste such as vegetable peelings, egg shells, orange peel, tea leaves, tea bags and vacuum-cleaner waste; paper can be included in small quantities, but it should preferably be shredded and soaked beforehand

∽ garden waste including weeds (nettles are excellent), vegetable remains including rhubarb (in spite of occasional advice to the contrary), woody prunings of no more than pencil thickness, old cabbage stalks if shredded, chopped with a spade or cut into pieces up to 7.5cm/3in long, spent potting soil and bonfire ash, lawn mowings in small quantities after being allowed to dry out and rotted straw in moderate quantities (see also Straw, page 44)

∽ gathered materials such as green bracken (gathered between late spring and early autumn) and autumn leaves (even pine needles) in moderate quantities – though leaves are probably better composted separately (see page 55)

∽ animal manure and bird manures, such as pigeon droppings, which can be incorporated or used as an activator (see below).

What not to use

∽ diseased vegetables, particularly any affected with clubroot or onion white rot and, to be on the safe side, potato or tomato plants affected with blight (as the resting spores of some diseases can survive in the cooler parts of a compost heap, and others survive relatively high temperatures, diseased plants should instead be burnt or buried)

∽ perennial weeds such as docks, couch grass, bindweed or ground elder, unless they have been dried out in the sun and killed, and any weeds treated with weedkillers

∽ woody material unless shredded

∽ scrap pieces of meat, which attract rats, or cat and dog wastes or litter, as they pose a health risk

∽ materials that do not rot such as plastic, tin, glass, or man-made fibres.

Building the heap Ideally you should pre-mix waste materials before putting them on the compost heap. The easiest way is to collect them in airtight plastic bags or rubbish sacks. Keep one purely for household waste and one for weeds and, when there is enough material, make them into one layer 15–23cm/6–9in thick. If the material is dry, water it to make it pleasantly moist but not sodden. Never make a thick layer of any one material, especially grass cuttings, which easily become compacted. This prevents air circulation and stops the biological activity in the heap.

The carbon/nitrogen ratio For a heap to provide the right environment for bacteria to flourish it needs to be about two thirds carbon source (by bulk) and one third nitrogen source. The carbon elements come from fibrous material – stems, straw, bean haulm and roots, while the nitrogen is derived from green leaves and manures. In the summer months the balance is normally satisfactory. In autumn and winter a shortage of fresh green material is likely to occur. You can remedy this by adding a source of nitrogen or biological activator to stimulate bacterial activity. Whatever you use, either incorporate it with pre-mixed waste, or sprinkle it thinly on each layer. Suitable materials include proprietary organic compost activators, animal or poultry manure, seaweed meal or concentrated seaweed extracts, blood, fish and bonemeal, or comfrey leaves in a layer two to three leaves thick. (Without an activator, compost will still be made eventually: activators merely accelerate the process.)

Moisture The compost heap needs to be damp, but not soaking wet. Water if necessary. In areas of very high rainfall it may be necessary to protect it with a cover to prevent it from becoming waterlogged.

Completion When the heap reaches the top of the bin, cover it with a sheet of heavy polythene film punctured with holes for ventilation. Make the holes about 2.5cm/1in in diameter and 30cm/12in apart. Then cover the whole heap with permeable insulating material, such as a thick layer of straw, matting, 5cm/2in of soil or an old carpet.

Turning When a heap is completed the temperature initially rises, then after a week or so starts to fall again. You can measure temperatures with a compost thermometer. In a good heap initial temperatures reach about 60–70°C/140–158°F, which will normally kill most weed seeds and pathogens. However, the outer 15cm/6in layers tend to dry out, and can remain cool. Once the temperature is falling the heap can be reactivated by dismantling and rebuilding it – a process known as 'turning' – so introducing a fresh supply of oxygen. It is easiest to turn it into an adjacent empty box. Alternatively, rebuild the heap on the same site, turning it 'sides to middle'. If this is difficult, slice off the outer 7.5–15cm/3–6in before using the compost, and put it aside to start the next heap. Compost heaps can, in theory, be turned once a week. That requires dedication! It is certainly beneficial to turn a heap at least once, replacing the covering afterwards.

Readiness In summer a heap made this way will normally be ready in three or four months; in winter it will probably take at least six to eight months.

Use You can either dig the compost into the soil or spread it on the surface, using up to a barrowload per square metre/yard.

Trench composting
On light and well-drained soil compost is sometimes made in trenches, which preserve heat well. This is inadvisable on heavy or poorly drained

soils, as they are likely to become waterlogged. The idea is to fill the trench with household waste and compostable material during the winter months so that it will be ready for planting with hungry crops, such as runner beans, in spring. Make the trenches about 30cm/12in deep and a convenient width. Add the waste in layers, as in a compost heap, covering each layer with about 1cm/½in of soil. Allow at least two months from filling the trench to sowing or planting. Ambitious gardeners have been known to make compost pits of roughly 1m/3ft depth and width in which to plant pumpkins the following season.

Wire mesh   *Cardboard*

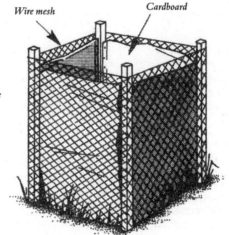

A simple compost bin can be made of wire mesh supported by strong posts and lined with cardboard, as here, or old carpet. Without the lining, it would be suitable for composting leaves to make leaf mould.

LEAF COMPOST

Autumn leaves decompose very slowly, and although they can be worked into compost heaps, if composted on their own they eventually decay into wonderful leaf mould. This can be used in sowing and potting compost, or when half rotted, as drainage material in pots, or for mulching. Simply pack the leaves into a wire-netting enclosure 60–90cm/2–3ft high (see above). They may take up to two years to rot down completely. You can also gather leaves in black plastic sacks, tie the sacks at the neck, and leave the leaves to decompose.

Leaves from trees grown on very alkaline and chalky soils make poor leaf mould. The best way to utilize them is to dig them into trenches.

THE USE OF COMFREY

The deep-rooting, hardy perennial plant comfrey, *Symphytum* spp., is an excellent source of liquid fertilizer and a valuable 'manure' in its own right. The leaves are exceptionally rich in potash, besides containing useful levels of nitrogen and phosphate, and rot down rapidly. No organic garden should be without its comfrey corner. (Half a dozen plants are sufficient for a small garden.) Although the common wild forms, *S. officinalis* and *S. asperum*, can be used successfully for manuring, the most productive form as a fertilizer is 'Bocking 14', a cultivar of Russian comfrey, *Symphytum × uplandicum*.

Cultivating comfrey
Very conveniently, comfrey thrives in light shade, provided it is not too dry, rapidly establishing itself as a ground-cover plant. Indeed the wild species, several of which have beautiful flowers, can become invasive. Even small pieces of broken-off root can sprout and form plants. While these forms are propagated by seed or division, 'Bocking 14' is a sterile clone, and is grown by division of established plants or from root cuttings. Either raise your own or purchase plants or cuttings.

Comfrey is best planted in spring or autumn – rather than in the heat of summer or during its dormant period in mid-winter. Plant in reasonably fertile soil, spacing plants about 75cm/2½ft apart. In the first season remove the flowering stems so that the plant can build up its reserves. Established plants can be cut three to four times a year, but plants may require some feeding to maintain this rate of growth. Beds can easily last for twenty years.

Comfrey leaves as a manure
Wilted comfrey leaves make an excellent compact mulch around plants. They can be used to line potato and tomato trenches or to mulch soft fruit. Layers of leaves, laid two to three deep, can be worked into a compost heap to stimulate bacterial action. However, comfrey should not be composted in bulk, as it rots into a slimy mass.

Concentrated liquid comfrey (comfrey manure or tea)
The simplest way to make this is in a large barrel, rain butt or rubbish bin, supported on bricks to raise it a short distance off the ground (see opposite). Either insert a tap near the bottom, or drill a 1cm/½in hole in the base, standing a jar beneath the hole to collect the juice. Stuff the barrel with fresh or wilted leaves, weighted down with a heavy board to compress them. Cover the barrel with a lid to keep out flies.

The concentrate will start to drip through within about ten days. More leaves can then be added to keep the process active. The concentrate will keep for several months if stored in a jar in a cool dark place. Dilute it from 10 to 20 times with water before use. Avoid getting it on your skin, and be warned: it can be smelly.

Comfrey leaves are packed into a bin and weighed down with a wooden board to make liquid comfrey fertilizer, which drips from the hole at the base into a jar.

Removable lid

Ash can

Wooden board and weights

Packed comfrey leaves

Hole

Jar

Comfrey plant

Comfrey concentrate can also be made by packing chopped leaves into an upright 15cm/6in diameter plastic pipe. (For more information on cultivation of and using comfrey, see the excellent HDRA leaflet, 'Comfrey for Gardeners' – see Further Reading, page 372.)

NETTLE MANURE

Also known as nettle tea, this is another useful, home-made general-purpose fertilizer, best made with young nettles cut in spring. Either make it in the same way as concentrated liquid comfrey (above), or half fill buckets with compacted nettles and cover them with water. Use the resulting liquid, without dilution, 'when it starts to smell' – well, that was the advice given to me by the late Robert Hart, of 'forest garden' fame.

WORM COMPOST

Worm composting is a method of recycling organic kitchen and garden waste, using compost worms to convert the waste into a rich end product, technically known as vermicompost. One of the pioneers of worm compost was the American biologist Mary Appelhof, author of *Worms Eat My Garbage* (see Further Reading, page 372).

Worm compost is highly fertile, being rich in humus and readily available plant nutrients. It can be used as a fertilizer, soil conditioner or potting-compost ingredient. It is not a bulky product, so is best concentrated where it can be most effective, for example sprinkled along seed drills when sowing, around roots or as a top dressing when planting, or worked into containers. It can be mixed with equal quantities of well-rotted leaf mould to make a sowing compost.

Making worm compost

Worm composting is easily adapted to small-scale, domestic use. It is not difficult, provided that you understand the basic principles and meet the necessary conditions. Basic requirements are a container (the worm bin or wormery), initially about a hundred worms, bedding material for the worms and a regular supply of kitchen or garden waste. In temperate climates it is best to start a system in spring or summer when worms breed most rapidly, allowing them to become well established by winter.

Siting the wormery Bins can be kept indoors, outdoors or in a frost-proof shed or garage. Indoor bins need a a close-fitting lid, solid base and internal drainage system. Outdoor bins can be free-draining, either without a base or with a slatted base. Worms cease to work at temperatures below about 10°C (50°F), so the bin will need insulation in cold weather. Bubble plastic, carpeting and polystyrene are suitable insulating materials, provided the ventilation system is not cut off. Portable bins can be moved in and out as required. Bins should never be in direct sunlight.

Types of bin A wide range of containers can be adapted as wormeries, and it is not difficult to make your own. Essentially the container must be strong, waterproof – so that moisture is kept in and rain out – and have means of ventilation and drainage. The greater the surface area, the better, as worms need air and work near the surface.

The most common types of bin are a converted rubbish bin, which can be used indoors or out, and a shallow wooden box, which is more suitable for outdoor use (see below). A typical box is 30cm/12in high,

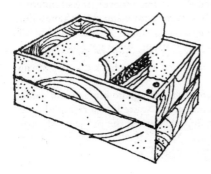

A shallow wooden box, lined with newspaper and filled with bedding, makes a worm compost bin. Drainage holes have been drilled in the base and the surface is covered with damp newspaper or a layer of cardboard.

with a 60 × 90cm/2 × 3ft base. The base is slatted or drilled with about a dozen 1cm/½in drainage holes, covered with a layer of damp newspaper. Worms will not escape through the holes, unless there is insufficient food in the box. In constructing a worm box, avoid wood that has been chemically treated. Various commercial models are available. In choosing one look for sturdiness, reasonable volume (the larger the capacity the better), ease of drainage from the base, a means of ventilation, ease of filling and emptying, and ease of turning or mixing compost.

The earthworms The most suitable worms are those that feed exclusively on decaying organic matter, such as the manure, brandling or tiger worm *Eisenia foetida* (commonly used for bait), the red worm *Eisenia andreii* and *Dendrabaena venera*. Suitable worms can be found in manure heaps or at the base of compost heaps, or bought from fishing shops or suppliers.

Bedding material A layer of light, airy but moist material in the bottom of the container, about 10–13cm/4–5in deep, provides the basic 'home' for the worms to burrow and feed in. Suitable materials are well-rotted compost, leaf mould or farmyard manure. Half the bulk can be newspaper shredded into 2.5–5cm/1–2in strips, moistened thoroughly, then mixed with the same volume of leaf mould, compost or manure. (Avoid newsprint with coloured ink.) To help prevent the contents from becoming acidic and to aid the worms' digestion, add a handful of soil or horticultural sand, or a sprinkling of ground limestone. Introduce the worms into the bedding material, then cover it with several sheets of damp newspaper to keep light out and moisture in. Leave the worms for several days before adding any food.

Feeding the worms Worms do best fed on a varied diet such as organic domestic waste, shredded newspaper and leafy garden waste. Avoid seeding weeds, diseased plant material and fish or meat, which may attract flies. Dried and finely ground egg shells can be incorporated to supply calcium. Either bury the food in pockets throughout the bedding, or spread it over most (but not the entire) surface in a layer up to 5cm/2in deep, covering it with a thick layer of damp newspaper. Only replenish the food supply when it is exhausted. If necessary the worms can be left for up to four weeks without feeding.

Maintaining the wormery Every few weeks or so fork gently through the compost with a hand fork to keep it aerated and to check that the worms are healthy. The contents must be moist but not waterlogged. The ideal temperature for worm activity is 18–25°C/64–77°F.

Extracting the worm compost The compost accumulates gradually below the surface layer, and from time to time, usually after about eight months where bins are used, it must be separated from the worms. You can then start the process again. There are several methods:

∾ Spread what has proved a popular food on the surface (covered with newspaper) and leave for about a week. This will bring most of the worms to the surface. Remove the top few centimetres/inches of undigested food and worms, empty out the lower compost for use, then replace the top layer on fresh bedding.

∾ On a sunny day spread the contents of the bin on a sheet of plastic in a layer 5cm/2in deep. Place thick sheets of wet newspaper in the centre. The worms will congregate under this, and can be collected and added to fresh bedding.

∾ If the wormery is a shallow box, push the compost to one side, and put fresh bedding and a fresh food supply covered with wet paper on the other. In due course the worms will move into the vacant side, allowing you to remove the mature compost. This should be done whenever the bedding layer has become too shallow to bury food in.

Worm casts

Worm casts, usually from worms reared on a seaweed diet, are occasionally offered for sale. You can, of course, collect them from the garden, most easily from lawns. They are a very rich source of nutrients, and benefit the soil and plant growth. Sprinkle them along drills before sowing, or use them to top dress young plants.

GREEN MANURES

Green manures or 'cover crops' are grown primarily to dig in, to increase soil fertility. If even a small piece of ground looks like being vacant for a few weeks or several months, it is worth sowing it with a green manure. Look on green manures as a supplementary source of fertility, never as the sole means of maintaining fertility and supplying plant nutrients. Depending on the crop used, the following are some of the many benefits of green manures:

∾ They increase the organic matter in the soil.

∾ They increase available nitrogen in the soil.

∾ They protect the soil surface over the winter, so preventing soil structure from being destroyed and soluble nutrients being washed out (overwintering manures also take up the nutrients and return them to the soil when they are dug in in spring).

∾ They help to smother weeds.

∾ They increase the drought resistance of the soil.

∾ They produce extra material for the compost heap or for mulching.

∾ In the case of deep-rooting green manures, they draw up nutrients from deeper levels and release them nearer the surface when dug in.

∾ In the case of some, the flowers attract beneficial insects.

Types of green manure
Green manures fall into three main categories, according to their uses:

Fast-growing leafy crops These quickly make a leafy canopy, which, when it is dug in, gives an almost immediate release of nitrogen. Mustard (*Sinapsis alba*) and rape (*Brassica napa* var. *napa*) (a rich source of nitrogen and phosphorus), fodder radish and the blue-flowered *Phacelia tanacetifolia* are examples. Note that all these, except for phacelia, are brassicas (crucifers) in the cabbage family, so avoid growing them in soil where there is clubroot infection.

Leguminous crops The *Leguminosae* family, typified by peas and beans, have nodules on their roots which fix atmospheric nitrogen in the soil, releasing it slowly for the crops that follow them in the ground. Their leaves also produce nitrogen when they rot down. Examples are various types of clover, alfalfa, bitter blue lupin, winter field beans, field peas, winter tares or common vetch and fenugreek (which will not fix nitrogen in cool climates). In some circumstances legumes grow poorly and fail to develop root nodules, because the bacterial rhizobium they need to do this is not in the soil. This usually occurs with non-native species, and can be corrected by using appropriate inoculants, which are mixed with the seed before sowing. They can be purchased from seed companies. Winter-hardy legumes such as field beans, tares and crimson clover can be used for overwintering; perennials such as alfalfa and some clovers can be used as long-term green manures.

Fibrous-rooted crops These develop dense fibrous root systems, which ramify through the soil, improving its structure. When dug in they increase the organic matter in the soil. Grazing rye (*Secale cereale*) and *Phacelia tanacetifolia* are in this category.

Using green manures
Green manures can be used as short-term summer 'catch crops', for overwintering or as long-term manures.

Short-term catch crops Fast-growing green manures are sown from spring to summer, between one crop being lifted and another being sown or planted, whenever a piece of ground becomes vacant. They are dug in a few weeks to a couple of months later. The area sown can be a whole bed or just a small patch or strip a metre/yard or so long. You can also sow green manure in greenhouses and polytunnels, rather than leaving ground bare – especially during the winter.

Overwintering These green manures are sown from summer to autumn and dug in the following spring. In cold areas they must be winter hardy. Grazing rye and field beans are particularly useful as they can be sown in late autumn, after the summer vegetables have been cleared. (See also Leguminous crops, above.)

Long-term Sowing perennial green manures is a productive way of utilizing pieces of land that are surplus to requirements. Not only will they improve the soil structure and keep down weeds, but they can be cut or mown to provide material for mulching or composting. The most suitable crops are legumes (see above).

Choosing a green manure

For good results it is essential to chose manures that suit your soil, your climate and your purpose. At the outset I strongly recommend sowing several different ones side by side – even just a row or two of each. This quickly indicates which will thrive in your conditions. Stick to those in future. See the chart on pages 64–65 for the characteristics of the different green manures. Those I use most in my own garden are *Phacelia tanacetifolia* and fodder radish in summer (they are cut down by the first hard frost to form a natural mulch) and winter tares, grazing rye, crimson clover and field beans for overwintering. These seem to suit our slightly acid clay soil, low rainfall (averaging 50cm/20in per annum) and winter temperatures that drop to -7°C/20°F, but rarely for more than a week at a time.

In fitting green manures into a rotation (see page 176), consider when they will leave the ground available for the next crop to be sown or planted. For example, overwintered green manures normally remain in the ground until late spring, making the ground unavailable for early sowing or planting.

Cultivation and management

Green manures can be broadcast, sown in narrow or wide drills or, in the case of field beans, sown individually (see Sowing methods, page 88). As a general rule they are dug in while still young and succulent, before the stems harden and become woody, or they start to flower. If they are very bulky they can be awkward to dig in. In this case cut off the top growth first. Leave it on the ground to wilt before digging it in, or put it on the compost heap, or use it for mulching. The remaining roots and stems will then be much easier to dig in. Turn them into the top 15cm/6in of soil.

Alternatively, bulky green manures can be cut down, then covered with heavy black film or old carpeting and left to rot.

It takes a while for green manures to break down in the soil, and research has found that in the immediate aftermath, seed germination of the next crop may be suppressed. In warm weather allow two to three weeks to elapse between turning in the manure and sowing, and up to four weeks in cold weather. Otherwise transplant seedlings into the ground, once it is reasonably firm.

MANURING POLICY: A SUMMARY

This is the kernel of the manuring policy I have used in my organic garden for many years:

- ❧ Whenever a piece of ground needs digging, work in organic matter. Depending on availability, I rotate farmyard manure, spent mushroom compost and home-made compost around the garden.
- ❧ Whenever a crop is planted, mulch it with an organic mulch unless mulching films are appropriate.
- ❧ During the growing season stimulate growth on underperforming plants with liquid or foliar feeds, applied on avaerage about once a month, but more frequently if necessary. I generally use seaweed-based stimulants.
- ❧ Every winter ridge up any vacant beds and mulch with bulky organic manure (see page 69).
- ❧ During the growing season sow green manures in vacant ground when opportunities arise, and in late summer/autumn sow several beds with an overwintering green manure.

GREEN MANURE CHART

KEY

Life cycle		Characteristics (Chars)		Usage	
A/HHA	Annual/half-hardy annual B	FGLC	Fast-growing leafy crop	ST	Short-term (sown spring–summer; average 2–3 months in soil)
Biennial		NFL	Nitrogen-fixing legume		
P/HP	Perennial/hardy perennial	NFL*	Not fixing in some soils	OW	Suitable for overwintering
		F	Fibrous-rooted	LTP	Long-term perennial (1 year+)
		DR	Deep-rooting		

CULTURE

Unless otherwise stated: sow in drills 20cm/8in apart; assume sowing spring–summer; cut down before flowering.

	Life cycle	Chars	Soil	Usage	Notes
Brassica napa var. *napa* Rape *see* Mustard (below)					
Fagopyrum esculentum Buckwheat	HHA	DR	Tolerates poor soil	ST	Grows rapidly. Pretty plant; leave some flowers to attract hoverflies
Lupinus angustifolius Bitter blue lupin	HA/HHA	DR NFL	Thrives in light acid soil	ST	Sow to June, seeds 3.5cm/1¼in deep; 13cm/5in apart. Not dense growing. Keep weed-free in early stages
Medicago lupulina Trefoil	A or B	FGLC NFL	Avoid acid soil Tolerates light dry soil	ST OW	Tolerates light shade Sow by August if overwintering
Medicago sativa Alfalfa, lucerne	HP	FGLC NFL* DR	Prefers alkaline soil Avoid acid soil Avoid waterlogged soil	ST LTP	Survives dry conditions once established. Can cut 2–3 times a year if grown as perennial. Pretty flowers; young leaves edible
Phacelia tanacetifolia Phacelia	A, B	FGLC	Tolerates all soils	ST	Last outdoor sowing August; can sow in greenhouses in autumn to overwinter. Survives light frost outdoors if sheltered. Can leave some flowers to attract hoverflies and bees
Raphanus sativus var. *oleifamis* Fodder radish	HHA	FGLC	Any soil	ST	Rots into soil after frost, making good winter ground cover

Secale cereale Grazing rye	HA		Most soils	OW	Sow end summer to early winter. Protect from birds after sowing. Dig in when flower heads felt inside stems. May suppress wireworm
Sinapsis alba Mustard	A	FGLC	Fertile moist soil Avoid soils infected with clubroot	ST	Can turn in 3 weeks after sowing. Turns woody rapidly. Good in greenhouses in winter. Frost tolerant
Trifolium hybridum Alsike clover	HP	NFL	Tolerates wetter and more acid soil than most clovers Avoid very dry soils	ST LTP	If used as perennial cut down before flowering to encourage new growth
Trifolium incarnatum Crimson clover	HA	NFL	Reputedly prefers light soil, but OK on heavy	ST OW	Sow by mid-summer if overwintering. Don't sow in cold areas. Leave some flowers to attract bees
Trifolium pratense Essex red clover	HP DR	NFL	Reasonably fertile; soil with pH>5.5	LTP	Can dig in after few months but more beneficial to leave longer; for cutting see Alsike clover
Trigonella foenum-graecum Fenugreek	HHA	FGLC NFL*	Well-drained fertile soil; drought tolerant when established	ST	Mice attracted to seeds. Relatively slow to become woody. Young leaves edible. Tolerates some frost
Vicia sativa Winter tares/ common vetch	HA NFL	FGLC	Avoid dry acid soil Best on heavy soil	ST OW	Sow late summer, early autumn, c. 4cm/1½in deep, 15cm/6in apart. One of hardiest green manures. Follow with leafy crop to utilize rapid nitrogen release
Vicia faba Winter field beans/ fava beans	HA	NFL	Best on heavy soil Not drought tolerant	OW	Sow by early winter 4cm/1½in deep, 13cm/5in apart. Keep weed-free early. Can cut down in spring and allow more growth before digging in. Makes excellent mulch. Can leave some plants to flower to attract bees. Flowers, leaf tips, small beans edible

4

DIGGING, MULCHING, WEEDING AND WATERING

Digging is the most basic garden operation. Once soil has been thoroughly dug, it is relatively easy to rake the surface into a fine tilth suitable for sowing or planting.

Digging is beneficial for many reasons. It gets air into the soil to encourage bacterial activity; it exposes heavy soil to the elements, which helps break down clods; it breaks up compacted soil so that plant roots can penetrate more deeply; and it exposes weed seeds and insect pests to birds. It is above all a means of working manure and other organic matter into the soil.

Digging is traditionally done with a spade, using a fork for lighter work. Both can be used, so choose whatever is most comfortable for you.

As mentioned earlier, heavy soils are best dug in autumn or early winter. Not only does this expose clods of soil to winter weathering, but clay particles are more likely to be destroyed by working in spring when the soils will be wetter. Light soils are best left until spring. Never dig light soils in very dry conditions, as this will accelerate the loss of moisture, which is always a risk.

The 'degrees' of digging, according to how much effort is involved, are forking, then plain or single digging, then double digging, also known as bastard trenching. Real trenching, which involves digging the ground two spits (that is, two spade lengths deep), is rarely justified except in exceptionally difficult soils.

Whatever method is used, any manure or organic matter being dug in can either be spread evenly over the surface at the outset, or kept 'at the ready' in small heaps or in a wheelbarrow.

Forking

Forking is simply turning over the top layer of soil with a garden fork – or spade if preferred. Manure can first be spread on the surface and forked in. Forking is generally done between clearing one crop and sowing or planting the next. After clearing early peas, for example, fork over the ground before sowing the next crop of, say, lettuces, beetroot or carrots. In spring, after the soil has been broken down by frost, it can often be forked over very easily. If you are fortunate enough to have a really good loamy soil, forking may be sufficient to keep it in good condition permanently, but most soils benefit from being dug annually, with occasional double digging until they are in good condition (see below).

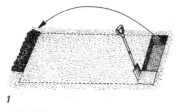

1

2

Single digging
Stage 1: Dig the width of the plot, removing the
soil to the far end of the plot.
Stage 2: Lay manure in the bottom of the trench.
Stage 3: Cover the manure with soil from the
adjacent strip, then fork it over so that soil and
manure are thoroughly mixed.

3

Single digging

The object is to work the top spit of soil, a depth of 23–25cm/9–10in, working in manure or compost in the process (see above). To allow room for manoeuvring, start by taking out a small trench, the depth of the spade and about 30cm/12in wide, across the width of the area you are digging. Remove this soil to the end of the plot, where your digging will finish (see Stage 1). Then dig the strip beside your trench, turning the soil into the first trench – and so on. If you are adding manure initially, lay it in the bottom of the trench (see Stage 2) before turning in the soil from the adjacent strip and forking over to ensure that the soil and manure are thoroughly mixed together (see Stage 3). Fill the last trench with the soil you removed from the first.

Double digging

Here a wider trench is made, about 40cm/16in wide, essentially to provide more working space. Again barrow the soil to the far end of the plot, so that you can use it to fill the last trench. Then fork over the soil at the bottom of the first trench as deeply as possible – to the depth of the fork or spade if possible – put in the manure, and fill the trench with the top spit of soil from the adjacent strip, mixing soil and manure together thoroughly as before. Then fork over the bottom spit of the adjacent strip to the depth of the fork, add manure and so on.

Although double digging is more work, it is worth doing. Experiments at Horticulture Research International in the UK indicate that even apparently good soil becomes compacted in the lower levels. When this compaction is broken up by deeper digging, roots penetrate more easily and extract water from lower levels, so conserving water in the upper layers. This is important because it is from the upper layers that the surface roots extract nutrients, and they can only do so when the soil is moist.

The effects of this deeper digging normally last for about three years. So theoretically most soils, certainly any with a drainage problem, would benefit from this treatment at least every third year; forking or single digging can be done in the years between. Where you have a thin sandy soil, or a shallow soil over gravel or chalk, double digging helps to deepen the topsoil.

Digging tips

- ∾ If you are digging a large area, divide it into smaller sections and tackle them one at a time. (Digging, it goes without saying, seems much less daunting in narrow beds.)
- ∾ Put the spade in as vertically as possible. That way you get through the ground faster and penetrate deeper.
- ∾ With heavy soil, digging is easier if you use the spade to make preparatory 'slits' in the soil at right angles to the trench. You can then remove the soil cleanly.
- ∾ As far as possible, dig out and remove the roots of perennial weeds such as dock, ground elder, bindweed, dandelion, couch grass and thistles. Remove all seeding weeds. Young annual weeds can be dug in. (See also page 74.)
- ∾ Do not attempt to break up the soil finely. Just turn it over and leave it rough, as frost action helps to break up the clods. Frost 'tilth' is very beneficial for soil structure. When you see it on the soil surface, leave it undisturbed for a week to get the maximum benefit.
- ∾ Do not bring subsoil to the surface, as it contains little organic matter or nutrients.
- ∾ Never dig when it is very wet (if the soil is sticking to your boots, it's too wet), very dry or very frosty. If you keep the soil covered with a light mulch of, say, bracken or straw, the surface is protected and will remain 'diggable' in adverse conditions. The mulch itself can be dug in. On heavy soils, aim to complete the digging by early winter, to allow plenty of time for frost to break down the clods.
- ∾ Where possible, allow at least six weeks for the soil to 'settle' before sowing or planting.
- ∾ Digging is hard work. Always go at it gently, taking smaller 'slices' of soil if the going is tough.

A problem in very small gardens is finding the space to double dig: there rarely seems to be a large enough vacant patch. So forking has to suffice, with organic matter applied mainly by mulching until an opportunity arises to dig more thoroughly and incorporate organic matter deeper into the soil. For this reason try to plan your garden so that crops which will mature at roughly the same time are adjacent – not always as simple as it sounds!

Winter ridging

With heavy clay soil it is very beneficial to ridge up the beds in winter. This gives maximum exposure to frost action, while allowing rainfall to drain off the ridges. The ridges can be mulched with organic matter. Ridging is really only practicable with gardens laid out in narrow beds (90–120cm/3–4ft wide). The way I do it is first to fork over a strip, roughly 30cm/12in wide, down the centre of the bed, then to spade the soil from each side on to the forked soil to make the ridge.

Making raised beds

For the concept of making free-standing raised beds, up to about 30cm/12in above ground level, see page 24. Make them as follows:

1 Start by forking over the whole area to a depth of 15–20cm/6–8in. If the soil is poor, double dig it.
2 Mark out the position of the beds, allowing about 38cm/15in for paths.
3 Spade 15–20cm/6–8in of soil from the path on to the bed area to raise it.
4 Rake the bed to level it, then shape it into a curved shape if required. Firm the sides with the back of a spade.

You can remake the beds every few years, double digging the ground at the time if it seems necessary to build up fertility.

Intensive deep beds

These are beds that are made outstandingly fertile, both by very deep digging and by working in large quantities of organic matter. For more on this, see Further Reading, page 372).

'NO-DIGGING'

The 'no-digging' system is advocated by many organic gardeners. In this system digging is abolished in favour of continually mulching the soil, with cultivation more or less restricted to light forking and hoeing. A small area of mulch is scraped away when seeds are sown or planting is carried out.

Compared to other soils 'no-dig' soils generally have higher organic matter, are therefore more fertile and moisture-retentive, and have a high, undisturbed earthworm population. The soil surface is protected in winter, which minimizes leaching, and the soil structure is not damaged through inappropriate digging.

The system has a few drawbacks. Deep-seated compaction problems cannot be remedied, incorporating manures deeply is harder and it can be difficult to eradicate serious perennial weed problems. Mulched soils are slower to warm up in spring, and the mulch itself may provide cover both for overwintering pests and, in slug-prone areas, for slugs.

No-digging is probably most suited to light soils with good underlying drainage and no serious weed problems. On heavier soils, or those with compaction or weed problems, it is advisable to dig conventionally for a few years to correct the problems, before adopting a no-dig approach. I have no first-hand experience of a total no-digging system, but certainly after years of working our heavy clay soil on a narrow bed system, we find that there is now far less need to dig. The more fertile your soil becomes, the closer you are to that nirvana where no digging is necessary.

MULCHING

Mulching is one of the most valuable practices in organic gardening. A mulch is any material laid on the surface of the soil. It can be organic, such as straw or compost, which eventually rots into the soil, or inorganic, such as polythene film, or even stone, gravel and coarse sand. Keeping the soil covered generally increases soil fertility and productivity, besides offering other benefits. It is effective both on outdoor beds and under cover in greenhouses and polytunnels.

Benefits of mulching
Depending on the material used, the following are some of the potential benefits of mulching:

- ∾ Mulching conserves soil moisture by preventing evaporation. This is most valuable in areas of low rainfall.
- ∾ It improves the soil structure by preventing compaction when the soil is walked on; by protecting it from winter weathering and the adverse effect of heavy rain; and by encouraging earthworm activity. (Perhaps surprisingly, earthworm activity seems to increase with both organic and inorganic mulches such as carpeting and heavy films.)
- ∾ It helps keep down weeds.
- ∾ It insulates the soil, by keeping it cooler in summer and warmer in winter.
- ∾ It lessens the need to cultivate, so gradually making a no-dig situation more feasible (see 'No-digging', above).
- ∾ Organic mulches add organic matter and some nutrients to the soil. They can eventually be dug in.
- ∾ Inorganic mulches laid under sprawling plants like bush tomatoes and trailing cucumbers keep them clean and reduce the risk of fungus diseases.

෴ Certain film mulches can deter pests – for example, shiny and chequered plastic films can deter aphids and other insects (see Inorganic mulches, below).

෴ Clear film mulches can be used to warm up the soil for early sowings.

Organic mulches

Organic mulches divide into those which are a source of nutrients and increase soil fertility (they will also keep down weeds if used thickly) and those used primarily to suppress weeds and/or conserve moisture. Most organic mulches should be applied in a fairly well-rotted state, or else nitrogen is taken from the soil in the early stages of decomposition. This is particularly true of mulches derived from wood, such as sawdust and pulverized or shredded bark. It is inadvisable to use them on vegetable beds until they are a couple of seasons old, although they can be used to mulch paths, or for visual effect, laid over plastic film mulches on paths.

The choice of mulching material is wide. Virtually any of the bulky, soil-improving manures mentioned in Chapter 3 can be used as mulches provided they are well enough rotted to be easily spread on the ground and around plants. Garden compost, straw, hay, lucerne hay and pellets, spent mushroom compost, wilted green manure tops, wilted comfrey, spent hops, seaweed, leaf mould and various recycled waste products are all good mulching materials. (For more on their characteristics and use, see pages 43–6.) In the US the marsh plant salt grass (*Spartium patens*) is a popular garden mulch, laid whole or shredded.

Any mulch should be loose enough in texture for air and water to penetrate through to the soil. Bracken and straw, for example, are very permeable. Fresh lawn mowings and fresh comfrey leaves become very compacted if put on in a thick layer. Allow them to dry out for several days before spreading them on the ground. (Never use any materials that have been sprayed with a hormone weedkiller.)

The thickness of the mulch depends on the material and, to some extent, on the reason for mulching. This is one of the things one learns with experience. On the whole the thicker the better, provided that plants are not in danger of being physically swamped. For a mulch to be of most benefit, I would suggest a minimum 2.5cm/1in layer of garden compost, 5cm/2in of mushroom compost or dried lawn mowings and up to 15cm/6in of straw, which 'settles' to much less.

Organic mulches with little or no nutrient value can be used to control weeds and retain moisture. These include peat substitutes such as coir and cocoa shell, flax-fibre mulching mats, recycled biodegradable paper mulches, newspapers laid several layers thick, cardboard, old carpets and matting, and the wood by-products mentioned above. Other than the purpose-made mulching mats, which are excellent for large plants, these materials are more appropriate for use around fruit trees and shrubs, or on paths and waste ground.

Inorganic mulches

These suppress weeds and help retain moisture, but supply no nutrients to the soil. In arid parts of the world plants are mulched with stones, gravel and even sand. In Spain twenty years ago we saw stone mulching in polytunnels: the stones conserved moisture during the day and radiated heat at night. Stone mulches probably need to be at least 7.5cm/3in deep to be effective.

Most of the inorganic mulches used in gardens today are made from some kind of polythene film, with new, potentially useful products continually being launched.

Mulching films vary in thickness from very light (typically 120 gauge/30 microns) to far more substantial and durable films of 500 gauge/125 microns. The following are examples of mulching films currently available:

Impermeable unperforated black film Keeps down weeds, and helps retain moisture and any warmth in the soil, but does little to warm up the soil. It keeps out rain except where planting holes are made.

Black perforated film Keeps down weeds, while allowing some water to penetrate through to the soil. Used for long-term mulching, particularly of strawberries.

Impermeable clear film Warms up the soil and to some extent helps retain moisture, but does little to suppress weeds other than as a physical barrier.

Opaque white film Reflects heat and light up on to plants. In dull climates it is used to mulch fruiting vegetables such as tomatoes and peppers to accelerate ripening. Also useful for mulching salads and oriental greens grown under cover. Suppresses weeds by acting as a physical barrier.

Double-sided black and white 'co-extruded' film A dual-purpose film laid with the black side down to suppress weeds and the white side uppermost to reflect light on to plants, as opaque film above.

Chequered and shiny films Primarily used to deter insects such as aphids, but to some extent suppress weeds and conserve moisture.

Lightweight black permeable fabric A soft fabric that is warm to the touch, easily cut and does not fray. It suppresses weeds, allows some moisture to penetrate, seems to have a warming effect on the soil and keeps plants clean. It is an excellent mulching film under cover, especially in winter. Though more expensive than plastic films it lasts several years if used carefully. It can also be used outdoors.

Permeable woven polypropylene films These dense but permeable films are primarily designed for long-term, weed-suppressing mulches on paths. They drain well, so weeds don't get established on the surface; earthworms seem to flourish beneath them. They can also be used for mulching sturdy plants but there is a risk that they will chafe tender plants. The edges tend to fray, but can be sealed with an electric hot knife or even with a candle. On paths they are best anchored with 15cm/6in long purpose-made metal staples. They can be covered with bark chips to make attractive-looking paths.

For fleece films and perforated transparent films, used to bring crops on sooner, see Crop covers, page 128.

Laying film mulches
On the whole it is easiest to lay film before sowing or planting.

1 Spread the film over the bed or areas to be covered.
2 Anchor the edges by weighing them down with bricks, clods of soil, pieces of timber or polythene bags filled with sand or soil (the most gentle option) and pin them down with tent pegs or purpose-made pegs.
3 With a trowel make slits in the soil at least 7.5cm/3in deep around the area being mulched, bury the film edges in the slits, and push the soil back on top to keep them in place. This looks neat when well done.

The same methods are used for anchoring insect-proof nets and fleeces (see page 131 and illustration, page 148).

In practice it is easier to lay films over slightly domed beds, which have the added advantage of not puddling after rain.

Sowing and planting through films
To sow large seeds, make holes or slits in the film at the required spacing with scissors, a knife or the point of dibber. Small seeds are best raised separately and transplanted as young plants.

Planting through slits in polythene film. Left: cut crossed slits in the film at suitable intervals for the plants. Right: ease the slits open and plant through them.

To plant through films, cut a cross (folding the segments back under-neath) or two sides of a triangle (folding the third back underneath) or a semi-circle (folding the straight side back underneath) large enough to ease the plant through. For planting potatoes under black films, see page 310.

As the plants grow, check that they are not being covered or restricted by the film. Enlarge the holes if necessary. Unless you are using perforated films, water carefully by the plant stem when necessary. Alter-natively, perforated or porous irrigation tube can be laid beneath the film (see page 80).

When to mulch

The golden rule of mulching is to remember that it generally maintains the status quo in the soil. So always mulch beds when the soil is warm and moist, and then it will remain that way. Mulching cold, very wet and very dry soils will be counter-productive. Mulching when planting or immediately afterwards often works well.

There is scope for mulching all year round. Here are some sugges-tions:

- ✿ In autumn mulch overwintering crops, such as celeriac, leeks, parsnips and winter radishes, to keep the soil warm, preserve soil structure and make lifting easier in frosty weather.
- ✿ In early spring mulch lightly after digging unless the soil is very wet. It will keep the soil surface in a beautiful condition before you make the seedbed.
- ✿ In late spring and summer mulch between rows in the seedbed after seedlings have germinated, and between growing crops such as peas, beans, onions and carrots, to keep down weeds and preserve moisture.
- ✿ In summer mulch tomatoes, cucumbers, courgettes and sprawling plants to keep their fruit clean and of good quality.

WEEDS

Weeds can be a serious problem in any garden. They compete for plant nutrients and water in the soil, and for space and light above ground. The weight of a barrowload of weeds is proof of how much they take from the soil. Weeds are very vigorous and will take over completely if unchecked. A row of vegetable seedlings can be smothered by weeds, which usually germinate and grow faster than cultivated plants. Some weeds harbour pests and diseases during the winter. So one way and another, weeds that adversely affect growing vegetables must go. Light weed cover can be tolerated, and it should be said, a fair number, when young and succulent, are edible in salads (see *The Organic Salad Garden*).

The weed problem falls into two parts: annual weeds, which germinate, flower and die in one year, and perennials, which go on from year to year and have very vigorous, persistent root systems.

Annual weeds

Typical annuals – groundsel (*Senecio vulgaris*), chickweed (*Stellaria media*), fat hen (*Chenopodium album*) – are easily dealt with by hand weeding or hoeing. Start as early in the year as you can to minimize the competition with the vegetables you are trying to grow. With most vegetable crops weed competition starts to become really serious about three weeks after the seedlings have germinated. So start weeding then if you haven't already done so. Interestingly, research has shown that it is the weeds between rows, rather than within rows, that are the most competitive. So work on them first.

At all costs, annual weeds must be prevented from going to seed. It is a much quoted and rather depressing statistic that one large fat hen plant can produce 70,000 seeds. Even small, insignificant weeds can produce a fair number of seeds. Take heed of the old proverb 'one year's seeding is seven years' weeding'. There's a lot of truth in it.

Annual weeds can be controlled in the following ways:

By spacing A very satisfying way of keeping weeds under control is to abandon the practice of growing plants in rows with wide spaces between them in favour of growing plants in blocks or patches, with equal spacing between them. When fully grown the leaves of neighbouring plants touch and form a blanketing canopy over the soil, which effectively prevents most weed seeds from germinating. Here again, research supports the practice: apparently the filtered light created by a canopy of leaves makes the weed seeds dormant. This system won't work with narrow-leaved vegetables like onions and leeks. You will need to weed or hoe between plants in the early stages – or better, mulch with dry lawn mowings, mushroom compost or some well-rotted organic material. Some weeds inevitably find their way through the mulch but they are relatively easy to pull up. A snag is that the mulch itself can be a source of weeds. Even so, it is worth using.

With mulching films Mulching plants with one of the many films now available (see Inorganic mulches, page 72) is an effective way of controlling weeds, even though the films are rather unsightly. There are two ways of laying film mulches. On the whole it is easiest to lay the film first, making holes and planting through them (see illustration, page 73). However in some cases it makes sense to get the plants established, then unroll the film over the plants, cut cross-like slits in it above the plants and gently pull the plants through.

With mulching mats Single large plants such as globe artichokes or squashes can be mulched with purpose-made mats. These can be cut from any heavy, light-excluding material such as heavy polythene film, pieces of old carpeting or some of the excellent biodegradable materials made of flax fibre, coir and so on. Cut the mats into squares or circles of 30cm/12in or more diameter, with a slit cut from the outside edge to the centre point. You can then open out the mat and slip it around the stem of the plant, in much the same way as collars are slipped around brassica plant stems to deter cabbage root fly (see illustration, page 148).

Bulky organic mulches Organic mulches (see page 71) – mushroom compost, for example – will to a large extent control weeds, though it may take a very thick mulch (7.5cm/3in deep) to suppress the more vigorous weeds.

Cultivation practices Weed seeds remain viable for many years and ground that has not been cultivated for some time holds a huge reservoir of seed. Many of these seeds will germinate on cultivation. The best course when cultivating ground that is likely to be full of weed seeds is to prepare it for sowing or planting (see page 86), leave it for a week or so to allow the first flush of weeds to germinate, then hoe them off before sowing or planting. You can encourage the germination of weed seeds by covering the ground with clear polythene film after preparing the soil. In the first season try to avoid deep cultivation, as this brings up more weed seeds from the lower layers. Just hoe shallowly, pull up weeds by hand or mulch around plants. Unless they have gone to seed, all annual weeds can be put on the compost heap.

Perennial weeds
Perennial weeds are more of a problem than annual weeds. The most common are couch grass (*Agropyron repens*), dandelion (*Taraxacum officinalis*), ground elder (*Aegopodium podograria*), docks (*Rumex* spp.), nettles (*Urtica* spp.), marestail or horsetail (*Equisetum arvense*), and hedge and field bindweed (*Calystegia sepium* and *Convolvulus arvensis*). There are of course others – every garden tends to have its own special 'worst weed'. Occasionally a cultivated plant runs riot and becomes a weed: Japanese knotweed (*Fallopia japonica*) is a prime example.

With perennial weeds it is important to recognize them, both by their leaves and by their roots. Use a good wild flower book for identification (see Further Reading, page 372). As a rule perennials either have long deep roots (dandelions, thistles) or rambling extensive roots (couch grass, ground elder, bindweed). Annuals generally have shallow roots and are easily pulled up. If in doubt, pull it out!

Perennials can be controlled in the following ways:

Persistent attack The main approach is to cut them down frequently and dig them out. With some thistles, bindweed, ground elder, couch grass and dandelion even small pieces of root can sprout, so it is important to remove the plant as completely as possible. The best time is during winter digging. In summer try not to hoe perennials off at ground level, which may encourage them to resprout, but pull them up by the roots. A piece of good news from the now defunct Weed Research Station: docks will die if you chop off the top 10cm/4in of root. Either bury the roots of perennials deeply or dry them out in the sun before putting them on the compost heap. Some of them have remarkable powers of recovery in second-rate compost heaps. All weeds manufacture food through their leaves, and by continual removal of the leaves the plants will be weakened. Ground elder is one plant that can eventually be defeated this way.

Mulching The mulching techniques mentioned above can be used to keep perennials within bounds while vegetables are growing. Vigorous perennials, and the sharp growing points of couch grass, tend to push through or up around the edges of the mulch, or re-emerge when the mulch is lifted.

Perennials on neglected sites
Perennial weeds can be discouraging for anyone tackling a neglected garden. This is where chemical weedkillers (herbicides) are tempting. The organic alternative is to blanket the ground so that all light is excluded.

The first step is to chop back the top growth with a hook, then to cover the ground with materials such as heavy-gauge black polythene film, old carpeting, even a single or double layer of cardboard. How long it needs to be left down depends on the weeds, soil and situation – anything from three months in the growing season to a maximum of a year. The mulch will, of course, also deter the annual weeds. Lift the covering from time to time and dig down to see to what extent the plants and roots have been weakened. If most of the remaining weeds can be pulled or dug out, start cultivation. It is advisable to plant through a weed-suppressing mulching film or material initially rather than sowing seeds. If cardboard is used, it will have become soft enough to plant through after several months' exposure.

When breaking in compacted or neglected ground, it may be necessary to rotovate several times to make the ground workable. In practice the first and second rotovations may simply cut the perennial roots up into pieces that regenerate. They will, however, have been disturbed and loosened, and with a little persistence can eventually all be removed.

WATERING

Even in the apparently wet climate in the British Isles, most vegetables benefit substantially from an increased supply of water, particularly in the drier regions of the country.

Plants require a constant throughput of water, which is taken in by the roots and evaporated through the leaves. They need enough water to keep the leaves turgid – growth is checked once they start to wilt – but it's a fallacy to assume that the more watering the better. Water washes nitrogen and other soluble nutrients out of reach of the roots and it encourages shallow, surface rooting, rather than the deep rooting that enables plants to utilize deeper reserves of nutrients and moisture. I'm personally convinced that generous watering reduces the flavour of fruiting vegetables such as tomatoes.

Water mainly stimulates leaf growth, which is what you want with leafy plants like lettuce and cabbage. With root and bulb crops, radish and onions for example, overwatering may result in excessive leaf growth at the expense of the roots. Requirements also vary according to the stage of development, giving rise to 'critical periods' for watering (see below).

Conserving water
In regions where water is an increasingly scarce resource, you should do everything you can to conserve it and minimize the need to water.

- Dig in as much bulky organic matter as possible, as deeply as possible, to increase the water-holding capacity of the soil. This is particularly beneficial on light, fast-draining soils.
- Far more water is lost through evaporation than drainage, so keep the soil surface mulched to prevent evaporation (see page 70). Wherever practicable, mulch immediately after watering.
- On sloping ground, lay out your beds across rather than down the slope to minimize erosion and loss of water.
- In dry weather minimize cultivation. Surface hoeing encourages evaporation, and deeper cultivation brings moisture to the surface, which then evaporates. Once the top few inches of the soil have dried out, they act as a mulch and the rate of evaporation is slowed down.
- Keep the ground weed-free. Weeds both compete for water and evaporate moisture through their leaves.
- Wind increases the rate of evaporation, so, especially in exposed gardens, erect artificial windbreaks (see page 20).
- Collect water from any conveniently sited roofs, with a down pipe leading to a lidded rain butt or barrel. (Lids help prevent the development of pests and diseases.) Rainwater is purer and softer than mains water.
- Where water is scarce, concentrate on watering during the critical periods (see below).

How to water
The golden rule is to water gently and thoroughly. Large water droplets destroy the soil surface and damage fragile plants and seedlings. These

should be watered with a fine rose on the can, the rose turned upwards for the gentlest spray.

The most common fault when watering is to underwater. The soil becomes wet layer by layer, and until the top layers are thoroughly wet, the root zone beneath will remain dry. This takes much more water than most people realize. It is salutary to poke your finger into the soil after what seems like a heavy shower; the soil is often remarkably dry. So never just sprinkle the surface for ten minutes or so. An occasional 'good heavy watering' is far more beneficial than light intermittent waterings. A good heavy watering is about 22 litres per sq. m/4 gallons per sq. yd. However, light soils need to be watered more frequently than heavy soils, though less water is required at each watering.

With established plants, direct water to the base of the plant. Where plants are spaced far apart, confine watering to a circular area around each, leaving the soil between them dry to discourage weed germination. You can water large plants like tomatoes and courgettes by sinking a porous clay pot into the ground near the plant and watering into the pot. Water seeps through gradually. Plants grown closely at dense spacing make heavy demands on soil water, and need generous watering. (This concept underlies the wide spacing adopted in arid regions.) Intensively grown cut-and-come-again crops also need plenty of water.

As a general rule, water in the evening to minimize evaporation, but allow time for leaves to dry before nightfall. This is important in poly-tunnels, where high humidity at night can encourage fungal disease.

Critical periods for watering

Germination Seeds will not germinate in dry conditions, so ground destined for sowing must be watered in advance.

Transplanting This is a delicate stage for plants. They should be trans-planted into moist but not waterlogged soil, and kept moist until they are established. Root hairs on 'bare root' plants are often damaged by trans-planting, which initially limits the plant's ability to absorb water. Water gently – daily in dry weather – applying no more than 140ml/¼ pint each time. Plants raised in modules are much less delicate, but must be watered thoroughly before transplanting.

Leafy vegetables Vegetables grown primarily for their leaves, such as brassicas, lettuce, endive, spinach and celery require a lot of water throughout growth. In the absence of rainfall, they would benefit from about 10–15 litres per sq. m/2–3 gallons per sq. yd a week. Where regu-lar watering is difficult, limit watering to a single, heavy watering – about 22 litres per sq. m/4 gallons per sq. yd – concentrated ten to twenty days before you estimate that the plant is ready for harvesting.

Fruiting vegetables For tomatoes, cucumbers, peas and beans – all vegetables grown for, in botanical terms, their 'fruits' – the critical time for watering is when the plants are flowering and the fruits start to swell. Heavy watering at this stage increases their yields appreciably. (For full details, see appropriate crop in the Vegetable Directory.)

Root crops These need enough water for steady growth, but too much water encourages lush foliage rather than root development. In the early stages, water only if the soil is in danger of drying out, at the rate of at least 4.5 litres per sq. m/1 gallon per sq. yd a week. More water is required in the later stages when the roots are swelling.

Watering equipment
In small gardens a watering can, with a fine rose for watering seedlings, is sufficient. In larger gardens semi-automatic systems potentially save time and water. Various types of hose or tubing can be operated on low water pressure systems, connected directly to a mains water tap, a water butt or a garden hose. These gently water a strip up to 50cm/20in wide.

Perforated polythene 'layflat' tube This cheap, flexible, but not very durable hose, is laid on the ground between plants. Water seeps out through small holes in the tube.

Porous pipe/seeper hose These stronger hoses are permeable along their length. They can be buried 10–15cm/4–6in deep in the soil in permanent beds or, where more flexibility is wanted, laid on the surface. Covering them with mulch prevents evaporation and the build-up of scale in hard water areas.

Drip/trickle irrigation systems In these systems water is delivered to individual plants through nozzles or emitters in fine tubes. Networks can be designed to water large areas, greenhouses and containers. On a large scale get professional advice and good-quality equipment.

On the whole, overhead sprinkler systems are not recommended in a vegetable garden. Water is wasted as much falls on bare soil and is evaporated; moreover, plants are more prone to disease when water is directed on to leaves rather than to the roots.

5

SEED, SOWING AND PLANTING

SEED

Seed quality

Most vegetables are raised from seed and, for the majority, minimum standards of purity and germination are laid down by law. This means that the seed you buy is normally of good quality. Seed, however, is grown all over the world and subject to the vagaries of climate. Inevitably in some years the seed harvest is better than others, which can be reflected in the quality of seed available.

Within the countries of the European Union vegetable varieties can only be sold if they are listed in the 'Common Catalogue' and the appropriate National List. The economics and costs involved mean that some old varieties have been withdrawn, and can only be obtained today through heritage seed libraries (see page 9).

Vegetable seed is widely sold in garden centres and supermarkets, but they tend to stock only the most popular types and varieties. Dedicated vegetable growers will find a far wider choice in the many mail-order seed catalogues.

Seed viability

All seed deteriorates with age, gradually losing its viability – that is, its ability to germinate. Deterioration is most rapid under damp or hot conditions. (See Seed storage, below.)

The natural viability of vegetable seed varies according to the species, and is affected by a range of factors. Tomato and legume seed can, under good conditions, keep for up to ten years; brassicas, lettuce, endive and chicory will normally last four or five years, but may fall off after a couple of years; the onion and leek family deteriorate after the second year; root vegetables such as parsnip, salsify and scorzonera lose viability rapidly, so it is advisable to use fresh seed each year.

Testing viability Rather than wasting time sowing seed of dubious viability, do a germination test before making your main sowing. Put a piece of foam rubber in a small dish (to retain moisture), cover it with a double layer of paper towelling, lay the seeds on top and put them somewhere warm (a temperature of 21°C/70°F is recommended), preferably covered or in a plastic bag to conserve moisture. If the seeds have not germinated within a couple of weeks, cut your losses and buy fresh seed.

Seed storage

You should always keep seed as cool and dry as possible, never in a hot kitchen or damp shed. Ideally it should be stored at temperatures below freezing: for every 5°C/9°F rise above zero, the storage life of seed is halved. Keep seed in an airtight tin or jar in a cool room or, if there is space, in a domestic refrigerator. An additional safeguard is to put a cloth bag or dish of silica gel crystals in the container to absorb atmospheric moisture. Periodically remove it and dry it in a low oven for a few hours before replacing it in the seed box. Cobalt-treated silica gel usefully turns from blue to pink when moist, indicating when it needs to be dried. Recently silica gel has become hard to buy in small quantities. An alternative, suggested by the Genetic Resources Unit at the Wellesbourne Gene Bank, is to use grains such as wheat or rice. Drive out any latent moisture by drying the grains for about an hour on a metal tray in a low oven. Then immediately put them into an airtight jar or tin to cool. Store seeds in paper or foil packets in the same jar. Never store seeds in plastic bags, which create a moist atmosphere.

Foil packs Vegetable seed today is often packed in hermetically sealed foil packs. Seed remains viable much longer in these than in paper packets, but once the foil packs are open, normal deterioration sets in.

Types of seed

Seed firms offer seed in different forms and with various treatments.

Naked seed This is the term for ordinary individual seeds. In the case of beetroot, the so-called 'seed' actually contains several seeds, which have to be thinned on germination.

Pelleted seed Individual seeds are coated with an inert protective material, making them into tiny balls. The technique is very useful for minute and odd-shaped seed, as it makes them much easier to handle. As a result they can be sown accurately, reducing or eliminating the need to thin seedlings subsequently. The protective coating normally breaks down in the soil, but with some types of pellet the coating can harden if the pellet dries out, preventing germination. To avoid this, sow shallowly at about twice the pellet's depth, in pleasantly moist soil; if conditions are dry, sow in watered drills (see page 88). Gently firm the ground after sowing to retain soil moisture, and if necessary water lightly to keep the soil moist until the seed germinates.

Pills Pills and split pellets are among other types of pellets, mainly used by commercial growers for sowing under cover but sometimes available to home gardeners. Sow them very shallowly, virtually on the surface.

Seed tapes and sheets Seeds are embedded into soluble tapes, or tissue-like sheets. The seeds are evenly spaced, generally about 1–2cm/½–¾in apart, so subsequent thinning is minimized and easily done. 'Sow' the tapes or sheets by laying them on the soil, or in a seed tray, covering with soil and keeping them moist in the normal way.

Chitted or pre-germinated seed The seed has just started to germinate – a tiny root can be seen – and is despatched by a seed firm in a small sachet ready for pricking out (see page 104). Such seed is a useful short cut for home gardeners, especially with seed such as cucumber that requires high temperatures to germinate but, once germinated, can be grown at some-what lower temperatures. You can also chit your own seed to give a head start to seeds that are unlikely to germinate if sown outside in cold soils – such as French beans and sweet corn. Use the technique for testing seed viability (see page 81). Sow the seeds as soon after they have germinated as possible, handling them extremely carefully when you do so as the tiny root tips are easily damaged.

Primed seed Seed is brought to the point of germination by the suppli-ers, then dried and packeted. Once sown, it germinates exceptionally fast, making this a valuable technique for seeds that germinate slowly when sown *in situ* in open ground, such as carrots, parsley and onions. Sow seeds as soon after receiving them as possible – and at least within three months. After that they may completely lose their viability.

Dressed and treated seed Seed is quite frequently treated or dusted with chemicals, either to combat soil-borne diseases which prevent germina-tion (especially in cold wet soils), or to overcome certain seed-borne dis-eases, such as celery leaf spot. Always wash your hands after handling treated seed. Seed treatments and dressings may affect long-term viability, so it is inadvisable to keep seed for a second season. Strictly speaking, organic gardeners should not use these seeds. Untreated seed is available from companies supplying organic gardeners, and other seed companies can often supply untreated seed on request.

Choosing varieties
Choosing between the many varieties available can be bewildering, especially for the novice gardener. There are some indicators of quality and suitability.

F1 hybrid seed Most new vegetable varieties are 'F1 hybrids', made by crossing two parent lines that have been inbred for several generations. Compared to standard 'open-pollinated' varieties, the resulting hybrid plants have exceptional vigour, quality and uniformity, often coupled with useful disease resistance. The seed is expensive, as the cross has to be remade every time seed is required. Personally I feel that the cost is almost always justified. (Incidentally, it is not worth saving seed from F1 hybrid varieties, as they will not breed true.) F1 hybrids are widely grown in commercial horticulture, partly because new varieties can easily and effectively be patented. This has been a factor in the loss of heritage varieties and explains the reluctance of some gardeners to use them.

Awards of merit As a result of assessment in formal trials, outstanding cultivars are given the Award of Merit (AM) by the Royal Horticultural Society in the UK, and Gold, Silver and Bronze medals in the All America Awards scheme (AAA) in the US.

'Suitable for organic growers' Since the late 1990s regular trials have been carried out in the UK to assess the performance of varieties in an organic system. The main qualities looked for are natural vigour (not least to outstrip weeds), and pest, disease and weather resistance.

Genetically modified seeds With the many serious, unresearched and unanswered questions over the long-term effects of this plant-breeding technique, I feel strongly that gardeners should not use genetically modified seed.

SAVING YOUR OWN SEED

Home gardeners are generally advised against saving their own seed because of the risk of cross-pollination and the difficulty in ripening seed in the unpredictable climate in the British Isles. It takes skill to save seed of high quality. However, you may want to save seed of a variety that is difficult to obtain, or of an outstanding plant of your own. It is also useful to save seed of cut-and-come-again salad crops, which utilize far more seed than is found in the average seed packet. This is relatively easy for those like cresses, corn salad, chervil and salad rocket, which naturally run to seed in spring and early summer when the weather is more reliable. They can sometimes be sown simply by crumbling the seed pods into the drills. Radish, broad and runner beans and peas are also easily saved. To be sure of maintaining quality, it is advisable to start again with commercial seed every few years. (See also Further Reading, page 372.)

Seed-saving guidelines

- ✿ Save from the best plants, never from diseased plants or plants that have bolted prematurely.
- ✿ Only save seed of one cultivar of any vegetable; otherwise there may be a risk of cross-pollination.
- ✿ If necessary, to avoid cross-pollination or provide protection, transplant a promising or 'special' plant into an out-of-the-way corner or into a greenhouse or polytunnel, and allow it to seed there.
- ✿ Keep plants well watered when they are flowering and when the seed heads are forming, but stop watering when the seeds pods start to turn from green to brown.
- ✿ Stake or tie tall plants to prevent them from falling on the ground and the seed pods from becoming soiled or diseased.

ﾍ As far as possible, allow the seed pods to dry naturally on the plant. Cut the stems at ground level just before the pods burst, and hang or lie them in a cool dry place, with newspaper beneath to catch seed from shattering pods.

ﾍ If there is a risk of seed pods being damaged by rain, birds or other pests, pull them up before they have dried and hang them upside down under cover, say in a greenhouse, to dry off completely. Place newspaper beneath to catch falling seed.

ﾍ When the pods are brittle dry, shake out the seed on to newspaper, blowing off any dust and debris. Store the seed in paper envelopes, jars or empty film cassette cans in cool dry conditions (see Seed storage, page 156).

WHERE TO SOW SEED

The majority of vegetables are raised from seed. Depending on the circumstances, they can be sown *in situ*, in a nursery seedbed or 'indoors'.

In situ This is sowing in the ground where the plants will remain until maturity. The method is mostly used for root vegetables such as beetroot, carrots, parsnips, radishes and turnips, none of which transplant easily, for large seeds like peas and beans, and for cut-and-come-again seedling crops (see page 156).

In a nursery seedbed A nursery seedbed is a piece of ground set aside for raising seedlings and young plants, which are sown in relatively closely spaced rows, from which they will later be transplanted into their permanent position. A seedbed is used primarily as a means of saving space in the main beds. Slower-growing vegetables, especially those that eventually require a lot of space, can be nurtured until ready to transplant, allowing the main beds to be used meanwhile for other crops. Leeks and brassicas, vegetables that transplant well, are often grown in seedbeds. The disadvantage of using seedbeds is that seedlings grow rapidly and soon become overcrowded unless thinned, and plant root hairs are inevitably damaged in pulling up the young plants. For this reason raising plants in modules is often preferable (see page 97).

'Indoors' This term implies sowing in a greenhouse or anywhere under cover or protected, in some kind of seed tray or modules (see also Sowing indoors, page 95). The main purpose is to extend the growing season, especially for the more tender vegetables. It is essentially used

ﾍ for tender vegetables which cannot be planted outside until after the danger of frost is over;

ﾍ to extend the growing season and obtain better or earlier crops of standard vegetables.

There are no hard and fast rules about which method to adopt for any vegetable. It will vary according to the region, the cultivar (some are bred to withstand colder temperatures) and what you are trying to achieve. Take lettuce: it can be sown under glass to provide an early outdoor planting; it can be sown in a seedbed early in spring for the early summer crop; and later sowings can be made *in situ*, when conditions are drier and transplanting is more risky. These plants are thinned out to the required distance.

The following pages describe sowing methods in some detail, largely for the benefit of new gardeners. It may sound a little complicated at first but soon becomes as instinctive as driving a car.

MAKING A SEEDBED

The term 'seedbed' is confusingly used both for any piece of ground where seed is sown and for a nursery seedbed, an area put aside for raising seedlings as described above. Both cases require the same approach to preparing the ground and sowing the seed.

Siting a nursery seedbed

✤ Make the seedbed in an open position, even though it may be tempting to tuck it into an odd corner or near a hedge. These spots are unsuitable as they are likely to be dry and partly shaded, and the seedlings will become drawn and spindly as they strain towards the light.

✤ The soil does not have to be very fertile, as young plants are undemanding. The lighter the soil, the better: avoid heavy and stony soils.

✤ Choose a site that is free of perennial weeds, as it will be difficult to weed without disturbing the seedlings. And avoid last year's potato plot, as tiny sprouting potatoes are a menace among small seedlings.

✤ There is a lot of capital locked up in a seedbed, so if it is likely to be plagued by cats, dogs, birds or even children, enclose it with a temporary wire-netting fence held in place with bamboo canes. Single strands of strong black cotton over individual seed rows will usually deter birds.

Getting a tilth

Tilth is an old word gardeners use to describe the state of the surface of the soil. For sowing average-sized seeds the soil surface needs to be firm but not consolidated, free of stones and lumps of soil, and raked to a 'fine tilth', with the soil crumbs roughly the size of breadcrumbs. The art of preparing a seedbed is essentially that of creating a tilth. How easy this is depends on the soil structure (see page 27). Soil with a good structure can often simply be raked in spring to create a tilth ideal for sowing seeds. It is more difficult to get a good tilth on soils that dry out rapidly with the surface almost turning to dust, or on soils that are sticky when wet then dry into solid, almost unbreakable clods – both conditions caused by poor structure.

The key is recognizing the precise point to start making the seedbed – and that comes with experience. The soil must be neither too wet nor too dry. If it sticks to your shoes as you walk on it, let it dry out for a few more days before tackling it. But don't wait until it is completely dry and dusty. The 'right moment' is particularly important on clay soils, which can turn from a wet and sticky state into hard clods almost overnight.

If you cover the soil with a light organic mulch after you have dug it over in the winter or spring, it will be much easier to make a good seedbed when the time comes. Just rake the mulch aside before starting to work. (Very wet soils should not be mulched, but should be exposed and allowed to dry out.)

These are the steps in preparing a seedbed:

1 If the soil is rough or fairly compacted, start by lightly forking or hoeing to a depth of 5–7.5cm/2–3in. This dries it out and makes it easier to work.

2 When the surface seems in the right state – that is, dry enough to crumble to a tilth (possibly the same day, or maybe a few days later), break down any clods with the back of the rake, rake it level, and rake off stones and any remaining lumps of soil. Small lumps can sometimes be crumbled in your hands.

3 Rake the soil gently backwards and forwards until you have the sort of tilth you want. The finer the seeds being sown, the finer the tilth should be. Large seeds like peas and beans are best sown in a fairly coarse tilth, which discourages weed germination. It may be necessary to repeat the raking procedure several times, perhaps over a few days, to get the soil just right for sowing. It will probably need one final raking just before sowing.

4 If you cannot sow a prepared seedbed immediately, cover it with a thin mulch of straw, hay, compost or even newspaper, to preserve the tilth and prevent it from drying out until you are ready. The strong winds which are common in spring dry out a surface in no time (see also Stale seedbed, below).

5 If you want to encourage weed seed germination before sowing vegetable seed, so that you can hoe them off, cover the prepared seedbed with transparent film (see also page 76).

In the past, shuffling over the soil or treading it before raking was recommended. That is now considered to be damaging to the soil structure, except perhaps on very light soils.

Stale seedbed

Preparing a seedbed about ten days before sowing – a 'stale seedbed' – is a useful practice to deter the bean seed fly and onion fly, pests which are attracted by the smell of freshly disturbed soil. The flies lay eggs in the soil, which hatch into maggots, which attack onion, leeks, peas and beans. The seedbed can be covered with very fine netting as an extra precaution.

Temperature

Seeds germinate at different temperatures, but rarely at soil temperatures below 5°C/41°F. Use a soil thermometer to measure the soil temperature or simply feel the soil. If it feels cold to the touch, the odds are that it is too cold for sowing. Almost all vegetable seeds germinate much faster in warm rather than cold soils; lingering in the soil before germination often proves fatal. So never be in a hurry to start sowing early in the year unless you can provide protective covering, such as cloches. Be guided by the weather and the soil conditions. This is a case where the early bird does not catch the worm and is far more likely to catch a cold.

SOWING METHODS

Seed can be sown in narrow drills, sown in wide drills, broadcast or sown singly. With all but the last, it is essential to *sow thinly*. New gardeners are always tempted to sow thickly – just in case! If you do, in practice, either germination is so good that masses of seeds germinate, and have to be thinned in time as otherwise none will be any use, or some other factor such as cold soil, bad weather, pests or the age of the seed prevents almost all the seeds from germinating – so you have to sow again anyway.

Sowing in narrow drills

This is the standard method of sowing outdoors in rows. It is used for fast-maturing plants like radishes, or for vegetables that are awkward to transplant such as carrots, beet, salsify and parsley, and lettuce in hot weather. It can also be used for cut-and-come-again seedling salads. Sowings in nursery seedbeds are normally made in narrow drills.

1 Try to choose a day when there is not much wind.
2 Prepare a seedbed with a fine tilth (see page 86).
3 Mark out your row with a garden line or twine attached to sticks or metal pegs. Mark each end with sticks or pegs. In the nursery seedbed rows can be as close as 10–13cm/4–5in apart for lettuces or leeks, and about 20–23cm/8–9in for brassicas.
4 Use the point of a trowel or hoe, or even a pointed stick, to make a straight, shallow, smooth drill along the length of the line. The drill can be anything from 1–5cm/½–2in deep, depending on the seed. As a general rule, seeds need to be covered by about twice their depth of soil.

Sowing in a drill. Left: use the point of a trowel or hoe to 'draw' the drill at an even depth. Right: space the seed thinly and evenly along the drill. After sowing, press the seeds gently into the bottom of the drill with a finger or the back of the trowel or hoe and cover the seeds with soil.

Most small seeds need to be just covered with soil and larger seeds such as lettuce by about 1cm/½in of soil. Exceptions are peas and beans, which are sown 3–5cm/1¼–2in) deep. As a general rule, sow slightly deeper on lighter soils than on heavy soil.

5 Put a few seeds in the palm of the hand, take a pinch at a time between the forefinger and thumb, and drop the seeds along the drill. This may seem laborious but is more accurate and less wasteful than shaking a packet at random along a row.

Methods of seed spacing. Top: evenly spaced seeds to minimize thinning. Below: station sowing with fast-maturing radish interspaced between evenly spaced, slower-growing parsnips.

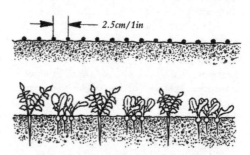

6 Either space the seed evenly along the drill, roughly 1–2.5cm/½–1in apart or 'station sow' – that is, sow in groups of three or four seeds, leaving a space between each group (see above). These will eventually be thinned to one per station. If the final spacing will be, say, 20cm/8in apart, sow groups 10cm/4in apart. Sowing evenly and station sowing prevent seedlings from becoming overcrowded, cut down the need for thinning and make weeding easier. In some cases two different vegetables can be intersown in the same row. The classic example of this is fast-growing radish sown between slow-growing

parsnips. The radishes are cleared before the space is required by the parsnips.

7 After sowing, press the seeds gently into the bottom of the drill with the side of your hand or the back of the rake or hoe.

8 Cover the seed with well-crumbled soil, using your fingers, or a hoe or trowel, and put in a label.

9 In dry weather the seedbed can be covered after sowing with clear film (see page 128), to help retain moisture until the seeds germinate. Remove it as soon as the seedlings appear above ground.

10 Once the seedlings are well established, put a 2.5cm/1in thick layer of dried grass cuttings or well-rotted compost between the rows as a mulch. This keeps down weeds and helps retain moisture in the soil. If the ground is not already moist, water before mulching.

11 Watch out for attacks from pests such as slugs, flea beetle and birds, which attack plants in the vulnerable seedling stages (see Chapter 7).

Sowing in wide drills. Use the blade of an onion hoe or draw hoe to make a flat drill of the depth required.

Sowing in wide drills

A 'wide drill' is a shallow, flat-bottomed drill, generally, but not necessarily, about 10cm/4in wide, the width of a hoe blade. The depth is adjusted as for a narrow drill above. Wide drills are convenient for sowing seeds that require little or no thinning, such as radishes or peas, or for those harvested as cut-and-come-again crops, for example seedling salads (see page 156). In this case several drills can be made side by side, the seedlings eventually spilling over the edges to make dense patches. A wide drill can be considered a halfway house between a standard drill and broadcasting; it is easier to weed than a broadcast area.

1 Prepare the seedbed in the normal way.

2 Use the blade of an onion hoe or draw hoe to make a flat drill of the depth required. If sowing fairly dense patches of salad seedlings, make adjacent drills as close as they can be without spilling soil from one into the next.

3 Sow seed evenly across the drill and press it in.

4 Cover with the soil from the edge of the drill.

Broadcasting. Left: scatter the seeds evenly over the soil. Right: rake the soil first in one direction, and then at right angles to the first direction, to cover the seed.

Broadcasting

In this method seeds are scattered over the surface of the soil and then raked in. Again, the method is used where little or no thinning is required, traditionally for early carrots, for turnips when grown for turnip tops, for sowing green manures, and also for mustard, cress, salad rocket and other cut-and-come-again seedling crops (see page 156). It is unwise to broadcast in weedy soil, as subsequent weeding is difficult.

1 Prepare the seedbed normally. If you suspect that the soil is very weedy, prepare it first, allow the first flush of weeds to germinate and hoe them off before sowing.
2 Scatter seed evenly over the surface.
3 Rake the soil first in one direction, then at right angles to the first direction, to cover the seed.

Sowing singly

Large seeds like beans, peas, sweet corn and squashes can be sown individually *in situ* in holes made to the correct depth with a small dibber. Before covering them with soil make sure that the seeds are at the base of the hole and not suspended in a pocket of air. Sow a few spares alongside to fill in gaps if there are casualties.

The less hardy seeds like cucumbers, marrows and sweet corn can be sown under jam jars to give them extra protection initially. Sow them in pairs, removing the weakest after germination.

SOWING IN ADVERSE CONDITIONS

Situations arise where one can no longer afford to wait for perfect sowing conditions. The worst effects of sowing in adverse conditions can be ameliorated.

Wet conditions

1 Cover the area you want to sow with cloches or clear polythene film several days beforehand.

2 If you have to sow while the soil is still sticky, put a wooden board alongside the row and stand on it while working. This takes your weight and prevents the soil from becoming consolidated.

3 Line the sowing drill with a sprinkling of sharp sand, potting compost (old compost can be used), vermiculite or finely crumbled leaf mould, and sow on this base.

Dry conditions

1 Make single or wide drills as appropriate.
2 Before sowing, use a small houseplant can to water the bottom of the drills only, until almost muddy.
3 Sow the seeds directly on the moist soil, pressing them in.
4 Cover the seed with the dry soil from beside the drill. This acts like a mulch and prevents moisture from evaporating, so keeping the seeds moist until they germinate. After sowing, pat the soil with the palm of the hand to consolidate it.

This method is invaluable for sowing in dry spells in late spring, as well as in mid- and late summer, and is recommended for slow-germinating seed such as parsley.

Thinning. Left: to avoid damaging seedling roots, nip off surplus seedlings just above soil level. Right: thin so that each remaining seedling stands clear of its neighbour. After thinning, firm back the soil.

THINNING SEEDLINGS

Seedlings, whether in their permanent rows or in a seedbed, can grow very rapidly and quickly deteriorate if they become overcrowded. To prevent this they must be thinned and surplus seedlings removed. Some thinnings – of onions, leeks and lettuce, for example – can be carefully transplanted to another site. When thinning, try to minimize the disturbance to the remaining seedlings.

✿ Thin when the soil is moist or water an hour or so beforehand. In hot weather thin in the cool of the evening.

~ Start thinning as soon as the seedlings are large enough to handle.
~ Remove intermediate seedlings so that the remaining seedlings stand just clear of their neighbours.
~ Preferably thin by nipping off the seedlings at ground level. This is much less disruptive to neighbouring seedlings than pulling them out. (See illustration, opposite.)
~ Gently firm the soil around the base of the remaining seedlings.
~ Thin in successive stages to offset any losses from pests or diseases. The final distance between plants depends on the vegetable.
~ Remove all thinnings and bury them in the compost heap, as their smell can attract the plant's pests.

TRANSPLANTING

Unless plants have been sown *in situ*, they will at some stage need to be transplanted into a permanent position. The term 'transplant' is generally used for young plants that are dug up from the soil – from a nursery bed, for instance – and moved elsewhere. They are often described as 'bare-root transplants', as opposed to plants that are raised in a pot or some kind of module, where the roots take on the compact shape of their container and suffer very little disturbance when planted. The transplanting guidelines below apply equally to plants that are purchased ready for planting, and to module-raised plants.

Stages in planting. Left: making a hole. Centre: firming the plant. Right: tugging a leaf to make sure it is firmly planted.

Transplanting is inevitably a shock and temporary setback to a plant, which can be offset by raising plants in pots or modules (see page 97).

Most vegetables can be transplanted if handled carefully. Young plants make new roots more easily than old ones and tend to recover sooner from transplanting, so on the whole the earlier plants can be transplanted to their permanent position, the better. The optimum stage varies from vegetable to vegetable. Lettuces can be transplanted when they have four leaves, brassicas when they are about 10cm/4in high, while beetroot, parsnips and carrots can only be transplanted when they are very small, before the tap root develops.

- Always transplant in cool, dull weather, never in the heat of the day.
- If the soil is dry, water both the seedbed and the soil into which the plants are being moved either the previous evening or several hours beforehand. Water plants in modules thoroughly before planting.
- Handle plants by the leaves rather than the roots, to avoid damaging the delicate root hairs.

- Use a trowel, dibber or smaller tool to make a hole that will be large enough for the roots without cramping them. Hold the plant in the hole as you replace the soil. If planting brassicas in dry weather, 'puddle' or water the hole first.

Transplanting. Handling the plant by the leaves – here a 'plug' or module-raised plant – lower it into a hole large enough for the roots.

- Finally firm the soil around the stem with your fingers and water gently, with a rose on the can. Firm planting is essential. Give a leaf a tug when you have finished: if the plant is wobbly, replant it.
- For planting distances, see individual plants in the Vegetable Directory, and Equidistant spacing, below.

On the whole it is beneficial to mulch after planting, both to keep moisture in and prevent weed growth (see page 70).

EQUIDISTANT SPACING

I highly recommend the practice of growing most vegetables at equidistant spacing, rather than in the traditional widely spaced rows with a lot of wasted space between them, especially in conjunction with narrow bed systems (see page 22). When converting spacing recommendations for widely spaced rows into equidistant spacing, add the in-row and inter-row spacings together and halve them. For example, instead of planting 20cm/8in apart in rows 30cm/12in apart, plant 25cm/10in apart each way. As a general rule, the leaves of adjacent plants should be just touching, or slightly overlapping, when mature. Some can stand being more crowded than others.

HEELING IN

If you buy bare-root plants but cannot plant them immediately, they can be 'heeled in' temporarily. Make a shallow V-shaped trench or hole, lay the plants in it close together, cover the roots and part of the stem with the soil, and water them.

You can also use this technique to prolong the useful life of mature vegetables which have to be lifted at the end of the season because the ground is needed – leeks, celeriac or parsnips, for example. Heeled-in plants will keep in reasonable condition for several weeks (see illustration, page 274).

SOWING INDOORS

The terms 'sowing indoors' or 'sowing under cover' are used for any situation where plants are raised in protected conditions, rather than being sown directly in the soil outside. 'Indoors' can be in a cold greenhouse or polytunnel, in a cold frame or under cloches, in a heated propagator (which can be in a greenhouse or in a room indoors), on a windowsill or elsewhere inside. The common denominator is protection from the elements. Costly facilities such as a heated greenhouse, though wonderful if available, are unnecessary. Sowing indoors is used in many circumstances:

- ❧ To start tender, half-hardy vegetables such as tomatoes, peppers, cucumbers and Mediterranean herbs such as basil that would not have time to mature if sown directly outside.
- ❧ For seeds that are exceptionally small, tricky to germinate, particularly vulnerable in the seedling stage or very expensive. Seed sown directly in the ground is always at risk from unfavourable weather and soil conditions, as well as from pests and diseases.
- ❧ To get earlier, out-of-season crops. For example, spring lettuce can be sown indoors in late winter and planted out in early spring for the first pickings.
- ❧ To extend the growing season for slow-maturing crops such as celeriac.
- ❧ To control temperature in the early stages. Some oriental greens will bolt prematurely if there is a sudden drop of temperature while they are in the seedling stage. This can be avoided if they are sown indoors. Conversely lettuces and onions will not germinate at soil temperatures above 24°C/75°F, which can easily occur outdoors in hot weather. They can be germinated in cool conditions indoors and planted out later.
- ❧ To save garden space. A maturing crop can be occupying cultivated ground while its successor is being raised indoors, ready for planting when the former is harvested.
- ❧ To raise high-quality plants – as a result of close attention and protection from hostile elements outside.
- ❧ To avoid buying plants from garden centres or nurseries. There is always some risk of importing pests such as vine weevil and diseases such as clubroot on bought plants, and once introduced these can be

a nightmare to eliminate. Moreover, most suppliers only offer a limited choice of varieties compared to those available in seed catalogues. Above all, it is intrinsically satisfying to grow your own and saves money.

With modern sowing composts and propagation equipment seeds germinate easily, and initially require relatively little space. The skill, especially for the tender vegetables, lies in providing good growing conditions after germination, in the weeks before planting out. If the temperature at this stage, particularly at night, is too low, seedlings and young plants may die off; if the light levels are inadequate, they will become weak, spindly and pale. They will need to be potted on and spaced out. Make sure that you have somewhere warm and light to keep plants in this interim period.

The great temptation with sowing indoors is to start too early. But tender vegetables cannot be planted out in the open until all risk of frost is over, which is often not until late spring or early summer. If plants are ready too soon they deteriorate while waiting to be planted. (For recommended sowing times for each vegetable, see the Vegetable Directory.)

Stages in raising plants indoors

Several stages are involved in raising plants, though not every stage is necessary in every case. Pricking out, for example, is eliminated by sowing in modules (see below). Potting on is only necessary for relatively large plants such as tomatoes and cucumbers.

Sowing Seeds are sown in light compost, either in a seed tray or small pot, or singly in some kind of module.

Pricking out Young seedlings are moved into a larger container, usually into richer compost, so that they have space to develop. Pricking out is unnecessary when seeds are sown in a module.

Potting on After a few weeks, small plants can be moved into larger individual pots or larger modules, to continue growing. It is not always necessary – plants may already be large enough to plant out – but plants that are potted on will be exceptionally strong, well-developed plants. If plants are to be grown to maturity in large pots or containers, they may be repotted later into even larger pots.

Hardening off To avoid a setback when they are planted out, plants need to be acclimatized gradually to lower temperatures and more exposure. Hardening off is unnecessary if the plants are being grown to maturity in greenhouses, and to a lesser extent if they are being planted into frames or under cloches.

PLANT-RAISING EQUIPMENT

The basic requirements are containers or modules, sowing or potting compost, and, in most cases, a propagator or some means of raising the soil temperature.

Standard containers

All sorts of things can be used for sowing. Where seed will be pricked out soon after germination, fairly small containers are sufficient. Unless the container is porous, it should have drainage holes in the base. Typical sowing containers are:

- ∾ Shallow plastic or clay seed pans or seed trays, which need be no more than 5–7.5cm/2–3in deep.
- ∾ Clay, plastic, fibre, polythene or sturdy paper pots: 7.5cm/3in diameter is generally large enough.

Improvised containers You can improvise cheap containers from plastic punnets, cartons, beakers, yogurt pots and other domestic items, simply by poking drainage holes in the base. Use a heated poker or knitting needle to make the holes. Plastic sandwich boxes with fitted lids make excellent 'seed trays'. I know of gardeners who successfully sow into used tea bags!

Modules

A 'module' is any container or 'cell' filled with sowing or potting compost, where a single plant is grown to potting or planting stage. Plants raised in modules, and modules themselves, are often known as 'plugs'. Module systems have several advantages:

- ∾ As the seedling has no competition from other seedlings it develops into an exceptionally good, healthy plant with a strong, compact root system.
- ∾ When the seedling is planted out, there is virtually no root disturbance. Vegetables that normally suffer if transplanted, such as Chinese cabbage, can be planted out very successfully from modules.
- ∾ The compact root system developed in modules enables planting to take place in conditions that would be unsuitable for planting a bare-root transplant – fairly wet soil, for example. Moreover, young plants can 'hang about' in modules without too much of a setback. (You can feed them with a seaweed-based fertilizer to keep them going.) Spare plants can be kept in the wings for planting in gaps, or in vacant ground as the space becomes available.
- ∾ A variety of plants can be raised in a small space. A forty-cell tray, for example, could easily be used for raising ten plants each of four different vegetables. In a small garden it is better to raise a few, first-class plants than lots of poorer-quality plants.

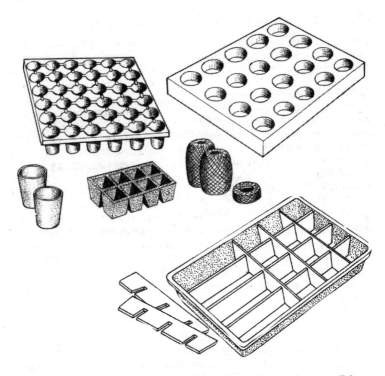

Types of container. Left to right, top row: moulded modular plastic tray, polystyrene cellular tray; centre row: small pots, fibre pots, expanded and compact Jiffy 7s; bottom: seed tray divided into modules.

The main drawback to modules is that they take up considerable space in a propagator, where space is always at a premium. A practical compromise is to sow in small seed trays or containers, then prick out into a module.

The following are purpose-made and improvised modules, which are filled with some kind of compost for sowing (see illustration, above):

- ∿ Moulded plastic and polystyrene trays, consisting of a number of round or square cells. The cell size can range from 1–7.5cm/½–3in diameter.
- ∿ Standard seed trays converted into cells with interlocking plastic or cardboard dividers.
- ∿ Fibre egg cartons or trays, in which seeds are sown in the egg compartments. When the time comes for planting, split the cartons apart and plant out the sections; the roots will grow through them. (Fur-

ther improvisation on this theme is to sow in half egg shells, placed in plastic egg boxes to keep them upright. The plant's roots will eventually penetrate the shell, so it can be planted out intact. If the shell is not already cracked when the time comes for planting, squeeze it gently to crack it and help the process along.)

☙ Any small pot or container used to raise a single, individual plant.

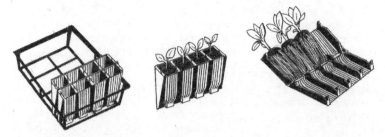

Root trainers. These deep, tapered modules, originally developed for raising tree seedlings, are excellent for raising vegetables. Designed to stand upright in a tray, they open out for planting and can be re-used.

☙ 'Root trainers': deep, tapered, hinged cells of corrugated plastic that neatly open out for planting. They are designed to stand upright in a purpose-made tray. The shape of the cells seems to encourage very good root growth. With care they last several seasons.

In other systems compost and container are integrated:

'Jiffy 7s' These are flat discs about 4cm/1½in diameter, originally made of compressed peat-based compost held in a fine net (see illustration, opposite). When watered they swell into small pots. Seeds are sown in them individually, and grown to planting stage. The whole 'Jiffy' is planted as the plant roots grow out through the net. Jiffy 7s are now also being made from the coconut waste coir, which is good news for those of us concerned about the exhaustion of peat reserves.

Soil blocks These were the precursors of modern module trays, and are still used by commercial growers. They are made as and when required by compressing loose soil or potting compost into a cube with a blocking tool, which also makes a small indentation in the upper block face into which the seed is sown. Depending on the size of the blocking tool used, blocks can range from tiny 'mini blocks' about 1cm/½in square to blocks 5cm/2in square or more. The mini blocks occupy the least space at the germination stage and can be transferred into a larger block for the later stages of growth. Blocks can be stood side by side in a standard seed tray. It is easiest to make blocks with proprietary blocking composts which contain an adhesive but, with skill, you can make blocks from ordinary soil or potting compost. It is a question of getting the moisture content correct. Some organic blocking composts have been introduced. To some extent soil blocks have been superseded by modules, and it is no longer easy for home gardeners to find the tools or appropriate compost. Soil blocks are nevertheless a practical propagation system, and worth using where available.

Seed-raising kits There are various kits on the market, in which compost in a container is either pre-sown with seed or ready for sowing. In some the container lid serves as a watering tray after germination. Kits can be very handy where propagation facilities are limited.

Sowing and potting compost
Compost is the general term for a mixture into which seeds are sown, pricked out or potted on. It is not compost-heap compost, which is too rich for plant raising. Ordinary garden soil is usually unsuitable for raising plants indoors, as it is too coarse, poor-draining and liable to be full of weed seeds.

Traditional sowing and potting composts were made by mixing sterilized sieved garden loam, peat and sand with chemical fertilizers. Apart from being laborious, and time- and space-consuming, this method is difficult to do well. Most gardeners today use commercially prepared composts.

Theoretically seed is sown in a very fine, almost inert sowing compost, then pricked out and potted on into a coarser, richer potting compost. In practice multipurpose composts are now widely used for all stages and prove very satisfactory. Organic fertilizers can be used to supply extra feed where necessary in the later stages of growth.

The committed organic gardener who is also concerned about the use of peat, which threatens to exhaust peat reserves, has a restricted choice of plant-raising composts. The well-established John Innes range of soil-based composts include peat and chemicals; most other composts are peat-based. However, composts are being developed from peat substitutes such as coir, forestry waste products and recycled municipal waste, sometimes enriched with worm casts. Watch the gardening press for suitable products.

Module composts Although standard potting compost can be used in modules, it can become compacted, and commercial growers use specially formulated composts which give better results. Suitable organic composts are being developed. Use them where you can, or use multipurpose composts or one of the home-made compost mixes below.

Home-made organic sowing compost Mix one part of coarse builder's or silver sand with two parts of leaf mould. Leaf mould is easier to handle if it is sieved through a 6mm/¼in sieve. It can be watered with liquid seaweed to enrich it. This compost would be suitable for germinating seeds and growing them to the pricking-out stage.

Comfrey potting compost This recipe, developed by organic gardener Terry Marshall, has proved very successful. The main ingredients are leaf mould and comfrey, preferably using the Russian comfrey cultivar 'Bocking 14'.

1 Cut the leaves of well-established comfrey plants in early autumn.
2 Take a strong plastic sack and put in a layer roughly 7.5cm/3in deep of well-rotted leaf mould, ideally 12–18 months old.
3 Cover with a similar thickness of comfrey leaves, pressed down lightly.
4 Alternate comfrey and leaf-mould layers until the sack is full.
5 Tie the sack at the neck, make a few ventilation holes with a garden fork and leave in a sheltered place until spring, when it will be ready for use.

This can be used as a multipurpose compost.

Worm compost mixes
Home-made worm compost (see page 57) can be the basis for sowing or potting compost. The ratio of the various ingredients is not critical. The following are the ratios recommended by the Henry Doubleday Research Association (HDRA):

∾ Sowing compost: mix 1 bucket of sieved leaf mould with 1 bucket of worm compost.
∾ General-purpose compost: mix 1–2 buckets of worm compost with 3 buckets of well-rotted leaf mould (or peat alternative) and 1 bucket of sharp sand or horticultural grit.

Add roughly 75g/3oz of ground limestone or calcified seaweed to every 45 litres/10 gallons of mixture – this is roughly a barrowful. The higher the proportion of worm compost, the richer the mixture will be.

PROVIDING A SOURCE OF HEAT

Most vegetable seeds will germinate satisfactorily at soil temperatures of 13–16°C/55–61°F. The ideal source of heat is from below – 'bottom heat', as it is called – which is easily supplied by a standard plug-in electric propagator. These small propagators are economic to run.

Domestic propagators range from units in which heat is supplied by a light bulb beneath the seed tray to electrically heated plates and coils placed beneath a seed tray. A propagating box can be built on greenhouse staging, using insulated electric cables buried in sand. Make sure that they are professionally wired.

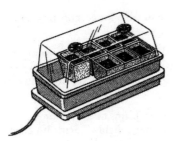

Small propagator with electrically heated base plate.

Whatever system you use, cover it with a sheet or dome of plastic, glass or heavy clear film to retain moisture and prevent the soil surface from drying out. Remove the cover daily and wipe off condensation.

There is no doubt that early sowings are faster and less erratic where a propagator is used. In the absence of a propagator, put seeds somewhere warm to germinate, such as an airing cupboard (but move them into the light as soon as they germinate), over a radiator or near a stove. Try to avoid direct sunlight, a very dry atmosphere or draughts. Once outdoor temperatures are rising, seeds can be sown in cold greenhouses, frames or under cloches outside.

PROCEDURES FOR SOWING INDOORS

Sowing in standard containers

1 Make the compost pleasantly moist. Composts vary in texture and ability to absorb moisture, but if the compost is at all dry, put it on a bench and water it with a rose on the can. Turn it over and over with your hands so that there are no dry pockets. (In some cases it is easier to fill the container with the dry compost, then stand it in a tray of water so that it can soak up water before sowing. This normally takes several hours.)

2 At this stage I often water the compost with a weak solution of sea-weed extract to stimulate healthy growth.

3 Fill the container with moist compost. Press it down with a small board or flat surface to make it reasonably firm and level, leaving a 1cm/½in space below the rim of the container. If you are using pots for sowing, you can put a layer of broken crocks or foam rubber at the bottom to economize on compost.

4 Sprinkle the seeds evenly over the surface, or else space them carefully 6mm–2.5cm/¼–1in apart, depending on the seed.

5 Cover the seeds by sieving a little dry compost or sharp sand over them. Sand seems to reduce the risk of seedlings being attacked by fungal diseases. As a general rule, seeds need to be covered to about twice their depth. Very small seeds, and some that require light to germinate, can be left uncovered. Firm the soil again after sowing.

Sowing in containers. First, fill the container with loose, moist compost. Second, make the surface smooth and level by pressing with a small board. Third, sprinkle or space seeds evenly over the surface. Fourth, cover seeds with sieved compost or sharp sand.

6 If necessary, water the surface lightly, or stand the container in water until the top surface is moist. The latter method is preferable with small seeds, which are easily swamped by overhead watering.

7 To prevent the compost from drying out, cover the container with a sheet of glass or polythene, or a fitted plastic dome, or slip it into a plastic bag. Remove the covering once the seedlings have germinated.

8 Put it into a propagator or somewhere warm.

Sowing in modules

Follow essentially the same procedure, but with most of the purpose-made module composts, it seems to be easiest to fill the modules loosely with dry compost, then to water them gently from above, and/or stand them in a tray of water for several hours, until they are thoroughly moist.

The aim in sowing in modules is to have only one germinated seedling in each cell or block. To achieve this, either sow one seed per cell, or sow several seeds and nip out all but the strongest seedling once they have germinated. (For the exception of multisowing, see below.)

If you are sowing only one seed, obviously germination rates must be high. To be on the safe side carry out a germination test before sowing (see page 81).

Large seeds are easily sown individually. Small seeds can be trickier to sow on their own. Either push them carefully off a piece of paper, or put them on a saucer and pick them up individually, spillikin-style, using the moistened tip of a piece of broken glass, a darning needle or a metal plant label. The former works best (though I am in constant trouble for recommending it!). A single seed adheres to the glass, but drops off neatly when the glass touches the compost (see below). Cover the seed gently with compost from the edge of the module.

To sow seeds singly in modules, pick up individual seeds on the moistened tip of a piece of glass. The seed drops off neatly when the glass touches the compost.

Multisowing This technique saves space and time. It is appropriate for the few vegetables that are not adversely affected by competition from close neighbours – leeks, onions, round beetroot and round carrot being examples. Several seeds are sown together in a cell, but the seedlings are left unthinned and are eventually planted out 'as one' at wider spacing than normal.

Post-germination treatment

- ∞ Examine your seeds daily as they can develop very fast. Every morning remove the cover, wipe off any condensation and then replace it.
- ∞ As soon as seedlings have germinated, remove them from the dark (if they were in a cupboard) – otherwise they will become weak and drawn. Remove any close-fitting lids or covers that would cramp growth.
- ∞ Keep them in airy, well-lit conditions, but keep very small seedlings away from direct or bright sun for a few days, as it can massacre them. If you cannot move them from a windowsill, prop up some newspaper or netting to shade them lightly.
- ∞ Once seedlings are sturdy and established, give them as much light as possible. If they are on a windowsill, give them a half-turn daily, so that they do not get drawn in one direction.
- ∞ Water gently to prevent them from drying out, but don't overwater. It is best to water fragile seedlings by standing the container in a tray of water so that it can soak the water up from below. If you are using peat-based or similar composts, particularly for soil blocks, take great care to prevent them from drying out. Rewetting dried-out compost can be very difficult.
- ∞ Prick out seedlings as soon as possible (see below).

PRICKING OUT

Seedlings can be pricked out as soon as they are large enough to handle. In most cases this is once they have developed two true leaves, as opposed to the first tiny 'seed leaves'. The purpose of pricking out is to give the seedlings plenty of space to develop, in a reasonably fertile compost. If they were initially sown well spaced out in multipurpose compost, there is no need to prick out.

Prick out into seed trays, preferably 5–7.5cm/2–3in deep, or into any kind of module or small pot. Only prick out healthy-looking seedlings: duds rarely recover. Most seedlings can be kept at lower temperatures once pricked out.

1 Prepare a tray or pot with potting compost as for sowing.
2 Water the seedlings first, allow the compost to drain, then lever them out gently with a miniature dibber or any small bladed tool (even a

*Pricking out. Once seedlings
become large enough to handle,
prick them out from the container
in which they were planted (left)
into a seed tray (right), handling
them by their leaves to avoid
damanging the delicate root
hairs. Ensure that they are well
spaced out.*

large nail can be used). Disturb the roots as little as possible. Handle the seedlings by the leaves, never by the root, as this could damage the delicate root hairs.

3 Make a small hole in the compost, large enough to take the root.
4 Hold the seedling slightly above the compost, ease it into the hole, then press soil firmly but gently around it, so that the seed leaves are just above soil level and there are no air pockets beneath it.
5 Water if necessary, using a fine rose.
6 Shade seedlings from direct sun for a day or two, especially if they show any signs of wilting.

POTTING ON

Often seedlings can remain in the container in which they have been pricked out until they are planted out. However, when they are going to be grown in large pots, as may be the case with tomatoes and peppers, or when they are outgrowing their containers before it is time to plant them out, it may be necessary to move them into a larger pot to give them room to develop. If they become overcrowded there is an increased risk of disease.

It is always best to move plants into larger containers in stages, rather than into very much larger containers in one move. Peppers that will eventually be grown in, say, 20cm/8in pots, should be potted first into pots of at least 7.5cm/3in diameter as an intermediate stage.

1 Water plants well in advance and allow to drain.
2 If you are using soil-based compost, put a good layer of drainage material such as old crocks in the bottom of the pot. (This is unnecessary with naturally well-drained peat-like composts.) Partly fill the pot with potting compost, tapping the base on a flat surface a couple of times to settle the compost.
3 Hold the plant in the centre so that the lowest leaves will be just above soil level.
4 Holding the plant in place, fill the pot with compost, leaving a 1cm/½in space below the rim.

5 Firm around the plant with the fingertips, tapping the pot on a surface from time to time to consolidate and level the compost.
6 Water lightly; water more heavily later when the plant is established.
7 Shelter the plant from direct sun for a couple of days.

Plants often grow very rapidly in pots and need plenty of ventilation. Never allow them to get overcrowded. If necessary move them a little further apart every day or so, so that the leaves of adjacent plants are not touching.

Sometimes plants start to outgrow their pots before conditions outdoors are suitable for planting, and it may not be practical to repot into larger pots. As a holding operation, stand the plants in their pots in trays lined with potting compost and, in the case of fibre or paper pots that will disintegrate, pack compost around them. Water the compost with a seaweed-based fertilizer. The roots will continue to develop and feed.

HARDENING OFF

Plants raised indoors tend to be 'soft' and need to be toughened up over a two-to-three-week period before they are planted out. The standard method is to gradually expose them to colder conditions, first by increasing ventilation, then by putting the plants in a cold frame or protected situation outdoors for longer periods each day. Initially either cover them at night (this is easy in a cold frame) or bring them back indoors. Eventually they will only need protecting on exceptionally cold nights.

Stroking or brushing is a method of hardening off plants which saves moving them outdoors and bringing them back in again at night or in cold weather. Using a piece of paper or cardboard, brush the seedlings backwards and forwards for up to a minute a day.

'Brushing' is an alternative method of hardening off, developed by the Japanese, which saves moving the plants outdoors. Seedlings are brushed or stroked to produce the toughening effect of exposure to lower temperatures and wind (see illustration above). Using a piece of paper or cardboard, literally brush the seedlings backwards and forwards for up to a minute a day over the normal hardening-off period. I believe a special brush is used commercially.

6

PROTECTION

Anyone wanting maximum returns and year-round supplies from a vegetable garden should invest in some kind of protection. This umbrella term embraces everything from cloches and frames to greenhouses, walk-in polythene tunnels, low tunnels and 'crop covers' made of perforated or fleece films. Protection (or 'protected cropping' or 'growing under cover', in horticultural jargon) offers many potential benefits.

BENEFITS OF PROTECTION

Extending the growing season
Plants normally start growing when the average daytime temperature reaches approximately 6°C/43°F in the spring. The date this happens varies from year to year, but can be any time from late winter in warmer areas to mid-spring in colder regions. Similarly, growth stops when the temperature drops below 6°C/43°F in the autumn. The days between these two points are termed 'growing days'. In the warmest parts of the British Isles there are over 300 growing days, in the coldest fewer than 250. Quite a difference!

Temperature also affects the rate of growth. Provided plants have moisture, the higher the temperature above 6°C/43°F, the faster they grow.

In varying degrees, protection raises the temperature of the soil and air around plants, and slows down the rate at which heat is lost from the soil at night. On sunny days in winter, temperatures can soar under glass or polythene, allowing plants under cover to grow when those outside are still gripped in arctic conditions.

All forms of protection effectively increase the number of growing days, by at least three or four weeks in spring and as much again in the autumn. Protection is therefore most valuable in cold, high, exposed and northerly areas where the growing season is shortest.

Extending the plant range
The combination of an extended growing season and higher temperatures enables more demanding, exotic crops to be grown. In cool climates, naturally semi-tropical plants such as tomatoes, peppers and yard-long beans may be only marginally successful outdoors, but they will be very productive under cover. Obviously the range can be increased further with the use of heated greenhouses, but that is outside

the scope of this book. This may be the place to point out that while it is fun to experiment with exotic vegetables – raising a few peanuts, for example – returns are inevitably low. In terms of feeding a family, resources can be put to more productive use.

Protection from frost

Some vegetables withstand frost well, but many are killed or damaged by frost. Cloches and other unheated forms of protection can only be relied upon to give protection against slight frost. They will not keep out severe frost. On cold clear nights, the air temperature under cover can fall as low as the temperature outside (in freak cases even lower), although the soil temperature is probably higher than that of exposed ground outside.

However, protection mitigates the effects of frost in several ways. Crucially, it protects plants from the wind. It is the combination of low temperatures and wind that is potentially lethal to plants. Secondly, protection keeps plants dry, and frost damage is more severe on wet foliage. Thirdly, frost penetrates less deeply under cover, so the soil thaws and warms up sooner after being frosted than would otherwise be the case.

Incidentally, whether in the open or under cover, plants are at most risk of frost damage when they thaw out rapidly. You can prevent damage by spraying the plants with water before the sun reaches them the following morning. This helps to thaw them more slowly. When heavy frost is expected, cloches can be sprayed before nightfall. The layer of ice formed offers extra insulation.

Shelter from the elements

It is well known that plants give much higher yields if protected from even the lightest of winds (see page 20). Severe wind is another question. The damage that can be caused by gales and bitter winds – both in winter and spring – is enormous. Wind desiccates leaves and batters and tears them, making it a struggle for the plant to survive, let alone grow. In coastal areas it is worth protecting plants from wind-borne salt spray. You can hugely improve the quality of leafy salad vegetables in the stormier months of the year by protecting them from the elements.

Benefits also stem from protecting the soil surface from heavy rain, which in winter washes nutrients out of the soil and in spring can wash away seeds and even seedlings.

Protection from pests and diseases

All forms of protection are a physical barrier and in varying degrees keep out birds, rabbits and other animals, and to some extent, flying insect pests. It is relatively easy to clear slugs and other soil pests out of greenhouses, tunnels and frames. Tomatoes under cover remain free of tomato blight, which is air-borne, for quite a while after outdoor plants have been infected. (I've noticed that plants nearest ventilator panels are usually infected first.)

The other side of the coin is that the high levels of humidity and higher temperatures under cover encourage some diseases and insects, notably aphids, thrips, red spider mite and whitefly. In winter animal pests such as moles, mice and even rats are attracted to the warm and sheltered environment.

MATERIALS USED IN PROTECTIVE CROPPING

In the past, glass was the main material used for greenhouses, garden frames and cloches, but today there are many plastics and other materials to choose from, most cheaper than glass. Each has advantages and disadvantages.

Glass

Light transmission Provided it is kept clean, glass transmits light very well. This is particularly important in winter, when low light levels limit plant growth.

Heat absorption Glass is an effective heat trap. During the day soil absorbs heat in the form of short waves but at night some of this heat is lost from the soil as long-wave radiation. Glass transmits incoming short waves but, unlike most plastic materials, to some extent holds back the outgoing long waves, so retaining heat that would otherwise be lost.

Durability Glass lasts for many years without deteriorating, although of course it is easily broken, making it a hazard where there are children.

Handling Glass is heavy and panes can be awkward to handle; some skill is required to erect glass structures. Breakages are less likely if all edges are rubbed with a carborundum stone when glass is first put up.

Rigid plastics and synthetic materials

Light transmission Some modern transparent rigid plastic materials transmit light almost as well as glass, though moisture tends to condense on them, cutting out light. The opaque plastics, such as glass fibre, appear to cut out light, but it has been demonstrated that plants grow well in the even, diffuse light that results. Some rigid plastics lose light either because the surfaces become scratched or because they discolour with time through exposure to ultraviolet light. Materials treated against ultraviolet light (UV-treated) will last longer. Store plastics out of sunlight when not in use.

Heat retention Rigid plastics generally retain less heat than glass. A few, such as polyvinyl chloride (PVC), are like glass in being relatively impermeable to long-wave transmission, so retain some heat at night.

Durability Compared to glass, most rigid plastics are relatively short-lived, lasting no more than four or five years before becoming brittle. Glass fibre is exceptionally durable.

Handling The materials are light to handle, and can be erected on a less substantial framework than glass. They are more flexible than glass, but when used as cloches will require more anchorage. They are much safer than glass where there are children. Of currently available products:

- Corrugated PVC sheeting transmits plenty of light, retains heat well, is strong and should last at least five years.
- Acrylic sheeting (originally known as 'Perspex') has good qualities of heat retention and light transmission, and is very durable. It is at present mostly used in frames.
- Glass fibre is very strong and durable, although opaque, which means that you cannot see the plants beneath without lifting it.

Semi-rigid plastics

Polypropylene board This is a double-layered corrugated plastic with fluted channels between the two layers. As it has the characteristics of double glazing, its thermal insulation is higher than glass. Light transmission is considerably lower than glass, but this is another case where plant growth seems to be good in the diffused light. It lasts three to five years, provided it has been UV-treated. It can be attached to metal or wooden frames, but use it with the flutes running horizontally at ground level, or moisture and dirt are sucked into them, causing discolouration.

Wire reinforced plastics These are cheap materials which can easily be bent into wide, high or narrow shapes as required. They are useful for making cloches and frames and short-term protective structures. With care they will last three or four years.

Polythene films

Cheap lightweight polythene films are used for making cloches, low tunnels, frames and walk-in polytunnels. The thickness or gauge of the film varies from very thin films, normally used for one season to make low tunnels, to much thicker films of 500–720 gauge/125–180 microns, used for polytunnels. Where these heavy films are UV-treated, the manufacturers guarantee them for four seasons. Some modern films are made with an antifogging additive, which makes condensation run down the inside of the film rather than forming on the leaves and increasing the risk of disease. It will only be effective for one season; for practical purposes the film subsequently reverts to conventional film.

Temperatures can rise very rapidly under polythene film during the day, and fall sharply at night, though as mentioned earlier, condensed moisture on the underside of the film helps prevent radiation from the soil.

Films can be battened to wooden frames or anchored over metal frames. (For perforated polythene films and fleece films, both used for crop covers, see page 128.)

CLOCHES

A cloche is any small unit used for protected cropping, which is easily moved from one part of the garden to another. Cloches are normally designed so that they can be placed end to end to cover a row of plants.

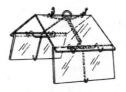

A 'tent' cloche, made of panes of glass held joined by a Rumsey clip and end panels held in place with angled canes.

A glass 'barn' cloche. When in use the ends should be closed with panes of glass.

A cloche made of corrugated PVC.

Types of cloche

Glass cloches The traditional cloche is made of panes of glass, held together in a wire frame with clips. 'Tent' cloches are made of two panes, low and high 'barn' cloches of four panes (see illustrations above). The flat-topped 'tomato' or 'utility' cloche has three panes, the roof pane being removable. Glass cloches offer good growing conditions (see page 109). Disadvantages are that they are expensive, easily broken, heavy to handle, somewhat awkward to erect single-handed and potentially dangerous to children.

Plastic and other materials Cloches are made today from a wide range of rigid and flexible materials, often semicircular in outline. Few retain heat as well as glass and they have a shorter life span, but they are lighter and easier to handle. In choosing from the many makes on the market, consider the factors outlined in What to look for in cloches, below.

Home-made cloches

DIY enthusiasts will have no trouble making serviceable cloches from the wide range of materials above. Most are now sold in suitable lengths and widths, and can be tacked, nailed, battened or screwed on to a wood frame. A tent shape is the easiest to construct. Polythene film is best secured between two pieces of wood. Make supporting frames as narrow as possible, so that the maximum light is admitted.

There are various devices for joining loose glass panels to make tent cloches, the best-known being the cleverly engineered Rumsey clip (see illustration, page 111).

Medium-to-heavyweight large plastic bags can be made into low cloches, which are useful for protecting tender herbs and salads in winter. Cut the bottom off the bag, bend two pieces of fairly heavy wire (you can use coat hangers) into a semicircular or barn outline. Slip one into each side of the bag and through the lower end to support and anchor the plastic. They can be straddled over an insulating layer of bracken, straw or dried leaves (see below).

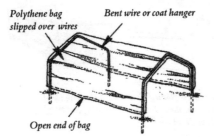

Polythene bag slipped over wires

Bent wire or coat hanger

Open end of bag

A simple home-made cloche made of a polythene bag slipped over bent wire or a coat hanger.

Side shelters Temporary shelters can be made from rigid PVC, polypropylene, wire-reinforced plastic or polythene film attached to a wooden frame. They can be kept upright simply by pushing pairs of canes into the ground on either side. Use them to protect tender plants like sweet corn and tomatoes in their early stages, or lean them against runner bean poles to make a protective tent over young beans. They can also be leant against a fence as a lean-to shelter.

A cloche used as a windbreak. The plant has outgrown the cloche, but the cloche, put on its side, continues to give some protection.

What to look for in cloches
When making or purchasing cloches, consider the following factors:

Light Choose cloches that let in plenty of light and are easily cleaned. The exception is cloches made of translucent materials, which give gently diffused light. Light is most important (a) where cloches are used during the winter to grow, rather than merely protect, vegetables and (b) in industrial areas where smoke in the atmosphere reduces the light.

Heat The less heat loss from the soil, the better. Note that there is less heat loss from a double layer of material, although this reduces the light. The boffins are uncertain as to whether the value of the heat gained outweighs the light lost!

Strength and stability Cloches are very vulnerable to wind. Avoid sharp angles, which catch the wind, and make sure that there is a secure means of anchorage, such as strong steel pins which protrude into the soil, flanges which can be pinned or weighted down, or overhead wire stays.

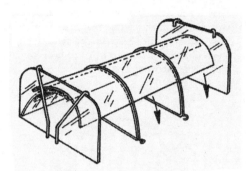

A cloche with built-in ventilation. The top can be rolled over or back as required.

Ventilation Cloches need some ventilation, especially in summer. Glass cloches have gaps in the top which can be adjusted for ventilation. In some cloches roof panels can be raised or rolled back for ventilation (see above). Small ventilation holes can be made in the roof of rigid and semirigid plastic and glass-fibre cloches. If there is no built-in ventilation, leave small gaps between the cloches when erecting them.

Through draughts Open-sided single cloches or open-ended tunnel cloche rows easily turn into destructive wind tunnels. Close them with end pieces, which interlock securely over the cloche or are self-anchoring with steel pins. Otherwise use panes of glass or clear material (rather than pieces of wood, which would block the light) as end pieces, securing them with canes set at an angle in the soil (see illustrations, pages 111 and 114, and Anchoring, below).

Handling Choose cloches that are easily erected – some are so complex they never get assembled! Look for handles that make it easy to move them for watering or other operations, or to move them around the garden. Cloches that stack on top of each other or fold flat when not in use are an asset.

Size When choosing cloches, bear in mind the main purpose for which they will be used. Cost tends to increase with size. Tent cloches and low tunnels are fine for seed raising and for low crops such as lettuce. Low barns, with sides 15cm/6in high, are adequate only for the young stages of tall crops such as tomatoes, sweet corn, peppers and peas. High barns, with sides 30cm/12in high, and flat-topped cloches give more scope for protection in the later stages. Some cloches have side extensions to increase their height, while in others the top pane can be raised slightly or removed to give more height. The height–width ratio of the semirigid cloches can be adjusted within certain limits. Several brands of cloche are available in varying widths.

Cloche management

Soil To get the best returns from cloches, put them on the best soil, working as much organic matter as possible into the top 15cm/6in or so. Soil under cloches is apt to dry out rapidly, so mulching (see page 70) is always beneficial. It also helps to keep down weeds, which thrive in the favourable environment.

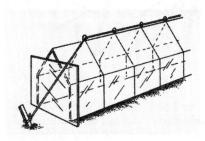

A cloche anchored with twine run through the handles and tied to sticks at either end.

Anchoring Winds can be devastating. Glass cloches and brittle plastics break, and lighter cloches are easily blown away in exposed positions – where, of course, cloches are most valuable. There are many ways of improving anchorage:

- Run twine through the handles and tie to canes or stout sticks at either end (see above).
- Push pea sticks into the ground alongside the cloches.
- Give extra support to tent cloches with pairs of bamboo canes stuck into the ground on either side and tied together above the ridge.
- Weigh down rigid plastic cloches with empty wine bottles tied together at the neck with heavy string or baler twine, and hung on either side of the cloche ridge.
- When securing the end panes of glass cloches, use a cane or stick pushed into the ground at a 45-degree angle. This is much less likely to work loose and cause friction against the cloche than an upright one (see illustrations above and page 111).

Watering With rigid cloches rain water runs down the sides of cloches and, provided there is plenty of organic matter in the soil, percolates through to the roots of plants under the cloches. Some makes of cloche are 'self-watering' in that rain water is diverted down flutes to the inside of the cloche. Apart from when watering small seedlings (which have not had time to develop an extensive root system), there is normally no need to remove cloches for watering; they can be watered overhead with hoses or cans. This indirect form of watering helps to conserve the tilth of the soil. Check to see if the soil is sufficiently moist by poking your finger into the soil in the middle of the cloche. If it feels dry 2.5cm/1in or so below the surface, it may be necessary to remove the cloche to water more thoroughly.

Ventilation On hot spring days and in summer, plenty of ventilation is required. For cloches without built-in ventilation systems (see What to look for in cloches, page 113) it may be necessary to remove alternate cloches in a row during the day. They can be replaced at night.

Coverage In frosty weather glass itself can become so cold that plants touching it will be frostbitten. To prevent this from occurring, make sure that plants are not in contact with the cloche sides. Height can be gained, and cloches raised to cover growing crops, in several ways:

- ❧ by using side extensions where available
- ❧ by standing cloches on bricks or wooden blocks
- ❧ by planting in trenches about 15–23cm/6–9in deep, with the cloches straddling the trench – only practicable in light, well-drained soils, as otherwise the trench will become a waterlogged ditch.

Planting distances have to be adjusted to some extent to take advantage of the width of a cloche.

Side shelter Some types of rigid cloches can be stood on their side and 'wrapped' around tall plants to act as a windbreak. Anchor them with a cane through the handles, or with canes pushed into the ground alongside (see illustration, page 112).

LOW POLYTHENE FILM TUNNELS

The cheapest form of protection is a tunnel of lightweight polythene film laid over wire hoops to cover a row of plants; sophisticated systems using high-quality hoops would cost more. On the whole, low tunnels offer less protection than cloches.

The most commonly used polythene film is 150 gauge/38 microns. It is flimsy and generally only lasts one or, at the most, two seasons. Heavier polythene films can be used but are harder to manipulate and pull taut. Film can be bought in rolls and then cut to the lengths required. It must be wide enough to cover the beds generously on each side. Use UV-treated film where available, and store film out of sunlight when not in use. The low tunnel shape stands up to wind surprisingly well, but if it does rip you can mend tears with purpose-made tape. Low tunnels can also be covered with perforated films (see page 129) and fine nets designed to exclude insect pests (see page 147).

Standard hoops are of galvanized steel wire, but hoops can be made from steel rods, flexible polythene piping or any material that combines flexibility with firmness. The surface must be smooth to prevent the film from being snagged. Some hoops have a ring at soil level for attaching anchoring strings or wire. Hoops are usually spaced about 90cm/3ft apart and pushed into the ground at least 10cm/4in deep.

The height and span of the tunnel depends entirely on the length of the hoops, and can be adjusted according to the crop being grown. To work out a suitable size of hoop, take a piece of fine wire and bend it into an arc. I designed many of mine to cover 1.2m/4ft wide beds, with the height at the centre up to 45cm/18in. There are often cases, however, where higher clearance is needed to cover taller crops.

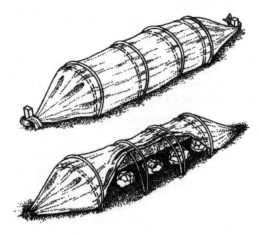

Low polytunnel. Above: the polythene film has been laid over wire hoops and is kept down with fine wire hoops. Below: the film has been pushed up for ventilation.

To keep the tunnel taut, the ends of the film need to be bunched together and anchored at either end in any of the following ways:

- ∞ Knot it around canes or pegs in the ground 60cm/2ft or so beyond the end hoop, pushed in at approximately a 45-degree angle (see above).
- ∞ Bury it into the ground.
- ∞ Weigh down the ends.

Often the film also needs to be kept in place along its length, to prevent the sides from flapping unduly. The method used depends on the type of hoop and the exposure to wind. Here are some suggestions:

∾ Run fine wire or strings over the top, hooked or tied to the base of the hoops on each side. Strings should be tied with a permanent knot on one side, but with a knot that is easily undone on the other. This makes it easier to move tunnels in finger-numbing weather.
∾ Peg the outer edges with purpose-made plastic pegs or metal tent pegs.
∾ Roll the edges around metal or plastic piping laid alongside. Some patented systems use a neat clip to hold the film tight around the pipes.
∾ Weight the edges with metal piping, wooden poles or small but strong polythene bags filled with soil or sand.

In windy situations it may be necessary to bury one side in the ground along the tunnel length, the edges covered with soil. Leave the other side free for access. Spare hoops can be anchored over the top to increase stability in severe weather.

For watering, ventilation and other operations, simply push up the film on one side. In hot weather the combination of high temperature and humidity under the film is conducive to pests and diseases – in which case push up both sides for maximum ventilation. In the Mediterranean, where low polythene tunnels are extensively used for early outdoor tomatoes, melons and other crops, square or round 'peepholes' are cut along the lengths of the tunnels, so that plants are sheltered but still get plenty of ventilation.

Snow should be brushed off low tunnels in winter, as sagging film can damage crops. If the vegetables are low-growing and robust, leave the snow to act as insulation.

Bearing in mind the limitations of their height, you can use low polythene film tunnels for the same purposes as cloches, as outlined below, but you should recognize that they offer less insulation and are less efficient. In cold weather both cloches and low tunnels can be used inside greenhouses and polytunnels as an extra layer of insulation.

YEAR-ROUND USES OF CLOCHES AND LOW POLYTHENE FILM TUNNELS

In temperate climates there is scope for using cloches all year round, especially in the absence of greenhouses or walk-in polytunnels. The possibilities are summarized below. Low polythene tunnels can be used the same way. For the main vegetable groups for cloche work, see Vegetable groups for strip cropping with cloches, page 365; for Season and month conversion chart, see page 15.

Spring

ℴ For preparing the ground for sowing. Put cloches on the ground several days to a week before sowing to dry out and warm up the soil; or if sowing is delayed cover a prepared seedbed to preserve the tilth.

ℴ For earlier crops of hardy vegetables. Sow or plant under cloches from late winter to early spring as weather conditions permit. Some vegetables can remain covered until mature or nearly mature. For suitable crops, see Group 1(b). Early potatoes can also be started under cloches.

ℴ For early sowings of cut-and-come-again salad seedlings. Sow *in situ*. The seedlings will appear at least ten days earlier than any sown in the open ground (see Cut-and-come-again, page 156 and Chapter 9).

ℴ To raise seedlings. Seeds sown in seed trays or pots can be protected under cloches. In late winter/early spring make early sowings of mainstream vegetables such as brassicas, onions and lettuce. Follow with sowings of half-hardy vegetables which cannot be planted outside until all risk of frost is past (Group 2).

ℴ For hardening plants raised in heat indoors. Seedlings and young plants raised in propagators can be hardened off by putting them in seed trays and pots under cloches. Move the cloches a little further apart each day, then leave them off during the day but cover them at night, finally removing them altogether unless frost threatens.

ℴ As an extra layer of protection in polytunnels or greenhouses. Air and soil temperatures under cloches will be several degrees higher than in the rest of the greenhouse. Use them to bring on salad crops, and for protecting tomatoes and half-hardy plants when first planted.

Summer

ℴ For half-hardy crops, primarily to improve yield and quality. Half-hardy crops (Group 2) can be sown or planted under cloches once risk of frost is past. Cloches can be removed if necessary for later stages of growth.

Autumn

ℴ To protect late-summer sowings and plantings. This includes late sowings of peas and dwarf French beans, lettuce, oriental greens, marginally hardy salads such as endives and chicory and cut-and-come-again salad seedlings (see page 156).

ℴ For ripening fruiting vegetables at the end of the season. Dwarf peppers and bush tomatoes can be covered completely; cordon tomatoes can be bent down and covered with cloches.

ℴ For drying onions and garlic for storage.

Winter

- To protect overwintering salads from the elements. This includes hardy salads such as winter lettuce, spinach, winter purslane, hardy oriental greens like mizuna and komatsuna, and less hardy salads that stand some cold weather such as endives and chicory.
- For autumn-sown/planted vegetables maturing the following spring and summer. For example, broad beans, spring cabbage (these only need to be cl, clodded in very cold areas), early summer cauliflower, hardy peas, onion seeds or sets, spinach/spinach beet/Swiss chard.
- As an extra layer of protection in polytunnels or greenhouses. See Spring, above.

Planning cloche use
To make the most of cloches, draw up a simple plan so that they will almost always be in use. Like all garden plans it must be flexible to allow for the vagaries of the weather.

Strip cropping The most productive way of using cloches is 'strip cropping'. This implies cultivating two adjacent strips of ground (each the width of your cloches) and planning the cropping so that you can simply move the cloches to and fro between the strips with the minimum of effort. The basis of strip cropping is to divide vegetables roughly into four groups, according to the months they will be under cloches. There will inevitably be some overlapping of groups. (See Vegetable groups for strip cropping with cloches, page 365.)

- Cloches are used first on Strip A for a Group 1 crop (mainly hardy autumn- or spring-sown vegetables) cloched during the winter and early spring. In late spring the Group 1 crop is cleared or no longer requires cloche protection.
- Cloches are then moved on to a Group 2 crop on Strip B. This would be a half-hardy crop requiring protection at least during the early stages of growth.
- By early summer the Group 2 crop will have outgrown the cloches. By then strip A will have been completely cleared and is replanted with a Group 3 crop (tender vegetables), which can be grown under cloches all summer.
- When this crop is finished in autumn, the cloches can be moved back to Strip B, where a Group 4 crop (maturing in late autumn or over-wintering) has been sown or planted.

Intercropping under cloches
Often two or three crops can be sown together under cloches to make the most of the space. For example:

- radishes with most crops
- peas with lettuce and radishes on either side
- dwarf French beans either side of sweet corn
- carrots and radishes on either side of French beans
- carrots, salad onions or cos lettuces intercropped with small lettuce
- turnips, lettuces, carrots or radishes alongside peas
- seedbed sowings of brassicas, onions, leeks and lettuces alongside a row of carrots
- quick-maturing salad seedlings (such as cress, salad rape, Mediterranean rocket, pak choi, mizuna) alongside tomatoes, sweet corn, French or runner beans (see also Intercropping, page 159).

A simple strip cropping plan is given below. The months are for general guidance. They were originally based on conditions in my East Anglian garden, but note that there is considerable variation from one region to another.

STRIP CROPPING PLAN

Season	Strip A	Strip B
October–April	Oct: winter hardy lettuce or Sugar Loaf chicory planted under cloches down each side. Nov: narrow band of peas sown down middle	
end April–May	Peas and lettuce unprotected	**Cloched** late April: dwarf French beans sown
June–October	**Cloched** Early June: peppers or bush tomatoes planted under cloches	Dwarf French beans unprotected
October–April		**Cloched** Mixture of oriental greens such as rosette pak choi, mizuna, mibuna, leaf radish and hardy salad seedlings

GARDEN FRAMES

The garden frame is in effect a bottomless box with a sloping lid or roof – a halfway house between a cloche and a greenhouse. More substantial than a cloche, it is less affected by wind, better insulated and offers more protection from frost. The disadvantage is that it is less flexible to use. In the past frames were constructed over 'hotbeds' of fermenting manure, and were extensively used for forcing early salads.

Frames can be portable or permanent, lean-to or freestanding, with a flat or sloping roof. The sides of permanent frames were traditionally of brick, wood or concrete. Modern portable frames more commonly have a timber, galvanized steel or aluminium frame, with transparent sides of glass, rigid or semirigid materials, or fairly heavy polythene film.

Glass-to-ground frames let in most light, which is an important factor late and early in the year. A solid-sided frame will generally have better

Top left: a horizontal trellis in a frame, propped up on upturned flower pots, keeping cucumbers off the ground. Top right: wood- or brick-sided frame with glass lid or 'light'; the glazing bar is propped on a piece of wood for ventilation. Bottom left: glass-to-ground aluminium frame. Bottom right: home-made lean-to frame erected against a fence, using polythene film battened to wooden battens which are secured on to a timber, half-buried for anchorage.

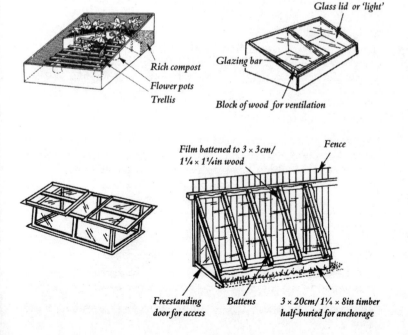

Rich compost
Flower pots
Trellis

Glass lid or 'light'
Glazing bar
Block of wood for ventilation

Film battened to 3 × 3cm/ 1¼ × 1¼in wood
Fence

Freestanding door for access
Battens
3 × 20cm/1¼ × 8in timber half-buried for anchorage

insulation, especially if built against a wall, but if it is too deep seedlings and young plants will be drawn towards the light and be weakened.

Frames are usually made lower at the front and higher at the back to make the best use of available light. A shallow frame for salad crops would be about 18cm/7in high in the front and 23cm/9in at the back. A deeper frame for cucumbers would be about 30cm/12in in front and 45cm/18in at the back. A simple lean-to frame against a wall to grow tomatoes would need to be at least 1.2m/4ft high at the back.

The roof or lid is traditionally a glass 'light' in a wooden frame but it can also be made of modern materials. The lights can be hinged or slide backwards: bear this in mind if selecting a frame to fit into a small area. If lids are of a lightweight material, there must be some means of securing them tightly in windy weather.

Many gardeners make their own frames, usually from timber coupled with glass and any of the synthetic materials mentioned earlier (see page 109). Most rigid and semirigid materials can be drilled or screwed to the frame bars. Polythene film should be at least 500 gauge/125 microns, and battened down. Glass is best fitted into 5cm/2in square glazing bars, dry glazed with sprigs to hold it in place.

The scope for using frames for winter and spring crops is greatly increased if they are heated. The simplest method is with electric soil-warming cables. An alternative is the old-fashioned hotbed method, using rotting manure.

Siting a frame

Frames should be in an unshaded position in the northern hemisphere, facing south if single span, or in a north–south direction if double span. As with cloches, make the soil in the frame as fertile as possible. Replace the top 15cm/6in with really good soil or potting compost if necessary.

Frame techniques

Ventilation Frames are relatively airtight, so ventilation is very important to prevent a muggy atmosphere, which encourages disease. Ventilate by propping up the lights or by sliding them open. In summer they can be removed completely.

Watering In winter water the soil at the base of the plant, rather than the leaves, to lessen the risk of fungal disease.

Frost In very cold weather give additional protection by covering frames with sacking or other insulating material at night.

Light Seed boxes in deep frames may have to be raised on upturned boxes or pots to prevent seedlings from being drawn towards the light.

Pest protection Set mouse traps in winter: they go for any goodies in a frame.

Use of frames

Broadly speaking, frames are used in the same way as cloches, although they cannot be moved from one crop to another so easily – if at all. Being more substantial than cloches, they are more suitable for providing frost-free protection in winter. The lights are easily removed to accommodate tall crops. Common uses include:

- ∿ raising plants in early spring in seed trays or modules, or *in situ* for transplanting
- ∿ hardening off seedlings and young plants
- ∿ growing early spring salads such as lettuce, radish, beet and young carrots
- ∿ growing half-hardy and tender crops in summer (cucumbers and melons do well in frames, especially if the plants are raised off the ground on a horizontal trellis – see illustration, page 121)
- ∿ blanching endives, dandelion and chicory in winter (the plants can be transplanted into frames and blanched under straw)
- ∿ forcing Witloof chicory in winter
- ∿ forcing early roots of mint and seakale in spring
- ∿ storing red and Dutch white winter cabbage
- ∿ overwintering mature lettuce and other hardy salads
- ∿ maintaining a winter supply of parsley, mint and other herbs, by lifting mature roots in autumn and planting in a frame.

PERMANENT GREENHOUSES

On economic grounds it is hard to justify the cost of building even an unheated greenhouse for growing vegetables. But if you have one, use it! Vegetables can be grown directly in the soil, or in pots and other containers on staging. The former is more productive and easier to manage. For this purpose a greenhouse glazed to ground level is the most suitable type, as it allows for maximum light at ground level. (As mentioned earlier, heated greenhouses are outside the scope of this book.)

In cool climates greenhouses are widely used in summer for growing tender vegetables such as tomatoes, cucumbers, peppers and aubergines. Much to my chagrin, their potential for growing winter crops after the summer crops have been cleared is largely overlooked. Except in very severe climates, they can be planted in autumn with oriental greens and traditional winter salad plants, or sown with a wide range of cut-and-come-again salad seedlings. Any plants remaining in spring can be cleared with little loss when the time comes to plant summer vegetables.

Cost aside, the major drawback to permanent structures is that where a crop – tomatoes in particular – is grown for several years consecutively in the same soil, the soil becomes 'sick' through the build-up of pests and diseases. As a result crop failure becomes increasingly likely. For organic gardeners there are no simple solutions to the problem: one way or another fresh, uncontaminated soil has to be imported (see page 152). One of the merits of walk-in polythene tunnels (see below) is that they can easily be dismantled and moved to a fresh site every two, three or four years to avoid soil sickness.

WALK-IN POLYTHENE FILM TUNNELS (POLYTUNNELS)

Small 'walk-in' polytunnels, on the lines of those used by commercial growers, offer vegetable lovers a viable and cheap alternative to a permanent greenhouse. Shaped like a giant semicircular cloche, they consist essentially of a frame of heavy-duty galvanized steel tubular hoops, linked with an overhead ridge bar, which supports a polythene film cover.

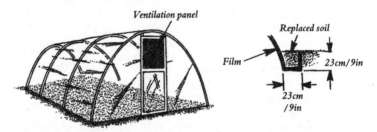

Walk-in polythene tunnel. There is a ventilation panel in the upper half of the door. The inset shows how the film edges are anchored in a trench 23cm/9in deep by 23cm/9in wide.

In basic models the hoops are sunk into foundation tubes knocked into the soil, the film being anchored by burying the edges in a shallow trench around the perimeter of the tunnel. The hoops can be concreted in to make a permanent structure. My personal feeling is that for vegetable growers this negates the benefits of mobility.

Polytunnels have enormous potential for extending the growing season and increasing productivity, at a fraction of the cost of a greenhouse. They are not the most beautiful garden features, but they can be disguised. In summer they can be screened off completely with climbing beans, cucumbers or marrows trained on poles or trellises alongside the tunnel, or with single or double rows of giant sunflowers, planted 23cm/9in apart each way. The light shade cast in summer by growing plants will cause no problems. One year we erected a metal arch over the doorway and planted it with runner beans and ornamental climbers (see illustration, page 207). Grow flowers and herbs in the soil around it – parsley and calendula have proved successful with me – or surround it with pots of plants to soften the appearance.

A typical 'off-the-peg' tunnel for home gardeners is 3 x 6m/10 x 20ft in size, with a height of about 2m/6ft at the ridge. A tunnel can be narrower, wider or longer, though if much longer than 10.5m/35ft supplementary ventilation is necessary in the centre. (Pest and disease attacks usually manifest themselves first in the centre of a long tunnel.)

Use UV-treated film of at least 500–600 gauge/125–150 microns but preferably up to 720 gauge/180 microns. If well fitted, this is normally guaranteed to last four years. The benefits from the durability of the heavier film far outweigh the slight loss of light. Lighter films cannot normally be expected to last more than three years before they tear or disintegrate and need to be replaced.

One of the drawbacks of polytunnels, in comparison with greenhouses, is the lack of ventilation. This leads to excessively high temperatures in summer and high humidity levels in winter, which encourage pests and diseases. Indeed, especially for organic gardeners, the main problems encountered in using polytunnels are the high summer temperatures. In choosing a model, or in making any structure covered with film, build in as much ventilation as possible. Where feasible, have a door at each end with ventilation panels in at least the top half. Rigid plastic windbreak 'net' is ideal for the purpose. Temporary 'blinds' of windbreak netting can be devised to cover polytunnels and provide shading in very hot weather.

The orientation of the tunnel has a bearing on temperature. If the tunnel is sited in essentially an east–west direction, the sun will bear down on the long flank of the tunnel all day. If it is sited in a north–south direction, the main impact will be on the narrow end, maximum daytime temperatures will be appreciably lower and greenhouse pests will be less likely to build up seriously. Where there is an option, organic gardeners are advised to choose a north–south orientation.

As there is no natural rainfall in a polytunnel, watering is essential. Having a tap in the tunnel, or an easy connection via a hose, saves time and energy.

To make best use of a polytunnel, site it on good well-drained soil, as far as possible on level ground, and away from overhanging trees. In exposed sites erect an artificial windbreak (see page 20) at least in the path of prevailing winds. This minimizes buffeting and heat loss in the winter months, increasing the useful life of the tunnel.

To erect a polytunnel:

1 Choose a calm, warm day. Warmth makes the film supple and therefore much easier to pull tight. Aim to eliminate slack areas, which flap in the wind and initiate tears in the film.
2 Mark out the site and erect the hoops first. Before putting on the film, cover those sections of the hoops that will be in direct contact with the film with self-adhesive anti hot-spot foam tape. The metal hoops become exceptionally hot mid-season, and the insulation can prolong the life of the film by a year. Alternatively, paint the hoops with white paint to reflect the sun.

3 Dig a trench around the outside, except where there will be doors, of 23–30cm/9–12in width and depth.

4 Ease the film over the frame, temporarily weigh down the far side with metal piping, stones or clods of soil and lay the edges of the near side in the trench. Cover it with soil. Anchoring the second side provides the main opportunity to get the film tightly over the tunnel with no wrinkles. Lay it in the trench, and partially fill the exposed edge with soil. Line helpers along the tunnel, each holding the outer edge of the film. Get everyone to heave together. (The weight of the soil enables the film to be pulled taut and so eliminate wrinkles.) Then cover the edge with soil from the trench.

5 Put in the doors according to the manufacturer's instructions. Insulate any rough edges by binding with rags or tape. Gather the film into folds as evenly as possible and batten it to the door frame. Make folds face downwards so that they will not collect dirt.

Note that extra ground space can be gained at a doorless end of a tunnel by pulling the film out to a point (as in low tunnels) and burying it in the ground.

To get the film taut over the frame of a polytunnel, weight the edges (here using soil) before pulling it tight.

Home-made polythene structures
With average handyman skills you can make useful small structures of varying shapes and sizes by battening film to a wooden frame, or anchoring it into the soil over a metal or galvanized pipe framework.

Polytunnel management

∾ Build up soil fertility with plenty of organic matter. This helps to make the soil moisture-retentive – an important point, as soil dries out rapidly in the high temperatures reached in the tunnel. In my experience it is inadvisable to use farmyard manure, as it introduces pests which are normally destroyed when manure is in the open.

꧁ Grow vegetables directly in the soil, or in any of the bed systems out-lined on page 22. I have even seen fancy potager-style beds laid out in a polytunnel.

꧁ Keep plants mulched as much as possible, both to control weeds and to conserve moisture. Either use organic mulches – straw mulches seem to encourage a good earthworm population under cover – or any synthetic mulching material (see page 72).

꧁ Make ventilation a priority. Temperatures and humidity build up rapidly even in winter, so always err on the side of over-ventilation. If necessary, cut semi-circular, dinner-plate-size 'portholes' in the sides of the polytunnel in summer, 30–45cm/12–18in above ground level, about 1.8m/6ft apart. Fold over the lower uncut edge and tape it down securely on the inside to prevent flapping. The portholes can be taped up again in winter if necessary.

Ventilation holes in a polytunnel. A semi-circular flap has been cut out of the polythene and temporarily taped to the inside wall of the polytunnel. Inset shows the hole taped up again in winter.

꧁ Repair tears in the film as soon as they develop, using strong purpose-made tapes. Polythene film is tougher than it appears and can stand a fair amount of patching. Tears quickly become more serious rips, but it is surprising how much shelter even a badly ripped polytunnel can provide, in comparison to open ground.

꧁ Discolouring green algae may develop on the surface of the film, init-ially on the more shaded side. Sponge or scrape it off gently. This is easiest to do when the film is wet, so hose it beforehand if necessary.

꧁ Make maximum use of semi-automatic watering systems (see page 80). Watering may be necessary even in winter, when frost can have quite a desiccating action.

꧁ Attach strings for supporting climbing plants to the overhead ridge bar.

Use of polytunnels

In essence, polytunnels are used in much the same way as cloches. Their height makes them pleasanter and more convenient to work in, and their size enables them to be planted extensively. The main uses are summa-rized here. (See also Cloches, page 111, Chapter 9 and the planning lists on pages 184–9).

Spring

∾ For early sowings in seed trays or pots for transplanting.
∾ For early *in situ* sowings of cut-and-come-again salads and oriental greens.
∾ For early sowings and plantings of other crops, for example carrots and salads.

Summer

∾ To grow half-hardy vegetables and herbs, such as basil, perilla, tomatoes, peppers, aubergines, iceplant and summer purslane.

Autumn

∾ To dry garlic and onions.
∾ To grow winter salads, oriental greens, overwintering brassicas such as calabrese, and cut-and-come-again seedlings for quality pickings during winter.

Winter

∾ To force Witloof chicory.
∾ For overwintering crops planted in autumn.
∾ As a wonderful haven for the winter gardener.

For more information on polytunnels, see Further Reading, page 372.

CROP COVERS

'Crop covers' is the term for various types of light films which can be laid directly on a crop to give protection. Originally known as 'floating' mulches, cloches or films, they are either perforated with slits or holes, or made of fabrics with considerable natural 'give'. This accounts for their main characteristic – an ability, within certain limits, to expand as plants grow, supported by the plants beneath. They can be very useful in vegetable growing, especially where there is no space for a greenhouse, polytunnel or frames.

Crop covers raise the soil and air temperature around plants, and have a sheltering, windbreak effect. As a result crops can be ready a couple of weeks earlier than they would be otherwise, will yield more heavily and will be of better quality. Crop covers also give some protection against flying pests. They are most valuable early and late in the year.

Think of covers primarily as a way of extending the growing season and improving quality. Unless you are using heavy fleece (see below), don't plant out much earlier than you would otherwise. Once planted, crops will grow much faster than they would in the open. Covers are a good method of capitalizing on the advantages of naturally early sites.

Covers are most easily managed on gently mounded raised beds, where they can fit snugly over the surface.

The main types of crop cover currently available are clear perforated polyethylene films and the much softer 'horticultural fleece' made from polypropylene combined with other compounds. Where they are available, always use films that are UV-treated. Films with reinforced edges last longer and are more easily anchored. This is a rapidly developing field, so watch out for potentially useful new products.

Clear perforated films

These light films are perforated either with many small holes of 1cm/½in diameter or with myriads of tiny slits. The latter type is more expensive but more 'elastic'. Perforated films will last for two seasons if handled with care.

You can make your own perforated film by burning holes in 200 gauge/50 microns film with a hot poker. Aim to make the holes about 1cm/½in diameter, spaced about 4–5cm/1½–2in) apart, so that there are roughly 200 holes per square metre/yard. Burning seals the edges so that the film won't tear, as it is likely to do if the edges are cut.

Perforated films are mainly used in spring in the early stages of growth. Their characteristics are:

- Soil warms up rapidly beneath them. In sudden hot spells temperatures can rise too high and damage plants.
- They offer very little protection against frost but give protection from the chill winds that increase the potential damage of frost.
- They are relatively impervious to rain and overhead irrigation.
- If they are left on too long there is a risk of plants becoming short of water, and possibly being chafed and damaged by the relatively harsh film.
- For every crop there is a critical point at which the film must be removed, either because of chafing or because of temperature rises. For this reason they are generally used only in the first few weeks of growth.
- They are normally laid directly on the crop, but can be laid over low tunnel hoops, to cover taller crops such as tomatoes and peppers in their early stages (see illustration, page 116).

Fleeces

These spun-fibre, 'non-woven' films have a soft, cheesecloth texture and drape easily over plants. They are made of varying thicknesses, sold with a number after the trade name, for example 'Agryl P 17' or 'Envirofleece 30', the number being the weight of the film in g/m^2. So the higher the number, the heavier the film. They are more expensive than perforated films. In comparison with perforated film, their characteristics are:

- ∾ Fleece is gentler in action, so there is less chafing of plants. It is more easily torn and less durable. Depending on thickness, and if handled carefully, fleece may last a couple of seasons.
- ∾ Fleece gives protection against several degrees of frost – the heavier the film, the greater the protection. Films of 17g protect down to –2 or –3°C/28–26°F, 30g films down to –5 or –6°C/ 23–21°F.
- ∾ You can further increase frost protection by covering the fleece with a layer of the mesh film used to deter insect pests.
- ∾ Fleece is more permeable to air and water, so less subject to temperature fluctuations, and retains moisture better. Fleece can be watered from above.
- ∾ Fleece gives protection against birds and flying insect pests, including aphids, cabbage root fly, carrot fly, flea beetle, butterflies and moths, provided it is securely anchored at soil level with no gaps between the film and the ground, and there are no holes in the fabric. Unless the weather is very hot, carrots can be grown under fleece until near maturity, and therefore protected from carrot root fly.
- ∾ Fleece can be left on plants much longer than perforated films, in a few cases until harvesting. Japanese radishes, for example, can be protected against cabbage root fly by covering with fleece until shortly before lifting. Normally it is removed after six to eight weeks.
- ∾ A drawback is that fleece is opaque, so it is hard to see how the crops are performing without lifting it.
- ∾ Fleece is not suitable for use in very windy areas.

Managing crop covers

- ∾ Before laying films, make sure that the ground is weed-free, as weeds germinate fast and flourish in the cosy environment underneath them.
- ∾ Lay perforated films immediately after sowing or planting. If doing so after sowing, sow in slightly sunken drills, so that the seedlings can get established before they 'hit' the film.
- ∾ As a rule fleece is more successful if laid after planting, as heavy rain after sowing makes it drape on the ground, damaging emerging seedlings. This may be avoided by sowing in sunken drills.
- ∾ Lay perforated film with a little slackness to allow for growth, but not overstretched or sagging. Lay fleece fairly taut, but fold the edges at the sides, so that it can be released in stages as the crops grow. (For large plants allow as much as 50cm/20in of slack).
- ∾ The most secure method of anchorage is to bury the edges in 5cm/2in deep slits in the soil, made on either side of the bed with a trowel. Push the soil back against the edge of the film to keep it in place. This is most suitable for perforated films, which are in place for shorter periods. The disadvantage is that gaining access to plants means unearthing the edges.

ॐ For easier access, anchor films and fleece at the edges with purpose-made plastic pegs, metal tent pegs, metal piping, or small but strong polythene bags filled with sand or soil. These are much easier to lift when access is required and more practical (as less abrasive) for fleece. Covers can also be carefully stapled to boarded edges with a staple gun.

Removing crop covers

The trick in using crop covers is knowing when to remove them. This applies particularly to perforated films, where the restricted ventilation means that once temperatures rise, plants may deteriorate rapidly. The optimum time varies with the crop and the conditions. Where relevant, details are given in the Vegetable Directory. In practice, keep a close eye on plants, and remove the film if there is any sign of stress – sooner rather than later. Remove crop covers from insect-pollinated crops such as tomatoes and courgettes at least when the flowers appear.

As growth under films is 'soft', sudden exposure to harsher conditions is a shock and setback for plants. Never remove films in bright sunshine or in cold weather: do so towards the evening on still, mild, overcast or damp days.

Water gently just after the covers are removed if the ground is dry, as will often be the case.

(For cultivation of bush tomatoes under perforated films, see Tomatoes, page 343.)

Main uses of crop covers

There is enormous scope for experimenting with the use of crop covers. Many of the uses suggested on page 117 for cloches can be applied to them. Here is a summary of potential uses:

Spring and early summer

ॐ Drape fleece over seedlings and young plants under cover and outdoors as extra protection if frost threatens.
ॐ Use crop covers for the early stages of many outdoor vegetables, including early potatoes, lettuce, outdoor bush tomatoes, beetroot, cabbage, cauliflower, celery, courgette, spinach, parsley, French beans, endive, red chicory and other leafy salad crops.
ॐ Grow radishes and carrots to maturity (the latter under fleece only).

Autumn and winter

ॐ Use fleece to cover overwintering lettuce, corn salad, spring cabbage, late sowings of beetroot, spinach, radish, oriental greens and cut-and-come-again seedlings, to increase growth and improve quality.
ॐ Use fleece as emergency frost cover, and drape it over outdoor crops and also crops under cover, for example late-maturing tomatoes and peppers, if frost is forecast.

7

PESTS AND DISEASES

Pests and diseases can take their toll of vegetables in terms of quality and quantity. While commercial vegetable growers spend a great deal of money on insecticides and fungicides to get high yields and unblemished produce for marketing, the organic gardening philosophy is to provide the optimum conditions for healthy growth and, if necessary, to accept that some vegetables will have imperfections. So what if there are a few holes in a cabbage leaf or the odd maggoty pea?

Although in theory vegetables can be attacked by a wide range of pests and diseases, in practice only one or two pose a serious threat in any season – perhaps carrot fly on carrots and parsnips, or clubroot affecting the brassicas. There are practical, non-chemical solutions to most of these pests and diseases. This chapter takes a broad look at likely problems, and means of prevention and control. Specific pests and diseases will be covered under the appropriate vegetables in the Vegetable Directory.

MAIN GROUPS OF PEST

The following are some of the main pests likely to be encountered in the vegetable garden, divided a little arbitrarily into different categories.

Insect pests

Caterpillars The larval forms of butterflies and moths attack a wide range of leafy plants, mainly brassicas, making holes in the leaves. They are usually highly visible.

Carrot fly larva feeding on a carrot, with adult fly (left) and larva (right).

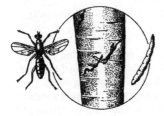

Beetles and weevils Adult and larval forms (grubs) cause damage to roots, stems, leaves and pods. Asparagus beetle, flea beetle, and pea and bean weevil are typical. (The Colorado beetle is a horrendous pest in countries where it is endemic.)

Root flies The young maggots of various species of fly attack root vegetables, most commonly carrots, onions and brassicas.

Cabbage root fly maggots attacking a young plant. Damaged plants normally wilt and die.

A wilted lettuce (above) is a sign of lettuce root aphid, which attacks the plants' roots (below).

Aphids This group includes greenfly, blackfly, whitefly, mealy aphid and root aphids. They pierce leaves and other parts of the plant and suck the sap, causing physical damage and often transmitting virus diseases in the process. Attacked leaves are often twisted, curled or blistered. Aphids may excrete sticky honeydew on leaves, which can be colonized by black sooty mould.

Soil pests

The larval forms of insects (see chart opposite) Several familiar insects have larval forms which live on the soil and feed on roots and stems. These include (the popular names for their adult forms are in brackets): cutworm (noctuid moths), wireworm (click beetle), chafer bugs (May and June bugs) and leatherjackets (cranefly, alias daddy-long-legs). They are generally most serious where grassland has been converted into vegetable plots. They are mainly night feeders. (For damage, see chart, overleaf.)

Nematodes/eelworm These microscopic soil pests live in the soil and in roots. Some are very serious pests – potato eelworm, for example. They debilitate affected crops, often causing the long-term problem known as soil sickness, where it becomes impossible to grow the crop in question. Cysts can persist in the soil for many years, in which case long-term rotation and growing resistant varieties are the only remedies.

Slugs and snails These are the bane of the organic gardener, as they thrive in environments rich in organic matter, feeding on a wide range of leaves and stems. They are mainly night-feeding, and live both in the soil and above ground, sheltering in debris. They are worst on heavy soils.

Soil pest	Larval form	Adult form	Time/nature of damage	Control measures
Cutworm / Turnip moth	3 pairs legs and sucker feet Fat caterpillar, distinct head Greenish or brownish grey Up to 5cm/2in long	Noctuid moths e.g. turnip, heart and dart moth and others	Spring to autumn Mostly night feeders Cut off stems of wide range of plants at soil level Make holes in potatoes and other root crops	Rain/heavy watering in early summer kills larvae Search soil by damaged plants and kill larvae Grow plants under fine nets to deter adults Biological control
Leatherjacket / Cranefly	Legless, no distinct head Fat soft body, but tough-skinned Earthy colour Up to 3.5cm/1¼in long	Cranefly or Daddy-long-legs	Most destructive early spring to summer Larvae eat roots in soil and bite through stems of wide range of plants at soil level Ragged feeding on lower leaves	Generally as cutworm Ensure soil well drained Clear and dig ground before autumn, especially if previously grassland Biological control on small scale
Wireworm / Click beetle	3 pairs short legs Shiny, tough, wire-like body Golden yellow, up to 2.5cm/1in long	Click beetle (Adults fling themselves into the air when lying on their backs)	Spring to autumn Worst in first 3 years after digging in grass Bite off stems of wide range of plants at ground level Make holes in roots and tubers	Hunt and destroy around damaged plants Plant potatoes initially in new ground to reduce numbers when crop lifted
Chafer bug / Cockchafer beetle	3 pairs strong legs Large brown head Tail end of body swollen Lies with characteristically curled body Whitish, inactive Up to 4cm/1½in long	May bug (cockchafer beetle) June bug (garden chafer)	Summer to autumn All kinds of roots gnawed 5cm/2in or more below the soil surface	Keep garden clean and weed-free Search soil near damaged plants and kill grubs Biological control on small scale
Millipede	2 pairs legs on most segments; slow-moving Most harmful ones are: Flat type: flat, light brown, 1.5–2cm/½–¾in long Thin snake type: smooth round body up to 2cm/¾in long Usually black and shiny; curl up when disturbed		Spring to summer Eat pea and been seeds and seedlings Also attack roots and tubers	Search near damaged plants and remove

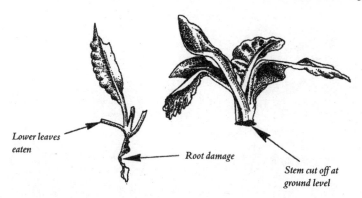

Lower leaves eaten

Root damage

Stem cut off at ground level

Typical soil pest damage. Left: eating the lower leaves and damaging the root. Right: cutting the stem off at ground level.

Greenhouse pests Glasshouse whitefly and red spider mite, along with aphids and thrips, are pests which can become very serious in the high temperatures that develop in greenhouses and polythene structures. Fortunately they can be controlled with biological control (see page 142).

Mammals In many vegetable gardens the most substantial losses are due to animals: rabbits, deer, mice taking peas and broad bean seeds, moles tunnelling unmercifully through rows of seedlings and uprooting plants, and cats and dogs scratching.

Birds In rural gardens large birds such as pigeons, jays and pheasants can cause substantial damage to greens, peas and other vegetables, particularly in winter. Small birds such as sparrows attack seedlings, especially lettuce, beet and spinach. The answer lies in deterrence. Some birds, of course, are beneficial in feeding on insect pests and weed seeds.

DISEASES

Most of the diseases which affect vegetables are caused by fungi, bacteria and viruses. They are infectious and can spread very rapidly in conditions that suit them. They are much harder to control, either with chemicals or by other means, than pests. Indeed, in many cases, once the disease has become obvious it is too late to do anything about it. Prevention is better – and easier – than cure. Grow resistant cultivars wherever available.

Fungal diseases Various fungi cause grey moulds and mildews – the greyish 'threads' are the mycelia produced by the fungi. Common diseases are grey mould (*Botrytis*) on lettuce, downy mildew on lettuce, tomato and cucumber, powdery mildew on cucumber, blight and stem

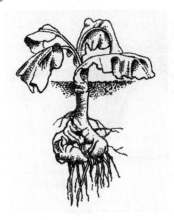

Clubroot: a disease on brassicas which produces distorted galls and swellings on the roots.

rot on tomatoes, various onion rots, celery leaf spot, leek rust and various blights, storage rots and galls. Fungi also cause damping-off diseases in seedlings, where seedlings either fail to germinate or collapse shortly after they have emerged. Fungal diseases can be spread by air-borne spores, and some, such as onion white rot, produce resting spores which last many years in the soil. Clubroot in brassicas is caused by a fungus-related 'slime mould'.

Bacteria Invisible to the naked eye, bacteria cause rots and cankers, sometimes slimy in nature, and are often secondary infections on plants that are already damaged. They are spread by air, by splashing water droplets, and even by particles of soil.

Virus diseases Still something of an unknown quantity, virus diseases debilitate plants. Cucumber mosaic virus is typical. The leaves become mottled and develop a yellowish mosaic pattern, the whole plant becomes stunted and dies. Virus diseases are spread in many ways: by propagating from infected plants, by aphids, eelworms, occasionally fungi and even by hand. If you suspect that a plant has a virus disease (obviously stunted growth and mottling are fairly common symptoms), it is wisest to pull it up and burn it to prevent the spread of infection. Some virus diseases, such as lettuce mosaic, are seed-borne.

Plant disorders
Inadequate growing conditions lead to what are dubbed 'physiological' diseases or disorders. They are not infectious. They can be caused by water shortage or faulty watering; temperatures that are too high or too low; poor nutrition or a mineral deficiency; even an excess of a chemical salt in the soil caused by the excessive use of artificial fertilizers. These can be prevented by good husbandry – see below.

THE BEST PREVENTIVE MEDICINE: GOOD HUSBANDRY

If this catalogue of plant ills seems unduly long, take comfort from the fact that strong, well-grown plants are not only less susceptible to pest and disease attacks but are more likely to recover from attacks that occur. The good husbandry that results in healthy plants has many facets.

The soil

Fertility Plants' fundamental requirement is fertile, well-drained soil with plenty of organic matter, a balanced supply of nutrients and adequate moisture.

Soil pH Clubroot, a serious disease on brassicas which produces distorted galls and swellings, is most likely in poorly drained and very acid soils (see page 30). A remedy is to lime to bring the pH to a slightly alkaline level, above 7. Potato scab is most likely to occur on alkaline soils – so don't lime if it is a problem.

Garden hygiene

Removing debris At some stage in their life cycle many common garden pests and diseases shelter on rubbish, under pieces of brick or slate or piles of decaying vegetable matter, or among dry leaves under hedges. Keep the garden clean to deprive them of a suitable environment. Store equipment and materials under cover. There are many examples of pests and diseases flourishing on plant debris:

- Downy mildew fungi overwinter in plant debris.
- Aphids overwinter in brassica stalks. Pull up remaining stumps of Brussels sprouts, hardy cabbages and sprouting broccoli before the aphids produce a winged generation in late spring.
- Flea beetles shelter in rubbish and weeds throughout the winter.
- Slugs and snails hide and lay eggs in shelter afforded by pieces of wood, mulching plastic, old cabbage leaves or the grooves in module trays.

Weed control Keep beds and paths free of weeds. Weeds harbour pests including cabbage root fly, carrot fly and the broad bean blackfly, as well as fungi, the slime mould which causes clubroot and some viruses. The lettuce virus disease beet western yellows is found in groundsel (*Senecio vulgaris*) and shepherd's purse (*Capsella bursa-pastoris*). In spring I've often found young leatherjacket grubs in the root systems of grass weeds and, I hate to say it, as we grow them for their edible flowers, in the fibrous roots of cultivated forms of *Bellis perennis* daisies.

Diseased plants Sources of infection often remain on diseased plant material. Never leave leaves, roots or old stems of diseased plants in the ground or lying around. Chop them up if necessary and put them on the compost heap (provided it reaches reasonably high temperatures), or bury or burn them.

Water tanks Keep these covered as they are a breeding ground for pests and diseases.

Cultural practices

By adopting certain cultural practices, you can often avoid diseases and pests, or limit their potential damage.

Rotation The rationale for rotation (growing plants in different beds or parts of the garden in a sequence over several years) rests on the fact that some serious soil-dwelling pests and diseases only attack plants of a particular family. They can be starved out if they are deprived of their favourite plant host – but conversely increase rapidly where it is being continually grown. Although there are limitations to the effectiveness of rotation in small gardens, it is a sound practice to adopt. For more on rotation, see page 175.

Plant raising Seeds which are slow to germinate because the soil conditions are poor, lingering seedlings unable to develop a good root system and those plants which somehow never 'get away' are most vulnerable to attack by pests and diseases.

When sowing indoors

- Keep all propagation equipment clean.
- Prick out early to avoid overcrowding.
- Raise plants in modules wherever feasible.
- Harden off well before planting outside.

When sowing outdoors

- Never sow or plant in very cold, very wet or very dry soil (see page 91).
- Make a firm seedbed with a good tilth (the best guarantee of quick germination (see page 86).
- Make a stale seedbed in advance of sowing where possible (see page 88). This can deter the bean seed fly and onion fly.
- Thin early to avoid overcrowding. Fungal diseases are most likely to develop and spread where plants are too close.

Planting healthy material Never propagate or plant diseased material. Discard potato tubers, garlic, onion or shallot bulbs with any signs of rot. Examine bought plants carefully for signs of clubroot swellings on the roots.

Timing and related tactics Pests and diseases can sometimes be avoided by choice of the sowing time. As far as possible base this decision on local knowledge. For example, in some areas flea beetle attacks are far more serious in spring than late summer – in which case avoid spring sowings of susceptible plants like turnip, radish and oriental greens unless protected under fine nets. Autumn-sown broad beans escape the worst of the blackfly aphids; very early and mid-summer sowings of carrots may avoid carrot fly; early plantings of potato often avoid potato blight. Onions raised from sets rather than seed escape onion fly attacks.

Interplanting Whereas monoculture encourages pests, interplanting can deter and confuse them. In my experience carrots sown mixed with annual flower seed (see page 161) suffer very little carrot fly attack. Similarly, interplanting French marigolds between tomatoes and peppers, when grown under cover, appears to prevent whitefly attacks. This may be due to the strong scent of the foliage. Underplanting crops like brassicas with green ground cover, such as clover, can distract pests and deter them from laying eggs on the brassicas.

Spacing Overcrowded mature plants compete for nutrients, light and water. If plants are too densely planted, humidity and lack of ventilation encourage disease. Plants under cover should be given maximum ventilation to prevent the build-up of pests and diseases.

Siting If growing both potatoes and outdoor tomatoes, plant the tomatoes as far as possible from the potatoes to cut down the risk of infection from potato blight.

Feeding Don't force plants by overfeeding, especially with nitrogenous fertilizers. The sappy growth that results is prone to pest and disease attack.

Watering Don't allow plants to wilt for long: wilted plants are the most vulnerable to aphid attack. Avoid watering so late in the day that leaves won't dry before nightfall, as damp leaves encourage fungal spores to develop.

Handling vegetables for storing Always handle vegetables that are being stored very carefully, especially potatoes, onions and garlic. The rots which destroy stored bulbs and tubers often start where they have been cut or even bruised. (A French garlic seller told me it broke her heart to see garlic being thrown about: it should be handled like eggs, she said.)

Choice of plants

Respect the climate Grow appropriate vegetables for your region. Attempting to grow semi-tropical crops outdoors in cool areas invites disaster.

Resistant varieties Where they are available, choose varieties that have been bred with resistance, or at least tolerance towards specific pests and diseases. Unfortunately there is no guarantee that the resistance is permanent as pests and diseases may quite rapidly develop new strains to overcome the resistance. Useful introductions include the swede 'Marian', which is highly tolerant of mildew and clubroot; lettuce 'Minetto', which has good resistance to downy mildew and mosaic virus; lettuces 'Avoncrisp' and 'Avondefiance' with resistance to lettuce root aphid; the parsnip 'Avonresister', with resistance to canker; and the mildew-resistant cucumbers 'Brunex', 'Tyria' and 'Cassandra'. There are many others. Watch out for new developments in the gardening press.

The environmental approach

The success of chemical-free organic gardening depends on building up a natural population of beneficial insects and predators. In gardens where pesticides are used regularly the predator populations are severely damaged. They recover gradually in the absence of spraying, eventually reaching a level where they make a very significant contribution to pest and disease control.

Get to know the 'beneficials' It is important to identify, and avoid destroying, beneficial predators. Some examples are ground or carabid beetles (which feed on slug and snail eggs), the devil's coach horse or rove beetle (which feeds on slugs, and soil pests including cutworms and leatherjackets), ladybird adults and larvae, which feed on aphids, as do the larvae of hoverflies and lacewings, and the parasitic ichneumons, which lay their eggs on caterpillars. (See also Further Reading, page 372.) In the soil, work on the basis that fast-moving grubs and related creatures, such as the centipedes, are beneficial; they need to be fast as their prey, small slugs and insects, are mobile. Plant eaters – therefore pests from our point of view – are the slower movers, such as some of the millipedes. Wasps, frogs and toads are all beneficial, though wasps, of course, are a pest if you have fruit trees.

Grow flowers to provide nectar and pollen Beneficial insects seek out plants that supply nectar and pollen, so try and plant some in the garden. The most suitable are flat open flowers, which enable the short-tongued beneficial insects to reach into them, and very small flowers. Among those that can be grown in a vegetable garden for other purposes – for use as culinary herbs, edible flowers or green manures – are pot marigold (*Calendula officinalis*), fennel (*Foeniculum vulgare*), thymes (*Thymus* spp.) and the green manure *Phacelia tanacetifolia*. There are many more. (See Further Reading, page 372.)

Eternal vigilance

This is perhaps the key to success as an organic gardener. Keep a close eye on plants to nip trouble in the bud. Spot caterpillar eggs on the undersides of brassica leaves and clutches of newly hatched caterpillars or aphids and destroy them. If a plant is wilting unaccountably, dig it up carefully: a soil pest may just be starting to attack and the plant can be saved and replanted. I have even washed cabbage root fly maggots off the roots of oriental greens and replanted them successfully!

CHEMICAL CONTROLS

A few chemical sprays are permitted under organic gardening standard rules, on the grounds that they break down rapidly into non-toxic components with no residual effects. They are therefore less harmful to the environment than standard chemical controls and do not act as 'broad spectrum' chemicals, which kill bees, pollinating insects, other beneficial predators and parasites as well as pests – and possibly affect birds and other creatures in the food chain. All the insecticides approved for organic use act as 'contact' poisons, killing pests on the surface at the time of or shortly after application. Because they are short-lived they are less effective than standard pesticides and fairly frequent spraying may be necessary. They can have a useful role where severe pest damage is threatening a crop and all other methods of control have failed.

The fact remains that they are chemicals, they do damage life other than the specific pest or disease being targeted and, with frequent use, the pests and diseases develop a natural resistance to them, so rendering the chemicals useless. So their use should always be minimized.

Spraying guidelines

If you are using chemicals, it is important to keep to the rules:

- Follow the manufacturer's instructions meticulously.
- Spray in the evening or in dull weather when fewer pollinating insects are flying about.
- Never spray water, ditches, ponds, rain tubs and so on, or allow spray to drift on to water.
- Never spray when it is windy, or allow spray to drift into neighbouring gardens.
- Try to make up no more spray than is needed, as the surplus will have to be disposed of.
- Never transfer chemicals to other containers such as beer or soft drink bottles that people might drink from.
- Store chemicals in tightly shut containers or tins, in a cool, dry, preferably dark place well out of the reach of pets and children.
- Wash hands and equipment very thoroughly after use.

Applying pesticides

The term 'pesticide' covers all chemicals used for controlling pests and diseases, both insecticides for controlling insects and fungicides for preventing fungus disease attacks. Pesticides are usually applied as dusts, liquid sprays or aerosols. It does not always follow that the same range of pests will be controlled by all forms of an insecticide – so study labels carefully to make certain.

On a small scale, there are handy puffer packs of dusts and aerosols, in both of which the chemical is in a form ready for use. Liquid sprays are made up from concentrated powder or solution and applied with a sprayer. As spray goes a long way, a 0.5 litre/1 pint capacity trigger pump hand sprayer, preferably with an adjustable nozzle, is adequate for average use in a small garden. For larger-scale work, use a portable compression sprayer, such as a knapsack sprayer, which is pumped up before use.

Some pesticides, but not all, can be mixed with others or with liquid fertilizers or foliar feeds and applied together. Check the manufacturer's recommendations before using a particular mixture.

The safer pesticides

The chart on the following page shows the safer insecticides currently approved for use in the UK by the organic standards authorities. Other potentially useful products such as quassia, neem, garlic oil and granulosis virus may be approved for use in future. Remember that these are not powerful chemicals, and results can be disappointing.

The fungicide Bordeaux mixture, which was used to control potato and tomato blight and celery leaf spot, is being withdrawn. Bicarbonate of soda solutions, which control powdery mildew, are not permitted under organic systems.

Home-made rhubarb spray

The recipe for this mixture was devised by organic pioneer Lawrence Hills to kill aphids, and many people have found it effective. Strictly speaking, using such mixtures is illegal under current EU legislation. However, I include it here for gardeners outside the EU and in the hope that the relevant restrictions will eventually be removed.

Chop up 1.4kg/3lb rhubarb leaves. Boil for ½ hour in 3.5 litres/6 pints water. Strain off liquid and cool. Dissolve 28g/1oz soapflakes in 1.2 litres/2 pints water, mix with the rhubarb liquid and spray.

Note: some rhubarb cultivars are considered more effective for this spray than others. 'Glaskin's Perpetual' is not recommended.

BIOLOGICAL CONTROL

For organic gardeners – besides the general hygiene measures and cultural practices mentioned above – the answer to pest problems lies in using biological control and traps, barriers, nets and other means to deter or control the most common vegetable pests.

Biological control is the use of a pest's natural enemy to control it. There are no harmful effects on beneficial insects, other forms of wildlife or human beings. As far as can be seen, there is no damage to the environment, as a biological control is specific to the pest and, once the pest is

SAFER PESTICIDES

Product	Comments	Effective against
Derris (rotenone)	Main active ingredient is rotenone Available as powder and liquid Can harm some beneficial insects; safe for bees Harmful to fish, so keep away from ponds Can mix with pyrethrum to make more effective insecticide	Aphids (greenfly, blackfly, cabbage mealy aphid) Small caterpillars Flea beetles and pollen beetles Turnip fly, some weevils, thrips, sucking insects, red spider mite Used at double strength it has some effect on Colorado beetle
Pyrethrum	Available as dust and spray Harmful to some beneficial insects and fish, but not very persistent Can be mixed with derris to make more effective	Same pests as derris, but particularly against insects such as aphids (blackfly, greenfly, cabbage mealy aphid), whitefly, red spider mite
Soft soap sprays based on fatty acids*	Available as dilute or concentrated liquid May damage small beneficial insects Best used as spot treatment on infestations	Aphids (blackfly, greenfly, cabbage mealy aphid), whitefly, red spider mite
Rape seed oil	Available as concentrate Biological control can be applied immediately after use	Controls greenfly, blackfly, whitefly, thrips, red spider mite Availability and effectiveness as soft soap sprays
Bacillus thuringiensis	Biological spray of bacterial spores Powder diluted to use as spray Harmless to all beneficial insects	Moth and butterfly caterpillars; cutworm caterpillars when feeding on leaves
Sulphur	Naturally occurring mineral Available as puffer or sulphur candle for greenhouse smoke	Powdery mildew

*Note: although insecticidal soap is a virtually identical product, for technical reasons it cannot currently be legally marketed as an insecticide in the UK.

eradicated, the control itself dies out. It has to be reintroduced when there is another infestation.

With the increased interest in avoiding the use of chemicals, a lot of research is being undertaken on biological control, and new forms are regularly being introduced. Watch out for them in the gardening press. In most cases successful use of biological control requires certain minimum temperatures and/or humidity levels. For this reason it is most widely used in the more controllable environment of greenhouses and polytunnels. Fewer are available for use outdoors.

Although it is often suggested that the beneficial agents for greenhouse pests require minimum average daytime temperatures of at least 18°C/64°F, in practice they start being active at about 10°C/50°F, becoming increasingly active as temperatures rise to about 16°C/61°F and above. (If there is a sudden temperature drop they become inactive again, but will revive when temperatures rise.) As pest populations can soar once established, it is always better to introduce controls early rather than later.

Applying predator mites in vermiculite to cucumber leaves to control red spider mite. The paper catches any spillage, for use on other leaves.

Applying biological control agents is relatively easy. In most cases they are despatched by specialist suppliers, generally in packs and sachets which are clipped or sprinkled on plants to release the agents (see above). Agents for use outdoors are usually sprayed or watered on the ground or on plants. Unopened sachets of *Bacillus thuringiensis* can be kept for two or three years in a cool dry place.

It is essential to identify the pest correctly in the first place and follow the instructions carefully. Choosing the optimum moment to apply the agent can be tricky. Temperature aside, the pest population must be sufficient to support the predator or parasite.

In greenhouses soft soap fatty acid sprays can be used early in the season to control whitefly, red spider mite and aphids, and biological controls applied once temperatures rise above about 10°C/50°F.

The nematode controls for slugs, and the more recently introduced controls for cutworm and chafer bugs, are expensive on a large scale, but can be very effective in limited areas, such as raised beds. They require moist conditions when applied and subsequently. Irrigation after use is recommended.

Effective biological controls are currently available for the following vegetable pests:

Outdoors

- ❧ Caterpillars – the bacterium *Bacillus thuringiensis* (see The safer insecticides, page 142) (use no more than necessary, as caterpillars may build up resistance)
- ❧ Slugs and small snails – parasitic nematode *Phasmarhabditis hermaphrodita*
- ❧ Red spider mite – the predatory mites *Phytoseiulus persimilis* (effective at day temperatures above 16°C/61°F)
- ❧ Leatherjackets – parasitic nematode *Steinernema feltiae*
- ❧ Chafer grubs – parasitic nematode *Heterohabditis megidis*.

In greenhouses

- ❧ Aphids – predatory midges *Aphidoletes aphidomyza* or parasitic wasps *Aphidius* spp.
- ❧ Whitefly – parasitic wasps *Encarsia formosa*
- ❧ Red spider mite – predatory mites *Phytoseiulus persimilis*
- ❧ Thrips – predatory mite *Amblyseus cucumeris*.

ALTERNATIVE METHODS OF CONTROL OF PESTS AND DISEASE

Here is a summary of alternative methods for the main groups of common pests. The emphasis is on cheap and easy methods.

Slugs and snails

Hunting at night Feeding slugs are easily found by torchlight, especially on warm muggy nights. The most effective way of controlling them is to collect them in yogurt pots, beer cans or buckets – depending on the scale of the problem. If you can't bear to squash them, achieve instantaneous death by pouring boiling water over them.

Hunting during the day Slugs can be found hiding in cool damp places such as under debris or mulching mats. Or put half grapefruit skins on the ground, skin side uppermost. Slugs will crawl into them and are easily collected.

Traps Various kinds of slug trap are on the market; baiting them with beer is often recommended. You can also make traps by sinking small containers, jars or plastic cartons, filled with beer, into the ground. In my experience these trap beneficial ground beetles as well as slugs, though theoretically this is avoided if the rim of the trap is well above ground level.

Deterrents Dry sharp materials such as grit, sand, coarse ashes, bran or broken egg shells can be placed around vulnerable plants to deter slugs. They are effective in varying degrees, though dry materials lose their efficacy if they become wet. Wide stretches of gravel path, of probably at least 2m/6½ft width, around a vegetable patch seem to keep out slugs.

Barriers Individual young plants can be protected with barriers made from plastic pots or bottles with the bottom removed, placed over the plants and pushed well into the ground. Barriers of self-adhesive copper tape are a very effective and long-lasting barrier on plant pots.

Cultivation Digging and hoeing exposes slugs to their natural enemies, birds.

Biological control Biological control (see above) will work in moist soils at temperatures above 5°C/40°F. Treatment with the appropriate nematode is normally effective for up to six weeks. This is a fairly expensive option.

Soil pests

Hunting See Slugs and snails, above. Soil pests can be found on the surface at night. During the day they can often be found lurking in the root system of – or near by – an obviously damaged plant. Even if a plant has to be sacrificed, at least the pest is prevented from moving on to the neighbouring plant.

Traps Many soil pests, including wireworms, cutworms and millipedes, can be attracted to traps made from scooped-out potatoes or carrots fixed on skewers just below the soil surface. Examine the traps daily and destroy any pests that have been caught.

Barriers The 'bottle barriers' suggested above for slugs and snails have some effect against cutworms and leatherjackets.

Cultivation See Slugs and snails, above.

Biological control See chart on page 143.

Caterpillars

Hand picking Keep a constant watch and pick them off as young as possible; ideally look for eggs and squash them before they have hatched.

Fine mesh nets (see below) Nets will protect plants both from adult moths and butterflies laying eggs which hatch into caterpillars, and from young caterpillars searching for food.

Flying insect pests: general controls

Many insect pests fly or have a flying stage. Horticultural nets and fleeces, primarily used to increase shelter and raise the temperature on outdoor crops, also offer excellent protection from insect attack. They will not, of course, be effective if the pest is already on the plants, or on or in the soil (as may be the case with flea beetle) when the plants are covered. It is essential that there are no holes in the materials and that they are very securely anchored at ground level. Any gaps will allow insects to crawl or fly inside. (For general use and anchorage methods, see Crop covers, page 128.)

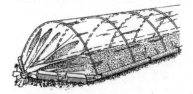

Low nets to deter flying pests. Left: anchored with weights. Right: anchored into the soil.

Net barriers Fine mesh nets (not unlike woven mosquito netting) are normally laid over low hoops and anchored in the soil. They offer long-term protection as they are very permeable and can be left in place throughout the life of the plant. Depending on the fineness of the net, they can keep out a wide range of pests including moths and butterflies, cabbage root fly, carrot fly, onion fly, pea moth and the cutworm moths, frit fly, pollen beetle, leaf miners, flea beetle (in varying degrees) and some aphids. They also offer protection against birds and rabbits. They have to be removed from insect-pollinated crops, such as outdoor tomatoes or dwarf beans, before they flower. Only very fine nets will completely exclude flea beetle, whitefly and thrips. For protection from flea beetle coverage of plants is only necessary for four to five weeks after sowing.

Horticultural fleece These soft, very light films (see page 129) are usually laid directly on plants with enough slack to allow the plants to grow. In most cases they are removed after several weeks as the high temperatures and lack of ventilation they encourage begin to be counterproductive. While in place they offer excellent protection against the insect pests listed above, including, if the films are very well anchored, flea beetle.

Aphids

Encouraging natural predators (See The environmental approach, page 140) Not spraying and planting nectar-supplying plants is very beneficial, as huge quantities of aphids are devoured by the larvae of hoverflies, lacewings and ladybirds – as well as by adult ladybirds.

Squashing by hand Colonies can be eliminated by squashing gently, so as not to damage the leaves.

Sticky yellow traps In greenhouses, sticky yellow glue traps, suspended above plants, will catch a fair number of aphids. Treat the traps more as a means of evaluating the build-up of the aphid population – prior to introducing biological control – than as a control measure.

Chequered and shiny films (see page 72) Shiny aluminium films and black-and-white chequered films, laid between plants, have been shown to deter aphids. For maximum effect at least 50 per cent of the ground should be covered.

Cabbage root fly

(For damage, see illustration, page 134.) Note that cabbage root flies emerge in spring to lay their eggs when cow parsley (*Anthriscus sylvestris*) is in flower. This is when preventive action is most needed.

Protective collars The adult fly lays eggs at the base of the stem of young brassica plants and the hatched maggots burrow into the roots, destroying the plants. You can prevent attacks by slipping collars around the stem at ground level when planting. The eggs are then laid on the collar and dry out. (The collars also provide shelter for beneficial beetles.) You can make collars from carpet foam underlay or any material that will lie flat and stay in place. Cut circular discs of 15cm/6in diameter and make a small

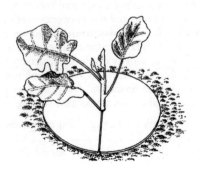

To prevent cabbage root fly, place a disc of carpet foam underlay or similar material, with a small hole in the centre and a slit from the hole to the edge, around the stem of a young plant.

hole in the centre, with a slit from the centre to the outside edge. Open it to place the disc neatly around the stem.

Barriers Make barriers from plastic pots or bottles with the base removed (see Slugs and snails, page 145). Alternatively take a plastic pot, cut a hole in the base large enough to slip a plant root through from above, plant it and bury the rim 1cm/½in deep in the soil. You may need to cut away the pot later to allow the stem to expand, but the pot gives protection at a critical time.

Deep planting Organic gardener Jack Temple recommended planting brassicas in shallow V-shaped trenches, about 10cm/4in deep. As the plants grow, gradually fill the shallow trenches with well-rotted compost. This encourages the growth of secondary roots higher up the stem, which take over if the lower roots are damaged.

Carrot fly
(For damage, see illustration page 132; for carrot fly barrier, see right.)

Carrot fly barrier made from polythene film battened to a light wooden frame. It is 60cm/2ft high with the lower edges buried in the soil.

Barriers Carrot fly is a low-flying insect, and can be deterred by surrounding the carrot bed with a barrier of heavy-duty clear polythene or fine woven mesh netting, at least 60cm/2ft high, buried 5cm/2in deep in the soil. The bed should be no more than about 1m/3ft across. One of many methods of doing this is to put posts at the corners of the bed, or along its length if necessary, staple wire to the top of the posts, then fold a sheet of polythene or net over the wire and bury it in the soil. Insert bamboo canes on either side of the film or net if extra support is needed. The illustration above shows polythene film battened to a light wooden frame.

Raised boxes Grow carrots in boxes or tubs raised to a height of 60cm/2ft, so that they are inaccessible to the carrot fly.

Mice

Traps Their main target is peas, and mouse traps are the best remedy. There is a tradition of covering pea seeds with holly leaves or something prickly to deter mice, but I remain unconvinced that this works.

Moles

Traps Unfortunately moles find the high earthworm population in an organic garden very inviting. They can be caught with traps set in their runs, or, if you have no objection to using them, chemical fuses. Other products on the market merely drive moles away – presumably to your neighbour's garden. Mothballs pushed into their runs, or pieces of foam rubber soaked in paraffin and set on fire, are also said to frighten them away. The traditional remedy of planting caper spurge is, in my experience, quite useless.

Rabbits

Fencing Effective fencing must be at least 90–120cm/3–4ft high, and of 2.5–3cm/1–1½in wire mesh, to prevent baby rabbits from squeezing through. It also needs to be buried at least 30cm/12in deep, bent outwards, to prevent rabbits from burrowing beneath. In severe cases an entire garden will need to be rabbit-proofed. Make sure that there are no entry gaps by gates.

Cats

Barriers Hawthorn twigs laid on the surface help to protect seeds and seedlings from cats, as do wire-netting pea guards bent over emerging seedlings (see below). Unfortunately cats love playing in and on fleece films and fine nets.

Birds

Cotton thread Small birds such as sparrows can destroy emerging seedlings and young plants. Deter them with single strands of black cotton above or on either side of the seedling rows, about 5cm/2in above ground. Use strong cotton such as button thread and put them in place immediately after sowing or planting. Tomorrow is often too late!

Wire net barriers You can give patches of vegetables reasonable protection from large birds by surrounding them with wire netting 60–90cm/2–3ft high. It is a nuisance for cultivation and access, but if

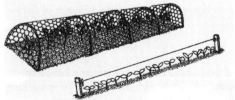

*Methods of deterring birds.
Above: a wire pea guard.
Below: a single strand of black
cotton suspended above seedlings.*

anchored simply with bamboo canes it can be moved fairly easily around the garden.

Cages Where bird damage is devastating, the last resort is growing vegetables in cages of nylon, wire or plastic netting. Mesh 10–15cm/4–6in square is sufficient to keep off pigeons. Cages also keep out animals like cats and, usually, rabbits, but prevent birds from scavenging for pests. Better, perhaps, to give temporary protection to vulnerable crops with netting over the hoops used for low polythene tunnels (see illustration, page 116). I try to find a space for tall and vulnerable winter crops like purple sprouting broccoli in the fruit cage.

Humming wire Various types of 'humming wire' 'sing' in the wind and can be effective deterrents. The wire needs to be at least 60cm/2ft above the ground, with lines running at different angles to catch the wind from various directions.

Scarecrows All manner of device can be erected to scare birds. They must be constantly moved and changed. Birds become used to anything! Typical deterrents include:

- windmills of many types, often incorporating a jangling sound
- plastic sacks with edges cut into fringes, or rags strung in lines over the rows of vegetables
- upturned bottles painted red, placed on canes or stakes; even ordinary wine bottles, stuck neck down into the ground
- hawthorn and other sharp twigs placed around growing crops
- life-like hovering hawks or other birds of prey, suspended from branches or attached on strong lines to posts or flexible canes
- old compact discs strung on wires.

Soil sickness
There are groups of diseases (and some soil pests) that build up in soil where the same crop is grown repeatedly over a number of years. The resulting soil sickness makes it impossible to grow a healthy crop. This most commonly occurs with tomatoes in greenhouses, where they are grown in the same soil for several years running. Botanically related crops such as peppers, aubergines and tomatillos will also be affected.

Unless the soil is completely replaced future crops have to be grown in containers raised off the ground, or protected from the contaminated soil by polythene film, or in growing bags (see page 171). Alternatives are to grow in soilless systems such as ring culture (see Further Reading, page 372) or in the case of tomatoes to graft them on to a disease-resistant rootstock. Putting chickens temporarily into a greenhouse or polytunnel, after it has been cleared, is a good way of ridding it of soil pests. They can be penned into a small area with wire fencing and moved daily.

8

SPACE SAVING AND PRODUCTIVITY

It is hard to express in words the satisfaction that comes from having a truly productive vegetable garden with no ground idle, no space wasted and an abundance to pick for the kitchen. Many would-be vegetable growers today have only a small plot and for them productivity is a necessity. Even where space is unlimited, time, energy and resources are saved if the vegetables required can be produced from a smaller area.

We twenty-first-century gardeners are fortunate. Plant breeders are giving us compact, fast-maturing, high-yielding varieties, often with disease or pest resistance; modern technology has brought us biological controls, horticultural fleece, polythene tunnels and fine nets to keep out insect pests. So we have the means to produce an abundance even in very small gardens. This chapter looks at some of the means of getting the most from small spaces. For planning a succession, so as to avoid gluts and gaps, see Chapter 9. Another aspect of productivity is siting plants in suitable spots, so as to maximize their performance; for plants' specific requirements, see individual plants in the Vegetable Directory.

VERTICAL GROWING

An obvious way of saving space is to grow plants vertically, the obvious candidates being climbing and tall vegetables.

Utilizing fencing

Climbing vegetables such as French and runner beans, marrows, cucumbers and the less vigorous pumpkins and squashes can be trained up wooden trelliswork, galvanized wire netting, pig netting, or the various types of rigid and flexible plastic, polythene or nylon net designed to support plants. Netting mesh of 5–10cm/2–4in square is suitable. Marrows will also cling to willow fences or hurdles. Suitable boundary fencing and wire fruit cages can therefore be put to good use growing vegetables. Most of these climbers naturally cling to the supports, though a little extra tying is sometimes required in the early stages, especially with marrows and cucumbers. Beans do not cling very easily to plastic-coated wire but can be encouraged to do so. Peas do not climb as strongly or to the heights of beans, but can be grown against mesh supports.

Utilizing walls

Where walls or fences are smooth-surfaced – made, for example, of brick, cement or wood – some additional support will be needed for climbers.

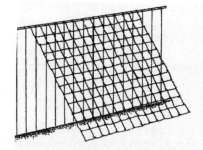

A sloping support for climbers erected against a fence.

Supports can be erected upright against the wall, or a foot or so away leaning towards the wall (see above). Suitable materials are trelliswork or any kind of mesh designed to support plants. One way of doing this is to construct a frame with galvanized pipes, chain-link fencing and Kee Clamp fittings (see below). They are easily erected and dismantled.

Avoid north-facing walls that get very little sun, but don't overlook the walls of the house. Why not pick beans from a bedroom window? Grow them up strings attached to eyes set in rawlplugs.

The height of low walls can be increased with a strip of trellis, rigid fencing or rigid windbreak material along the top, or with Kee Klamp panels of galvanized piping and chain-link fencing (see below). You can build home-made lean-to frames (see illustrations, page 121) and small greenhouses against a wall or fence, so saving space and materials.

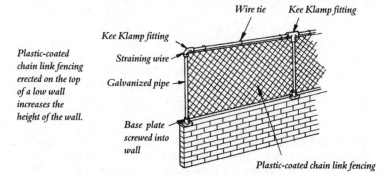

Plastic-coated chain link fencing erected on the top of a low wall increases the height of the wall.

Wire tie · Kee Klamp fitting · Kee Klamp fitting · Straining wire · Galvanized pipe · Base plate screwed into wall · Plastic-coated chain link fencing

Provided the position is not too exposed, 'growing bag' panniers can straddle a low wall (see page 172); plant pots and other containers can be placed on walls where space is short. They can also be hung on railings and fences. Naturally sprawling plants like pumpkins and many of the squashes can be allowed to clamber over low walls.

The warm position at the foot of sunny walls is ideal for sun-loving plants such as tomatoes, peppers, aubergines and Mediterranean herbs like basil and rosemary, and in spring for early salads.

The soil at the foot of walls dries out rapidly, so work in plenty of humus and keep it well mulched to retain moisture. Extra watering may be necessary in the lee of walls.

Vegetables on structures

Arches and pergolas Climbing vegetables can be trained up structures like arches and pergolas. Help them to get off the ground in the early stages by erecting some kind of mesh, trellis or even strings fastened overhead and looped around the plant stem just above soil level.

Wigwams and tepees The classic method of supporting climbing runner and French beans is on double rows of bamboo canes or poles, crisscrossed near their tips; the structure can be kept rigid with horizontal canes resting on the crossover points and lashed firmly to the canes. Sometimes strings are hung from the horizontal canes to support intermediary plants. Equally picturesque, and potentially taking less space, are 'wigwams' or 'tepees' made from bamboo canes or poles – any number from three to a dozen or more. Rustic hazel and willow tepees serve the same purpose. Canes for supporting climbing beans need to be at least 2.4m/8ft long. Push them well into the soil and tie them securely near the top. Wigwams and tepees are suitable for any climbing beans, trailing marrows and the less vigorous squashes, and for cucumbers. Some tying in may be needed in the early stages. For decorative effects sweet peas (*Lathyrus odoratus*), tuberous nasturtiums (*Tropaeolum tuberosum*) and canary creeper (*Tropaeolum peregrinum*) are among plants that can be planted with them. Smaller wigwams can be made for peas. The stems need a little more support, so either wrap netting around the canes, or run extra strings from top to bottom, buried in the soil or pegged down firmly. The plants will then successfully grow within the structure.

Spiral stakes Climbing cucumbers can be trained up the flexible galvanized-steel spiral stakes primarily designed for tomatoes.

Hoops Climbing vegetables that are not too rampant can be supported on hoops made from lengths of supple young wood, such as hazel, willow or dogwood. Tie two pieces together securely to make an arch 1.2–1.5m/4–5ft at its apex, pushing both ends into the ground firmly. (They may even root, which makes the structure more rigid. Just remember to pull it out at the end of the season, before it becomes a tree.) Solid but flexible polythene hoops can be used in the same way. Overlapping arches make a pretty edge to paths. For this and other supports for climbing beans, see illustrations, page 207. When grown on arches the mature beans, cucumbers and marrows hang down in an appealing way, ready to be picked.

Be aware that climbers, especially beans and trailing marrows, can become very weighty plants, and may well reach a height of 2.4m/8ft or more. Supports must be very strong to withstand the weight. Pinch out the growing points when the plants reach the top of the supports.

Vegetables as screens

Use tall-growing vegetables and climbing vegetables trained on supports to screen off unsightly features such as rubbish bins, domestic oil-storage tanks and compost heaps. These vegetables can also be used to mark divisions between one part of a garden and another, and occasionally as windbreaks. Jerusalem artichokes are tough enough for this role. Other tall vegetables that can serve as screens are cardoons (they take a lot of space in every direction), red orache, the giant spinach *Chenopodium giganteum* 'Magentaspreen', sweet corn and, in warm climates, the grain amaranths. Sunflowers too can be planted in rows two to three deep and as close as 15cm/6in apart each way. If you need to justify this theatrical extravagance, remember that the seeds are edible. Climbing beans will also twine up the stems of sunflowers and tall varieties of sweet corn and maize. Get the sunflowers or sweet corn well established and, when they are about 75–90cm/2½–3ft high, plant pot-raised beans at the base. The supporting plants sometimes need staking to keep them upright. (For this and other decorative ways of growing climbers, see *Creative Vegetable Gardening*.)

Low hedges On a smaller scale, peas can be grown as low hedges, the leafless and semi-leafless types being perhaps the most suitable. The tendrils of neighbouring plants twine together, so they are virtually self-supporting, taking on the appearance of a green barbed-wire fence. Grow them in a band at least 30cm/12in wide. The delicate fern of asparagus makes an attractive screening hedge, 90–120cm/3–4ft high. It is most effective from summer to late autumn, when it loses its colour.

MAKING THE MOST OF DIFFICULT SITUATIONS

Ground cover Provided they have been planted in fertile soil, marrows and pumpkins can romp over waste ground and into derelict corners. They make excellent ground cover. They can also be trained neatly in circles to save space (see illustration, page 165).

Shaded areas Most vegetables grow best in an open sunny site, so shady corners of the garden, where the soil is often dry and poor, tend to be wasted. Where it is feasible, use such corners for the compost heap, making comfrey compost, storing equipment and so on. Otherwise build up the soil fertility and try vegetables that tolerate light shade and grow reasonably provided they are well watered. (For the full list, see page 362.) Early in the year most of these vegetables and herbs can be grown under fruit trees or ornamental trees such as flowering cherries, before the tree foliage becomes dense. The exceptions are the tall growers: Jerusalem artichokes, lovage and angelica.

Dry situations A few vegetables perform reasonably in fairly dry positions. (For the full list, see page 363.) Some with relatively deep taproots such as Sugar Loaf chicory and Swiss chard need moisture in the early stages, but later tolerate dry situations better than most leafy vegetables. Mature rhubarb plants, presumably on account of their deep root system, also tolerate dry conditions well.

Moist situations Provided they are not waterlogged, some plants, often of marsh origins, tolerate damp situations. (For the full list, see page 363.)

VEGETABLES IN FLOWER BEDS

Many vegetables have beautiful colour, texture or habit, and are pretty enough to be grown in flower beds, so saving space in the vegetable garden. Except where they are being used as edgings, plant them in small groups or irregular-shaped patches, rather than in rows. The exception is large plants such as courgettes, which can be planted singly. Vegetables are much more demanding than flowers, so if you are growing them in flower beds make sure that they have enough space and light to develop, and that the soil is reasonably fertile.

Although outside the scope of this book, common culinary herbs – especially their more colourful and variegated forms – along with the many edible flowers, are perfectly suited to being grown in flower beds. My two favourites are the variegated nasturtium *Tropaeolum majus* 'Alaska' and Chinese or garlic chives. All parts of the nasturtium are edible in salads – buds, flowers and leaves – while the young green seedheads can be pickled as a caper substitute. Chinese chives have pretty leaves with a mild garlic flavour, sometimes used as a vegetable, and dainty white edible flowers.

For more on the concept of decorative kitchen gardens and potagers, and on the use of edible flowers and herbs in salads, see *Creative Vegetable Gardening* and *The Organic Salad Garden*. Decorative qualities of particular vegetables and varieties are noted in individual entries in the Vegetable Directory. For planning purposes, see also page 364, where vegetables suitable for flower beds are listed in groups according to their height.

CUT-AND-COME-AGAIN (CCA) SYSTEMS

I am convinced that the secret to getting the maximum out of limited space is to make full use of cut-and-come-again (CCA) techniques.

These depend on the fact that many leafy vegetables will regrow after they are first cut, giving two, three or occasionally more cuts from one sowing. CCA can be done at the seedling stage or with semi-mature or mature plants for a successive supply of leaves.

Seedling CCA

To appreciate what CCA seedlings are about, think back to the mustard and cress we all grew on moist blotting paper during our schooldays. The seedlings were cut when about 2.5cm/1in high and that was it. But if the same cress is sown in soil, where it can grow eventually up to 30cm/12in high before running to seed, and is cut repeatedly when 4–5cm/1½–2in high, it might resprout two or three more times over a few weeks – producing a surprising amount of 'greenery' in all – in a very short time, in a very small space.

Apart from the fact that CCA is a highly productive system, at this young stage seedlings are at their most nutritious and tastiest, making them ideal for use raw in salads. Salad rocket, 'cutting' lettuces, cress, salad rape, endive, Sugar Loaf chicory, pak choi and mizuna are a few of many which make delicious salad seedlings. After one or two cuts, some can be left to grow a little larger for cutting between 10–15cm/4–6in high. They will be a little coarser by then, but excellent as cooked greens. Spinach, leaf radish, Texsel greens and many of the oriental greens are suitable for this treatment. For a complete list of vegetables that can be grown as CCA seedlings, see page 359. In commercial parlance these small leaves are now widely known as 'baby leaves'.

A patch of cut-and-come-again seedlings. Those on the right are ready for cutting; those on the left have been cut and will resprout.

Sowing CCA seedlings CCA seedlings can be sown in single drills, broadcast or sown in wide drills – the latter probably being the most efficient method (see Sowing methods, page 88). As the seedlings will not be thinned, aim to space seeds about 1cm/½in apart. Never sow on weedy ground, as weeding among the seedlings will be almost impossible. Weeds can be controlled by laying a mulching fabric on the soil, cutting wide bands out of it to expose the soil and sowing in the exposed band of soil. Broadly speaking, outdoors CCA seedlings are best value from spring to early summer, then from late summer to early autumn. In many cases mid-summer sowings in hot weather are liable to bolt prematurely. Under cover the optimum time for CCA seedlings is very early spring and autumn.

Harvesting and culture Cut the seedlings when they reach a usable size, with scissors or a sharp knife. Cut about 2cm/¾in above soil level, always cutting above any tiny seed leaves or the lowest pair of leaves, as it is from these axils that new growth emerges. For the seedlings to maintain a high level of productivity over several weeks, or in some cases months, the soil must be reasonably fertile and they must always have plenty of water.

Mature CCA
There are several vegetables where, if you cut the mature head just above the lowest leaves rather than pull the plant up by its roots, a secondary head or heads will develop later in the season. This is the case with spring

Cabbages sprout at these points

5–7.5cm/2–3in

Double-cropping cabbage. A cabbage can produce a secondary crop of five heads after the initial head has been cut to a stump.

and summer cabbage – both green and red types. To encourage the process, make a shallow cut in the top of the remaining stalk (see above). Sometimes as many as four or five medium-sized cabbages will develop from the edges of the cuts. Similarly, if an overwintered lettuce is cut in spring, leaving a few basal leaves, a slightly misshapen second head will develop four or five weeks later. This is far quicker than starting the lettuce from seed, which can take three months. (In my experience the secondary heads of summer lettuce tend to be bitter – but it is worth experimenting.) For successful double cropping, the soil must be fertile and the plants must have plenty of water. It works best early in the year when plant growth is naturally fast.

Secondary leaves More frequently when a head is cut, the stump will throw out a second crop of loose leaves rather than forming another head. It can continue to do this over many months. Chinese cabbage and pak choi, Sugar Loaf and red chicory, and broad- and curly-leaved endives are typical of plants that act this way.

Increased frost resistance Apart from the productivity in double cropping, the reduced head size seems to give the plants increased tolerance of low temperatures and more resistance to frost. Whereas a heavy frost would kill a large, leafy plant of Sugar Loaf chicory, a relatively bare stump will survive winter, and be ready to produce further leafy growth the following spring. This characteristic can be utilized by planting such crops in polytunnels in late summer or early autumn. They may well remain productive throughout winter (especially in mild winters) but, even if they are merely stagnant in winter, they will survive, ready to burst into growth as soon as temperatures rise on warm spring days – a time of year when vegetables are most scarce.

Cutting the head of a Salad Bowl lettuce. The cut stump (below left) will almost immediately start producing more leaves.

Semi-mature CCA

Many other vegetables respond well to CCA treatment at a semi-mature stage. Cut across the plant before the head has formed (in the case, say, of a Chinese cabbage planted too late to mature) or, in the case of naturally loose-headed plants, cut across the head (see above) or simply harvest single leaves, leaving the plant to resprout. Besides those mentioned above, the following respond well to this CCA treatment: Salad Bowl lettuces, curly kales, salad rocket, chrysanthemum greens, Texsel greens, all the purslanes, and most of the oriental greens including oriental mustards, mizuna and mibuna. Interestingly, with russet-tinged loose-headed lettuces, the secondary growth tends to be a deeper red colour.

INTERCROPPING

'Intercropping' is when two or more vegetables, with complementary growth habits, are grown in the same piece of ground to maximize its use. Rows of one may alternate with another, or different crops may alternate within a row. In typical intercropping one vegetable would be fast-maturing and the other slow. In 'undercropping' one would be tall and the other low or spreading, so more or less growing beneath it. There are many forms of intercropping. (For intercropping to create decorative effects, see *Creative Vegetable Gardening*.)

Intercropping within rows

Slow- and fast-maturing crops are grown in the same row, the fast-growing crop being harvested before the slower one requires the space. There are several options:

∾ Sow both crops at the same time. They are usually station sown (see illustration, page 89).

∾ Plant them at the same time. This is easiest if the plants have been raised in modules (see page 97).

∾ Plant one crop, and then sow the second crop between the established plants.

Root vegetables are among the slowest to develop. Parsnips, Hamburg parsley (and the herb parsley, which has a substantial root), salsify and scorzonera are typical root crops which can be station sown, with faster-maturing crops sown between the stations. Suitable quick growers include radish (often used as a marker for slow-germinating seeds), small lettuces such as 'Tom Thumb' which are only about 10cm/4in diameter, small types of pak choi and almost any of the CCA salad seedlings (see page 359).

Intercropping around individual plants

Large plants Intercropping is feasible with large, slow-maturing plants, typically brassicas such as cauliflower, purple sprouting broccoli and Brussels sprouts. When fully grown they require a lot of space, but even when grown at equidistant spacing there is plenty of space between them for a month or so after planting. Celeriac is another suitable slow-growing vegetable, but it is intercropped for a shorter period than the bulky brassicas as it is more closely spaced. There are several options for intercropping around individual plants:

∾ Plant small fast-maturing crops between them, for example small lettuces, small types of pak choi and corn salad.

∾ Encircle plants with bands of CCA seedlings or a circle of radishes. Either make a discrete circle around each plant, or a continuous weaving figure of eight between a series of plants. I usually sow CCA seedlings in 5–10cm/2–4in wide bands. Colourful patterns can be created by using red 'Salad Bowl' or 'Lollo' varieties of lettuce. It is often possible to take two cuts of the seedlings before all the space is

Left, undercropping: lettuce planted between sweet corn. Right, intercropping: rows of cut-and-come-again seedlings sown in lines between young brassicas.

needed by the developing brassicas. Resist any temptation to leave them longer, or else the brassicas will suffer from the competition. Use any fast-growing CCA seedlings (see page 359).

∾ Sow bands of CCA seedlings, or single rows of radish as criss-crossing lattice between plants (see above).

Climbing plants Where climbing squashes, cucumbers or beans are grown on tripods or trained up canes, fast-growing crops can be sown or planted between them in the early stages, before the climbing plants shade the ground too densely. (For quick-maturing vegetables, see page 358.) I have also been fairly successful with vegetables that tolerate some shade in summer, such as Sugar Loaf and red chicory, land cress, spinach and corn salad.

Mixed sowings

A variation on the double-cropping theme is to mix different seeds and sow them together in broadcast patches or wide drills to make optimum use of limited space. The seeds selected can either develop at different rates, so that the fastest growing are harvested first, or be chosen to mature more or less at the same time so that they can be cut as salad or stir-fry mixtures. The companions have to be chosen carefully so that the more vigorous will not smother the weaker. Sow fairly thinly for this reason. The following are some successful combinations, but there is plenty of scope for experimenting with your own:

∾ Carrots plus annual flowers. Mix the carrot seed with the seed of annual flowers or ornamental grasses in roughly a 50:50 ratio by volume. Use no more than four or five annuals, choosing those with feathery, rather than dense foliage. Either sow them all together or sow close, alternating rows of carrot seed and mixed annuals. The flowers make for a colourful patch all summer, but the carrots develop satisfactorily among them, suffering little from carrot fly attacks. The pest seems to be deterred, or simply confused, by the flowers. Suitable annuals include love-in-a-mist (*Nigella damascena*), blue flax (*Linum usitatissimum*), cornflower (*Centaurea cyanus*), godetia, nemesia, scabious (*Knautia arvensis*) and the 'light-leaved' everlasting flowers such as rhodanthe. This also works well with parsnips. (See also *Creative Vegetable Gardening*.)

∾ Carrots plus pak choi – a Chinese practice, which worked well for me when I mixed two teaspoons of carrot seed with one of pak choi. Harvest the pak choi first, leaving the carrots to develop.

∾ Leeks and spring onions. Sow together in spring. Start to pull the spring onions in mid-summer, leaving the leeks to mature.

∾ Radishes and/or spring onions with, say, carrots, turnips, parsnips or parsley. Sow very thinly and pull the carrots and onions carefully when large enough to use, so the remaining crop is not disturbed.

∾ Salad mixtures. Traditional continental salad mixtures are known as '*misticanza*' in Italy, '*mesclun*' in France and, more recently, as 'saladini' in the British Isles. They may contain over a dozen different species, emerging and developing in turn over a twelve-month period. Seedsmen also offer interesting mixes, for example of red and green varieties of lettuce, or mixed types of Italian chicory.

'Oriental Saladini' mixture grown in a seed tray.

∾ Stir-fry and braising mixes – mixes of vegetables that can be cut from 10–13cm/4–5in high for cooking. Typically they include kales, mustards and oriental greens. The mixture known as 'Oriental Saladini' is entirely Asian vegetables (see page 295).

Intercropping between rows

Here a fast-growing crop is sown or planted alongside, or between, the rows of a slower-maturing one. The quick crop is cleared before the space is required for the later stages of the main crop. This system is less suitable where equidistant spacing has been adopted but, nevertheless, often proves a useful means of saving space.

Take care not to overdo it. Remember that both crops must have enough space, light and moisture to develop, and there must be room to cultivate and pick. For these reasons it is advisable to sow or plant the main crop rows a little farther apart than usual. To sustain both crops, the soil must be fertile and more watering than normal may be required. Water generously when the plants are getting established, and then mulch to preserve moisture in the soil and minimize the need to weed.

As a rule intercropping is inadvisable with sprawling and spreading vegetables, such as potatoes and globe artichokes – but there are always exceptions!

Here are some suggestions for intercropping:

- Between rows of shallots – carrots, small lettuces such as 'Little Gem' and 'Tom Thumb', small cultivars of pak choi, chrysanthemum greens, corn salad, turnips for pulling young and spring onions.
- Between and alongside dwarf cultivars of French, runner and broad beans – any of the above, as well as standard lettuces, winter brassicas, leeks, spinach, Swiss chard (all of which will continue to develop when the beans are finished).
- Between rows of winter brassicas – carrots, small summer cabbages, lettuces, corn salad, winter purslane, land cress, red chicory (which seems to thrive when overshadowed), small cultivars of pak choi, chrysanthemum greens, kohl rabi and beetroot. (See also Intercropping around individual plants, page 160.)
- Between bands of spring-sown peas (dwarf types are the most suitable) – winter brassicas, turnips, carrots, leeks, spinach, chard, lettuces, beetroot and oriental mustards.

This example of successional intercropping has proved successful in my vegetable garden:

1 Mid-spring, two bands of peas are sown 75cm/2½ft apart.
2 Mid- to late spring, a row of Brussels sprouts is planted between the two bands of peas spaced 60cm/2ft apart.
3 At the same time, radishes are sown between half the sprouts and land cress between the other half.

Undercropping: the long, the short and the tall
Various forms of intercropping utilize combinations of tall, dwarf or sprawling habit.

Undercropping sweet corn Sweet corn leaves cast relatively little shade, which makes sweet corn ideal for intercropping. The resulting combinations often look decorative. Bear in mind that sweet corn must be planted in block formation, rather than in single rows, to facilitate cross-pollination. Possibilities include:

- marrows, gherkins, less vigorous pumpkin varieties trailing between plants

ରୋ summer vegetables such as amaranths, beetroot, dwarf French beans, lettuce and red chicory (see illustration, page 161).

ରୋ hardier vegetables which will continue growing after the sweet corn is harvested – for example, oriental mustards, mizuna and mibuna, chrysanthemum greens, red chicory and parsley.

Sweet corn itself can be planted successfully between rows of brassicas. For training climbing beans up sweet corn, see page 155.

Double-cropping potatoes Although potatoes are naturally sprawling, so not generally recommended for intercropping, I have found the following two examples feasible:

ରୋ Trailing marrows between rows of early potatoes. The marrows are vigorous enough to hold their own until the potatoes are lifted.

ରୋ CCA salad seedlings or radishes sown in the ground above potatoes when the potatoes are planted. They will normally be ready for cutting before the potatoes have come through the ground to disrupt them.

Intercropping climbing vegetables See page 161.

SPACE-SAVING CULTIVARS

Dwarf cultivars

You can save space by growing dwarf cultivars, which can be planted closer than standard cultivars. Dwarf peas, for example, take less space than tall peas, require less netting or fewer pea sticks and are easier to intercrop. The drawback is that most dwarf cultivars are lower yielding, though improved heavier-yielding varieties are continually being developed. There are now excellent dwarf cultivars of tomatoes, peppers, aubergines and savoy cabbages among others. (For details, see the Vegetable Directory.)

Bush forms of trailing plants

The compact bush forms of squashes, marrows and cucumbers occupy less space than the trailing forms, so are excellent in small gardens. Remember that trailing pumpkins, marrows and squashes can be trained around in circles to make them much more compact. Peg down the leading shoots with sticks or bent pieces of wire. You may have to do this daily to keep up with them as shoots can grow very quickly indeed (see illustration, opposite).

SPACE-SAVING SYSTEMS

Narrow beds

Adopting narrow beds as the basic unit in the vegetable garden, and planting within the beds at equidistant spacing, is intrinsically a productive and space-saving way of growing vegetables (see pages 22 and 94).

A pumpkin can be grown in less space if the shoots are trained around in a circle, temporarily pinning down the leading shoots as they grow with wire pegs.

Raised beds and mounds

Raised beds (see page 23) increase the surface area that can be cultivated. So do raised mounds, an idea that originated in China but was later taken up in Germany. (See *Forest Gardening*, Further Reading, page 372.)

Reducing paths

In very small gardens paths take up valued space. Replace them with occasional stepping stones, to give a solid base from which to work in wet weather. I have seen very neat concrete stepping stones which had been moulded in seed trays.

Protected cropping

All forms of protection enable you to use the cultivated area more intensively and productively (see Chapter 6).

Successional sowing

A common failing with new gardeners is to sow too much at any one time. This leads to gluts which, unless the surplus can be frozen, dried or stored for winter, are a waste of space and effort. With appropriate vegetables it is more economic to maintain a succession by sowing little and often – on average every two to three weeks during the growing season. As the rate at which vegetables grow varies during the season, the golden rule is to watch until the first sowing has appeared above ground, then to sow the next and so on, rather than sowing at strictly regular intervals. Successional sowing is most suited to fast-growing vegetables that are eaten young, such as radishes, young carrots, lettuce and CCA seedlings. (For a full list, see pages 358–60.)

Catch cropping

This is the term for a quick-growing crop that is sown in the gap between one crop being cleared and another long-term one being planted. The first could be winter brassicas cleared in spring, the later crop tender summer vegetables such as tomatoes or sweet corn or the winter brassicas, which are not planted out until early to mid-summer. Any of the fast-growing vegetables suggested for successional sowing could be used as a catch crop (see page 360). Fast-growing green manures such as mustard and *Phacelia tanacetifolia* can also be used as catch crops (see page 61).

Gap filling
Sometimes gaps appear in plantings before they reach maturity, usually because of pest damage. Typically, this can happen with winter greens or a bed of lettuce. In the case of greens, there may still be time to transplant one of the faster-growing brassicas, such as calabrese or one of the oriental greens, into the gaps. You can replace lettuce casualties if, when raising plants initially, you had sown or transplanted a few spares into modules. Alternatively sow a few seeds of a fast-growing crop in the gap (see pages 358–60).

Continuity
Careful planning, so that there is always a supply of fresh vegetables, supplemented with stored vegetables where necessary, is the essence of productivity. For more on planning for continuity, see page 179.

Seed sprouting
Seed sprouting is arguably the most space-saving way of producing an edible crop. Seeds are germinated in some kind of container and the small sprouts eaten, normally within a few days of starting them off. No soil is required. An enormous range of vegetable seeds can be sprouted, making a valuable contribution to the diet, particularly in winter.

For successful germination the seeds need warmth and moisture – but as the combination of warmth and moisture encourages the growth of moulds, the germinating seeds must be cooled regularly to keep them fresh and healthy. This is normally done by rinsing them frequently with cold water. Always purchase seeds that are intended for sprouting. Many seeds today are treated with chemicals, and it would be dangerous to sprout and eat them. See also Bean sprouts, page 208. For further reading, see *The Organic Salad Garden* and *Salads for Small Gardens*.

Growing in containers
See below.

CONTAINER GARDENING

In small gardens it is often convenient to grow some vegetables in containers, utilizing space on paths, paved areas, patios, balconies, flat roofs, windowsills and even on low walls. Producing large quantities of vegetables from containers is hard work, but you can grow useful supplementary crops this way. Containers also provide a practical solution to the problems of growing in greenhouses where soil sickness has developed (see page 151).

Patio gardening has become so popular that there are now many specialist books on the subject. This section looks briefly at the main features to consider when growing vegetables in containers.

Types of container
Almost anything can be used as a container, provided it is strong enough to withstand the combined weight of wet soil and the mature crop. If you are growing large vegetables the container must be stable. There must always be a means of drainage, the only exception being growing bags of peat- or coir-based compost which absorb moisture without becoming stagnant. Where containers are used on a balcony or flat roof, they must be lightweight in themselves. Some containers are designed to be mounted on castors so that they can be moved around easily – a very useful feature.

The main types of container are:

- clay and plastic pots, wooden boxes, tubs, barrels (whole or cut in half), hanging baskets
- proprietary growing bags made of strong plastic, purchased pre-filled with potting compost (see page 171)
- window boxes
- domestic and garden artefacts converted into containers, such as watering cans, old tyres (piled high or cut in half and suspended from a balcony or railing), coal scuttles, picturesque old wheelbarrows, cattle troughs, 9 litre/2 gallon plastic cans with the tops cut off – the scope is endless.
- Purpose-made containers (see The vertical polytube, page 172).

Building containers against a wall You can make containers by boarding or bricking up an area against a wall, using the existing foundation as a base, whether it is shallow soil or concrete. Long ago I saw a beautiful crop of runner beans growing on a concrete path against a house. The 'box' they were in was made from two wooden drawers with the bottoms knocked out, standing on top of each other. Around them a loose wall had been built of rounded bricks, washed up on a nearby beach. They kept the boxes in place and added a decorative touch.

A board can be fitted across a windowsill and plants grown in pots behind it, to give the impression of a window box.

Size of container
For growing vegetables, the larger the container the better. This is partly to enable it to withstand the desiccating effects of exposure to wind and

sun, and partly to hold as large a volume of soil or potting compost as possible.

As a rough guide, seedlings can be grown in a soil depth of 7.5–10cm/3–4in, lettuces and plants of similar size need a soil depth of about 15cm/6in, while containers with a depth and width of 20–25cm/8–10in enable a much wider range of vegetables to be grown.

Drainage

Creating good growing conditions in containers is a balancing act between allowing free drainage and conserving moisture. Good drainage is essential to prevent the soil from becoming stagnant and plants waterlogged.

Drainage holes Garden pots are made with drainage holes, but you will have to drill holes in the base of tubs and wooden boxes – or burn them out with a hot poker. The holes should be at least 1cm/½in in diameter, about 7.5cm/3in apart, and preferably slanted so that they are less likely to become blocked. They can be covered with concave pot crocks, or coarse drainage material, to keep them 'open'. Containers can be raised off the ground on bricks, blocks or small pieces of wood to allow water to drain away. An alternative is to have them flat on the ground, but to drill drainage holes in the sides of the container, 2.5cm/1in or so above the base. You can make window boxes on sloping sills level, and free-draining, with wooden wedges. Containers on balconies or windowsills should have some sort of drip tray underneath to prevent water from dripping down walls.

Drainage layer To ensure good drainage in the container fill the bottom with a layer at least 1cm/½in deep of broken crocks, pieces of brick, small stones, charcoal or coarse ashes. If for any reason there are no drainage holes, increase this to 2.5cm/1in. This layer can be covered with 2.5cm/1in or so of dry leaves, or pieces of moss or turf (face downwards) before you put in the soil/compost mixture – again to help drainage. A drainage layer is unnecessary if the medium is pure coir- or peat-based compost.

The growing medium

Most garden soil is unsuitable for containers, as it quickly becomes compacted with frequent watering. The soil mixture should be as 'open' and porous as possible, with a high level of humus. (The term 'compost' is widely used for any mixture used in containers.) With the frequent watering that is unavoidable with container growing, whatever growing medium is used becomes stale and impoverished, and should be renewed annually.

Home-made composts Use good-quality potting compost or good garden soil as the base, mixed with roughly equal quantities of well-rotted garden compost, comfrey compost or worm compost, and smaller quantities of mushroom compost (see Chapter 3). Soil-based compost can be lightened with handfuls of all or any of the following: potting compost, peat substitutes, vermiculite or coarse sand. They will contribute to the porosity of the soil but will not supply any nutrients or humus. Using fresh manure is inadvisable in the confines of a container.

Proprietary composts The choice is normally between potting compost, which is usually peat-based (though organically approved substitutes are becoming available), and soil-based composts formulated for growing in containers. For large vegetables the potting compost needs to be a richer formula than that used for plant raising (see page 100). Composts based on peat or peat substitutes are lighter and more suitable where weight is a factor; their disadvantage is that they dry out and lose nutrients rapidly. Soil-based composts (such as the well-known John Innes range) are heavier, but retain moisture and nutrients better, though they are not as free-draining.

Seaweed-based compost An equal mixture by volume of seaweed, decomposing straw and garden compost makes an excellent growing medium. Put it in the containers two or three months before planting and leave it to rot down well.

Retaining moisture
In dry weather and in areas of low rainfall, the biggest problem with containers is preventing them from drying out. If they are against a wall they may be effectively shielded from rain. Be prepared to water plants in containers twice a day in really hot weather. If you are using containers extensively it is worth setting up a trickle irrigation system.

Preventing evaporation A lot of moisture is lost through evaporation from the sides and the soil surface. To offset this:

- Line containers with heavy-duty polythene with drainage holes punched in the bottom.
- Mulch the surface with bark or gravel chippings, stones or any other suitable material, in a layer as much as 5cm/2in deep.
- Place a pot inside a larger container, filling the gap between them with soil or pebbles to minimize evaporation.
- Stand pots in dishes or trays of gravel, and water through the gravel.
- Cut small holes or squares in the upper surface of a growing bag, rather than cutting it away completely as is often recommended. This reduces the area exposed to evaporation (see illustration, overleaf).

Water-absorbent materials Various inert proprietary granules and urea-based products such as Fytocell can be mixed into container composts. They absorb moisture and help to keep the soil moist.

Planting through small holes in a growing bag minimizes evaporation.

Watering with wicks Moisture-absorbing wicks can be made from strips of soft cloth, wool or string, twisted together. These allow water to seep gently into the container. A friend waters pots by burying narrow strips of cloth in the bottom of the pot, which protrude through the drainage hole into the gravel base on which the container is standing. A 'bucket and wick' system can be used to keep plants watered during brief absences. Stand a full bucket near the pots, with long wicks reaching from the bucket to the pots (see below).

A 'bucket and wick' system for watering plants during brief absences.

Site and protection

Containers are very vulnerable to the desiccating effect of both wind and sun. As far as possible, avoid exposed positions and spots where they would be in full sun all day. In summer, leafy crops such as lettuce, spinach, salad rocket and peas can be grown in light shade. (See also page 363.) Cloches or nets can be fitted over containers to protect them from wind: wire-framed, bell-shaped cloches are suitable for round containers. Inverted glass jars can be used in spring as mini cloches where seed is sown in containers. (See also Chapter 6.)

Protecting window boxes Windows boxes in exposed positions on high buildings or balconies are particularly exposed to wind, which can tear leaves to shreds. Protect them with:

ꙮ small windshields across the ends, made with hessian, netting, matting or even twigs to break the force of the wind

ꙮ small low cloches, or polythene film or windbreak netting anchored over small wire hoops.

Maintaining fertility

With the exception of herbs and cut-and-come-again seedlings, most container-grown vegetables will require supplementary feeding during the growing season, on average on a weekly basis. Diluted seaweed or liquid comfrey are suitable (see page 56). Concentrated and strong feeds should be avoided in containers. (For specific feeding recommendations, see the Vegetable Directory.)

Top dressing The top layer of soil in a pot becomes impoverished and depleted during the growing season. Once or twice during the season, or whenever any roots are exposed on the surface, 'top dress' it with a layer 2.5cm/1in or so deep of well-rotted manure or garden compost. This is particularly recommended for hungry vegetables like tomatoes, oriental greens or any of the beans.

Earthworms Contrary to popular belief, earthworms are beneficial to fertility in pots, boxes or any other containers, but they will only remain in the container if the soil is kept moist.

Compost-filled growing bags

The various types of growing bags, made from heavy-duty polythene film filled with prepared compost, have been a feature of home gardening for many years. The average size of propietary bag is about 1m/3ft long, 30cm/12in wide and 15cm/6in high, though half-size bags are sometimes available. Vegetables are planted directly into the compost in the bags. The original bags used peat-based compost incorporating chemical fertilizers, but organic growing bags are now available.

Alternatively, home-made growing bags can be made from any strong plastic sacks. Ideally open them initially down the middle rather than across the ends, and fill them with good-quality compost or soil mixture as recommended for standard containers.

An ingenious 'growing bag pannier' (see illustration, overleaf), which can be hung over a fence, branch or any horizontal rail, was devised by tomato grower Terry Marshall. Hold an unopened growing bag in the middle, shake the contents so that they divide evenly between the two ends, and place it straddled over a supporting fence or rail. Make a slit on each side about 7.5cm/3in below the centre, and plant in the slits. Cascading tomatoes look most effective grown this way.

Where to use Growing bags are useful where space is limited, where there is little soil or where the soil is polluted or diseased. They can be laid anywhere convenient – on the ground, on a path, on a patio and so on. If they are placed against a wall or fence tall plants like tomatoes and climbing cucumbers and beans can be trained upwards. Supporting frames can be made or purchased for this purpose.

Managing growing bags Where growing bags are used in greenhouses to avoid soil sickness it is important not to perforate the base, or else they will become infected with the soil diseases. Otherwise they can be perforated to improve drainage.

Watering Proprietary growing bags are shallow, filled with light compost and dry out rapidly. Moisture is absorbed slowly, so watering 'little and often' is advisable so that they neither dry out nor become waterlogged. Apply regular feeds, following the supplier's instructions where appropriate. To limit evaporation only cut small holes in the top of the bag (see illustration, page 170).

Doubling bags The late Bernard Salt experimented with growing cucumbers in two growing bags, and found that this resulted in far higher yields. The bags were stacked one on the other with matching holes made in the base of one and in the top of the other. (See *Gardening under Plastic*, Further Reading, page 372.)

Reusing the compost The compost can generally be used several times, first for a demanding crop like tomatoes, then for an undemanding follow-on crop like salad seedlings. Lastly the spent compost can be spread on the garden as a mulch or used for seed-raising.

The vertical polytube
From time to time, unusual containers are designed for growing vegetables in a confined space. The 'vertical polytube' was one example. Invented and patented by Maurice Howgill in the 1970s it was essentially a polythene tube approximately 1m/3ft high and 30cm/12in in diameter, supported on a frame. The tube was filled with compost and holes

Tomatoes take up little space when grown through slits on each side of a growing bag pannier, straddled over a fence or any horizontal rail.

were made all around the tube at every level. In these almost any vegetable could be grown, simply planted through the hole into the compost. From roughly the equivalent of 1sq. m/1sq. yd of ground space Mr Howgill produced 100 leeks, 100 sticks of celery, 10 Brussels sprout stalks, 9kg/20lb of tomatoes and so on. As far as I know the vertical polytube was never marketed, but it illustrates the principle that growing plants vertically is a means of increasing the productivity of small gardens.

What to grow in containers

Vegetables With ingenuity a surprising range of vegetables can be grown in the relatively confined conditions of pots, boxes and other containers, provided there is plenty of humus in the soil mixture and they are well watered and fed regularly. Taking the cost of the containers and compost into account, it may be hard to justify on economic grounds, but who can put a price on the satisfaction of cutting a lettuce from a window box or picking spinach from the patio? Tomatoes are the most widely grown container crop, but peppers, cucumbers, Swiss chard, beet, dwarf beans (and in suitable situations climbing beans), salad plants such as lettuces, endives, spring onions, corn salad, land cress, purslane, radishes and the many cut-and-come-again seedlings are among the many other possibilities. Courgettes can be grown in large boxes or troughs; early potatoes in boxes, bags or tubs; carrots in deep boxes. A deep box standing on a path can serve as a seedbed for brassicas, leeks or lettuce. Containers can be made more colourful by interplanting a few flowers – such as trailing lobelia and hanging petunias – or edible flowers like pansies and nasturtiums.

Herbs Many perennial herbs such as thyme, marjoram and savory tolerate dry conditions and do very well in containers, even if neglected! Fine specimens of rosemary and bay can be grown in large tubs; Mediterranean annuals such as basil thrive in containers. Parsley, chives, mint and chervil are among culinary herbs that are more demanding, but will flourish with attention.

Windowsill gardening

Where space is at a premium indoor windowsills can be utilized for containers. Because of fluctuating room temperatures and the unevenness of light a windowsill is not the easiest place to grow vegetables. Most likely to succeed are cut-and-come-again salad seedlings. Spring sowings are probably the best bet and a useful means of filling the famous Vegetable Gap (see page 179). Sow in seed trays filled with good potting compost: it should be possible to get at least one, often two cuts. Give the boxes a half turn daily so that seedlings are not too drawn towards the light. (See Mustard, Salad Rape and Garden Cress, page 284.) Herbs such as basil can do well on indoor windowsills, as can dwarf forms of sweet and chilli peppers.

9

PLANNING

Whatever size your garden is, it is worth drawing up a plan each year with the aim of making the best use of available space. The plan should be flexible and treated as such. All sorts of unforeseen factors – early seasons, late seasons, bumper crops or failures – will drive a coach and horses through a rigid plan. But an unplanned, haphazard approach inevitably results in a waste of precious resources.

The main questions to consider are what to grow, where to grow it and how to plan for continuity – in other words, how to keep the pot boiling.

WHAT TO GROW

The first step is to work out priorities. Is the main purpose to keep the family in vegetables all year round? Or if the garden is small in relation to the size of the family, is the object to grow 'gourmet' vegetables, or those – peas, lettuce and tomatoes spring to mind – that taste so much better when home-grown? Or is saving money a priority? In this case avoid growing basic vegetables such as root crops (except possibly young carrots and new potatoes), onions, Brussels sprouts and cabbages, all of which are nearly always cheap to buy, and concentrate on salad crops, peas and beans, and maybe sweet peppers and aubergines, which tend to be expensive. (For examples of plans based on the first two criteria, see the Feed the Family and Gourmet Plans on pages 184–7.)

Family preferences In drawing up a list of priorities, don't ignore family preferences. In a surprising number of gardens vegetables are wasted because it turns out that no one in the family really likes them. Whoever grows the vegetables either has to convert the family to wider tastes (the best course), or alter his or her plans.

Climatic factors Don't waste space on vegetables which don't do well in your area. In cold areas outdoor tomatoes and cucumbers, sweet corn and even runner beans are risky. Grow extra salads, roots or greens instead.

Freezer If you have a freezer, modify your plan accordingly. It may be worth growing more peas, beans or calabrese – all of which freeze well – to give greater variety during the winter months. (For other vegetables recommended for freezing, see page 362.)

Storage space Most root vegetables can be stored outside, either in the ground or in clamps. But onions, garlic, pumpkins and other winter squashes should be stored in frost-free sheds or cellars; grow them only if you have storage space.

ROTATION

Traditionally the cornerstone of garden planning – and a key factor in deciding where to grow each vegetable – is the rotation system. This is the practice of grouping together closely related vegetables and growing them in a different bed, or different part of the garden, each year, generally over a three- or four-year cycle, for the following reasons:

Pest and disease control The main reason for rotation is to prevent the build-up of serious soil pests and diseases. These attack botanically related vegetables, and when their 'host' plants, to use the scientific term, are continually grown in the same soil, they can build up to epidemic proportions. If, however, an unrelated crop is grown in that soil for a few years, their numbers decline – or they fail to build up in serious numbers in the first place. The phenomenon known as soil sickness, where yields gradually decline year after year, is generally caused by soil pests such as eelworm (nematodes) and soil-borne diseases such as clubroot and onion white rot. (Clubroot can persist for twenty years; onion white rot for eight.) Rotation is the best form of preventive medicine. Rotation should also be practised in greenhouses and polytunnels. Soil sickness frequently develops if tomatoes, and related crops such as peppers and aubergines, are grown in the same soil for three or more consecutive years.

Soil fertility Leguminous crops such as peas and most beans contribute to soil fertility by releasing nitrogen into the soil when they are dug in (see page 61). For this reason they are often grown before brassicas, which have high nitrogen requirements. Crops also vary in the level of nutrients they require, and the depths at which they extract them. Ringing the changes allows depleted soil nutrients to be replenished naturally.

Weed control Plants with dense foliage and sprawling habit – potatoes and pumpkins are prime examples – largely prevent weed germination while they are in the ground, whereas onions and carrots form a poor canopy, and are susceptible to weed competition. There is far less of a problem where they follow potatoes or pumpkins. Potatoes are considered a good 'cleaning' crop, partly on account of their dense leafy canopy, partly because the earthing-up process exposes weed seeds and soil pests to birds. (Slugs and wireworm are also removed from the soil when the potatoes are lifted.)

Rotation groups
The following are the most important plant groups for rotation purposes:

∾ Brassica/crucifer (cabbage) family: broccoli, Brussels sprouts, cabbage, calabrese, cauliflower, kale, kohl rabi, oriental greens (for example Chinese broccoli, Chinese cabbage, choy sum, komatsuna, mustards, pak choi, Senposai), radish, salad mustard, salad rape, salad rocket, Texsel greens, turnips, swedes. In terms of rotation, brassicas that are in the ground for several months, such as cauliflower and winter cabbage, are far more significant than quick-maturing crops such as radish and salad rocket.

∾ Legume (pea and bean) family: beans (including broad, French and runner), peas, leguminous green manures (including field beans, tares and clover – see page 60).

∾ *Solanaceae* (potato) family: aubergines, peppers, potatoes, tomatoes.

∾ *Allium* (onion) family: garlic, leeks, onions, shallots.

∾ *Umbelliferae* family: carrots, celeriac, celery, parsley, parsnip.

In practice, the onion family are often grouped with the legumes, while root crops, including carrots and parsnips, are grouped with the *Solanaceae* (potato) family.

Many vegetables, for example courgettes, sweet corn, Swiss chard, spinach and most salads, pose little problem from the rotation point of view and can be fitted in wherever convenient, often as catch crops before or after the main plantings in each section. However, if lettuces have been attacked by root aphids, avoid planting in the same place for at least a year.

Here is a simple, three-year-cycle rotation plan:

	Plot A	*Plot B*	*Plot C*
Year 1	Legumes	Brassicas	Potatoes
Year 2	Brassicas	Potatoes	Legumes
Year 3	Potatoes	Legumes	Brassicas

In this rotation the nitrogen-fixing root nodules of the legumes enrich the soil for the brassicas that follow. Members of the onion and umbelliferous families, salad plants and other vegetables are fitted in where possible. See the plans on pages 184–7 for examples of planting sequences.

Rotation practicalities

Flexibility of the bed system The simple, traditional rotation plan above may be too inflexible for the modern gardener, implying as it does that one third of the garden is given over to each major group. Dividing a garden into six, seven or more narrow beds gives far more flexibility. It makes sense to treat legumes, brassicas and potatoes as the main groups (perhaps allocating more than one bed to them as needs dictate), but in addition allocating beds to alliums, umbelliferous crops and perhaps salads, and earmarking spare beds for 'miscellaneous' use. For many years the bed allocation in my garden was roughly as follows:

Brassicas	3½ to 4
Potatoes	4
Legumes	1½ to 2
Alliums	2
Salads	3
Other roots	1
Miscellaneous	4

I try to leave at least a three-year gap before returning to brassicas, potatoes, legumes or alliums in any bed.

Sequence In practice, it doesn't matter very much which group follows which. Arguments can be made in favour or against most sequences. The important factor is to ring the changes between the main rotation groups.

Time scale The longer the rotation cycle the better: rotation over a five- or six-year cycle is highly recommended where feasible. While a three- to four-year cycle is sound practice, in reality a cycle of six or seven years is needed to rid a garden of pests like eelworm and some soil-borne diseases.

Rotation in very small gardens
In very small gardens effective rotation is notoriously difficult, not least because the soil pests are to some extent mobile themselves. Moving a crop a few metres/yards in one direction will achieve little. Try to rotate, but at least:

- Avoid following a crop with another in the same botanical group.
- Leave as long a time gap as possible before replanting with another of the same group.
- Go in for diversity and intercropping, both of which slow down pest and disease attacks.
- Watch for soil problems developing, and if they do, stop growing the affected vegetables.
- Draw consolation from 'the case for not rotating', below!

The case for not rotating
As far as I know this was first expounded in the 1980s by Dr Bleasdale of the then Vegetable Research Station at Wellesbourne. It hinges on the facts that:

∽ some soil pests and diseases are mobile, so rotation in limited areas is probably ineffective
∽ some serious pests and diseases survive many years in the soil, for example, potato cyst eelworm up to six, and clubroot and onion white rot possibly as long as twenty
∽ grouping together vegetables in the same botanical group *can* result in pests and diseases spreading more rapidly – a common example of this being potato blight spreading to nearby tomatoes.

A solution, especially in small gardens, is to grow vegetables in the same area *until* a problem arises. For example, onions can be grown on the same bed until there are signs of onion white rot developing. Then they can be moved to another bed with healthy soil. Where clubroot is a risk, a bed can be put aside for brassicas, and kept at a higher pH with more frequent liming, to counteract its impact.

Rotation summary

∽ Don't lose sleep over rotation! Rotate as much as you can.
∽ At the very least avoid planting vegetables from the same group in the same area in consecutive seasons.
∽ Organize your garden in small beds to increase flexibility.

GROUPING FOR CONVENIENCE

Within the limitations of rotation, it is useful to group together vegetables that:

∽ mature at roughly the same time – this makes it easier to clear a patch of ground, dig it over thoroughly and possibly sow a green manure
∽ will be sown or planted at roughly the same time – this enables a cleared piece of ground to be put immediately to maximum use.

Typical groupings could be:

∽ spring-sown salad crops such as spring onions, early carrots, lettuce and cut-and-come-again salad seedlings
∽ crops which overwinter in the ground, such as leeks, celeriac, kohl rabi, Brussels sprouts and kales
∽ half-hardy summer vegetables, such as courgettes, tomatoes, sweet corn and peppers.

Herbs It makes sense to plant frequently used culinary herbs as near to the kitchen as possible, or along the edges of beds so that they are easily accessible in bad weather.

Perennial vegetables Perennial vegetables such as asparagus and rhubarb are best planted in beds or areas set aside for them, or at the extremities of vegetable beds. They would not normally be included in rotation plans.

PLANNING FOR CONTINUITY

One of the main concerns in planning is to have a constant supply of vegetables for the household. Vegetables can be grouped according to their season of availability: bear these groups in mind when planning for continuity.

Short-season availability Asparagus and sweet corn are typical of vegetables that are available for a limited season only.

Long-season vegetables Many basic vegetables are available over a long period. They include:

- ∾ vegetables which stand for weeks or months on maturity, for example leeks, brassicas such as purple-sprouting broccoli, parsnips, celery
- ∾ quick-maturing vegetables which can be sown in succession over several months, for example lettuce, summer radish, spinach
- ∾ vegetables where a long season of supply is manipulated by sowing different types or varieties, maturing at different seasons, for example cabbage and cauliflower.

Storage vegetables Many basic vegetables can be used fresh during the growing season, then lifted and stored for winter. Typical examples are potatoes, onions and carrots. They can be supplemented by vegetables that are frozen or preserved by other means.

Forced vegetables Witloof chicory can be forced in the dark for winter cropping, while rhubarb and seakale are among perennials which can be forced for an early crop.

The Vegetable Gap

In temperate and cool climates the most difficult period for producing fresh vegetables is from late winter to late spring – the so-called Vegetable Gap or Hungry Gap. Careful planning is necessary to fill this gap. This is where all forms of protection pay handsome dividends. The gap can be filled with:

- ∾ remaining supplies of hardy overwintered vegetables
- ∾ autumn- and winter-sown/planted salads and oriental greens over-wintered under cover
- ∾ cut-and-come-again seedlings sown under cover in late winter, followed with outdoor sowings in early spring under cloches or fleece, and finally sowings in the open
- ∾ forced vegetables
- ∾ sprouted seeds
- ∾ winter- and spring-sown crops of standard outdoor vegetables grown under cover (peas, broad beans, lettuce).

For a list of vegetables for the Vegetable Gap, see page 362; see also Mind the Gap, page 367.

DRAWING UP THE PLAN

1 Draw an outline plan of the beds, numbering or naming them.
2 Designate a rotation group (or miscellaneous group) to each bed.
3 List vegetables being grown (with approximate quantities) divided into 'main rotation crops' and 'others'.
4 Allocate 'main' vegetables to the appropriate bed, indicating how many months they are likely to be in the ground.
5 Where time and space allow, precede or follow these main crops with a short-term crop in the same rotation group *or* a miscellaneous crop.
6 Fit remaining crops into appropriate or 'miscellaneous' beds.

An example of practical sequences of a maincrop followed by a short-term crop would be with potatoes:

∾ Lift early potatoes in early summer and follow with courgettes.
∾ Lift mid-season potatoes in mid-summer and follow with autumn lettuce.

For other examples of practical sequences, see the plans on pages 184–7.

SAMPLE PLANS AND PLANNING INFORMATION

The Feed the Family Plan and Gourmet Plan on pages 184–7 are intended to be used as starting points for drawing up a garden plan. They are planned for gardens of sizes typical of vegetable plots in many gardens. They assume intensive use of the plot but exclude the use of protected cover, which would increase the output and extend the season enormously (see Chapter 6).

The Planning Information chart on pages 188–9 summarizes key information which is a help in planning, such as:

∾ how long vegetables are in the ground
∾ how much space they eventually occupy
∾ months in which they are available fresh
∾ whether the growing season can be extended with protection
∾ whether they can be stored for winter.

There are also lists on pages 358–66 of vegetables suited to different situations, purposes, seasons and treatments, which you may find useful. For a note on hardiness, see page 191.

In all these plans, lists and charts, dates are given as generalized seasons, rather than specific months, to enable them to be interpreted widely (for Season/month conversion chart, see page 15). The underlying facts are based on my records in East Anglia (see below). All measurements are approximate. The Planning Information chart includes a 'value for space rating' (see below).

Note on East Anglian climate

This information is for guidance only, and is based on records kept at Montrose Farm in Norfolk, UK.

~ Winter: average annual *minimum* temperature –7°C/29°F. This temperature is rarely maintained for more than a few consecutive days. Vegetables which overwinter in the open in most winters include spring and savoy cabbage, leeks, spinach, sprouting broccoli, corn salad, Brussels sprouts, kales.

~ Summer: average mean temperature in the *hottest* month (usually July) 15.6°C/60°F. Aubergines, peppers and outdoor tomatoes cannot be relied upon to produce good crops outdoors.

Frost We normally experience first frosts in early October. We can have the last frost as late as the first week of June. (I rarely plant tender crops outside, unless protected, until late spring/early summer.)

Rainfall Between 1991 and 2001 annual rainfall ranged from 41cm/16.14in to 75.5cm/29.7in. *When* it falls is unpredictable. In different years the highest rainfall was recorded in March, June, August, September and November!

Value for space rating (VSR)

Vegetable yields vary enormously according to locality, season, soil fertility and the cultivar grown, so I have always felt that quoted yields are relatively meaningless. I originally devised the 'value for space rating' (VSR) as an attempt to evaluate which vegetables would give the best returns in a small garden. It claims to be no more than an arbitrary guide. In calculating the index the two principal factors I considered were:

~ the length of time the vegetable is in the soil before it can be eaten or harvested

~ the approximate number of helpings yielded per square metre/square yard under average conditions.

So quick-growing, high-yielding vegetables score most points and slower-growing, lower-yielding vegetables fewer points.

Additional points are given for:

~ vegetables which are available fresh in winter and in times of scarcity
~ vegetables which are of far better quality when home-grown
~ vegetables which are normally difficult or very expensive to buy.

Guide to the VSR

★   worth growing if you have space and can intercrop at some stage
★★   reasonably productive
★★★   very good value
★★★★   exceptionally high returns

Notes on the Feed the Family Plan (pages 184–5)

The plan is designed to grow as much food as possible for a family over a year. It is for a rectangular garden 5m wide by 9m long. (A similar slightly smaller plot could be planned based on imperial units.) Assume that it lies in a north–south direction. The main vegetable area is divided into four long narrow beds, A–D, each 1m wide, separated by paths 33cm wide.

Each bed is planted mainly with one rotation group, for example legumes or brassicas, but crops from other groups are included. (The plan does not include maincrop potatoes or cauliflowers.) The brassica bed sometimes breaks rules by following a quick-maturing brassica with another brassica. (Gardening rules are made to be broken, especially in small gardens!)

The beds are rotated over a four-year cycle. Bed A in year 1 becomes bed B in year 2 and so on.

Cropping within the beds is planned in 1m strips, numbered i–ix. Some sowing, planting and clearing dates are indicated to make the plan easier to follow.

In drawing up a Feed the Family plan remember that most vegetables mature naturally between early summer and mid-winter. The gap between late winter and late spring is only filled with careful planning. (See Fresh Vegetables for the Vegetable Gap, page 362, and Mind the Gap, page 367.)

A garden this size could include:

- 5m × 2m wide polytunnel at the south end. Suggested cropping: summer – tomatoes, peppers, aubergines; winter to spring – oriental greens, winter salads, calabrese, spinach or Swiss chard.
- 5.5m × 2m area for compost heaps and frame at the north end.
- 1m border along eastern edge for permanent beds of asparagus and rhubarb, a three-year bed of perennial broccoli, or pumpkins trained in circles.
- 60cm border along western edge, to include a seedbed, some globe artichoke plants interplanted with herbs and perennial vegetables such as sorrel and Good King Henry. (Alternate the globe artichokes and perennial broccoli on a three-year basis.)
- Jerusalem artichokes planted as a hedge along one of the boundaries.

Notes on the Gourmet Plan (pages 186–7)

The plan is for a year-round supply of vegetables chosen for their flavour and quality when home-grown and/or because they are often difficult or expensive to obtain through normal channels. It is for a garden 5m wide by 9m long. (A similar slightly smaller plot could be planned, based on imperial units.) Assume that it lies in a north–south direction. The plot is divided into four narrow beds, A–D, each 1m wide and 7m long, separated by 33cm-wide paths. At each end of the garden 1.5m long strips are used for perennial and climbing vegetables, compost bins and frames.

Cropping within the beds is planned in 1m strips, numbered i–vii. Rotation and key as for Feed the Family Plan, above.

FEED THE FAMILY PLAN

Main vegetable area 5m wide (including 33cm paths) × 9m long. For notes on the plan, see page 182.

KEY: CCA = cut-and-come-again; o/w = overwintering; sdlgs = seedlings

Strips 1m square	Bed A (Legumes)	Bed B (Brassicas)	Bed C (Potatoes/Roots)	Bed D (Onion family)
(i)	1 BROAD BEANS (o/w), clear late spring/early summer 2 KALE plant early/mid-summer, in ground all winter	1 KALE (o/w), clear late spring 2 LETTUCE plant early summer, clear early autumn	1 MINI CAULIFLOWER sow early spring, clear early summer 2 MAINCROP CARROTS sow early summer, lift autumn	1 SHALLOTS plant late winter/early spring, lift mid/late summer 2 CCA SDLGS ROCKET/RADISHES for rest of summer 3 BROAD BEANS sow mid–/late autumn to overwinter
(ii)	1 BROAD BEANS sow early/mid-spring, clear late summer 2 SPRING CABBAGE plant late summer to o/w	1 SPRING CABBAGE (o/w), clear early summer 2 WITLOOF CHICORY sow/plant early summer, lift early winter	1 EARLY POTATOES plant early/mid-spring, lift early summer 2 RED CHICORY sow/plant early summer	1 STORAGE ONIONS plant late winter/early spring, lift late summer 2 BROAD-LEAVED ENDIVE plant late summer, use until winter
(iii)	1 SHELLING PEAS sow early/mid-spring, clear mid-summer 2 LETTUCE sow/plant mid-summer	One half: RED CABBAGE plant early spring, lift by autumn One half: SUMMER CABBAGE plant mid/late spring, clear late summer/early autumn	1 SECOND EARLY POTATOES plant mid-spring, lift mid-summer 2 FLORENCE FENNEL plant mid-summer	1 EARLY LEEKS plant late spring, use autumn/early winter 2 HARDY WINTER SALADS e.g. LAND CRESS, CORN SALAD, WINTER PURSLANE interplanted between leeks in late summer
(iv)	1 SPRING ONIONS (o/w), use in spring 2 DWARF FRENCH BEANS sow/plant late spring/early summer (can plant among spring onions)	One half MUSTARD, CRESS, SALAD RAPE CCA sow sdlgs early spring 2 CALABRESE or ROMANESCO CAULI sow/plant late spring, clear early autumn One half: SWEDES sow/plant late spring	1 SECOND EARLY POTATOES plant mid-spring, lift mid-summer 2 SUGAR LOAF CHICORY sow/plant mid–/late summer, interplant with hardy 'TREVISO' CHICORY	1 'LEAF LETTUCE' PATCH early successional sowings mid- to late spring for crops late spring to late summer 2 SPRING ONIONS sow late summer to overwinter, intercrop with WINTER SALADS as iii

	/late spring, crop until early autumn 2 SWISS CHARD sow/plant late summer between peas (crops until following spring)	sow early/mid-spring 2 CHINESE CABBAGE plant early summer, intersow with ORIENTAL CCA SDLGS cropping until winter	CELERY plant late spring, clear early autumn 2 TURNIP TOPS sow mid-autumn One half: HAMBURG PARSLEY sow mid-spring, in ground all winter	spring 2 SWEET CORN plant late spring/ early summer, intercrop early summer with SUMMER SALADS e.g. ICEPLANT, SUMMER PURSLANE
(vi)	1 PEAS (as v) 2 CCA SDLG SPINACH sow late summer between PEAS or MOOLI RADISHES; sown/ planted late summer between peas	1 CHRYSANTHEMUM GREENS and LETTUCE sow/plant early spring, clear mid-summer 2 ORIENTAL GREENS e.g. BROCCOLI, CHOY SUM, PAK CHOI, MIZUNA plant mid-summer	1 EARLY CARROTS sow early spring, cleared early summer 2 STORAGE BEETROOT sow/ plant early summer, lift autumn	1 CCA CURLY ENDIVE sow mid/late spring, intercrop with radishes 2 COURGETTES AND MARROWS plant early summer, crop until frost
(vii)	1 FRENCH BEANS, RUNNER BEANS, OUTDOOR CUCUMBERS, CLIMBING SQUASH grown on supports on vii, viii and ix, sow/plant late spring/early summer, pick until frost	1 CCA KALE SDLGS or TURNIPS sow early spring 2 HARDY ORIENTAL GREENS plant late summer/early autumn e.g. MUSTARDS, KOMATSUNA, MIZUNA	PARSNIPS sow/plant early spring, in ground all winter	1 LETTUCE plant early spring, clear early summer 2 HARDY LEEKS plant early summer, use until mid–/late spring following year
(viii)	1 o/w ONIONS for use early summer 2 See vii	1 TEXSEL GREENS CCA SDLGS sow early spring 2 MID– & LATE BRUSSELS SPROUTS plant late spring/early summer, interplant late summer, see iii D	1 CCA SDLG LETTUCE sow early spring 2 CELERIAC interplant late spring/early summer, in ground all winter	1 SWISS CHARD plant early spring, clear early/mid-autumn. 2 BULB ONIONS plant early/mid-autumn to overwinter
(ix)	See vii	One half: 1 CCA SPINACH SDLGS sow early spring 2 SAVOY CABBAGE plant early/ mid-summer One half: 1 KOHL RABI sow/plant early/mid-spring, ready early summer 2 PURPLE SPROUTING BROCCOLI plant early/mid-summer for spring	1 EARLY BEETROOT sow/ plant early/mid spring, cleared early summer 2 OUTDOOR TOMATOES plant early/mid summer, cleared by frost 3 GARLIC plant mid–/late autumn	1 GARLIC o/w, lift mid–/late summer 2 'LEAF LETTUCE' patch successional sowings in late summer to crop early autumn to winter

GOURMET PLAN

Main vegetable area 5m wide (including 33cm paths) × 10m long. For notes on the plan, see page 183.
KEY: CCA = cut-and-come-again; o/w = overwintering; sdlgs = seedlings

Perennial beds 1.5m wide	PUMPKINS trained in circle, 3 or 4 plants alternating every 3 years with freshly planted globe artichokes	GLOBE ARTICHOKES, 2 plants alternating every 3 years with PUMPKINS	ASPARAGUS BED	RHUBARB
Strips 1m wide	Bed A (Legumes)	Bed B (Potato family/Roots)	Bed C (Onion family)	Bed D (Brassicas)
(i)	1 BROAD BEANS (o/w), cleared late spring/early summer 2 CALABRESE planted early/mid– summer, finished autumn	1 EARLY POTATOES successional planting in i, ii & iii from early spring, lifting starts early summer 2 FLORENCE FENNEL plant early/mid–summer	SWISS CHARD sow/plant late spring, cut until winter	1 RED CABBAGE plant early spring, cleared autumn 2 CCA SALAD SDLGS e.g. CRESS, SALAD RAPE, ROCKET, MUSTARD sow autumn
(ii)	1 BROAD BEANS as i 2 LETTUCE OR CCA SALAD SDLGS OR MOOLI RADISHES sow/plant early summer	1 EARLY POTATOES lifted mid-summer 2 RED CHICORY plant mid-summer	1 EARLY LEEKS plant late spring, used autumn/early winter + CORN SALAD, LAND CRESS interplanted between leeks in summer for winter use	1 TEXSEL GREENS sow spring or CCA SALAD SDLGS 2 BRUSSELS SPROUTS plant early summer; interplant with RED CHICORY
(iii)	1 DWARF MANGETOUT PEAS sow late winter/early spring, finished mid-summer 2 CHINESE CABBAGE plant mid/late summer, lasts until frost	1 EARLY POTATOES lifted mid-/late summer 2 ENDIVE and SUGAR LOAF CHICORY plant mid-/late summer for use autumn	1 SALAD ROCKET and RADISHES sown spring 2 LATE LEEKS plant early summer, use until mid-/late spring next year	1 EARLY LETTUCE plant early spring 2 PURPLE SPROUTING BROCCOLI plant early/mid-summer, interplant with SUGAR LOAF CHICORY

(iv)	1 TALL PEAS several bands, sow mid-/late spring, finished early autumn 2 SWISS CHARD or SPINACH intersow or plant between peas late summer	CELERIAC plant late spring/early summer, in ground until following spring	1 SPRING ONIONS sown late winter/early spring, cleared by early summer, and/or CCA SDLGS 2 SWEET CORN plant early summer, interplant with MIZUNA and MIBUNA GREENS	1 MINI CAULIFLOWER sow/plant early spring, cleared early/mid-summer 2 LETTUCE or BROAD LEAVED ENDIVE sow/plant early/mid-summer
(v)	as iv CHARD and SPINACH crop until following spring	PARSNIPS sow or plant early/mid-spring, in ground until spring	1 SHALLOTS plant late winter/early spring, lifted early autumn + WINTER PURSLANE intersow or plant in summer	1 SUMMER ENDIVE plant early/mid-spring, cleared early/mid-summer 2 ORIENTAL BRASSICAS interplant hardy and less hardy (see vi)
(vi)	DWARF FRENCH BEANS for use fresh, sow/plant late spring/early summer, crop until early autumn	1 EARLY CARROTS sow/plant late winter/early spring, lifted early summer 2 BUSH TOMATOES plant early summer, cleared by frost 3 GARLIC plant mid-/late autumn	1 GARLIC planted previous autumn, lifted late summer 2 HARDY RED CHICORY and /or CHRYSANTHEMUM GREENS plant late summer	1 ORIENTAL SALADINI and CCA SALAD SDLGS sow spring 2 ORIENTAL BRASSICAS (see v) e.g. hardy: MUSTARDS, MIZUNA, KOMATSUNA, SENPOSAI; less hardy: PAK CHOI, CHOI SUM, FLOWERING RAPE, CABBAGE
(vii)	DWARF FRENCH BEANS for use dried, sow/plant late spring/early summer, lifted early autumn	1 EARLY BEETROOT sow/plant early/mid-spring, lifted by early summer 2 OUTDOOR TOMATOES/PEPPERS plant early summer 3 ONIONS (o/w) plant mid-/late autumn	1 o/w ONIONS planted previous autumn, lifted early/mid-summer 2 COURGETTES plant early/mid-summer 3 SPRING CABBAGE plant early autumn	1 SPRING CABBAGE planted previous early autumn, cleared early summer 2 WITLOOF CHICORY sow/plant early summer, interplant with SUMMER PURSLANE
Lower strip 1.5m wide	COMPOST HEAP/FRAME	COMPOST HEAP/FRAME	Climbing MARROWS and CUCUMBERS, alternating with climbing beans every year	Climbing FRENCH and RUNNER BEANS, alternating with marrows and cucumbers every year

	Jan	Feb	Mar	Apr	May	June	July	Aug	Sep	Oct	Nov	Dec	Ave. weeks to maturity	Ave. spread cm/in	VSR
♦ Amaranthus													6–8	10–20/4–8	***
Artichoke, Jerusalem													28–32	30–60/12–24	*
Aubergine													21	60/24	*
♦ Bean, broad (autumn sown)													28–32	38–45/15–18	**
♦ Bean, broad (spring sown)													12–16	38–45/15–18	***
♦ Beans, French													8–10	30/12	***
♦ Bean, runner													8–10	30/12	***
♦ Bean, salad													9–11	15/6	**
♦ Beetroot, storage													12	24–30/10–12	**
♦ Beetroot, salad													7–9	24–38/10–15	**
Broccoli, Chinese													34–38	68/27	***
Broccoli, purple sprouting													7–8	15/6	**
♦ Broccoli raab													30–36	45/18	*
♦ Brussels sprouts													9	23–30/9–12	**
♦ Cabbage, Chinese ■													32–36	30/12	*
♦ Cabbage, spring													14–20	30–38/12–15	*
♦ Cabbage, summer													20–25	45/18	**
♦ Cabbage, winter													10–13	28/11	***
♦ Calabrese													12–18	5–8/2–3	***
♦ Carrots, early													18–24	20–25/8–10	**
♦ Carrots, main													14–16	15–20/6–8	*
○ Cauliflower, mini													28	45/18	**
Celeriac													16–18	30/12	**
Celery, self-blanching													12–14	15–25/6–10	**
♦ Chicory, red													12–14	15–30/6–12	***
♦ Chicory, Sugar Loaf ■													24	25/10	*
Chicory, Witloof													7	15–30/6–12	**
♦ Choy sum, hybrid rape													4–8	15–20/6–8	***
♦ Chrysanthemum greens ■													12	10/4	***
♦ Corn salad ■													8–12	60/24	**
♦ Courgettes													12	45/18	**
♦ Cucumber, outdoor													13–16	30/12	**
♦ Endive ■													10–14	30/12	*
♦ Fennel, Florence															

CCA   cut-and-come-again seedlings
VSR   Value for Space Rating (see page 181)
♦   season can be extended and/or quality improved with cloches
■   can also grow as CCA seedlings; assume a VSR rating one or two stars high
○   for other types of cauliflower, see chart on page 232

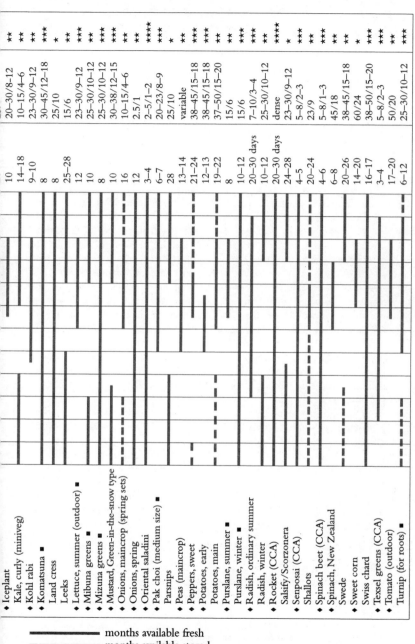

Vegetable		Months available					Spacing / Yield	VSR
◆ Iceplant						10	20–30/8–12	**
Kale, curly (miniveg)						14–18	10–15/4–6	**
◆ Kohl rabi						9–10	23–30/9–12	**
Komatsuna ■						8	30–45/12–18	***
Land cress						8	25/10	*
Leeks						25–28	15/6	**
◆ Lettuce, summer (outdoor) ■						12	23–30/9–12	***
◆ Mibuna greens ■						10	25–30/10–12	**
◆ Mizuna greens ■						8	25–30/10–12	***
◆ Mustard, Green-in-the-snow type						10	30–38/12–15	***
◆ Onions, maincrop (spring sets)						16	10–15/4–6	**
◆ Onions, spring						12	2.5/1	**
◆ Oriental saladini						3–4	2–5/1–2	****
◆ Pak choi (medium size) ■						6–7	20–23/8–9	***
Parsnips						28	25/10	*
◆ Peas (maincrop)						13–14	variable	**
◆ Peppers, sweet						21–24	38–45/15–18	***
◆ Potatoes, early						12–13	38–45/15–18	***
◆ Potatoes, main						19–22	37–50/15–20	**
◆ Purslane, summer ■						8	15/6	**
◆ Purslane, winter ■						10–12	15/6	***
◆ Radish, ordinary summer						20–30 days	7–10/3–4	***
Radish, winter						10–12	25–30/10–12	**
◆ Rocket (CCA)						20–30 days	dense	****
Salsify/Scorzonera						24–28	23–30/9–12	*
◆ Senposai (CCA)						4–5	5–8/2–3	***
Shallots						20–24	23/9	**
◆ Spinach beet (CCA)						4–6	5–8/1–3	***
◆ Spinach, New Zealand						6–8	45/18	**
Swede						20–26	38–45/15–18	**
◆ Sweet corn						14–20	60/24	*
Swiss chard						16–17	38–50/15–20	***
◆ Texsel greens (CCA)						3–4	5–8/2–3	***
◆ Tomato (outdoor)						17–20	50/20	**
◆ Turnip (for roots) ■						6–12	25–30/10–12	***

▬▬▬▬▬ months available fresh
▬ ▬ ▬ ▬ ▬ months available stored
▭▭▭▭▭ months available both fresh and stored

For other vegetables, see main text
Bean sprouts, mustard, rape and cress are available all year round: VSR ★★★★

VEGETABLE DIRECTORY

A NOTE ON THIS SECTION

This directory describes the cultivation of over eighty vegetables. The aim here is to grow vegetables for ordinary household consumption, not to produce enormous, prize-winning specimens for exhibition purposes, which is another story altogether.

The text here is written largely in note form, so as to be able to include as much information as possible and, I hope, to make it easy to find information. (Forgive me if it isn't!) Sometimes I have suggested alternative ways of cultivation. Try them out as opportunities arise, and stick with whatever suits your conditions best. There are no absolute rights and wrongs in gardening and, with experience, gardeners develop their own improved solutions to the everyday problems that arise. All sowing, planting and harvesting dates in these notes should be treated as approximations. There is a world of difference, gardening wise, between different regions and indeed between one year and the next. Be guided by practice in your own locality. Similarly, planting distances, pot sizes and other measurements need not be followed slavishly. They are there as guidelines.

Throughout this section, refer to Chapters 1–9 for explanation of all gardening techniques (such as sowing in modules), methods of pest and disease control if none is given, and methods of crop protection. The term 'under cover' implies unheated greenhouses or polytunnels, cloches or frames. The term 'manure' includes garden compost and other substitutes for animal manure. For season and month conversion chart, see page 15. For publication details of my other books referred to in the text, *The Organic Salad Garden*, *Creative Vegetable Gardening* and *Oriental Vegetables*, see Further Reading, page 372.

Abbreviations

VSR   Value for space rating (see page 182).
PP   Potager potential, indicating plants with decorative qualities, such as good colouring or pretty foliage
CCA   cut-and-come-again
cv   cultivar or variety
^   recommended for organic gardeners

Varieties

Choosing between the many varieties or cultivars (cvs) available today is not easy. 'Improved' varieties are introduced every season with much fanfare and, while some live up to the claims made for them, others fall short. Varieties suggested here have been chosen primarily because they are reliable or have outstanding qualities such as early maturity, high yields, good resistance to pests or diseases, natural vigour (all qualities recognized in Awards of Merit, see page 84) and in my view good flavour – although that is inevitably a subjective judgment. I have also made extensive use of the government-financed trials into varieties suitable for organic growers, carried out jointly over the last twelve years by the National Institute of Agricultural Botany and the Henry Doubleday Research Association. As far as possible, varieties recommended are those I have grown successfully myself. There are certainly others that are equally good, and new ones will be introduced in the coming years. There are now ongoing trials to assess varieties suitable for commercial organic production. Where recommended varieties are currently available to organic gardeners, I have included them, marked ^.

Unfortunately, with the combined pressures of modern marketing and European Union legislation, cultivars (including some excellent ones), come and go at an increasing rate. I apologize now for the fact that some I recommend may no longer be available in a few years' time. If only one knew which.

Seeds of the less-known vegetables and cultivars are not always available from general outlets such as stores and garden centres. They can, however, be obtained from specialist mail order seed companies, who advertise in the gardening press. (See Seed suppliers, page 375, and current gardening magazines.) They offer an excellent service. When you are buying seed, the smallest quantity sold is normally sufficient for small gardens – except where required for cut-and-come-again purposes, which need more seed. (For seed storage, see page 82.)

Some recommended cvs are recently introduced and although being used by commercial growers may not yet be available to amateur gardeners. I've included them in the hope that they will shortly become available.

Note on hardiness

Hardiness is the term used in temperate climates to describe a plant's ability to survive winter in the open without protection.

Half hardy: does not survive frost 0°C/32°F
Moderately hardy: survives at least –5°C/23°F
Fully hardy: survives to –15°C/5°F

In practice, factors such as wind speed, soil type and drainage, and plant maturity all affect a plant's hardiness at any specific temperature.

AMARANTHUS, LEAF (Chinese spinach/Indian spinach/Calaloo)
Amaranthus spp.

These short-lived tender annuals are grown for the exceptionally nutritious leaves and young stems. The leaves vary in size from small to 15cm/6in long, and in colour from pale, almost yellow, to dark green, some types with prominent red markings. Larger-leaved types are generally more vigorous but less subtly flavoured. Height from 20–35cm/8–14in depending on type. Note: 'grain' amaranths are different species, cultivated for their seeds. (See *Oriental Vegetables*.)

Site and soil
Requires warm climate, ideally temperatures of at least 20°C/68°F. In temperate climates normally needs protection or sheltered situation. Does best in light, well-drained soil, though tolerates heavier soil. Also tolerates fairly dry and fairly acid soil.

Cultivation
Delay sowing until soil temperature at least 10°C/50°F. Seed is tiny and can be mixed with sand to make sowing easier. Amaranthus is best sown *in situ* rather than transplanting. Seed germinates best in dark, so cover after sowing. Sow under cover in late spring/early summer, outside during summer.

Cultivation options:
1 Grow as a CCA seedling crop. Sow in single or wide drills about 10cm/4in apart. Start cutting when plants are 10cm/4in high, usually about 5 weeks after sowing. There will be some regrowth but for continuous supplies sow in succession at 2–3-week intervals.
2 Grow to pull young plants whole. Sow in drills as above or in rows 25–30cm/10–12in apart. Thin to 8–10cm/3–4in apart each way. Pull plants when about 23cm/9in high, on average 6–8 weeks after sowing.
3 For continual harvesting of semi-mature plants, sow as (2) above, but thin to 13–18cm/5–7in apart each way, depending on variety. The more vigorous varieties require most space.

Cutting can start once plants are 10–15cm/4–6in high. Either cut the whole plant back to about 3cm/1¼in above soil level (making sure some basal leaves remain) and leave to regenerate or allow plants to grow larger and cut individual leafy stems as required. Cutting the central stem or rosette of leaves formed in the centre encourages side shoots to develop.

Can also be raised from soft cuttings taken in summer – possibly using plants bought for consumption!

You can apply liquid feed during growing season. During the growing season remove any flowering shoots that develop, to encourage further leafy growth. If plants are left to flower at the end of the season (especially where grown under cover) they will often self-sow and reappear the following year.

Harvesting and use
As suggested above. Regular picking is essential for prolonged lush growth, and to prevent the stems from becoming woody.

Cook like spinach; amaranthus is excellent steamed. Very young leaves can be used raw in salad.

Cultivars
There is much confusion over named varieties. 'White-leaved' varieties are most tender and 'buttery'. 'Green-leaved' and 'red-leaved' are coarser, more colourful and generally more productive.

VSR ★★★; PP red-leaved forms

AMERICAN CRESS see Land cress

ARTICHOKE, CHINESE *Stachys affinis*

This hardy annual produces small, ridged tubers about 5cm/2in long and 2cm/¾in wide, with attractive almost translucent pearly skin. The plants are sprawling, with mint-like foliage, growing up to 75cm/2½ft high. (See also *Oriental Vegetables*.)

Site and soil
Does best in open site in light rich soil. Can be treated as ground-cover plant in appropriate situation. Needs moisture during growing season if tubers to become reasonable size; tolerates moderately damp situation.

Cultivation
Requires a growing season of about 6 months. Plant in early spring as soon as soil is workable. Plant largest available tubers upright about 5cm/2in deep and 30cm/12in apart each way. For an earlier start, plant tubers in potting compost, in small pots or a seed tray. Plant upright 4cm/1½in deep and 4cm/1½in apart. Plant outdoors once they have started to sprout. (You can also use this technique if only small tubers available, to give them a better start.)

Keep weed-free in early stages, until plants are well established and blanketing the soil. Earth up stems to a height of 7.5cm/3in when plants are 45cm/18in high to make them more upright. Nip off flowering shoots and very straggly stems to concentrate energy on tuber formation. Can be fed with liquid feed during the summer.

Harvesting and use
From late summer onwards gently prise away soil to see if tubers large enough to use. Lift just before required as tubers shrivel rapidly once exposed because of their small size. Keep some large tubers to replant

following year. If frost threatens, cover plants with cloches or heavy fleece or mulch with bracken, straw, etc.

Raw tubers have crisp texture, nutty flavour: excellent sliced raw in salads. If cooking, scrub, boil or steam whole then slip off skin. Also excellent in stir-fries.

Cultivars
Currently no named cultivars available.

VSR ★

ARTICHOKE, GLOBE *Cynara scolymus* Scolymus Group

The globe artichoke is a handsome, silver-leaved plant growing up to 1.2m/4ft high with a spread of 90cm/3ft or more. It is moderately but not fully hardy. The edible parts lie in the immature bud: first the tiny pads at the base of the bracts, last the fleshy 'heart' or 'bottom' beneath the bristly, inedible 'choke'. When young the top 5cm/2in or so of stem is edible – and quite delicious. The whole bud can be eaten at a very young stage. Unpicked buds develop into beautiful purple thistle-like flowers.

Site and soil
Requires sunny site, ideally sheltered from strong wind. Avoid frost pockets. Thrives in maritime climate. Soil must be well drained and fertile. Work in plenty of well-rotted manure or compost before planting. In high-fertility soil plants grow large, are more prolific and remain in good condition longer.

Cultivation
There are several ways to start: purchase young plants; or take offsets (shoot with attached root taken from outer sections of established plant); or raise from seed.

Offsets are normally taken in spring, with best results from slicing off two or three small offsets and planting as one, rather than single offsets. Select a productive plant and use a sharp spade to slice off clump with plenty of fibrous root attached. Make sure at least three shoots are left on the original plant to provide current season's crop. Plant 90cm/3ft apart each way, or up to 1.2m/4ft apart in areas where they flourish. Make a hole large enough for the offsets, trim off any unruly roots and plant slightly below ground level. This compensates for the tendency of growing roots to push plants upwards. Cut back tips of leaves after planting to limit transpiration. Until established protect plants with windbreak or fleece in windy or cold areas, or shade and keep watered in hot weather.

For an earlier (i.e. early summer) crop in the first season, take offsets in autumn in mild areas. In cooler areas take small offsets in autumn, pot up in large pots, overwinter under cover and plant out following spring.

To raise from seed, sow indoors in seed tray or modules late winter, and harden off well before planting out late spring. Or sow in seedbed outside as soon as soil workable in spring. Plant at spacing for offsets above. A problem with seed-raised plants is that quality is enormously variable. In second season dig out poor plants and gradually improve stock by taking offsets from best plants.

Once growing well mulch to control weeds. You can apply liquid feed in the summer if plants not growing vigorously. Apply heavy top dressing of manure every spring.

Leave plants as long as they are vigorous and productive. Secondary stems develop around original plant and may in turn become strong primary stems. If clumps become very dense you can remove some of the central stems to prevent overcrowding. Once productivity declines, dig up old plant, take offsets from it and replant offsets in fresh site. This may be necessary after 3–4 years.

Where winter temperatures fall much below about -7°C/19°F, especially on heavy soil, earth up base of plants in autumn and cover with dry leaves or heavy fleece as protection. (There is some risk of this attracting sheltering creatures and slugs, which cause damage.) Remove protection in spring.

Harvesting
In the first season a single head on the primary stem is produced towards end of season. In subsequent years these heads are produced earlier; after they are cut side shoots develop, in most seasons producing a crop of secondary heads later in season. Either cut in tight bud stage, or delay until just starting to open, with more colour, and probably better flavoured. Cut with about 15cm/6in of stalk. Must cut before scaly bracts harden.

Cultivars
'Green Globe', 'Vert de Laon', 'Violetta di Chioggia' (purple).

VSR *

ARTICHOKE, JERUSALEM *Helianthus tuberosus*

This is a very hardy plant with nutritious, sweet-flavoured and non-starchy tubers, which can grow 3m/10ft tall.

Site and soil
Open or shady site; tolerates most soils unless waterlogged or very acid. Useful for breaking in rough ground because of fibrous root system. In small gardens use as screen, windbreak or in odd corners.

Cultivation
Plant tubers from late winter to mid-spring, 10–15cm/4–6in deep, 30cm/12in apart (or wider spacing for heavier crops), rows 90cm/3ft

apart. Egg-sized tubers are best; you can cut very large tubers so that each section has three 'eyes' or buds.

Earth up stems when 30cm/12in high for extra support. In mid-summer pinch out or cut back tops to keep height down to 1.5–2m/5–6½ft and concentrate energy in the developing tubers. Remove any flower buds that develop. Irrigate in very dry weather to prevent tubers from becoming excessively knobbly. In late summer it is advisable to stake plants individually, or support groups of plants with strong canes and twine. Yields are lower if plants damaged by autumn gales.

Cut stems down to about 7.5cm/3in when leaves wither in late autumn. Leave tubers in soil during winter months, except where water-logging a risk. Cover with cut stems to protect soil and make lifting easier in frosty conditions. Alternatively clamp like carrots (see page 212).

Harvesting and use

Tubers usually ready from late autumn onwards. Lift as required for use, as they are thin-skinned and dry out rapidly. Remove all tubers eventually. Even tiny tubers remaining in the soil will spread uncontrollably, usually leading to deterioration in quality. Save good tubers for replanting the following season.

Tubers are very knobbly and often muddy, so scrub, then boil or steam in skins (20–25 minutes) and peel just before serving. Can also be baked or stir-fried. Make excellent soup. Scrubbed raw tubers can be sliced into salads.

Cultivars

Named cultivars are not widely available.
'Fuseau' – long, narrow, less knobbly tubers.

VSR ★

ASPARAGUS *Asparagus officinalis*

Asparagus is grown for the young shoots or spears produced for a relatively short season in spring and early summer. Opinions differ on whether 'green' spears, normally grown on the flat, are better flavoured than white spears, which are obtained by earthing up and other methods. Plants can remain productive for twenty years, so are grown in a permanent bed, making them a luxury in small gardens. Make optimum use of the space by intersowing with parsley, which can be left to self-seed among the asparagus.

Site and soil

Asparagus thrives on light soil but tolerates a wide range of soil type, provided it is well drained. Preferred pH neutral to slightly alkaline: acid soils should be limed. To avoid pest and disease problems, don't make asparagus bed on ground previously used for asparagus or potatoes. It is essential that ground is completely free of perennial weeds before planting. Work in plenty of well-rotted organic matter beforehand.

Cultivation

Asparagus plants are naturally male or female (berry-bearing). Male plants give highest overall yields and live longer; female plants have lower overall yield and larger individual spears, but self-seed, leading to loss of vigour and overcrowding with self-sown seedlings. (In my garden some self-sown seedlings have proved very productive – though not necessarily where I would have chosen to plant them!) In the past asparagus beds were mixture of male and female. Modern hybrid cvs of all-male strains are considered the most productive cvs available, though some good strains of old cvs are worth growing.

Beds can be started in various ways:

1 Plant purchased one-year-old crowns (roots) in spring. These establish much better than two- or three-year-old crowns. If planted year 2000, first cut normally 2002. (Some new hybrid cvs being introduced can be cut lightly season after planting, i.e. 2001. Be guided by supplier's information.)

2 Plant purchased young plants, raised in modules, in spring/early summer. First harvest as above. Some cvs offered have been raised by micro-propagation. Treat in the same way.

3 Raise from seed sown in modules late winter. (Cheapest method, but normally means waiting an extra year, i.e. if sown 2000, first cut 2003.) Can be grown in single rows, or beds of double rows 30cm/12in apart, with beds separated by at least 90cm/3ft. Single row is the simplest system, described below.

To raise from crowns, plant as soon after receiving as possible; they quickly become desiccated. Work organic matter into area being used for bed. Make trench about 30cm/12 wide and about 20cm/8in deep, for planting at average depth of 13cm/5in. (Asparagus can be planted up to 30cm/12in deep. Deeper planting results in fewer but larger spears. Adjust trench depth accordingly.) Mound up soil in bottom of trench about 7.5cm/3in high. Spread claw-like roots gently on mound, spaced 30–38cm/12–15in apart (see overleaf). Cover with 5cm/2in of light soil. At end of season cut off foliage when it has lost its green colouring, 10cm/4in above soil level. Fill in trench completely. (This method helps to keep plants disease-free.)

To raise from purchased modules, plant in spring at same spacing and depth as crowns above, covering roots with soil.

To raise from seed, sow late winter/early spring in modules at temperature of 13–16°C/55–60°F. Harden off and plant in permanent position in early summer. Plant on the flat.

Planting one-year-old asparagus crowns. Spread the roots over a small mound in the bottom of the trench.

Keep beds weed-free, weeding by hand if possible to avoid damaging shoots or crowns. Otherwise little attention needed. Irrigation rarely necessary. In exposed situations you can keep fern in place by surrounding bed with twine tied to canes. At end of season cut stems back 10cm/4in above ground to prevent crowns from being rocked in winter winds. Mulch with well-rotted manure or compost in autumn. From second season onwards you can earth up stems to height of about 10cm/4in to increase white stem.

Harvesting

If plants are vigorous you can cut lightly in second season after planting, cutting initially over about a 4-week period; then leave plants to build up reserves. Otherwise wait until third season. In subsequent seasons you can extend cutting period to 6–7 weeks. Start cutting mid-spring when spears 13–18cm/5–7in long. Insert sharp knife or asparagus knife 5cm/2in below ground level, taking care to avoid damaging other shoots.

Pests and diseases

Asparagus beetle Tiny black and yellow winged beetles defoliate plants from late spring to autumn. Squash beetles and larvae by hand or spray with derris.

Violet crown rot Soil-borne disease causing crowns to rot. Often caused by poor drainage. No remedy. Burn plants and start new bed in fresh site.

Cultivars

All-male hybrids: †'Backlim' F1, †'Gijnlim' F1, 'Boonlim', 'Grolim', 'Purple Passion'.
Standard: †'Connover's Colossal' (Sore's selection).
(† = outstanding in 1998–2002 RHS trials)

VSR ★

ASPARAGUS PEA *Lotus purpureus*

This is an ornamental, somewhat bushy plant, with delicate foliage, pretty rust-coloured flowers and odd-shaped four-winged pods, which have an interesting and unusual flavour. Grows up to 45cm/18in tall with up to 60cm/2ft spread.

Site and soil

Open sunny site, rich light soil. Looks pretty lining paths and planted in groups.

Cultivation

Sow outside *in situ* mid- to late spring. Thin so that plants are 30–38cm/ 12–15in apart. Or start indoors in modules mid-spring, transplanting outside when about 7.5–10cm/3–4in high. Give some support with twigs to keep lower leaves off the ground; protect against pigeons.

Also makes nice patio plant. Grow single plants in 25cm/10in pots.

Harvesting and use

Ready early to late summer, generally within 10–12 weeks after sowing. Pick pods when no longer than 2.5cm/1in or else they become tough. Not a heavy bearer, but keep picking to encourage further growth.

Boil pods in minimum water; serve with sauce or butter. Or eat cooked and cold in salads.

Cultivars

No named cultivars.

Note: Don't confuse with the tropical climbing bean, *Psophocarpus tetragonolobus,* which is also known as Asparagus pea.

VSR ★; PP

AUBERGINE (Eggplant) *Solanum melongena*

The aubergine is a bushy tropical and sub-tropical plant, producing an extraordinary range of fruits. The types most widely grown are glossy, deep purple-skinned and cylindrical in shape. The skin colours of other types include white, pink, pink-flecked, green, even orange fruits, ranging from finger-thin to round, egg-shaped to Chinese varieties over 30cm/ 12in long. Some varieties have prickly stems and spines on leaves. Dwarf forms are about 30cm/12in high; standard varieties are on average 60–75cm/2–2½ft high with a spread of up to 60cm/2ft.

Site and soil

Will only mature reliably outdoors in warm parts of British Isles; needs warm sheltered site unless grown under cover. Growth is poor below 20°C/68°F; optimum temperatures considerably higher. Requires well-drained, reasonably fertile soil.

Cultivation

Sow indoors early spring, in modules or seed tray in propagator, at temperatures of 20°C/68°F. Prick out when about 5cm/2in high into

9cm/3½in pots. In early stages of growth maintain minimum night temperature of 15°C/59°F. Keep in good light: aubergines require high light intensity to thrive. Can be potted on into 15cm/6in pots. Either plant out in a greenhouse bed or grow finally in 17.5–20cm/7–8in pots in good potting compost. Plant when first flowers appear. Don't plant outside until all danger of frost is passed. Space standard varieties 40–45cm/ 16–18in apart. Dwarf forms can be as close as 30cm/12in apart.

Buckets of water placed among aubergines help create a beneficial humid atmosphere.

Plants require high humidity. It is beneficial to place buckets of water (or seed trays lined with plastic and filled with water) between plants so that constant evaporation takes place. Encourage plants to fruit on laterals (side shoots) rather than the main stem. To this end remove growing point of main stem when plants are roughly 20–25cm/8–10in high. This encourages side shoots to develop. With large-fruited varieties it is advisable to restrict fruit to a total of about five per plant. Remove embryonic fruits that develop on the main stem and, once a good crop is setting, remove straggling and surplus side shoots and new flowers.

Once fruits start to set, feed with a tomato fertilizer every 10 days to 2 weeks. A general feed can be applied earlier if plants are not flourishing. Keep plants well watered and mulched. Tall varieties may become top heavy and need staking with canes. Support weak side shoots with twigs or split canes. Plants are very susceptible to frost. Cover with fleece if frosts are imminent in late autumn.

Pests and diseases

Greenhouse pests Aphids, red spider mite, whitefly, thrips. May be problems under cover. Use biological controls. Keep greenhouse damped down regularly to discourage red spider mite. Interplant with French marigolds to deter whitefly.

Harvesting

It is not always easy to determine the optimum moment to pick. Indicators are smooth, plump, healthy-looking glossy skin in some varieties. (Others never become glossy.) At end of season plants can be lifted whole and hung in a cool place for a couple of weeks.

Cultivars

'Moneymaker' F1 – early, glossy purple fruits, good yield.
'Black Beauty', 'Long Purple', 'Black Enorma' – purple fruits, reliable.
'Bambino' – very compact with small round purple fruits.
'Snowy' F1 – productive, white egg-shaped fruits.
'Slim Jim', 'Japanese Pickling', 'Little Fingers' – reliable small-fruited varieties.

VSR ★; PP 'Bambino'

BEAN, BROAD *Vicia faba*

This hardy bean is grown primarily for the large shelled green or white (occasionally pink) beans inside the pods, though very young pods are eaten whole and young leafy tops are picked for spring greens. Most types are over 1.2m/4ft high, but dwarfer, smaller podded types are generally 30–38cm/12–15in high. Among distinct types are very long Longpods, the shorter, possibly better-flavoured, later-maturing Windsor type, small-seeded 'industrial' beans (well flavoured and freeze well) and pink-seeded varieties.

Site and soil

Well-dug soil, preferably manured previous winter. Autumn-sown crops benefit from shelter and well-drained soil. Rotate to avoid development of soil-borne foot and root rots: infected plants keel over and collapse.

Cultivation

Theoretically broad beans are hardy and most varieties could be sown in late autumn (November). This will produce the earliest crops for picking in late spring. In practice seeds are very liable to rot in wet winters, so autumn sowing is something of a gamble: spring sowings may catch up with them. Autumn sowings and late winter/very early spring sowings generally avoid blackfly attacks in spring. Unless wet winters are the norm, it is worth trying an autumn sowing followed by a spring sowing to provide a succession. Experiment with local conditions. Broad beans germinate at low temperatures.

Sowing options:
1 In mild areas sow outdoors from mid-autumn (October) to early winter in fairly sheltered position. Plants need be no more than 2.5cm/1in high before the onset of winter.

2 Outdoors from late winter (February) to mid-spring.
3 In modules or seed trays under cover or in cold frame from early to mid-winter, planting out in early spring. Useful method for early crops in cold districts, or where overwintered beans are attacked by soil pests or mice (an increasing problem in some areas).

Sow 4–5cm/1½–2in deep in drill or with dibber. Discard seeds with holes in them – usually made by bean seed weevil. These may not germinate. Many spacing systems are successful. Theoretically highest yields are from two plants per 30cm sq./12in sq. You can space plants 23cm/9in apart each way in staggered rows or patches. Sow some 'spares' to fill gaps.

Can be protected with cloches or crop covers from late autumn until early spring. Earth up stems of autumn-sown beans for extra protection. Medium and tall types require some support. Put strong canes into ground at corners of patch or end of rows: attach wire netting, bean netting or strands of twine to hold in plants. Pinch out tops when in full flower to help pods swell and prevent infestations of blackfly.

After picking put plants on compost heap. Or cut off stems at ground level and dig in roots, as nodules on roots return nitrogen to the soil.

Pests and diseases

Blackbean aphid/blackfly Young shoots are often covered with masses of black aphids. Pinch out tops, or spray with liquid derris. Burn infested shoots.

Mice These unearth seeds after sowing. Start off plants in modules.

Chocolate spot Dark brown spots on leaves eventually coalesce into blotches. May kill plants in wet seasons. No remedy. Burn infected plants and grow at wider spacing in future. Keep weed-free.

Harvesting and use

Pick green tips about 7.5cm/3in long, when beans still in flower before pods form. Wash twice and steam briefly. Eat small immature pods whole, boiled or sliced. Mature beans ready late spring to late summer, depending on sowing date. Eat when young and tender. Pick frequently. Freeze when young or use small-seeded varieties.

Cultivars

Spring sowing recommended unless otherwise stated.
'The Sutton' – excellent dwarf; spring sowing or autumn sowing under cloches or frames.
'Jade', 'Stereo', 'Medes', 'Optica' – semi-dwarf, small-seeded, suitable for freezing.
'Aquadulce Claudia', 'Super Aquadulce' – productive hardy Longpods (autumn-sown).

'Red Epicure' – reddish beans, good flavour.
'Witkiem Manita' – fast-maturing.
'Jubilee Hysor' – productive Windsor type.

VSR ** spring sown, * autumn sown

BEAN, FRENCH (Kidney, haricot bean) *Phaseolus vulgaris*

French beans are tender climbing or bushy annuals. Climbers can grow over 2.4m/8ft high; dwarf plants are on average 45cm/18in high with a 30cm/12in spread. The immature pods are eaten whole; semi-mature pods are shelled and the young beans eaten as 'flageolets'. Mature pods are shelled and the beans used fresh or dried for winter use. (Mature beans are often called 'haricots'.) Cultivars vary in their suitability for different purposes.

Types

Standard French bean Pods round in cross section, 12–20cm/5–8in long, green, yellow, purple and purple-flecked.

'Filet' or 'Kenya' types Very fine, pencil-thin pods of similar length. Usually green or flecked.

Flat-podded types Mostly climbing varieties. Wider pods, 20–30cm/ 8–12in long. Wide range of pod colour; most shelled beans white.

Waxpods Mostly yellow-skinned, succulent 'waxy'-fleshed types.

'Bobby beans' Short, round podded types up to 10cm/4in long, developed for industrial use to cook or freeze whole. (Currently no varieties on offer to home gardeners.)

In my view waxpods, filets, purple and flecked and some flat beans are the best flavoured. Most modern cvs are stringless when young. Dwarf forms crop earlier, and are suitable for growing under cloches in cold areas. Taller forms crop over a longer period and potentially give higher yields. Both are excellent value and decorative in small gardens. Purple-podded cvs have beautiful deep purple flowers.

Site and soil
Avoid exposed sites as plants are easily damaged by winds; otherwise open but unshaded site. French beans do best on well-drained, light, fertile, slightly acid, moisture-retentive soil. Advisable to rotate around garden. Prepare ground thoroughly. For climbing cultivars, you can trench soil beforehand (see Runner bean, page 205).

Cultivation
Never sow or plant in cold weather or wet soil; seeds are liable to rot or

plants succumb to soil pests and diseases. In adverse conditions far better to start indoors (see below). Germination very poor at temperatures below 10°C/53°F. Warm soil beforehand with cloches if necessary. Note: white-seeded types require slightly higher temperatures to germinate than dark-seeded ones.

Sowing programme:
1 For a crop in early summer, sow early spring (warm areas only) or in mid-spring under cloches. Give plenty of ventilation; remove cloches during day in late spring, completely by early summer. Alternatively use crop covers.
2 For main summer crop, sow outdoors late spring to mid-summer.

To start indoors, put beans on moist paper towelling until they swell, to initiate germination and ensure viability. Discard any that fail to plump out. (Seed swelling is not an infallible guide to viability: for extra 'guarantee' wait until a tiny shoot emerges from plumped seed.) Or sow in modules or seed trays and plant out after hardening off. Alternatively sow swollen or germinated seeds *in situ* under cover or outside, handling seed very carefully to avoid damaging the tiny shoot. Sow 4–5cm/1½–2in deep. For highest yields space plants 23cm/9in apart each way. Two outdoor sowings, three weeks apart, ensure a long season.

French beans are self-pollinating, so there are no setting problems as with runner beans. Prop up plants with brushwood or small sticks to prevent them from flopping over and getting muddied. Earth up stems if plants are leaning over. Prolong cropping of later sowings of dwarf varieties by covering plants with cloches in early autumn.

Pests and diseases

Slugs Very attracted to young plants.

Black bean blackfly (See Broad bean, page 202). Spray if becoming serious.

Bean seed fly Can prevent germination and attack seedlings; worst in cold wet soils. Prevent by sowing in stale seedbed and covering with fine net until seedlings established.

Harvesting and use
Beans ready 60–70 days after sowing. Pods edible as long as they can be snapped in half. Some flat types tender even when pods look swollen with developing beans. Pick young beans regularly to get a heavy crop; otherwise beans soon become stringy and cease cropping. Beyond 'snap pod' stage you can shell and eat young beans at green flageolet stage.

To dry beans for winter, preferably leave plant unpicked until end of season so that pods dry on plant. Pull up entire plant and hang in airy place to dry. When pods brittle, shell beans and store in airtight jars. Note: Beans contain toxins which are broken down by cooking. Don't eat them raw.

Cultivars

Dwarf

For early crops: 'Masterpiece Stringless', 'Deuil Fin Précoce'.

For heavy yields: 'Safari' (filet), 'Tendergreen', 'Purple Tepee', 'Cropper Tepee', 'Montano'.

For flavour: 'Delinel' (filet); 'Roquencourt' (yellow waxpod); 'Purple Tepee', 'Royalty' (purple-podded).

For flageolets and drying: 'Chevrier Vert', 'Borlotto Lingua di Fuoco/Firetongue' (see below).

For drying: 'Dutch Brown', 'Horsehead', 'Coco de Prague'.

Climbers

'Borlotto' (see below), 'Cobra', 'Blue Lake' (multipurpose), 'Empress' and 'Purple Podded' (purple pods and flowers), 'Hunter' (flat-podded), 'Kingston Gold' (yellow), 'Rob Roy' (speckled).

'Borlotto Lingua di Fuoco/Firetongue' (red-splashed pods, red and white seed). There are dwarf and climbing forms of this variety.

VSR ★★★; PP

BEAN, RUNNER *Phaseolus coccineus*

A tender, vigorous, prolific bean, most types climbing up to 2.4–3.8m/ 8–10ft or more. There are also some bushy dwarf types, which crop earlier but are lower yielding. It was originally introduced from South America for ornamental flowers and is useful for screening. The beans, which are long, flattish and often over 30cm/12in long, have a more pronounced flavour than French beans.

Site and soil

Likes well-cultivated, rich, light, well-drained but moisture-retentive soil, with plenty of organic matter; not too acid. Plants must be able to root deeply — need at least 38cm/15in topsoil. It is advisable to rotate around garden. Sheltered position best to encourage pollination by bees. Will grow in full sun or partial shade. Dwarf cvs excellent in flower beds.

Cultivation

Prepare ground previous autumn if possible. Dig trench one spit deep, 38–45cm/15–18in wide. To help retain moisture during growing season put in a layer of strawy manure, garden compost or equivalent, even shredded newspaper before replacing topsoil. Allow ground to settle thoroughly before sowing. You can work in general fertilizer before sowing, but this is normally unnecessary. Never sow in cold or wet soil. Start germination indoors if necessary (see French beans, page 203).

Sowing programme:
1 For main crop, sow mid-spring (warm areas) and late spring (cold areas).
2 For later crop, cloched in early autumn, sow dwarf cultivar in early summer.

Sow seeds 5cm/2in deep, 15cm/6in apart; highest yields obtained from two plants per 30cm sq./12in sq. Climbers can be grown in double rows 30–38cm/12–15in apart.

It is best to erect supports before sowing or planting beans. Beans climb vertically or at an angle and to some extent can be trained horizontally. They will cling to bean sticks, canes, heavy string, wire, 10–15cm/4–6in mesh wire or nylon net, but not plastic-coated wire unless helped by tying in. Essential to erect strongly anchored supports for climbing cvs, at least 2.4m/8ft above ground. For end supports of double rows, use 5 × 5cm/2 × 2in timbers or piping. Plants become very weighty when cropping. The most common support systems (see opposite) are:

∾ wigwams and tepees of 1.8–2.7m/6–9ft-long canes or poles
∾ criss-crossing poles or canes, linked and tied at the crossover point with horizontal canes, wires or string
∾ strings, wire or nylon mesh net suspended from a framework of posts or pipes and wires: stretch straining wires between end posts 30cm/12in and 2m/6½ft above ground, and attach netting or strings firmly to top and lower wires
∾ training on arches, trellis, willow hoops, supports attached to walls – many ingenious systems can be devised.

If growing beans near a wall, make sure the roots are in fertile soil with plenty of moisture. If growing by a hedge, slope the canes towards hedge to minimize competition for moisture. Young growths may need twisting or tying around supports initially. Water copiously in dry weather as roots should never be allowed to dry out. Water well when flower buds first showing if weather is dry. Mulching with well-rotted manure, rotted lawn mowings or compost valuable. Pinch out leading shoots when plants reach top of supports.

Flower-setting problems

These seem to be increasing, especially in dry summers. High night temperatures may be a cause, especially several consecutive nights of 16°C/61°F. Flowers mainly pollinated by bees. Early crops may fail to set if weather cold and bees not flying. White-flowering cvs appear to set better in hot climates and where pollination difficult. Planting in groups

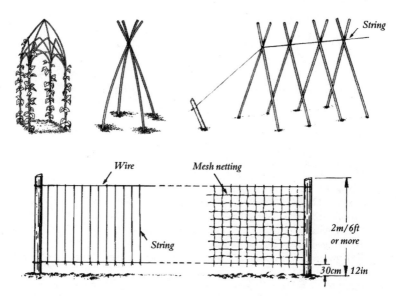

Runner bean supports. Top left: beans growing up an arch. Top centre: a tepee of 1.8–2.7m/6–9ft long canes or poles. Top right: criss-crossed canes or poles, secured with twine. Above: (left) strings 15cm/6in apart, or (right) mesh netting, attached to horizontal wires secured to 2m/6½ft poles.

to provide more shelter for insects may help. There is conflicting evidence that syringing flowers with water, as sometimes advocated, helps setting; however, watering the soil at the base of the plants when the buds first appear seems to encourage flowering as well as setting.

Artificial dwarfing

To convert climbing cvs into earlier-flowering dwarf cultivars 'pinch' plants – i.e. nip out growing point when plants about 20cm/8in high. Secondary side shoots will now develop. Nip out their tips above the second leaf.

Pests

Slugs and black bean aphid See French beans, page 203.

Pollen beetle May attack open flowers, but chemical spraying inadvisable as will damage bees.

Harvesting and use

Ready from mid-summer till frost. Keep picking young beans to ensure continuous cropping and reduce stringiness. Don't be put off by 'bumpy' look; they can still be quite tender. Old cvs generally develop 'stringy' pieces along pod edges which have to be peeled off; modern cvs are stringless, but best picked regularly when young. Runner bean seeds can be dried for winter use (see French beans), but very long cooking is required and they are coarser than dried French beans. White-seeded 'Czar' beans can be dried and used as lima or butter beans.

Cultivars

Dwarf
'Gulliver', 'Pickwick' – 'stringless'.
'Hammond's Dwarf', 'Hestia' (bicoloured).

Climbing
'Butler', 'Desirée', 'Polestar', 'Royal Standard' – 'stringless'.
'Czar', 'Desirée', 'Mergoles', 'White Emergo', 'White Lady' – white-seeded.
'Red Rum' – exceptionally early.
'Achievement', 'Enorma', 'Liberty', 'Scarlet Emperor' – old but superbly productive cvs.
'Painted Lady' and 'Sunset' (recently reintroduced) – lovely bicoloured and apricot pink flowers respectively.

VSR ★★★; PP

BEAN SPROUTS (Mung beans) *Phaseolus aureus*

Mung beans are small (rarely over 0.5cm/¼in long), round and normally green in colour. The germinated seeds (sprouts) are widely used in Chinese cookery and are probably the world's most popular 'fast food'. They are highly nutritious – rich in minerals, protein and vitamins – and very tasty. (For sprouting of other seeds, see *The Organic Salad Garden*.)

Cultivation
Can be grown indoors all year round, but most valuable in winter months. Only sprout a few at a time; 55g/2oz enough for three to four helpings as beans undergo sevenfold increase in weight and bulk during sprouting. Key to producing good long crunchy sprouts seems to lie in growing them under pressure; this can be achieved by weighting them. Ideal temperature for sprouting 20°C/68°F; avoid markedly higher or lower temperatures. Sprouts are whiter and more attractive if sprouted in the dark, so either put them in a cupboard, or cover them with tinfoil to exclude light. Commercial sprouters can be used (see illustration opposite, bottom left); but home-made sprouters are just as successful. The following is my own 'cheap and simple' loose sprouting method:

Far left, top: unless they are in a self-draining container, sprouting seeds need to be rinsed twice a day. Far left, bottom: a self-draining sprouter. Left: seed sprouting on a base.

1 Make container by punching holes roughly 1cm (less than ½in) apart in base of plastic carton such as ice-cream tub. This allows water to drain through easily.

2 Soak beans in water overnight so that they swell; remove any discoloured or unhealthy-looking seeds.

3 The following morning, drain beans, and refresh by putting in a strainer (see above, top left) and rinsing them with water until just moist.

4 Put drained beans in a layer at the bottom of the container: 0.5–1cm/ ¼–½in deep is normally sufficient in a small carton.

5 Cover with damp piece of cloth (to retain moisture) and tinfoil (if necessary to exclude light).

6 Put weight on top. Experiment with suitable weight for the container. I use a roughly 900g/2lb weight on a 13cm/5in diameter carton. If the weight does not fit easily on the container, put it on a saucer on top of the beans to distribute the weight evenly. (It is hard to believe that the sprouts can push up such a weight in order to grow, but they will!)

7 Put the sprouts in a cupboard, or somewhere dark and moderately warm, to sprout.

8 Every morning and evening remove weight and coverings, hold the container under the tap, and run cold water through to rinse the sprouts. Allow water to drain through the container without dislodging the beans; they should be just moist after rinsing.

9 Replace cloth, weight and foil if used.

10 Repeat until ready for use.

The following alternative method for sprouting on a base (see above right) will not produce such long or crunchy sprouts, and rinsing is a little more awkward. However, the sprouts root into the base and stand upright. For the base, use several layers of paper towelling or flannel laid in a dish. Prepare the sprouts as above. Cover the dish with foil to exclude light if necessary. Rinse by carefully pouring water in and out. When ready the sprouts will have to be cut from the base.

Harvesting and use
Depending on the temperature, sprouts will be ready within 3–6 days. The ideal length for eating is 5–7.5cm/2–3in long; quality deteriorates when sprouts are larger and seed leaves start to develop. If sprouts not eaten immediately, keep in fridge in water, rinsing daily. Best to eat within a couple of days. Green seed coats may sometimes still be attached to sprouts. No harm in eating them, but they are easily removed by tipping sprouts into a bowl of water, allowing seed coats to rise to the surface, then skimming them off with a slotted spoon.

Sprouts can be used raw or very lightly cooked. They should not be eaten raw in very large quantities.

VSR ★★★★

BEETROOT *Beta vulgaris*

A moderately hardy biennial, about 15cm/6in high and up to 25–30cm/ 10–12in in spread, beetroot is grown primarily for its roots, used fresh and stored, but the young leaves are also edible. The roots are round, obelisk or cylindrical in shape, and red, white, yellow or red with white rings in colour. Longer-rooted types are slower-maturing, considered well flavoured and often grown for storage. The leaves are normally reddish and are quite pretty in flower beds.

Site and soil
Open site; prefers rich, light, sandy soil, though grows in any fertile soil, preferably manured for previous crop. Preferred pH 6.5 to about neutral. Very acid soils should be limed, but avoid overliming as beet susceptible to mineral deficencies on alkaline soil.

Cultivation
On poor soil you can apply tomato fertilizer (high in potash) 10 days before sowing to encourage plant growth. Beet 'seeds' are a cluster of seed, so several seedlings germinate close together. 'Monogerm' seeds are single, therefore require less thinning; worth getting if available. Beetroot normally sown *in situ* as only very young seedlings can be transplanted. However responds well to being sown in modules. You can also multisow in modules. Only round types suitable. Sow three seeds per cell; if numerous seedlings germinate, thin to four to five seedlings. When seedlings 5cm/2in high, plant modules about 20cm/8in apart each way. Germination poor at temperatures below 7°C/45°F; delay sowing or warm soil beforehand with cloches/crop covers. Beetroot is liable to 'bolt' (run to seed) if sown early in cold conditions. Use bolt-resistant cultivars for early sowings. Sow about 2cm/¾in deep.

Small beet ready 9–12 weeks after sowing; useful catch crop and good for intercropping.

Make several sowings for continuous supply:

1 For small beet ready in late spring/early summer, sow bolt-resistant round cultivar late winter/early spring under cover or in cloches or frames. You can remove cover mid-spring. Space seed 2.5cm/1in apart, rows 20cm/8in apart; or sow in patches, spacing seeds 5cm/2in apart either way; or sow in 18–23cm/7–9in wide flat drills, spacing seeds 5cm/2in apart. These are traditional spacings. Research has shown that early beet can also be spaced much further apart to encourage very rapid growth. Recommendation is either to grow in rows 23cm/9in apart, thinning to 8cm/3¼in apart, or to space plants 15cm/6in apart each way. Yields from early sowings can be doubled by growing under crop covers. Remove after 4–5 weeks. Early sowings require little thinning if roots pulled young and eaten small.

2 For small beet in early summer, sow bolt-resistant round cultivar outside in early/mid-spring, spacing as above. Thin to 7.5–10cm/3–4in apart. Optimum spacing for pickling beet 20 plants per 30cm sq./12in sq.

3 For mini beet of ping-pong ball size, sow mid-spring to mid-summer at 2–3 week intervals for continuous supply. Sow in rows 15cm/6in apart thinning to 2.5cm/1in apart. Small even-sized beet ready about 12 weeks after sowing. Use round F1 varieties below ('Pronto' F1 very suitable) or bolt-resistant varieties such as 'Bikores'.

4 For main summer supply and winter storage, sow round or long cultivars, late spring or early summer outside. Station sow 7.5cm/3in apart in rows 20cm/8in apart, or sow at equidistant spacing 13–15cm/5–6in apart. Thin to one seedling per station.

5 Round cultivars, outside early/mid-summer, to leave in soil for pulling during winter in mild areas. Thin to 7.5–10cm/3–4in apart.

Keep beet weed-free. Water enough to prevent soil from drying out.

Pests

Sparrows Very attracted to small seedlings. Take protective measures.

Harvesting and use

Beets mature 60–90 days after sowing, but can more or less be eaten at any size. Pull salad beets from late spring to mid-autumn; maincrop beets can be pulled from mid-summer onwards. If soil is well drained you can leave beet in soil for winter in mild areas. Can cover with layer of bracken or straw for extra protection. Lift storage beet in early/mid-autumn, to prevent them from becoming tough. Lift carefully, twist off stems (cutting will cause bleeding), gently rub off adhering soil.

Storage

In boxes Only store healthy undamaged roots. Place them in layers in a wooden box or some kind of container. Put largest roots at the bottom, and smaller roots, which dry out faster, in the upper layers to use first. Cover each layer with sand, sieved ash or light soil. Put the box in a frost-free shed or cellar. Take precautions against mice if necessary.

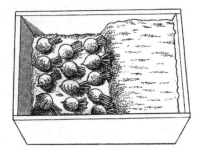

Beetroot stored in a box. The stalks have been twisted off and the roots stored in layers covered with sand.

In clamps Although less convenient, if there is no space under cover beet can be stored in clamps outside. (Clamps can also be made on the floor of a shed or cellar; less protection will be needed.) Make a clamp on well-drained soil, ideally in a sheltered position such as against a wall. Start with a layer of straw 20cm/8in or coarse sand 5–7.5cm/2–3in deep. Pile the roots on top in a heap with sloping sides which can be circular or any convenient shape. The final heap should be no more than 60cm/2ft high. Cover it with more straw of a similar depth, and finally with a thick layer of carpeting or about 7.5cm/3in of soil. This can be taken from around the perimeter of the clamp, so making a small ditch to drain away water.

Use

Beetroots can be eaten cooked, hot or cold and grated raw. Small beets are excellent pickled. Cook young leaves and stems like spinach.

Cultivars

'Boltardy', 'Moneta', 'Pablo' F1 – bolt-resistant, round.
'Bikores'; Detroit 2 selections: 'Bolivar', 'Crimson Globe' and 'Tardel'; 'Monogram' (monogerm) – round maincrop.
Suitable for general use or mini beet: 'Action' F1, 'Red Ace' F1, 'Pablo' F1, 'Pronto' – round, deep red, neat varieties.
'Cylindra', 'Cheltenham Green Top', 'Cheltenham Mono' (monogerm), 'Forono' – long types.
'Burpee's Golden' – lush edible foliage, yellow roots (which don't bleed).
'Albina' – white roots (which don't stain).

'Bull's Blood' – decorative deep red foliage, fairly hardy.
'Chioggia' – old cv with attractive white rings in beet, good flavour.

VSR ★★★ young, early beet and mini beet, ★★ maincrop beet; PP

BEET, LEAF see Spinach group

BEET, SPINACH see Spinach group

BROCCOLI, CHINESE (Chinese kale) *Brassica oleracea* var. *algoglabra*

This is a sturdy brassica that grows about 45cm/18in high with 25–38cm/10–15in spread. Its widely used name 'Chinese kale' is somewhat misleading, as it is in reality more akin to Western sprouting broccoli in habit and flavour. It is grown for its succulent well-flavoured flowering shoots, which are excellent cooked.

Site and soil
Fertile, moisture-retentive but well-drained soil. Tolerant of both fairly high temperatures and – once beyond seedling stage – slight frost.

Cultivation
Can sow from late spring to early autumn but, like most oriental greens, naturally crops best from mid- to late summer sowings, maturing towards the end of summer and autumn. You can plant late summer-sown crop under cover for winter pickings, as small plants harvested whole or large plants cropped over a longer period. In both cases plants require plenty of moisture throughout growth to retain their succulence. Keep well watered and mulched, especially in dry weather.

For small plants, sow by broadcasting or in rows about 10cm/4in apart, thinning to about 13cm/5in apart. Use small plants whole when the flowering shoots start developing.

For large plants, sow *in situ,* or in modules, or in a seedbed. When seedlings are about 7.5cm/3in high transplant to permanent position, spacing plants about 30cm/12in apart. (If sown *in situ*, thin in stages, using intermediate plants.) In good soil closer spacing may be equally successful. Pick main central head first, then side shoots as they develop.

Pests and diseases
As Cabbage, page 223. Pollen beetle can be a serious pest in some areas.

Harvesting and use
Mature plants ready within 10 weeks; young plants 2 weeks earlier. Pick shoots while still in flower bud stage.

Peel stems if outer skin has become tough. Steam, use in stir-fries or cook like sprouting broccoli (see page 216).

Cultivars

'Green Lance' F1.

For crosses that have been made with Chinese broccoli and other brassicas, see Hybrid broccolis, below.

VSR ★★

BROCCOLIS, HYBRID

Plant breeders have recently produced novel types of broccoli (i.e. brassicas grown for their flowering heads and shoots) by hybridizing different kinds of brassica. They are grouped here as hybrid broccolis, though they will be found in seed catalogues linked to an assortment of vegetables. Their parentage includes oriental brassicas, notably Chinese broccoli, calabrese, cauliflower and sprouting broccoli. In the main they are fast-growing, productive and excellent in flavour. More hybrids are likely to be developed in future. The following notes are on currently available hybrids, listed roughly in order of their productivity. All respond well to being sown in modules and transplanted.

'WOK-BROCC'/'SPRITE'

Chinese broccoli and purple sprouting broccoli hybrid. Very productive provided it is grown on fertile soil with plenty of moisture throughout growth. On average 30–38cm/12–15in high with similar spread. Usually forms a small head of about 2.5cm/1in diameter and, at the same time or shortly after, a flush of shoots up to 1cm/½in thick and up to 23cm/9in long down the stem. Moderately hardy, surviving –5°C/23°F in sheltered situation. Very delicate flavour.

Cultivation

Main sowing from early spring to early/mid-summer. You can also make earlier sowing late winter in gentle heat under cover, to plant outside. Make final sowing late summer to transplant under cover for winter use. Sow in modules and transplant at the four-to-five-leaf stage. Space plants 30–38cm/12–15in apart each way. For succession make two or three sowings at about 6-week intervals.

Harvesting and use

Plants generally ready 10–13 weeks after sowing. Essential to pick regularly to encourage more spears to develop. May continue producing over 6–8 weeks, with three or four flushes of growth. Excellent for stir-frying lightly, or for eating raw.

VSR ★★★

'BORDEAUX' FI

Purple sprouting broccoli and calabrese hybrid. Described as annual form of purple sprouting broccoli (see page 216), as it does not require a cold period (vernalization) to produce flower spears, but is superior in flavour. Grows to about 75cm/2½ft tall with 60cm/2ft spread. Prefers moderately fertile soil.

Cultivation
Make one or two sowings from February to June to pick from July into winter. Plant 60–75cm/2–2½ft apart each way.

Harvesting and use
Plants mature 4–5 months after sowing. Pick shoots when 10–15cm/4–6in long. Keep picking to encourage more growth of tender shoots. Can be picked over several weeks depending on the season. Will stand moderate frost. Cook like purple sprouting broccoli. Considered superior in flavour.

VSR ★★

'TENDERSTEM' FI
Calabrese and Chinese broccoli hybrid. Resembles calabrese in appearance, growing about 45cm/18in high with a similar spread. Stems below crowns exceptionally long, succulent and tender. Heads very even in size. Appears to perform well in relatively poor soil.

Cultivation
Sow in modules from March to July, sowing in succession every 2 weeks for regular supply from mid-summer to mid-autumn. Plants tend to mature together, so for most households it is sufficient to raise a small number at each sowing. Space plants 30cm/12in apart each way.

Harvesting and use
Ready for harvesting about 4 months after sowing. To encourage fleshy side shoots, remove central growing point – i.e. tiny broccoli head which develops on main stem at roughly same time as shoots. Normally you get flush of four or five fleshy shoots, 18–20cm/7–8in long. Smaller shoots may develop subsequently, but better results from successional sowing. Moderately hardy. Heads survive light frost and may become sweeter at low temperatures. Steam or stir-fry.

VSR★★

BROCCOLI RAAB (Cime di rapa, Brocoletto, Asparagus broccoli)
Brassica rapa Ruvo Group

This is a fast-growing brassica, grown for its immature flowering stems. A traditional crop in Europe, especially Italy and Portugal, it is grown as an annual or, where winters mild, as an overwintering biennial. It tolerates light frost. Its maximum height is about 30cm/12in, and its spread up to 15cm/6in. It has a distinct fresh, mustard greens flavour. Steam, cook lightly, or use small pieces raw in salads.

Site and soil
Reasonably fertile, moisture-retentive soil.

Cultivation
Cool-season crop, cultivated throughout the growing season in cool, temperate climates, and in spring and autumn in warm climates.

Sowing options:
1 First sowing can be made under cover in late winter; final sowing under cover in early autumn.
2 Otherwise sow in succession outdoors at roughly 3–4-week intervals from early spring (as soon as soil workable) to late summer. Don't sow in mid-summer if weather hot and dry.

Sow by broadcasting or sow thinly in rows about 10cm/4in apart. If harvesting young (see below), no need to thin; if larger plants are required, thin in stages to 15cm/6in apart, eating thinnings.

Pests and diseases
Theoretically susceptible to all common brassica pests (see page 223), but because so fast-growing normally trouble free, apart from flea beetle attacks at seedling stage. Cover with fine nets or fleece after sowing to protect from attacks.

Harvesting and use
With fastest-maturing types you can normally start cutting within 7–8 weeks of sowing.

Either start cutting while still leafy and about 10cm/4in tall, or wait until the immature flowering shoots are developing, and plants are 20–25cm/8–10in tall. If cut above lowest leaves, will continue to resprout for 2–5 weeks, depending on cv and conditions. Leaves, stems and flowering shoots are all edible. Stop picking as soon as stems start to toughen.

Steam, boil briefly or use small pieces raw in salad.

Cultivars
Old continental varieties named 40-day, 60-day, 90-day on basis of average maturity time from sowing. The earliest-maturing varieties were skimpier; the later ones hardier and used for autumn and overwinter sowings.

'Sessanta' (60 days) – productive, general-purpose cv.

VSR ★★★

BROCCOLI, SPROUTING *Brassica oleracea* Italica Group

Sprouting broccoli is a reasonably hardy, biennial brassica, grown for its flowering shoots. Purple forms grow over 90cm/3ft high, with a similar spread in good soil. White forms are somewhat smaller, less prolific and less hardy, but have excellent flavour. It is a traditional standby in the Vegetable Gap, though may not survive severe winters.

Site and soil
As Cabbage, page 220. Avoid very exposed site. Well-drained soil is advisable.

Cultivation
Sow mid- to early summer, in seedbed or in modules. Sow early-maturing cvs first to get succession. A few plants sufficient for most households. Plant out firmly during summer, spacing at least 60cm/2ft apart each way. Advisable to earth up and stake as plants grow. (See Brussels sprouts, below.)

Pests and diseases
As Cabbage, page 223. Birds such as pigeons are the most likely pest, especially in spring when greens are scarce.

Harvesting
Season extends from late winter to late spring; individual plants may crop over 2 months. Snap off shoots before flower buds open, when about 10cm/4in long. Keep picking regularly to encourage further cropping; inadvisable to strip a plant completely at one go.

Cultivars
The traditional early and late strains of both purple and white forms have been superseded by far more productive cvs.
Purple varieties (in approximate order of maturity): 'Rudolph', 'Red Spear', 'Red Arrow', 'Red Head', 'Claret' F1, 'Cardinal'.
White varieties: 'White Eye' (early), 'White Star' (late).

VSR ★★

BRUSSELS SPROUTS *Brassica oleracea* Gemmifera Group

This winter brassica is very hardy, the hardiest cvs surviving –10°C/14°F. It is grown for its tight leafy buds, which are picked from the stem, and for the sprout 'top', which can become very substantial in some traditional varieties. Its height ranges from about 35cm/14in high for the earlier, dwarf varieties to late, hardier types 75cm/30in high with a spread of 45cm/18in or more. Most sprouts are green, but there are well-flavoured, though less productive, red varieties.

Site and soil
As Cabbage, page 220. Soil must be fertile but not freshly manured.

Cultivation
Firm ground and long growing season are keys to success. Brussels

sprouts are grouped loosely as early, mid-season and late according to maturity from September to March, though the groups overlap considerably. For continuous supply, sow varieties from each group in succession, sowing early-maturing cvs first. However varieties are being developed which can be sown at different times to give a long cropping season (e.g. 'Maximus').

Sowing options:

1 Sow under cover late winter/early spring at temperature of about 18°C/64°F. Keep at about 10°C/50°F after germination so that seedlings develop sturdily. If sown in seed trays thin to 7.5cm/3in apart. Otherwise sow or transplant into modules at least 5cm/2in deep, or strong, anchoring tap roots may not develop, and mature plants may 'lodge' or keel over. Plant out mid-/late spring. Excellent method.

2 Sow in seedbed in open early/mid-spring; thin to 7.5cm/3in apart. Plant out late spring (ideally) or early summer.

3 If ground is available sow two or three seeds *in situ* early/mid-spring. Remove superfluous seedlings after germination.

Plant as Cabbage (General cultivation, page 220). Can be planted directly into ground vacated by peas, beans or any other early crops without digging over first. Plant dwarf types 60–75cm/2–2½ft apart, tall types 90cm/3ft apart. Provided they are not cramped, young plants can be interplanted between other established crops; or small plants and CCA seedlings can be sown or planted around them (see page 156).

A strong support for a tall Brussels sprout variety.

Draw soil around stems 1 month after planting to increase stability. Keep weed-free. During summer stake tall sprouts (and dwarf plants in exposed areas) to prevent 'rocking'; two ties are often necessary (see left). If plants not growing well in mid-summer, apply a general organic fertilizer. Otherwise they require little attention.

Stopping

'Stopping' is the practice of removing topmost sprout in mid-summer to encourage sprouts to mature at same time, rather than in succession. Useful where sprouts required for freezing.

Only stop early-maturing cvs. Stop them when lowest sprouts are roughly 1cm/½in in size. In autumn and winter remove yellowing leaves to improve air circulation and prevent sprouts from becoming diseased and rotting.

Pests and diseases
As Cabbage, page 223.

Mealy aphids A particular problem with Brussels sprouts as they get right inside the sprout.

Harvesting
Ready for harvesting from late summer to early/mid-spring; most crop for a period of 2–3 months. Pick the lowest sprouts first and eat sprout tops, which are delicious, last. Some weigh nearly 2kg/over 4lb! Pull out the stumps when finished as aphids have a tendency to overwinter in them.

Cultivars
Today's F1 hybrids are far more productive than the older open-pollinated cvs. The following are all F1s, listed in approximate order of maturity, though in practice some varieties stand for 2–3 months, straddling several categories. For precise information on cropping for specific varieties, consult seed catalogues.

Early: ^'Oliver' F1, 'Peer Gynt' F1.

Autumn to Christmas: ^'Maximus', 'Romulus', ^'Diablo', 'Bridge', 'Silverline', 'Topline'.

Late: ^'Exodus', 'Montgomery', 'Trafalgar', ^'Cascade', 'Wellington', ^'Braveheart'.

'Falstaff' – red sprouts.

VSR ★

CABBAGE *Brassica oleracea* Capitata Group

The most widely grown brassica of all, cabbage is ideally suited to a cool maritime climate. Most types of cabbage form dense heads, but loose-headed cvs and immature spring cabbage can be used as 'spring greens'. Cabbages are divided into broad groups (see below) according to main season of maturity; in practice there is considerable overlap between groups. With appropriate choice of cvs, they can be cut fresh from garden all year round. They are generally used fresh, but the Dutch Winter White type and some red cabbages can be stored for winter. Red and ornamental cabbages are very decorative when growing.

Types

Spring cabbage For use mid-spring until summer.

Summer cabbage For use early summer to autumn.

Autumn cabbage For use mid-autumn and into early winter.

Hardy winter cabbage For use mid-autumn until following spring.

Dutch Winter White cabbage For use mid-autumn until moderate frost, then stored until following spring.

Red cabbage Red forms of summer and autumn cabbage. Stand for many weeks when mature without deteriorating. Distinct flavour. Excellent cooked – notably in recipes using apple. Also pickled, and sliced very finely into salads. I've found cooked cabbage dishes freeze surprisingly well. In my experience less prone to pests and diseases than other types of cabbage. Main cropping season for summer types mid-summer to mid-autumn. Main cropping season for autumn types mid-autumn to early winter. Some autumn cvs suitable for lifting and storage before heavy frost.

Ornamental cabbage Very decorative form with distinctly variegated foliage. For cultivation, see Ornamental kales (page 268).

Site and soil – all types
Open, unshaded site; rich, moisture-retentive soil. Acid soils should be limed to reduce risk of clubroot. Rotate over minimum 3-year cycle to avoid build-up of clubroot and brassica cyst eelworm. Has high nitrogen requirement; excellent crop to follow nitrogen-fixing green manure. Needs to be planted in firm soil, and will not grow well in freshly manured or freshly dug ground.

General cultivation – all types
Sowing options:
1 Sow in seed trays, prick out and transplant to permanent position at three-to-four-leaf stage.
2 Sow in modules. Plant out as above.
3 Sow in seedbed. Thin to required spacing.
4 Sow *in situ*. Thin to required spacing. Mainly used for spring cabbage, mini cabbage and CCA greens.

Only plant sturdy, straight-stemmed plants. If necessary dig ground several weeks ahead of planting and leave the soil to settle. For summer plantings it is sufficient to clear previous crop, rake soil and plant without forking the soil. In very light soil and exposed situations plant in shallow furrows, 10cm/4in deep. As the plant grows fill in the furrow with soil, earthing it up around stem to increase stability. This also encourages secondary roots to develop, which helps plants withstand cabbage root fly attacks (for preventive measures, see page 223). Plant with lower leaves just above soil level. Size of cabbage can be controlled by spacing: the wider the spacing, the larger the head. Cabbage grows well at equidistant spacing.

Keep plants weed-free; remove dead and rotting leaves. Growth will be poor if checked through lack of water. In dry weather water at rate of 22 litres per sq. m/4 gallons per sq. yd per week. Most critical period for watering is 10–20 days before crops mature. One heavy watering at this point very beneficial.

Harvesting – all types
Pull up cabbages when required. Some cvs bolt soon after maturing; others stand in good condition for weeks or months.

Intensive systems – all types
There are several ways of increasing the productivity of cabbage:

1 Double cropping (see illustration, page 158). This technique works best with spring and early summer cabbage, but in suitable conditions can be done successfully in mid-summer (especially with red cabbage). It enables two crops to be obtained from a plant. Instead of pulling up the plant when required, cut the head off the stalk, leaving a couple of leaves or leaf nodes on the stalk. Make a shallow cross in the cut surface of the stalk to encourage development of new growths. Several months later as many as four or five small secondary heads may develop. Ground must be fertile and plants well watered for this to succeed. Give organic feed to boost growth when new heads start to develop.

2 Mini cabbage – small, compact cabbages of tennis-ball size with no wasted outer leaves; exceptionally tender in salad. Only certain varieties are suited to mini cabbage production. Sow *in situ,* or in seed trays, or in modules, from early to late spring. Space or plant out 13cm/5in apart each way. Neat little heads ready about 20 weeks after sowing. Suitable cvs: 'Elisa' F1 and 'Puma' F1 (standard green); 'Protovoy' F1 (savoy); 'Primero' F1 (red).

3 CCA greens catch crop – useful technique for getting quick returns from small area in summer/early autumn. Use spring cabbage cvs (see below). Sow spring to early summer. Sow *in situ* spacing several seeds per station 10cm/4in apart each way. Thin to one seedling per station after germination. Within 8 weeks leaves will be 10–13cm/4–5in high. Cut as young greens, cutting stems above lowest leaves or leaf nodes. Then leave all plants to resprout to give second cutting; or leave every third plant to heart up; or pull up completely and use ground for follow-on crop.

Cultivation of spring cabbage
For use mid-spring to summer, sow in mid-summer in cold areas and in the first two weeks of late summer in warm areas. Plant early to mid-autumn.

For a follow-on crop, sow under cover (in cold frame or under cloches) in early autumn, planting out in spring. Plant in shallow drills, 30cm/12in apart each way. Or space plants 10cm/4in apart, rows 30cm/12in apart. Pull soil around stems a few weeks after planting to give extra protection. In very cold areas protect with cloches until early/mid-spring. When growth starts in spring hoe round plants, and if necessary apply an organic top dressing to boost growth. Leave one plant in three to heart up; use others young as spring greens.

For spring greens in summer and autumn, continue sowing as above from early spring to early summer. Only certain varieties are suitable (see below).

Cultivation of summer cabbage

For use early summer to autumn, sowing options:
1 Late winter (warm areas), early spring (cold areas) in heated propagator, at roughly 13°C/ 55°F. Harden off well before planting out mid- /late spring. Use early summer cv.
2 Early to late spring in open, planting late spring to mid-summer for succession. Space plants 35–45cm/14–18in apart, according to size of head required.

Cultivation of autumn cabbage

For use mid-autumn and into early winter, sow mid- to late spring. Plant by early summer 50cm/20in apart.

Cultivation, harvesting and use of Dutch Winter White cabbage

For use mid-autumn until moderate frost, then stored until following spring, sow mid-spring. Plant early summer 50cm/20in apart.

Use during autumn and lift remaining plants before heavy frost for storage. Pull up by roots. Store in frost-free shed or cellar, either with roots intact or cutting heads with 5cm/2in stem attached. To store, suspend whole plants; or put heads into net bags and suspend them; or pile heads or plants on a layer of straw on the floor – convenient if below 0°C/32°F temperatures are likely, in which case the heads can be given extra coverage. Examine the plants regularly during winter months and gently roll off diseased outer leaves. Can also be stored in garden frames, raised off ground by placing on wooden slats and covered with straw. Essential to ventilate on sunny days to discourage pests and diseases. Excellent raw as coleslaw and stir-fried.

Cultivation of hardy winter cabbage

For use mid-autumn until following spring, sow late spring. Plant by mid-summer 50cm/20in apart. You can earth up stems to give extra protection in winter. Remove any rotting leaves.

Cultivation of red cabbage

For standard cultivation, see summer and autumn cabbage, above. For very early crop of summer cvs, sow in modules in early autumn, over-winter the seedlings under cover, and plant out in early spring as soon as the soil is workable. I have found this system produces exceptionally fine, heavy heads, perhaps because in this area of low rainfall the plants have benefited from the early start.

Pests and diseases – all cabbage types and other brassicas

The following are the most common pests found on cabbages and other brassicas. For organic gardeners, growing brassicas under fine nets is highly recommended to keep out the flying pests, such as flea beetle, aphids and whitefly, cabbage root fly, butterflies and moths with destructive caterpillars, and birds. For other control measures, see Chapter 7.

Flea beetle Nibbles holes in young leaves, often at seedling stage. Spray or dust as soon as noticed. Attacks worse in dry weather. Keeping soil moist deters attacks.

Mealy aphids Grey green, waxy-looking aphids, in colonies on leaves and stems causing puckering throughout summer, but worst in late summer. Squash by hand, spray or try moving ladybirds on to attacked plants. Can stunt plants seriously. Aphids overwinter in stumps so pull out and burn by early summer.

Cabbage whitefly Clouds of small white insects fly up when plants disturbed throughout summer. Not normally seriously damaging, but you can spray when they are first noticed. These also overwinter in stumps, so pull out and burn by early summer.

Caterpillars Eggs laid by various types of cabbage white butterflies and moths, mainly from mid-summer to autumn. Watch out for eggs (mainly on leaf undersides) and young caterpillars. Squash or spray them, or use biological control.

Cabbage root fly Potentially one of most serious pests. Adult flies (which emerge roughly when cow parsley (*Anthriscus sylvestris*) is in flower) lay eggs at base of young brassica plants; hatched grubs tunnel into roots causing plants to collapse. Standard advice is to dig up and burn attacked plants. However, with oriental greens, I have washed off grubs, trimmed back foliage and successfully replanted! Physical barriers best preventive measures (see page 148).

Slugs and snails Damage most serious in early stages; keep a constant watch and destroy.

Birds Attacks first occur at seedling and young plant stage. In winter mature plants often attacked unless grown under nets.

Clubroot (finger and toe) Soil-borne disease resulting in grotesque swellings (resembling dahlia tubers) on roots. Plants collapse and die. Lift diseased roots very carefully and burn them; never compost them. Difficult to eradicate because spores can last twenty years in soil. Rotation, improving drainage and liming to raise pH to slightly alkaline level help prevent and control. Heavy mulching may be beneficial. The good news is that brassicas with clubroot resistance are increasingly likely to appear in the near future. In infected soils raise plants in modules or pots – 15cm/6in pots are ideal – and plant out at late stage to give them a head start. Or concentrate on fast-growing brassicas, such as Texsel greens, broccoli raab and CCA oriental seedlings, which will be ready before the plants become seriously infected.

Cultivars

Spring cabbage
Spring cabbage mostly have small, pointed heads, though a few, such as 'Spring Hero', are round.

For headed cabbage: 'Duncan', 'Durham Early', 'Pixie', 'Offenham 1-Myatt's Offenham Compacta', ' Pyramid' F1, 'Spring Hero' (don't sow until late summer or may bolt prematurely).

For spring greens: 'Sparkel', 'Excel' F1, 'Greensleeves', 'Mastergreen' and cvs above.

For all-season greens: 'Duncan', 'Mayfield' F1, 'Advantage' F1.

Summer cabbage
Some varieties have pointed heads, but most have round, medium to large heads.

'Hispi' F1, 'Kingspi' F1, 'Spitfire', 'Duchy' F1 – pointed.

'Golden Cross' F1, 'Derby Day', 'Elisa' F1, 'Patron' F1– suited to early sowing.

'Stonehead' F1, ^'Castello' F1, 'Minicole' F1 – reasonably compact cvs which stand well.

Autumn cabbage
Typically compact dark green heads which stand well into late autumn/early winter.

Use summer cabbage cvs: 'Stonehead' F1, ^'Castello' F1, 'Minicole' F1, ^'Colt' F1, 'Freshma' F1.

Dutch Winter White
Typically smooth round heads with thin leaves.

'Hidena' F1, 'Lion' F1, ^'Bingo' F1, ^'Impala' F1.

Hardy winter cabbage
Group contains several distinct types of healthy-looking, well-flavoured cabbage.

January King type: flattish heads, blue red tinge, generally stand until mid-winter, excellent flavour: 'January King Hardy Late Stock 3', ^'Marabel' F1, 'Flagship' F1, 'Robin' F1.

White × savoy hybrids: crisp white inner leaves; some cvs stand into late winter – 'Celtic' F1, ^'Tundra' F1 (longest standing), ^'Roulette' F1.

Savoy type: distinct crinkled emerald green leaves, hardiest of all (surviving –10°C/14°F), and often standing into mid-spring. Under organic systems the earlier maturing cvs are generally the most successful: ^'Capriccio' F1 (early), ^'Midvoy' F1 (early/mid), 'Rigoletto' F1, 'Wivoy' F1, 'Ormskirk' F1, 'Tarvoy' F1 (all late), 'Wintessa' F1 (very late).

'Colorsa' F1 — beautiful savoy × red cabbage cross, with pink-tinged internal leaves. Excellent cooked or in salads, very hardy.

Portuguese cabbage: 'Couve Tronchuda', 'Braganza' — distinctive type with sturdy open habit, prominent broad white midribs, somewhat savoyed leaves with undulating edges. Hardy, handsome and well flavoured. Sadly seed rarely available. Grow it if you find it!

Red cabbage

For summer: ^'Primero' F1, 'Ruby Ball' F1, 'Normiro' F1.

For autumn: 'Red Rookie' F1, 'Rodeo' F1.

For winter and storage: ^'Autoro' F1, 'Hardoro' F1, 'Rodima' F1, 'Red Drumhead', 'Huzaro' F1.

VSR ★★ intensive systems, ★ standard heads; PP red cabbage

CALABRESE (Italian broccoli, green sprouting broccoli, summer broccoli) *Brassica oleracea* Italica Group

A fairly compact brassica growing 60cm/2ft tall, calabrese forms a central, green, cauliflower-like head 9–14cm/3½–5½in in diameter. After this is cut, broccoli-like flowering side shoots can be produced. Calabrese is a delicious vegetable, considered to have good anti-carcinogenic properties. It is moderately hardy in its leafy phase but the flowering shoots are susceptible to frost. It is a productive brassica for small gardens as most cvs mature in under 4 months and can be closely spaced.

Site and soil

As Cabbage, page 220, but tolerates poorer soil.

Cultivation

Either sow in modules and plant out, or sow *in situ* (three seeds per station, thinning to one after germination). Doesn't transplant well from seedbed. Space plants 30–38cm/12–15in apart each way. The wider the spacing, the larger the initial head will be.

Sowing programme:

1 For succession, sow from early/late spring until late summer.

2 For very useful early spring crop under cover, sow late summer/early autumn. Plant under cover late autumn/early winter. Plants may not survive in very severe winter, but it's worth a gamble. Recommended to use an early cv.

Mini calabrese: for high yield of small domed heads for single harvest, space plants 23–25cm/9–10in apart. Cut central head when nearly tennis-ball size. Use recommended varieties.

Calabrese must grow steadily; water well in dry weather. Organic top dressing or foliar feed in summer can be applied after cutting central head to stimulate growth.

Pests and diseases
As Cabbage, page 223.

Harvesting and use
Main season early summer until frost, depending on cv. Pick main head just before flower buds open; side shoots then develop. Pick constantly to encourage more shoots to develop. If attacked by caterpillars, soak in salted water before cooking to entice them out.

Boil or steam heads until just tender. Thick shoots can be peeled, then boiled or steamed. Freezes well.

Cultivars
Although most cultivars can be sown in succession throughout the growing season, most are best suited to sowing at certain seasons – i.e. early (early/mid-spring), mid (late spring/early summer), late (mid-/late summer).

Early: 'Trixie' F1 (small plant but good clubroot tolerance), ^'Green Belt' F1, ^'Decathlon' F1.

Mid: 'Crown and Sceptres' F1, ^'Monterey F1', ^'Belstar' F1.

Late: 'Corvet' F1, 'Marathon' F1, 'Flash' F1, 'Triathlon' F1.

For mini calabrese: 'Kabuki' F1.

For new types developed by hybridizing with oriental and other vegetables, see Hybrid broccolis, page 214.

VSR ★★

CAPSICUM see Pepper

CARROTS *Daucus carota*

With careful planning and successive sowing of different types, you can have carrots available in the garden for at least nine months of the year. The flavour of home-grown carrots is far superior to that of bought carrots. Most carrots are orange-fleshed, but white- and yellow-fleshed heirloom varieties, primarily used for fodder, are surprisingly sweet. Varieties with purple skin, purple and orange flesh, green skin and flesh and other combinations can be found. Watch for future introductions from the plant breeders.

Types
Carrots are classified according to types, with considerable overlapping between groups.

Earlies Mature within 12–18 weeks. Short or round roots of Paris Market type. Mostly used fresh, but some Nantes cvs also suitable for storage. Generally sweet-flavoured. Include:

- ∾ round/square-rooted cvs – suitable for difficult soils, e.g. heavy and shallow soils
- ∾ Amsterdam cvs – finger-shaped, smooth, excellent raw
- ∾ Nantes cvs – cylindrical and somewhat larger.

Maincrop Mature in 18–24 weeks. Larger, longer carrots, used fresh but, because of their bulk (which means they dry out more slowly), also suitable for winter storage. Include:

- ∾ Chantenay cvs – top-shaped, medium-sized, reputation for good flavour
- ∾ Berlicum cvs – larger, cylindrical, later maturing
- ∾ Autumn King cvs – tapered, potentially highest yielding, but unsuitable for heavy soils and areas with short growing season
- ∾ Intermediate cvs – longer but less weighty roots than Autumn King (includes Heirloom cvs 'Intermediate James Scarlet' and 'New Red')
- ∾ Imperator – very thin roots, 25–30cm/10–12in long. Recently introduced mainly for commercial 'cut and peel' use. Roots chopped into 5cm/2in lengths with rounded ends; skin rubbed off and sold for use raw. Very sweet; ideal for crudités and dips.

Site and soil
Sheltered situation for early carrots; open site for maincrop. Carrots thrive in light, deep, fertile, stone-free, well-drained soil. Roots cannot penetrate and swell in heavy clay or compacted soil. Need very fine seedbed. Never sow in weedy ground, as difficult crop to keep weed-free. Dig in plenty of well-rotted compost or manure several months beforehand; growth apt to be sappy and the roots tend to fork in freshly manured ground. Carrots also fork – on encountering a stone – in very stony ground. Foliage pretty, so can look good in flower beds (see page 364) and in a potager.

Cultivation of early crop
Especially useful crop, maturing early summer onwards. Use round, Amsterdam or Nantes cvs. Minimum soil temperature for germination 5°C/41°F, but at 10°C/50°F seeds germinate three times faster. Worth trying primed seed; often helps to overcome adverse weather conditions during germination. See Carrot fly, below, for thinning.

Sowing options:

1 Sow under cloches or in cold frames, late winter (in warm areas), early spring (colder areas). Warm up soil beforehand if necessary. On very light soils broadcast seed, or sow in 7.5–10cm/3–4in wide bands, spacing seeds 2cm/¾in apart. No thinning of seedlings should be necessary. On heavy soils can be sown in bands or drills 15cm/6in apart. Thin to about 5cm/2in apart. Remove cloches or frame lights in mid- or late spring when temperatures rise. Carrots ready in early summer.

2 Sow at same time as above, and cover with perforated film or fleece. Sow in sunken drills, laying films over the top of the drills. Remove perforated films when the carrots have about five leaves (usually after about 10 weeks); fleece can be left until maturity unless weather very hot. Nantes F1 cvs recommended for this method.

3 Multisow *round cvs only* in modules indoors in propagator in late winter, up to four seeds per 4–5cm/1½–2in cell. Transplant outside 'as one' after hardening off, spacing 7.5–10cm/3–4in apart. Can be protected with cloches, films and so on. (Long-rooted cvs are unsuitable for multisowing in modules as roots twist around each other. They can be sown singly in modules, but must be planted out before the tap root starts to develop.)

Cultivation of later supplies, using 'early' types as they mature faster

Sowing programme:

1 For summer supply of fresh carrots, sow in succession in open from early spring until mid-summer. Sow in drills 15cm/6in apart. Thin in stages to about 4–5cm/1½–2in apart for medium-sized carrots, or wider spacing for larger carrots. Very wide spacing – up to 10cm/4in apart – has been shown to encourage quick maturity and growth in early carrots.

2 For young carrot crop in late autumn/early winter, make final outdoor sowing late summer (colder areas), early autumn (warmer areas). Cover with cloches or fleece early or mid-autumn.

3 Sow under cover (in unheated greenhouse or polytunnel, or outdoors under fleece) in mid-autumn, preferably using Nantes F1 cvs. Success depends on severity of winter, but can result in very early carrots in late spring.

Cultivation of maincrop sowings for fresh use and storage

Use any maincrop cvs. Sow mid-spring to mid-summer. Sow in drills 15cm/6in apart. Thin as for later supplies (1) above.

Mini carrots

Using appropriate varieties carrots can be grown densely, for harvesting young within 11–13 weeks of sowing. These rapidly grown carrots are smooth and have little central core, which makes them exceptionally tender. Sow *in situ* outdoors from mid-spring to mid-summer at 2–3-week intervals. Sow thinly in rows about 15cm/6in apart, spacing seeds about 4cm/1½in apart so that thinning is unnecessary; or thin early to that spacing. Alternatively sow in shallow drills 10–15cm/4–6in wide, spacing seeds about 2cm/¾in apart.

General cultivation

Carrots are very susceptible to weed competition in early stages, so weed seedlings carefully. Once established, leaves blanket soil so weeding is less urgent. Mulch between rows to retain soil moisture. Carrots require only moderate amounts of water: excessive water encourages leaf growth at expense of roots. Root splitting often occurs when heavy rain follows dry period. Can be prevented by watering just enough to stop soil drying out completely and keeping soil mulched.

Pests

Carrot fly The most serious pest on carrots. Fly lays eggs at base of plants; when hatched tiny maggots tunnel into roots. Foliage becomes bronzed, seedlings die, larger plants are weakened and mined carrot roots don't store well. There can be several generations of flies each year. Adult flies are low-flying, so most successful methods of control are to grow carrots within 60cm/2ft high barriers, or in boxes raised off the ground, or under fine nets or cloches (see illustration, page 147). Take precautions when cow parsley (*Anthriscus sylvestris*) is in flower, as this is when flies migrate to carrot plants. The following practices minimize damage:

∾ Sow early (generally before mid-spring) and late (towards beginning of early summer) to avoid worst attacks.

∾ Sow thinly to minimize need for thinning, as smell of thinnings attracts adult flies. Thin in evening or in still conditions. Nip off unwanted seedlings just above ground level, rather than pulling them up. Bury all thinnings in compost heap. Water and firm remaining plants after thinning.

∾ Where problem is serious, aim to lift early carrots by early autumn, maincrop carrots by mid-autumn. This prevents another cycle from hatching and lessens following year's attacks.

∾ Remove all carrot debris; never leave it on the ground.

∾ Grow cvs with some resistance, such as the fodder carrots (which are pale but quite edible). New cvs with some resistance are being introduced, but only give up to 50 per cent resistance.

∾ Mingle carrot seed with seed of annual flowers and sow together (see page 162).

Cutworm Can damage young roots. Water heavily when you notice larvae. (See also page 133.)

Harvesting

In light soils pull roots out carefully as soon as they reach required size. In heavy soils it is advisable to fork out to avoid breaking roots; water soil beforehand if dry.

Storage

Carrots withstand light frost, but are damaged by heavy frost. They can be stored in various ways:

In the ground This is the best method for retaining flavour, but is only feasible in light, well-drained soil with few slugs. Impractical where mice and rats likely pests. Unless you are getting very early frosts, allow foliage to die back, then cover plants with black polythene film. Cover film with generous layer – up to 30cm/12in thick – of straw, bracken or insulating material. On exposed sites put low hoops over the top to help keep insulation in place.

Indoors Lift before heavy frost. Cut off leaves 1cm/½in above roots. Reject all diseased and damaged roots. Lay roots in layers in boxes or tubs, each layer separated by 1cm/½in of sand, sifted ashes or light soil, as with beetroot (see illustration, page 212). Put in frost-free shed or cellar. Cover with fine mesh if mice likely to be a problem.

In clamps outdoors Make clamp in sheltered spot, preferably against an outside wall on well-drained soil. Can start with a 5–7.5cm/2–3in layer of straw, or 5cm/1in layer of coarse sand or ashes. Pile carrots on top in a tapered heap, to a maximum height of 60cm/2ft. Cover with 20cm/8in layer of straw and, in cold areas, a 15cm/6in layer of soil. This can be taken from around base of heap to improve drainage.

Cultivars

Organic gardeners need carrots with exceptional vigour early, to overcome weeds, and later good leafy tops to keep down weeds; also the ability to bulk up rapidly, to compensate for the later sowing organic gardeners often adopt to avoid the worst carrot fly attacks.

Earlies: ^'Nairobi' F1, 'Nantucket', ^'Newmarket' F1, ^'Maestro' F1, ^'Napoli' F1 – Nantes types, suitable for use fresh and stored.

Maincrop: ^'Bangor' F1, ^'Bolero' F1, ^'Berlicum Bejo' (Berlicum type); ^'Autumn King Vita Longa', ^'Flyaway' F1(Autumn King type); 'Chantenay Red Core';'Newport' F1 (Imperator type; requires very deep soil).

Round carrots (improved modern cvs):'Rondo', 'Pariska', 'Parmex'.

Mini carrots: 'Amini', 'Ideal', 'Mignon', most Amsterdam and Nantes types such as 'Amsterdam Forcing 3 Minicor', 'Newport' F1

VSR ★★★; PP

CAULIFLOWER *Brassica oleracea* Botrytis Group

Cauliflowers are brassicas grown for their characteristic flower heads or curds, which are up to 20cm/8in diameter. Standard forms are white or creamy; purple- and green-curded forms are considered exceptionally flavoured. Plants on average 45–60cm/18–24in tall, spreading well over 75cm/30in. By nature cool-season crops, not suited to high summer temperatures. Grown as annuals or overwintering biennials. Cvs vary in hardiness. (For the perennial form of cauliflower, see Perennial broccoli, page 233.)

Types

Cauliflowers are classified according to season of maturity (see chart overleaf). For fresh cauliflower from spring to autumn, sow suitable varieties from each group at appropriate times. All-year-round production only feasible in frost-free areas.

'Romanesco' type Has lime green curds, with very pretty, pointed florets forming a pinnacle rather than rounded head. Excellent flavour. Cultivate as autumn cauliflower. (Often listed as calabrese in seed catalogues.)

Site and soil

Require moderately fertile, deeply dug, moisture-retentive soil, preferably neutral to slightly alkaline (pH of 6.5–7.5). Mineral deficiencies may develop on acid soils. Rotate in brassica group. Should be planted in firm ground. Avoid freshly manured soils which encourage leafy growth, rather than curd formation.

Cultivation

It is widely agreed that cauliflowers are not the easiest crop to grow organically. The secret of success is steady growth, with plenty of moisture both at young plant stage and when maturing. Growth checks are caused by delayed transplanting, or spells of drought, resulting in deformed and small curds. In areas with dry summers winter cauliflowers and mini cauliflowers are probably easiest to grow. Cauliflowers require long growing season and develop into large plants. Where space is limited concentrate on mini cauliflowers and summer/autumn heading group, which mature fastest of standard types.

For sowing times and spacing for different groups, see chart overleaf.

For autumn-sown early summer type, sow in modules or seed trays, then pot into small pots or modules (5–7.5cm/2–3in), overwinter in well-ventilated frame or under cloches; harden off well before planting out as soon as conditions suitable in early spring. For mid-winter-sown early summer type, sow in modules in heated propagator at 21°C/70°F and plant out after hardening off mid-spring for follow-on crop.

CAULIFLOWER TYPES AND PLANTING CHART					
Type	Sow	Plant	Spacing	Harvest	Weeks to maturity (average)
Winter (spring heading)	Late spring	Mid-summer	63cm/25in	Early to late spring	46–50
Early summer	1 mid-autumn 2 mid-winter	Early spring Mid-spring	53cm/21in	Early summer Mid-summer	36 20
Summer/ autumn	Mid-/late spring	Late spring to mid-summer	60cm/2ft	Late summer/ early autumn	21–23

In practice there is overlapping between groups and latitude over spacing and timing. Seed germinates best at about 21°C/70°F. Sowing in modules is generally recommended, but they can also be sown in a seedbed for transplanting or in situ, and thinned to required spacing. Aim to transplant within 6 weeks of sowing.

Plant at equidistant spacing. As a general rule, the later the maturity the wider the space required. To get heads maturing in a sequence, rather than all at the same time, either plant a few at a time over several days, or plant seedlings of different sizes at the same time.

If conditions are dry during growth, water if possible at the rate of 22 litres per sq. m/4 gallons per sq. yd every two weeks. Otherwise give one heavy watering 2–3 weeks before harvest. Early summer cauliflowers are most susceptible to water shortage. Cauliflowers grown at wider spacing than normally recommended develop more extensive root systems and withstand water shortage better.

Maturing curds can be protected from the sun by bending a leaf over them until required. Overwintering cauliflowers can be protected in severe weather by gently tying the leaves together over the head. In good modern varieties curds are naturally protected by leaves.

Pests and diseases
As Cabbage, page 223. Cauliflowers can be grown under fine nets in the early stages to protect against aphids and to some extent pollen beetle, which may attack them.

Harvesting and use
Cut curds when firm and tight. They do not normally stand well for many days after maturity. Individual cauliflower florets freeze well.

Mini cauliflowers
Cauliflowers can be grown at close spacing to produce small curds of 5cm/2in diameter, ideal for small portions or for freezing. Suited to growing in 90–120cm/3–4ft wide beds. Small curds mature at more or less same time, so best to make several successive sowings.

Sowing options:
 1 For early summer crop, sow in late winter, in modules or seed trays in propagator at 20–25°C/68–77°F. Plant out after hardening off.
 2 For early summer to mid-autumn crop, sow in early spring to mid-summer, in modules, in a seedbed or *in situ*.
 3 For early summer crop, sow in early autumn, in modules or seed trays. Overwinter in cold frames and plant out following spring.

Space plants 12–15cm/5–6in apart each way. If sowing *in situ*, sow 2–3 seeds per station, thinning to strongest seedling after germination.

Keep ground well watered and weeded throughout growth. Normally few pest problems as in ground for fairly short time. Small curds ready 14–16 weeks after sowing. Growth is fastest in late spring/early summer. Cut heads when 4–7.5cm/1½–3in diameter. Cook or freeze whole. Curds 'go over' quickly, so don't leave them for long once they are a usable size.

Cultivars
Winter (spring heading): 'Walcheren Winter Armado April', 'Ace Early', 'Jerome' F1, 'Arcade' F1, 'Purple Cape' (purple), 'Vilna' and 'Wanfleet' (late).
Early summer: 'Beauty' F1, 'Mayflower' F1, 'Linmont' F1, 'Montana' .
Summer/autumn: 'Lateman', ^'Plana' F1, ^'Limelight' and 'Alverda' (green), ^'White Rock', 'Nautilus' F1, ^'Lindon' F1, 'Fremont' F1, 'Memphis' F1, 'Mexico' F1.
Romanesco type: 'Minaret' F1, 'Amfora' F1.
Mini cauliflowers: 'Idol', 'Lateman', 'Clarke' F1, 'Candid Charm' F1.
Note: These are early summer cvs, the type currently recommended for mini cauliflowers. Their drawback is rapid deterioration once mature. Future trials may indicate that some autumn cvs are more suitable, and stand longer when ready for harvesting. Watch gardening magazines and catalogues for developments.

VSR * most types, ** mini cauliflowers

PERENNIAL BROCCOLI
Perennial form of cauliflower, popularly known as perennial broccoli. In spring produces small central cauliflower head and masses of broccoli-like side shoots with small heads. Very useful in the Vegetable Gap.

Cultivation and harvesting
Sow in spring in modules. Plant out after hardening off, spacing plants about 90cm/3ft apart. May need staking in windy situation. Protect from birds, especially in winter/spring. Keep mulched and well watered.

Cut main head first and side shoots once heads about 4cm/1½in diameter. Young stems and small leaves also edible. When plant starts to run to seed and coarsens, cut back all remaining shoots. Vigour gradually declines, so best replaced every 2–3 years.

Cultivars
Only known cv 'Nine Star Perennial'.

VSR ★★

CELERIAC (Turnip-rooted celery) *Apium graveolens* var. *rapaceum*

Bushy biennial plant, 45cm/18in high, 30cm/12in across. Primarily grown for knobbly well-flavoured bulb-like root at base of stem. Good substitute for celery as hardier and less prone to disease. Celery-like leaves useful for flavouring.

Site and soil
Open site, but tolerates light shade provided plenty of moisture. Needs fertile soil, rich in organic matter.

Cultivation
Must have long growing season with plenty of moisture throughout.

Sowing options:
1 Late winter/early spring in a heated propagator.
2 Mid-spring in cold greenhouse or under cloches.

Sow in modules or in seed trays. Germination of seedlings is often erratic. Be patient!

When seedlings large enough to handle prick out 6cm/2½in apart, preferably into modules or containers 7.5cm/3in deep. Don't start hardening off outside until weather is warm as any sudden drop in temperature stimulates flowering, and plants will bolt prematurely rather than forming swollen roots (see Celery, below).

Plant late spring/early summer 30–38cm/12–15in apart, base of stem at ground level. Water thoroughly in dry weather; keep plants mulched. Weekly liquid manure from early summer onwards very beneficial. Remove lower ageing leaves as season progresses to expose swelling root.

Pests

Celery leaf miner (celery fly) Most common pest, tunnelling into leaves and causing blisters. Remove diseased leaves and burn. Growing under fine nets prevents attacks. Never plant seedlings with blistered leaves. In my experience some recovery after watering with seaweed-based Maxicrop.

Slugs Attack in early stages.

Harvesting and use

Can be used from early autumn until late spring. Can normally be left in soil throughout winter. Will survive -10°C/14°F if very well protected with thick layer of straw or bracken tucked between plants to cover root. Or cover plants with frost-proofing grade of fleece. In very cold areas lift in autumn before severe frost, trim off outer leaves leaving central tuft attached, and store under cover in boxes of sand. In spring plants remaining in the ground can be lifted and heeled in, so that ground can be cultivated for other crops.

Celeriac bulb can be grated raw in salads, puréed, boiled, used in soups or served with cheese sauce. Unfortunately rough outer skin harbours dirt; scrubbing it clean is a (worthwhile) chore!

Leaves normally remain green all winter. Flavour is strong, but use sparingly in salads or for celery seasoning. Can also dry leaves for use as celery substitute in cooking.

Cultivars

'Balder', 'Monarch', 'Snow White'/'Snehvide' – among many good cvs.

VSR *

CELERY *Apium graveolens* var. *dulce*

Celeries are distinctly flavoured biennial plants grown mainly for their crunchy stems. They are essentially cool-season crops. There are several types, which display varying hardiness (see below). Self-blanching types and leaf celery are easier to grow in small modern gardens than traditional trench celery.

Types

Self-blanching celery Long-stemmed plants, on average 45cm/18in high. Not frost hardy, so mainly used as summer crop. In standard cvs (previously known as Gold type) stems cream or yellowish. Can be partially blanched by planting close, to make stems whiter and possibly sweeter. In American Green cvs stems are green, naturally well flavoured and supplementary blanching is unnecessary. Some varieties have a beautiful pink flush to the stem. Mainly used raw but can be cooked.

Trench celery The classic English celery, with long pink or white stems, growing up to 60cm/2ft high. Tolerates light frost, and survives moderate frost if protected with straw etc. in winter. Red- and pink-stemmed varieties are slightly hardier. To develop full flavour and texture, it requires some form of blanching to exclude light. Mainly used raw but can be cooked.

Leaf or cutting celery Very hardy, robust plant closely related to wild celery. Can survive -12°C/10°F. Branching bushy plant with glossy leaves and thin, fine stems. Height from 30–45cm/12–18in, depending on cv. Naturally vigorous and can be grown as CCA salad seedlings. Otherwise mainly used for soups and flavouring in winter months. Rarely affected by pests or diseases. The deeply curled-leaved variety 'Parcel' is an exceptionally decorative plant.

Site and soil – all types

Open site, very rich, moisture-retentive soil with plenty of organic matter. Does best in alkaline soils; very acid soils should be limed to raise pH to 6.5. Celery is a marsh plant in origin, so plenty of moisture throughout growth essential. Leaf celery less demanding than other types.

General cultivation – all types

Seed germinates at 10–15°C/50–59°F and requires light to germinate, so sow on the surface, or lightly covered with sand. Seedlings may bolt prematurely if temperature falls below 10°C/50°F for more than 12 hours. Hence it is inadvisable to sow too early. Keep surface damp until germination. Prick out seedlings as soon as large enough to handle. Plant at five-to-six-leaf stage after hardening off well. Delay hardening off until weather is warm. If cold weather threatens give extra protection.

Cultivation and harvesting of self-blanching celery

Sow in seed trays or modules early spring in propagator, or mid-spring under cover. Alternatively, buy plants late spring/early summer. Plant early summer after risk of frost is past. Usually planted in block formation at equidistant spacing to get a blanched effect and upright growth, but can plant in rows. Space plants 15–28cm/6–11in apart. The wider spacing gives thicker stems, while close spacing gives a higher overall yield of smaller stems, with more of a central 'heart' of little leaves. Plant with base of stems at soil level. Reject any plants with blistered leaves (see Celery fly, page 234).

Take precautions against slugs. You can cover with fleece for 2 weeks or so after planting to protect against frost and cold in early stages. Remove perforated plastic after 4 weeks. Tuck straw around 'Gold' cvs in mid-summer to increase blanching. In dry weather water weekly at rate of 22 litres per sq. m/4 gallons per sq. yd. Otherwise plants are liable to bolt or become stringy. Feed weekly with liquid manure from early summer onwards.

On average, stems ready for cutting 16–18 weeks after sowing. Will stand until frost though condition deteriorates as season progresses. Green cvs have shorter period of peak quality. Best to cut before outer leaves become pithy. Can cut individual stems at soil level, or lift whole plant. In the US celery is lifted before the first frost and stored in cellars for winter use.

Cultivation, blanching and harvesting of trench celery

Where possible prepare soil in advance by digging a trench 38–45cm/ 15–18in wide and about 30cm/12in deep, and working in manure or compost. On well-drained land this can be done the previous autumn. After preparing it, fill in to about 5cm/2in below ground level. This slightly sunken bed enables water to be retained when celery is growing. For seed raising, see above. Plant in single rows with plants 30–45cm/ 12–18in apart.

Trench celery can be blanched either by using collars, or by earthing up the plants as they grow. The latter is more complicated and requires more space for access. (For details, see old gardening books.) To blanch with collars, start in mid-summer when plants about 30–38cm/12–15in high. Use purpose-made collars or strips of heavy, brown, light-proof paper (paper sacking works well) about 15cm/6in wide. Don't use black polythene film as it attracts slugs and causes sweating. Tie collars loosely around stems, to allow for expansion. Use two ties and tie in a bow so easily removed to inspect stems. Tie collars close to leafy tops, but do not cover leaves. Blanch in two or three stages as the stems grow, at roughly 3–4 week intervals. Collars can overlap each other. In well-grown plants the total length of blanched stem would be about 38cm/15in. Lower collars can be removed and replaced if necessary. At the same time remove decaying or rotten leaves and sheltering woodlice or slugs.

Cut from early autumn onwards. Cutting can continue into mid-winter if plants are protected from frost.

Cultivation and harvesting of leaf celery

Cultivation/sowing options:

1. For single plant, sow in spring in seed trays or modules. Plant outside 23–25cm/9–10in apart. Or plant initially 13cm/5in apart, removing intermediate plants when young and leaving remainder to grow larger.
2. Multisow in modules, up to eight seeds per cell, planting out in 'clumps' 20cm/8in apart. These will be very fine-stemmed.
3. For extra-quality plants during winter, sow in mid- to late summer to plant under cover in autumn.
4. For CCA seedlings make successive sowings *in situ* throughout growing season.

Plants can be cut frequently, starting about 4 weeks after planting. Will regrow and remain productive over many months, though eventually will run to seed in spring. Leave a few plants to seed in second season. Young seedlings can be transplanted to wherever required.

Cut CCA seedlings when 10–13cm/4–5in high.

Pests and diseases

Slugs, celery fly See Celeriac, page 234.

Celery leaf spot Debilitating disease, leaving small brown spots on leaves and stems. Seed-borne and difficult to control organically. Dusting leaves with old soot may prevent attacks.

Use good-quality seed; unwise to save your own. Burn any diseased foliage.

Cultivars

Self-blanching
Standard type: 'Celebrity', 'Lathom Self Blanching', 'Lathom Galaxy'.
Green-stemmed: 'Tango' F1, 'Greensleeves', 'Hopkins Fenlander', *'Victoria' F1 (good flavour).
Pink-stemmed: 'Pink Blush' F1, 'Pink Champagne'.

Trench celery
'Mammoth White', 'Mammoth Pink', 'Martine' (red).

Leaf celery
Amsterdam cvs; 'Parcel' – very decorative form with deeply crinkled, parsley-like leaves.

VSR ** self-blanching, * trench celery, *** leaf celery; PP leaf celery 'Pink Champagne' and 'Parcel'

CHENOPODIUM GIGANTEUM 'Magentaspreen' (Tree spinach)

An unusual relative of the edible weed fat hen or lamb's quarters, this is an easily grown, productive and spectacularly colourful annual which deserves to be better known. The mature plant grows up to 1.8m/6ft high, with a 25–38cm/10–15in spread. In most stages the undersides of the leaves and leaf tips are magenta pink, with a floury texture. The raw young leaves have a pea flavour. The mature leaves can be cooked like spinach. It is exceptionally fast-growing.

Site and soil
Not fussy. Tolerates fairly exposed situation, relatively infertile soil and fairly dry conditions, though thrives in fertile sheltered situations.

Cultivation and harvesting
In practice this is a plant that self-seeds once a few plants are left to seed, reappearing early each year. This is the easiest way to grow it.

Alternatively:
1 For single plants to be harvested young, sow in spring *in situ* or in modules, spacing plants about 23cm/9in apart. Start picking leaves as soon as plants about 10cm/4in high. Nip out the growing point to

encourage bushiness. Plants may stay productive over many weeks, but eventually shoot up and become coarser.

2 For plants to be grown to full height, plant towards back of a bed or border. Strip off leaves individually as the plant grows. To establish plants for future, leave a few to seed in late summer.

3 For CCA seedlings, sow *in situ* throughout the growing season. Early and late sowings can be made under cover in spring and late summer/early autumn. Start cutting as soon as usable size.

Although 'Magentaspreen' can become invasive, seedlings are very easily uprooted.

VSR ★★★

CHICORY *Cichorium intybus*

This large group of biennial and perennial plants is closely associated with Italy. They are robust, tolerate a wide range of climate and soil conditions, and are rarely seriously troubled by pests and diseases. The main season of use is from mid-summer to spring.

Chicories are characterized by slightly bitter flavours, which may account for their lack of popularity. By shredding the leaves to sweeten them, using seedlings and blanching where appropriate, and blending them with milder-flavoured leaves in salads, you can make them refreshingly palatable. Most types can also be cooked, which subtly changes the flavour. Red chicories are very decorative, hence their wide use in restaurants and supermarket salad packs.

Red chicory, Sugar Loaf chicory and Witloof or Belgian chicory are the types most widely grown in gardens. All produce tall, beautiful spikes of sky-blue flowers when they run to seed in the second season. The flowers are edible in salads. (For the more unusual types of chicory, see *The Organic Salad Garden*.)

RED CHICORY (outside Italy widely known as 'radicchio')
Ground-hugging plants, typically with variegated or reddish green, loose-leaved heads early in season, becoming deeper red and forming tight little hearts with sweeter, crisp inner leaves in cooler weather. Improved modern cvs develop deeper-coloured, tighter heads much earlier.

Most cvs are moderately hardy. The narrow-leaved, non-hearting Treviso types are exceptionally hardy. Some cvs can be forced (see below). Grows best in fertile, moisture-retentive soil but very adaptable. Useful for intercropping, as tolerates light shade from overhanging plants. Natural season from summer to early winter, but can be extended to following spring by growing under cover in winter.

Cultivation

Germination can be erratic, especially for *in situ* sowing in summer (see Sowing in adverse conditions, page 91).

Sowing options:
1 Broadcast. Traditional method, suitable for older cvs. Broadcast seed in patches in weed-free soil, from late spring to mid-summer. This system can also be used for sowing chicory mixtures (see Saladini, page 321). Curiously, plants seem to thin themselves out, some growing larger at expense of weaker ones. If they appear overcrowded in late summer thin to 10–13cm/4–5in apart.
2 Sow *in situ* in rows. Space rows about 30cm/12in apart. Thin plants in stages to required spacing.
3 Sow in modules and transplant. I have found this the best method for getting good-quality heads of improved modern cvs. (If not using modules, sow in seed trays and prick out.)

Sowing programme:
1 For early summer crop, sow in mid- to late spring. Only use recommended cvs as most bolt rather than hearting from early sowings. Transplant outside after hardening off. Protect with cloches or crop covers in early stages.
2 For main summer and autumn outdoor crop, sow as above from late spring to mid-summer. (Treviso cvs can be sown by broadcasting, sown *in situ* or raised as single plants in modules. They will stand outside until the following spring.)
3 For winter/early spring crop under cover, sow mid-/late summer, transplanting under cover in late summer/early autumn.

Space plants 20–35cm/8–14in apart depending on cv. Traditionally chicory plants are trimmed back to 8–10cm/3–4in above ground level after planting to stimulate growth, especially in hot climates.

Keep weed-free; otherwise little attention needed. In late autumn you can cover remaining plants outside with low polytunnels, cloches or straw to extend the season. During winter outer leaves (especially of plants grown under cover) may develop rots. Remove infected leaves carefully. Plants often recover in warmer spring weather.

Forcing

Some Verona cvs and Treviso can be lifted in late autumn and forced in the same way as Witloof chicory (see below). Resulting chicons are beautiful: white with pink tips.

Harvesting

Once hearts form, either cut a little above ground level or cut individual leaves as required. Leave stumps to resprout; they normally produce further leaves over many weeks.

Cultivars

Red Verona type (traditional): 'Rossa Bella', 'Palla Rossa Verona'.
Variegated (traditional): ' Castelfranco , 'Sottomarina'.
Modern cvs: 'Cesare' (early sowing), 'Indigo', 'Palla Rossa Bella',
   'Augusto', 'Leonardo'. (Unfortunately seed of good new cvs is very
   expensive, so not widely available in home gardener catalogues.
   Improved cvs sometimes sold as plants.)
Treviso type: 'Treviso', 'Versuvio' F1.

VSR **; PP

SUGAR LOAF CHICORY

Mature plants form dense, conical heads not unlike cos lettuce. Inner
leaves creamy and naturally blanched, so sweeter than most chicories –
hence its name. Flavour still slightly bitter, but very refreshing. Highly
productive, as can be grown as CCA seedlings and/or for heads,
and responds to CCA treatment at every stage. Once established, plants
appear to have excellent tolerance to drought, possibly because of deep
roots. Reasonably hardy. Natural cropping season summer to autumn.
Most cvs tolerate light frost in open, but if grown under cover in winter
and kept trimmed back withstand much lower temperatures. Can be
grown almost all year as seedling crop.

Cultivation

Sowing programme for CCA seedling crop (any cv can be used):

 1 Make first sowing early spring *in situ* under cover. Sow by broadcasting, or in narrow drills 7.5–10cm/3–4in apart, or in wide drills. Start
   cutting when leaves 5–8cm/2–3½in high. Continue as long as leaves
   tender. You can then thin to 20–25cm/8–10in apart, allowing remaining plants to heart up. For continuous cutting keep plants well watered.
   Apply occasional liquid feeds to stimulate growth if seems necessary.
 2 Continue with outdoor sowings as above, as soon as soil is workable.
   You can sow at intervals throughout summer, but spring sowings are
   generally most useful. (Leaves liable to coarsen rapidly in hot summer
   weather.) You can protect with crop covers or cloches in the autumn
   to prolong season of usefulness.
 3 For winter crop, make final sowing early autumn under cover.

Sowing programme for headed crop:

 1 For early summer crop, sow modern cvs in seed trays or modules in
   spring. Plant about 25cm/10in apart.
 2 For main summer and autumn crop, sow any cvs in early and mid-
   summer as above or *in situ,* thinning to 25–30cm/10–12in apart.
   Plants can be covered (see Red chicory, above) in late autumn before
   frost to prolong season. Before frost heads can be pulled up by roots.
   Will keep for several weeks in refrigerator, cold cellar or frost-free
   shed. Protect with straw if necessary.

3 For winter crop under cover, sow in mid- to late summer, transplanting under cover in early autumn. Even if there is not time for large heads to develop, plants will resprout over a long period if cut at semi-mature stage.

Cultivars

Traditional Italian 'cutting' chicories: 'Trieste', 'Milano' – mainly used for CCA seedlings; will also form heads.
'Jupiter' F1 – versatile headed cv suitable for any sowings.
'Snowflake', 'Poncho' – headed types suitable for summer sowings.

VSR ★★★★ CCA seedlings, ★★★ headed

MIXED CHICORIES
'Misuglio'/'Misticanza' is an Italian mixture of various types of chicories, which can be broadcast together to make a colourful patch. Can be productive over several months. Various sowing times recommended: spring for summer crop, summer for crop that may overwinter successfully if protected; late summer/early autumn under cover. Worth experimenting to see what is most successful locally.

WITLOOF OR BELGIAN CHICORY
The parsnip-like roots are forced in darkness to produce white buds or 'chicons' during winter. Much more easily grown than people imagine. Either used raw in salads or cooked by braising, incorporating into cheese, ham or egg dishes, etc. Newer cvs much improved and easier to force.

Cultivation

Being closely related to dandelion, Witloof chicory is not fussy about soil. Avoid freshly manured ground, which can cause over-lush growth and fanged roots.

Sow in late spring/early summer, either thinly, *in situ,* in drills about 30cm/12in apart, or in modules for transplanting. (Chicory does not otherwise transplant very successfully.) Thin or plant about 23cm/9in apart.

Little further attention required during summer, other than weeding, and watering in very dry weather. Mulching advisable.

Forcing

Chicory can either be lifted and forced indoors, or forced *in situ* either outside or under cover. Indoor methods are more convenient; *in situ* methods are said to produce better-flavoured chicons.

In pots indoors As long as ground is not heavily frosted, you can lift roots any time from autumn to the end of the year.

1 Dig them up and leave somewhere sheltered, such as a lean-to shed, for a week or so to allow moisture to pass back into the roots from the leaves.

Forcing Witloof chicory indoors.

Lift roots in early winter; leave for about a week, then trim off the leaves 2.5cm/ 1in above the root. Store until required for forcing between layers of sand or soil.

Pot several roots close together into a flower pot and cover with a pot of similar dimensions. When chicons are ready for harvesting, cut about 2cm/¾in above soil level, leaving the root to resprout.

2 Trim off the leaves about 2.5cm/1in above the root.
3 Trim off wispy side roots. It is advisable to discard any roots that are less than 4cm/1½in diameter across the top, though they may produce small chicons. Trim root tips back to about 20cm/8in if too long for pots.
4 Store roots until required for forcing. Either lay them flat between layers of sand in boxes in a shed, or lay them in a 30cm/12in deep trench in the garden, covered with soil.
5 To have a succession, force a few at a time in a 23–30cm/9–12in flower pot. Fill with soil or old potting compost to support the roots. All nourishment comes from the roots, so good soil is unnecessary. Select three to five roots of roughly the same size. Pack them upright, fairly close together in the pot, with the necks about 2.5cm/1in above the soil.
6 Water lightly. Cover the pot with another upturned pot of the same size. Block the drainage hole with tinfoil or a stone to exclude light.
7 Put the pot somewhere indoors at a temperature of 10–18°C/ 50–64°F.

8 Inspect from time to time. Remove any rotted leaves and water lightly if dry. Firm chicons normally develop within about 3 weeks.
9 Cut them about 2cm/¾in above the root. If they are not eaten immediately, wrap them in brown paper or tinfoil to prevent them greening. Can be kept in the fridge. Roots left after the first cut may resprout to produce a smaller second crop of loose, but tender, blanched leaves.

They can be forced in boxes or any container of sufficient depth: allow at least 20cm/8in headroom for the chicon.

In situ *in a greenhouse/polytunnel*

1 Prepare the roots as above.
2 Instead of planting in pots, plant in greenhouse soil, e.g. in the ground under the staging.
3 Devise a method of excluding light completely – e.g. cover the area with black polythene film anchored over wire hoops (see below) or erect boxes or boards to black out the area.

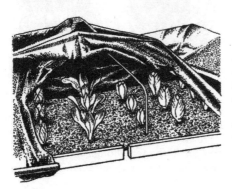

Forcing red Treviso chicory (left) and Witloof chicory (right) by planting in the ground under greenhouse staging. Roots are blanched by covering with black polythene film anchored over steel hoops.

Chicons normally take longer to develop than when forced in pots indoors. If temperatures rise rapidly in spring may get aphid attacks or develop rots. Use them up quickly!

In situ *outdoors*

1 In late autumn cut back the leaves as for lifted chicory.
2 Cover the stumps with 15–20cm/6–8in of sand, light soil, or sieved ashes, making a ridge over them.
3 You can cover the ridge with cloches or low polythene film tunnels to bring on the chicons sooner.
4 Chicons push through from late winter to early spring, depending on the weather. Scrape away the covering to cut them.

Cultivars
'Apollo', 'Zoom' F1.
Red forms of Witloof chicory, of the Treviso type, are now becoming available.

VSR *

CHINESE CABBAGE (Chinese leaves) *Brassica rapa* Pekinensis Group

This mild-flavoured Asian cabbage is much faster-growing than Western cabbage. They are usually light green in colour. Only a few of the many types are cultivated in the West. Chinese cabbage is not very hardy but withstands some frost if protected. It is excellent for CCA cropping at a semi-mature stage under cover in winter.

Types

Hearted/headed type Popularly known as 'Chinese leaves' in the UK and Napa cabbage in the US. Characteristic white-marbled veining on leaves; crisp hearts of tightly folded leaves. Squat 'barrel' forms particularly compact; tall cylindrical forms slower-growing and generally later maturing.

Loose-headed/semi-headed type Loose rosettes of leaves instead of distinct heart. Used mainly as CCA crops at semi-mature and seedling stage. The 'fluffy top' loose-headed cvs have beautiful creamy centres, crêpe-like leaves. Used at mature stage. Excellent salad vegetable.

Site and soil
Fairly open site, though tolerates light shade in mid-summer, provided it has plenty of moisture and is not crowded. To maintain fast growth it requires very fertile, moisture-retentive soil, limed if acid. Chinese cabbage has exceptionally high water requirements throughout growth.

Cultivation
Most types best sown summer for late summer/early autumn crop. Ideal crop to follow peas, early potatoes and broad beans. Like many oriental greens, tends to bolt prematurely if sown early in year – although a quick crop of CCA seedlings is often feasible in spring. Bolting tendency exacerbated by low temperatures in early stages, by dry conditions and by being transplanted.

For CCA seedlings, sow *in situ,* by broadcasting or in drills. Use loose-headed cvs only, as many hearted cvs have rough-textured leaves at seedling stage. Make first sowings under cover in early spring. Follow with outdoor sowings as soon as soil workable. You can protect with crop covers or cloches. Continue sowing outdoors until late summer. Make final sowing under cover early autumn. Cut seedlings when usable size, leaving to resprout unless plants have started to bolt and coarsen.

For headed crop:

1 For main crop, sow *in situ* or in modules from early to late summer. Space plants about 30cm/12in apart.

2 For early crop, you can try sowing late spring/early summer in propagator, using bolt-resistant cvs. Maintain minimum temperature of 18°C/64°F for first 3 weeks after germination. Protect plants with cloches or crop covers after planting.

3 For late crop, sow end of summer, transplanting under cover early autumn. Either grow at standard spacing, or space plants about 13cm/5in apart, for regular cut of small leaves during winter. Can be very productive.

Mulch after planting. Keep weed-free and well watered. Unlike most brassicas, Chinese cabbage has very shallow roots, and therefore needs frequent, moderate watering rather than single heavy watering. Water essential throughout growth and especially when plants nearing maturity. Responds to liquid feeds throughout growth unless soil very fertile.

Pests and diseases
As Cabbage, page 223. Subject to all common brassica problems. Growing under fine nets to deter flying pests is highly recommended.

Harvesting and use
CCA seedling crops ready from 4–5 weeks after sowing. Headed types ready 9–10 weeks after sowing, loose-headed types 2–3 weeks earlier. Cut heads about 2.5cm/1in above base and leave to resprout. Plants overwintered under cover naturally run to seed in following spring, producing tender flowering shoots. Cut these for use like broccoli. Heads can be lifted before onset of frost and stored for several weeks in cool, dry, frost-free conditions, or in a fridge.

Use Chinese cabbage raw in salads, or cook lightly, e.g. by steaming or stir-frying. Its delicate flavour is completely destroyed by boiling.

Cultivars
'Blues' F1, 'Tango' F1, 'Kasumi' F1, 'Yakimo' F1 – barrel type with reasonable bolting resistance.

'Green Tower' F1, 'Jade Pagoda' F1 – tall cylindrical type.

'Ruffles' F1 (previously 'Eskimo') – fluffy-top loose-headed type; reasonable bolting resistance.

Santo/Minato Santo – loose-headed type.

VSR ★★ headed and fluffy top, ★★★ CCA; PP fluffy-top types

CHOY SUM GROUP

'Choy sum' is a convenient group name for various closely related Chinese greens, grown for their delicately flavoured young flowering shoots and stems, and eaten like broccoli. The most productive types are purple-flowered pak choi and hybrid flowering rape. For other types of choy sum, see *Oriental Vegetables*.

PURPLE-FLOWERED PAK CHOI (Hon tsai tai) *Brassica rapa* var. *purpurea*
Pretty, branching plant, with purple stems and yellow flowers, growing over 30cm/12in high with a spread of 25–45cm/10–18in when it reaches maturity. It is adapted to cool weather and is fairly hardy, surviving -5°C/23°F. This makes it a useful winter vegetable.

Site and soil
Fertile, moisture-retentive, well-drained soil, as growth must be rapid to produce tender shoots.

Cultivation, harvesting and use
Sowing late summer for autumn/early winter crop is most successful. For follow-on crop under cover, sow late summer and plant under cover in early autumn. Sow *in situ* or in modules. Space about 38cm/15in apart in good soil; plants can be a little closer in less fertile soil. Plants normally ready in less than 2 months from sowing. Keep cutting shoots when 10–15cm/4–6in long, before buds open. Will produce more shoots over several weeks or months.

Eat raw in salads or lightly cooked (see Chinese cabbage, above).

VSR *; PP

HYBRID FLOWERING RAPE *Brassica rapa* var. oleifera
The cv 'Bouquet' F1 has been developed from rape plants traditionally grown for the extraction of oil from their seeds. It is an attractive, productive plant, with light green, prettily savoyed leaves, chunky succulent stems and heavy clusters of yellow flower buds. When fully grown it is about 45cm/18in high with similar spread, but it is normally grown closely and harvested young. It grows best in cool weather and survives light frost. It has an excellent flavour used raw or lightly cooked. In Japan it is also used as cut flower.

Site and soil
As Purple-flowered pak choi, above.

Cultivation and harvesting
For outdoor crop and winter crop under cover, sow as for purple-flowered pak choi, above. Early summer sowings are sometimes successful. Space plants 13–20cm/5–8in apart.

Cut shoots while tender before buds open, but with a hint of yellow colour showing. First cuts can be made when plants are no more than 20cm/8in high, within 8 weeks of sowing. Leave plants to resprout.

VSR **; PP

CHRYSANTHEMUM GREENS (Chop suey greens, Shungiku)
Xanthophthalmum coronarium (previously *Chrysanthemum coronarium*)

This decorative form of garden chrysanthemum is grown for the aromatic, distinctly flavoured and nutritious leaves, which are deeply serrated or rounded depending on the variety. It grows to about 15cm/6in high with similar spread in the leafy phase and up to 60cm/2ft when flowering. It becomes quite a shrubby plant if picked continually. The flowers are creamy yellow.

Site and soil
Not fussy about soil or site, though grows more lushly in fertile soil with plenty of moisture. Will tolerate light shade in summer.

Cultivation
Naturally healthy. Grows best in cool weather and seems to tolerate low light levels in winter. Sometimes becomes bitter at high temperatures. Withstands light frosts in the open, and lower temperatures if protected. Small and fast-growing, so very useful for catch cropping and intercropping. Does well in containers.
    Can be grown as CCA seedlings or as single plants. Can be sown for much of the year, but has a tendency to run to seed rapidly in hot weather and dry conditions. Spring and mid-summer/autumn sowings probably most productive and useful. Very fine seed, so sow shallowly. For single plants, sow *in situ,* or in seed trays or modules. Space plants 10–13cm/4–5in apart. For CCA seedling crop, sow thinly, either broadcast, or in single or wide drills, spaced 13cm/5in apart.

Sowing programme:
 1 For very early crop, sow early spring under cover.
 2 Follow with outdoor sowings as soon as soil workable.
 3 For autumn crop, sow towards end of summer; crop can be covered with cloches or crop covers to improve quality.
 4 For good-quality winter crop, sow early autumn under cover.

Harvesting and use
First cut of CCA seedlings can normally be made 4–5 weeks after sowing when 5–10cm/2–4in high. The younger the leaves the more tender they are. Leave the plants to resprout. Single plants normally ready 6–8 weeks after sowing. Can be cut or pulled whole, or individual leaves can be cut as required. Continue cutting regularly in order to keep plants tender. Remove any flower buds which appear. Cut back hard if stems start to become woody; plants often regenerate. Leave a few plants to run to seed at the end of the season; they may self-seed usefully. Leaves wilt rapidly, so use as soon after picking as possible.
    Use young leaves sparingly in salads. Older leaves are strong-flavoured and best cooked – lightly steamed, stir-fried or made into soup.

May become bitter if overcooked. They blend well with other Asian greens in stir-fries. Flower petals are edible raw in salads, but remove the centre, which can be bitter.

Cultivars
New cvs, such as 'Maiko', are broader-leaved and more productive than old; but currently named cvs are rarely listed in seed catalogues.

VSR ★★★; PP

CLAYTONIA *see* Purslane, winter

CORN SALAD (Lamb's lettuce, mache) *Valerianella locusta*

A low-growing, small-leaved, hardy annual, whose meek appearance belies its exceptional robustness. It is mild-flavoured and an invaluable ingredient in winter salads. Rarely more than 10cm/4in high with a similar spread, it is ideal for intercropping and undercropping.

Types

Large-leaved Somewhat floppy leaves and habit. Often called 'English' or 'Dutch' type. Use for any sowings.

'Vert'/'Green' type Dark green, shiny leaves. Plants squatter, perkier but smaller than large-leaved type. Popular in Western Europe, reputedly hardier than large-leaved, but probably less productive. Normally only used for later sowings.

Site and soil
Undemanding plant, tolerating both full sun and light shade in summer. Adaptable to wide range of soil and conditions. Growth more lush in fertile, well-cultivated soil, but tolerates poor soil, fairly dry and fairly moist situations.

Cultivation
Can be grown as single plants or as CCA seedlings. Former probably more productive method.

Sowing programme:
1 For late spring/early summer crop, sow late winter/early spring under cover.
2 For summer use, sow early/mid-spring outdoors.
3 For autumn use, sow early/mid-summer outdoors. May bolt prematurely in hot weather.
4 For winter and spring use, sow late summer/early autumn outdoors. These sowings provide invaluable pickings throughout winter until mid- to late spring. Can protect with cloches/crop covers, even bracken, in early winter to improve quality.

5 For productive, good-quality winter crop, sow early autumn under cover. Will continue growing on warm days when the outdoor plants stop growing.

As plants are small, seed is usually sown *in situ*, in narrow or broad drills about 10cm/4in apart, or by broadcasting. Thinning normally unnecessary. Can also be sown in seed trays or modules for transplanting, spacing plants 10cm/4in apart each way. Germination can be slow in hot weather. Sow in moistened drills, or cover beds with moist sacking or fleece until seeds germinate. Broadcasting and sowing in wide drills most appropriate for CCA seedling crop.

For good use of space, can be broadcast or planted between brassicas. Or sow between maturing onions or shallots, to follow on when onions lifted. Rarely troubled by pests or diseases, other than powdery mildew on autumn and winter crops. Ventilate well if grown under cover.

Harvesting
Mature plants ready in 12 weeks; seedlings several weeks earlier. Cut CCA seedlings as soon as they are usable size. They will resprout at least once, maybe several times. With single plants pick individual leaves as required, or cut across head leaving plant to resprout, or pull up the whole plant. (This is done where corn salad is marketed, as otherwise it wilts rapidly after picking.) Plants eventually run to seed in spring. Young flowers are edible in salads. Leave some plants to self-seed: saves you the trouble of sowing! Seedlings are easily uprooted if in 'wrong' place.

Mild flavour. Excellent in salads, especially complementing sharp-flavoured winter salad plants.

Cultivars
Large-leaved: 'Dutch', 'English', 'Italian', 'Valgros' – standard type.
'Green': 'Coquille de Louviers', 'Verte de Cambrai', 'Verte d'Etampes' ,
    'Jade', 'Cavallo', 'Vit', 'Vollhart'; productive new cvs: 'Fiesta', 'Trophy',
    'Gala'.

VSR ★★★

COURGETTES (Zucchini) *Cucurbita pepo*

Courgettes are the young, immature fruits of what are known in the British Isles as marrows but elsewhere as summer squash – see Marrows, page 281. Modern courgettes are bred for thin skins and excellent culinary quality. They are tender annuals, forming compact bushes of 60–90cm/2–3ft spread and about 45cm/18in high. Typical courgettes are 10–13cm/4–5in long, and light or dark green, yellow or striped; there are also round types. The flowers are edible. Leaves range in colour from pale yellow to mottled – some being very beautiful. (For more information on decorative qualities, see *Creative Vegetable Gardening*.)

Site and soil
As Cucumber, page 254.

Cultivation
Courgettes are naturally prolific: well-grown plants can produce twenty courgettes, so three or four plants are sufficient for most households.

For plant-raising, see Cucumber cultivation, page 254. Courgettes require soil temperature of 13–15°C/56–60°F to germinate. Sow indoors a month before last frost expected. There is no advantage in starting prematurely as plants are extremely susceptible to cold weather; very fast-growing once established. For a follow-on crop, you can make a second sowing in early summer, as cropping season is short. Harden off and protect as for cucumbers.

Plant sturdy plants when two leaves formed and third starting to develop (see illustration, page 255). Plant 90cm/3ft apart. Planting through mulching film, or mulching after planting, is recommended. Can be grown under fine nets to protect against aphids, which transmit mosaic virus. If weather dry after planting, water gently, but not in full sunshine as young plants easily scorched. Further watering generally unnecessary except on very light soils. Leaves develop an unnatural blotchy look when short of water – good indication that heavy watering is necessary. Once plants are flowering apply seaweed-based feed if not growing vigorously. Feed also later in summer if growth slowing down.

Pollination
Marrows have separate male and female flowers; pollination by insects is normally necessary to get fruit. Female flowers distinguished by small, embryonic fruit behind petals (see illustration, page 253). In very cold seasons and early in year fruits may fail to set, and hand pollination is advisable. Select fully open male flower, strip off petals and push it into centre of female flower. You can leave it there or use it to pollinate another flower. There is a natural tendency for male flowers to be produced early in year – and for female flowers to be produced later. Frustrating! No practical remedy other than waiting.

Pests and diseases
As Cucumber, page 256.

Cucumber mosaic virus Common problem; some recently introduced cvs have some, but not complete, resistance (see below). Grow under fine nets.

Harvesting and use
Courgettes can be ready within about 8 weeks of sowing. First fruits are sometimes misshapen. Golden rule: the younger the courgette, the better the flavour. For very small courgettes pick when flower still in bud; otherwise pick at point where petals drop off when courgette touched.

Courgettes must feel firm to the touch. For use as courgettes, pick long types from very small up to 10–13cm/4–5in long; round types up to about 6cm/2½in diameter. Essential to pick almost daily to encourage further cropping. Once marrow-sized fruits develop, productivity slows dramatically. If marrows are required, leave a few courgettes to develop. Some cvs produce far more acceptable marrows than others (see below). Plants are destroyed by first frost.

Many methods of cooking; peeling normally unnecessary.

Cultivars
Most F1 hybrids reliable and productive.

'Aphrodite' F1, 'Patriot' F1, 'Kojak' F1 (no spines on stems and leaves) – good-quality courgettes.

'Defender' F1, 'Supremo' F1, 'Tiger Cross' F1 – some mosaic virus tolerance.

'All Green Bush', 'Ambassador' F1, 'Early Gem' F1, 'Zebra Cross' F1, 'Badger Cross' F1, 'Tiger Cross' F1 – suitable for courgettes and marrows.

'Jemmer' F1, 'Gold Rush' F1, Parador' F1 – yellow-fruited.

'Rondo de Nice', 'Leprechaun' F1, 'Eight Ball' F1 – round fruit.

VSR ★★

CRESS *see* Mustard

CUCUMBER *Cucumis sativus*

Cucumbers are warmth-loving plants that will not stand any frost. Most forms are climbers, in varying degrees. The typical cucumber is a long green fruit, mainly used raw.

Types

Greenhouse/indoor Smooth cucumbers are often 45cm/18in long, though 'mini cucumber' group fully mature when 10–15cm/4–6in long. Vigorous plants requiring high temperatures in region of 18–30°C/ 64–86°F and high humidity to grow successfully. In temperate climates must be grown in greenhouses or polytunnels. Delicate, demanding crop, not easy to grow organically. There is a distinct division between old and new varieties:

- ∾ Old cvs – produce fruit on side shoots, so must be trained accordingly. (Nip out the growing point above the first six or seven leaves to encourage fruit-bearing side shoots). Male flowers must be removed, as fruits became bitter and misshapen if pollinated. Today these types are mainly grown for showing (see Further Reading, page 372).

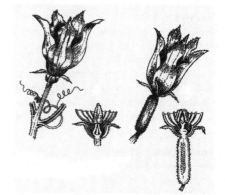

Typical cucurbit (cucumber/ squash family) flowers: male flower (left), female flower (right), and cross section.

✍ Modern 'all-female' hybrid cvs — require minimum night tempera-ture of 20°C/68°F. Fruit develops on main stem, so plants are easily trained as cordons up single string. Bred to have almost entirely female flowers, so pollination problem doesn't arise. Seed very expensive.

Ridge outdoor Shorter and rougher-skinned. Known as 'ridge' because traditionally grown on ridges to improve drainage. Mostly dark green, but there are also white-, cream- and yellow-fruited forms; some are round or oval-shaped. Much more rugged than greenhouse type with greater resistance to pests, diseases and low temperatures. All can be grown outdoors in temperate climate. Flowers must be insect-pollinated to set fruit, so never remove male flowers. Several distinct groups within type:

✍ Traditional cvs — fairly stubby, rough, prickly-skinned cucumbers. Plants are naturally sprawling rather than true climbers, but there are some non-trailing bush cvs, resembling bush courgettes. Bush cvs mainly grown in US; not highly productive, but suited to cultivation in large containers.

✍ Japanese and 'Burpless' hybrid cvs — welcome product of plant breed-ing. Relatively smooth, approaching greenhouse cucumbers in qual-ity and length; arguably better-flavoured. Climb up to 1.8m/6ft, depending on cv, with fruits up to 30cm/12in long. Key quality nat-ural vigour and robustness. Suitable for cultivation outdoors or in unheated greenhouses or polytunnels. Productive and highly recom-mended for organic gardeners.

✍ Gherkins — short, thin or stubby, prickly-skinned fruits on average 5cm/ 2in long, grown for pickling. Can also be used fresh. Sprawling plants.

✍ Round/oval-fruited 'Heirloom' cvs — fruits pale green or lemon colour, often apple- or lemon-shaped. Juicy and considered well flavoured.

Site and soil

Sunny sheltered site; tolerate light shade in summer. Protection against wind essential, especially in early stages. Soil must be reasonably fertile, moisture-retentive, humus-rich with good drainage. Very acid soils should be limed. Can prepare ground by making individual holes or trench 30cm/12in deep, 45cm/18in wide. Fill with well-rotted manure, old straw or compost, and cover with 15cm/6in soil to make a small mound to improve drainage. Rotate to avoid the build-up of soil diseases, especially in greenhouses.

Cultivation

The following applies mainly to ridge cucumbers, although all-female greenhouse cucumbers are grown much the same way. They require higher temperatures and more care to succeed well.

Grow ridge cucumbers outside or in unheated greenhouses or polytunnels. They can also be trained horizontally in frames (see page 256). Never grow ridge and all-female cvs in close proximity, or else the latter will be adversely affected by cross-pollination. Sow indoors mid-spring, in a propagator, or at minimum temperature of 20°C/68°F. As cucumbers don't transplant well, sow individually in modules or sow 2–3 seeds per 5–7.5cm/2–3in pot, thinning to strongest after germination. Sow seeds 2–2.5cm/¾–1in deep. The long-established recommendation to sow seeds on their edge has been disproved by organic growers Michael and Joy Michaud. In experiments with cucumbers, courgettes and winter squash, they found that seed germinated equally well sown flat or sideways.

Seeds usually germinate fast and keeping them healthy afterwards in cold spring weather can present a challenge! To prevent damping-off diseases, keep just moist but don't overwater. Try to maintain a minimum temperature of at least 15°C/60°F after germination. Keep in good even light, or else they become elongated and drawn. Harden off well and plant outside late spring/early summer, provided there is no risk of frost.

Plant sturdy plants at the two-to-three-leaf stage (see above). Plant with the neck of the stem just above ground level, not buried, as a precaution against neck rot. Plant climbing cvs 38–45cm/15–18in apart; sprawling and bush cvs 75–90cm/2½–3ft apart. If necessary protect with cloches or fleece in the early stages, especially if weather becomes cold, windy or wet. Stagger sowing dates to prolong season as cucumbers only crop for limited period.

Alternatively sow *in situ* under individual jam jars or cloches, thinning to one seed after germination. This method avoids transplanting. Nothing is gained by sowing in cold soil: wait until soil temperature is around 20°C/68°F, or simply feels warm to the touch.

Keep plants weeded and well watered; mulching recommended. From mid-summer onwards apply organic feed if plants not prolific. Protect young seedlings against slugs.

Cucumber, courgettes, marrow or squash plants are ready for planting out when they have two strong seed leaves and a third just developing.

Chitted cucumber seed and young plants are often available from seed suppliers – useful where propagation facilities are limited.

Training

Modern climbing cvs of ridge cucumbers require support. Older cvs climb less vigorously, but cucumbers will be of better quality if grown against a support and encouraged to climb even 1m/3ft or so.

Outdoors, train plants against trelliswork, up canes (they can be grouped in 'tepees' or tripods), or against wire or nylon netting, rigid pig net or equivalent. Mesh of about 23cm/9in square is adequate. Tie in if necessary. Allow for up to 1.5–1.8m/5–6ft growth.

In greenhouses growth is more vigorous and higher. Firm supports are required, or train up strings attached to overhead wires. Simplest to train plants up single stem. Remove side shoots which develop but do not remove any flower buds. Nip out growing point when plant reaches top of support, or at this point allow a couple of side shoots to develop and trail downwards or train them horizontally. With long-fruited cvs remove side shoots from the lower 30cm/12in of stem so that fruits won't trail on ground.

Cultivation in greenhouses

Raise plants as above. If planted in growing bags, plant two per standard bag. Main problem is build-up of greenhouse pests: prevent by maintaining high humidity. Mulch plants and paths with straw, which helps maintain humidity after spraying and keeps roots cool. In hot weather damp down with water at least once daily. If roots develop on the surface, top dress with good soil mixed with garden compost. Plants benefit if shaded from very bright sun.

Water regularly and once fruits are developing feed weekly with organic feed. With all-female cvs watch for occasional male flowers (see illustration, page 253) and remove.

Cultivation in frames

Useful method for growing ridge cucumbers in cold districts if no greenhouse/polytunnel available. Train cucumbers off the ground, for example on a horizontal trellis (see illustration, page 121). Keep frames well ventilated during the day. In hot weather spray regularly to keep down red spider mite. Top dress as above if roots appear on the surface.

Pests and diseases

Aphids Problem in some seasons.

Slugs Particularly serious in early stages.

Red spider mite Problem in warm dry weather especially under cover. Foliage becomes rusted. Burn badly infected leaves. Use biological control under cover. It may also be successful outdoors in hot summers.

Mosaic virus Leaves become mottled and distorted. Burn young infected plants and leaves from older plants. Older plants may recover, though yields will be lowered.

Powdery mildew White patches develop on leaves. No remedy. Grow resistant cvs where available.

Harvesting

Outdoor cucumbers crop mid-summer to early autumn. Indoor cucumbers ready couple of weeks earlier. Keep picking to encourage growth. With long cucumbers you can cut half of fruit while on plant, leaving rest attached. Bottom will callus over and can be used later. Small cucumbers can be pickled like gherkins.

Cultivars

Standard ridge cvs: 'Bedfordshire Prize', 'Marketmore' (good mildew resistance), 'Masterpiece'.

Japanese and 'Burpless' hybrids: 'Burpless Tasty Green' F1, 'Kyoto', 'Slice King' F1, 'Tokyo Slicer' F1, 'Chinese Long Green', 'Burpee Hybrid' F1.

All-female with good mildew resistance: 'Carmen' F1, 'Brunex' F1, 'Tyria' F1, 'Passandra' F1 (mini cucumber).

Heirloom and unusual: 'Sunsweet' F1 (lemon-shaped), 'Crystal Apple' (pale, round), 'White Wonder' (white-skinned fruits 20cm/8in long).

Gherkins: 'Conda' F1, 'Eureka' F1 – among many.

VSR ★★

ENDIVE *Cichorium endivia*

Endives are salad plants in the chicory family (confusingly called 'chicory' in many European countries) with lively green colouring and a distinct slightly piquant flavour. They are cool-season plants, at their best at temperatures of 10–20°C/50–68°F, often becoming coarse and bitter at higher temperatures. They are more pest- and disease-resistant than lettuce, and much better adapted to the low light levels and humidity of autumn and winter. Most cvs tolerate light frost. In the past plants were usually blanched to make them sweeter, crisper and creamier-coloured. With the improved modern cvs this is no longer essential. Endive has become a popular ingredient in supermarket salad packs.

Types

Curled (Frisée) Very pretty, fine, indented leaves; fairly flat head of 20–25cm/8–10in diameter. Type most suited to summer cropping, but some cvs reasonably hardy and grow well in winter. Ever-increasing choice of good cvs, each suited to sowing at certain periods. Be guided by catalogue and packet information.

Broad-leaved/Batavian (Scarole/escarole) Generally larger plants up to 30cm/12in diameter; most spreading in habit, but some older cvs fairly upright. Outer leaves broader and coarser than curled types; often incurved, creamier-coloured leaves in centre. Broad-leaved types fairly disease- and cold-tolerant; grow well in low light levels of winter, so useful lettuce substitute in late-summer to late-spring period. Withstand –9°C/16°F if sheltered and kept cut back. Respond well to CCA treatment as mature plant.

Newer cvs often intermediate between two main types.

Site and soil

Summer crops need reasonably high fertility (dig in plenty of manure and compost) and good supply of moisture throughout growth. Winter crops need good drainage, but tolerate lower fertility: excess nitrogen can lead to lush growth, making them more prone to rotting. Open site normally best; summer crops tolerate light shade.

Cultivation

Can be grown as single plants or CCA seedlings. Curled types most suitable for CCA seedlings. For single plants sow *in situ*, or in seed trays for transplanting, or in modules. Germination sometimes erratic. Seed germinates best at 20–22°C/68–72°F; hence poor germination is sometimes experienced in hot weather. Keep seedlings cool until germinated.

Sowing in seed trays and modules advisable in hot weather: transplanted crop reputedly grows faster and less bitter. Sow CCA seedlings by broadcasting, or in narrow or wide drills about 10cm/4in apart. Early sowings may bolt prematurely if temperature drops below 5°C/41°F for several days.

Space single plants 25–35cm/10–14in apart, depending on cv. With some new cvs natural blanching enhanced by close spacing at 25cm/10in apart each way. *

Sowing programme:
1 For early summer supply, sow early spring under cover in modules or seed trays, to plant outside. Or sow *in situ* for early crop CCA seedlings.
2 For main summer supply, sow mid-/late spring by any method.
3 For autumn supply outside, sow early/mid-summer by any method. In autumn you can protect with cloches/crop covers to improve quality. May stand well into winter in mild areas. Use hardy cvs for later sowings.
4 For autumn/winter crop under cover, sow mid-/late summer in modules or seed trays; plant under cover in autumn. Use hardy cvs. Cut heads and leave to resprout during winter.
5 For winter CCA seedlings under cover, sow late summer/very early autumn *in situ* under cover. Use hardy cvs.
6 For late spring supplies, sow hardy broad-leaved cvs in modules under cover late autumn. Overwinter as seedlings; plant early in year under cover or outside. May bolt prematurely but worth trying.

Keep winter crop reasonably well watered and mulched to prevent 'tipburn' – leaf margins drying out.

Blanching
Whether blanching is necessary is largely a matter of taste. Many modern cvs have fairly tight heads, so leaves are to some extent blanched naturally and have only a hint of bitterness. Curled types look very attractive blanched to near whiteness. Plants can be completely blanched by excluding all light, or partially blanched so that outer leaves remain green. Normally ready within about 10 days, but can vary. Use quickly once ready or they will deteriorate.

Blanch a few plants at a time when fully mature – generally about 12 weeks after sowing.

Leaves *must* be dry or else plants will rot when covered. Curled types most prone to rotting. Blanching can be done in various ways.

Partial blanching
1 Cover centre of plant with inverted dinner plate or something similar (see opposite), or with small purpose-made blanching caps. Be warned: both can attract slugs.
2 Tie up heads of tall-leaved types with twine or raffia.

Complete blanching

1 Cover plant with several layers of permeable black mulching fabric anchored at the edges.
2 Cover plant with a bucket, or large inverted flower pot with drainage hole blocked to exclude light, or sufficiently large blanching cap.
3 Lift and replant under cover in darkened area as for Witloof chicory (see page 242), but without cutting back the leaves. This was traditionally done in frames or cellars.

Harvesting and use

Cut across head when mature. Plants normally resprout several times, though they are less likely to do so after blanching. Endive responds well to CCA treatment at any stage, though plants may run to seed rapidly in hot weather. Protected winter crop can remain productive throughout winter into early spring. CCA seedlings often ready within 5 weeks of sowing. Number of cuts depends on sowing time and cv.

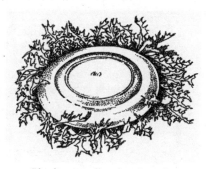

Blanching an endive using a large plate.

Mainly used raw in salads, but can be cooked: often braised.

Cultivars

Curled

For summer and autumn supplies: 'Ione', 'Frisela', 'Moss Curled'.
For autumn and winter supplies: 'Sally', 'Pancalière' (fairly hardy, suitable any sowings); 'Ruffec' and 'Wallonne' types, e.g. 'Minerva' (hardiest).

Broad-leaved

Versatile cvs: 'Elysée', 'Grosse Bouclé 2', 'Jeti', 'Stratego'.
Hardiest: 'Cornet de Bordeaux', 'Géant Maraîchère' (various improved races), 'Ronde Verte à Coeur Plein' ('Fullheart').

VSR ★★; PP curled type

FLORENCE FENNEL
(Sweet fennel, Finocchio) *Foeniculum vulgare* var. *azoricum*

Fennel is a beautiful, feathery-leaved annual, growing about 45cm/18in high. It is cultivated for the crisp, aniseed-flavoured 'bulb' formed by the overlapping bases of the leaves. In origin a Mediterranean marsh plant, it thrives in warm, moist conditions. (For cultivation of the perennial herb fennel, see herb books – see Further Reading, page 372.)

Site and soil
Must have well-drained, moisture-retentive soil, rich in organic matter. Prefers light sandy soil, but tolerates heavier soil. Avoid exposed sites.

Cultivation
There is a risk of fennel bolting rather than hearting if it is sown too early in the year, or checked by dry or cold spells. Steady fast growth is required. Raising plants in modules is highly recommended as bolting can be triggered by transplanting. Some modern cvs have good bolting resistance, but are not infallible!

Sowing programme:
1 For early summer crop, sow mid-/late spring, using bolt-resistant cvs. Soil temperature must be at least 10°C/50°F. Preferably sow in modules; otherwise sow in seed trays, prick out when seedlings very small, plant at four-to-five-leaf stage.
2 For main summer crop, sow in early summer, as above, or *in situ*, thinning to distance required.
3 For autumn crop outside or to plant under cover for early winter pickings, sow late summer in modules.

Space plants 30–35cm/12–14in apart each way.

Watch for slugs in early stages. Keep well watered; mulch to retain moisture and keep down weeds. Traditionally bulb earthed up when starting to swell to blanch it, but not essential. Tolerates light frost; cloche protection or fleece cover in autumn prolongs season.

Fennel can be grown successfully in 13cm/5in pots.

Harvesting and use
Plants mature in 10–14 weeks. Cut bulb at least 2.5cm/1in above soil level, but leave root in ground. It normally resprouts, producing small tasty shoots, delightful in salads. Such trimmed-back plants survive more frost than large leafy plants.

Use bulb raw or cooked (excellent braised). Can use fern and finely chopped stems for seasoning and in salads. If plant runs to seed use fresh or dried seed similarly.

Cultivars
'Rudy' F1, 'Selma', 'Zefa Fino', 'Cantino' – good bolting resistance.

VSR ★; PP

GARLIC *Allium sativum*

Garlic is a hardy plant generally growing up to about 30cm/12in high. The characteristically flavoured bulbs form underground. Mature bulbs are used fresh and stored for winter; the uniquely flavoured immature bulbs, known as 'green' or 'wet' garlic, are used fresh. In China garlic is also grown for its young green leaves, used fresh or blanched, and for the young flower stems (for cultivation, see *Oriental Vegetables*). Garlic cloves are white, pink and purple, and range from strong to mild in flavour. There are many strains, with much confusion over naming. Where available, use strains adapted to your region. Always buy stock certified free of disease. Garlic is widely acknowledged to have therapeutic qualities.

Site and soil
Open, sunny site. Does best on light, well-drained soil. Moderate level of fertility sufficient. Avoid freshly manured soil and very heavy, poorly drained soil, unless taking special measures (see below). Lime soil if acid. Garlic responds to potash; you can work fresh bonfire ash into ground before planting. Reasonable levels of moisture needed in growing season. Must rotate as member of onion family. Types vary in their capacity to store well.

Cultivation
Tolerates wide range of climate but may not form bulbs if grown at temperatures over 25°C/77°F. Most strains require cool period of 30–60 days with temperatures of 0–10°C/32–50°F — one reason for planting in autumn. Short storage types should be planted in autumn.

Plant plump, healthy-looking cloves, ideally about 1cm/½in diameter, broken off from garlic bulb. Discard puny cloves — or plant them further apart to compensate for their size. Alternatively plant 2cm/¾in apart to harvest as young green leaves. Garlic requires a long growing period. The earlier it is planted, the better. On suitable soil (see above) plant early to late autumn *in situ*. Otherwise plant late winter/early spring as soon as soil workable, using cvs recommended for spring planting.

Push cloves into the soil or make hole with a small dibber. Planting depth variable. On light soils plant up to 10cm/4in deep. Plant less deeply in heavier soil, but cover cloves by at least 2.5cm/1in soil. Plant flat end downwards — it's not always obvious which is which! For highest yields space cloves 18cm/7in apart each way. Alternatively space cloves 7.5–10cm/3–4in apart in rows 25–30cm/10–12in apart.

Where no alternative to growing on very heavy or poorly drained soil, put layer of coarse sand or potting soil beneath bulbs when planting to improve drainage. Work soil into ridges about 10cm/4in high, and plant in the ridges, at normal depth. Plant cloves individually in modules in autumn and overwinter in cold frames. Plant sprouted cloves outside in spring. (This produces excellent crops.)

Once established, garlic requires little attention other than the occasional weeding. Some strains produce flower stem as part of normal growth. Cutting this back by half 2–3 weeks before lifting is said to increase bulb size by as much as 20 per cent.

Harvesting

Unlike onions, garlic should be lifted when leaves start to turn yellow, generally mid- to late summer. Better to lift garlic too soon rather than too late, or bulbs shatter and may start sprouting. Bulbs may be quite deep; dig up carefully. Always handle garlic very carefully, as bruises lead to rots in store.

Dry garlic outside for 7–10 days, ideally in sunny, breezy conditions. If weather is wet, hang in greenhouse or conservatory with good through draught. It doesn't need to be 'baked' excessively in the sun.

Store hanging in bunches or plaited, or laid on wooden shelves or in boxes, in dry, frost-free conditions. Unless it is suspended, cut off the stem, leaving about 5cm/2in attached. If plaiting, moisten the leaves first to make them supple. In some varieties leaves more 'durable' than others. Ideal storage temperature 5–10°C/41–50°F. Bulbs keep 6–12 months, depending on cv. Provided bulbs are healthy, some can be kept for planting the following season. There is some evidence that home-saved strains gradually adapt to local climate.

Bulbs accidentally left in the soil often resprout the following spring, producing clusters of flavoursome leaves. Use these like chives.

Cultivars

The following strains performed well in trials in the UK.

'Cristo' (strong flavour, high yield), 'Long Keeper Improved', 'Ivory', 'Marshall's Mediterranean', 'Thermidrome' (short storage) – all performed best from autumn planting.

'Cristo', 'Snow Wight'/'Solent Wight'/'Mersley Wight' – good from both autumn and spring planting.

VSR ★

ELEPHANT GARLIC *Allium ampeloprasum*

Named on account of its enormous white bulbs and cloves, up to 10cm/4in diameter. Technically type of leek. Flavour varies from mild to quite strong. Plant in autumn a month before frost expected, or sow in modules as for garlic, above. Alternatively plant in early spring. Plant at least 2.5cm/1in deep and 20cm/12in apart. Normally ready mid-summer. Harvest as onions.

GARLIC CHIVES/CHINESE CHIVES *Allium tuberosum*

Chive-like plant; light-coloured leaves have delightful garlic flavour. Used fresh and blanched in China. Pretty white flowers also edible. For cultivation, see *Oriental Vegetables* and *The Organic Salad Garden*.

HAMBURG PARSLEY *Petroselinum crispum* var. *tuberosum*

This very hardy, dual-purpose form of parsley forms edible roots 17–20cm/6½–8in long, up to 7.5cm/3in diameter, closely resembling parsnips. The deep green glossy foliage remains green even in severe winters and can be used as a parsley substitute. This is an easily grown and useful winter vegetable.

Site and soil
Will grow in open site or semi-shade; appreciates moist situation. Tolerates poorer soil than most root crops. Soil preferably manured in the previous autumn.

Cultivation
Requires long growing season to develop large roots.

Sowing programme:
1 Sow early/late spring in drills 25cm/10in apart. Thin to 13cm/5in apart. Germination slow; seed can be mixed with radish seeds to mark rows. Alternatively station sow, sowing radish or small lettuce cv such as 'Tom Thumb' or 'Little Gem' between stations. Can also be sown in modules. Plant out before the tap root starts to develop.
2 Can also be sown mid-summer, to overwinter and give earlier crop in the following year.

Keep weed-free; mulch and water in dry summer.

Harvesting
Ready late summer until mid-spring following year. Can be left in soil all winter. Can be covered with bracken, leaves, etc., to make lifting easier in frost. For accessibility in winter can be lifted mid-/late autumn and stored in moist sand in shed, but some flavour may be lost in the process.

Scrub roots before cooking; they discolour if peeled. Roots are sweet-flavoured. Excellent roasted under joint, mashed with swedes, grated in salads, fried as chips. Can be dried for flavouring. Use leaves for flavouring and garnishing.

VSR ★; PP

ICEPLANT *Mesembryanthemum crystallinum*

The fleshy leaves and stems of this sprawling plant are covered with tiny bladders that sparkle in the sun. It is not frost hardy – its typical habitat is the Mediterranean seashore. It can be cooked as a spinach substitute (though it is not very appetising in my view), but its unusual appearance, succulent texture and refreshing, slightly salty flavour make it an unusual and worthwhile salad ingredient.

Site and soil

Not fussy about soil provided it is well-drained. Sunny site, sheltered from cold wind. Tolerates light shade in mid-summer: e.g. can be inter-cropped beneath sweet corn.

Cultivation

Naturally perennial in hot climates; treat as half-hardy annual in cool climates.

Sow indoors in seed tray or modules mid-/late spring. For early pickings, plant under cover late spring. Plant main crop outside mid-/late spring after risk of frost is over and when soil is warm. Young plants very susceptible to cold conditions. Protect with cloches in early stages. Alternatively sow *in situ* outdoors after risk of frost is past. Space plants about 30cm/12in apart each way. Can be treated as ground-cover plant.

Watch for slugs in early stages. Plants require little attention once established other than removing any flowers that appear.

For a late summer/autumn crop under cover, take stem cuttings from established plants in early summer. They root within a few weeks. Plant under cover when rooted.

Mature plants, rather unexpectedly, survive light frost. Cloche in late summer to extend season and maintain quality. Plants under cover may still be usable well into early winter.

Harvesting

First picking sometimes a month or so after planting. Pickings may continue over several weeks. Pick young leaves and small 'branches' of leaves and stems. Pick constantly to encourage more tender growth and prevent plants from running to seed. Older leaves and stems become coarse. Succulent leaves and stems are relatively slow to wilt. May keep fresh several days in fridge.

VSR ★★; PP

K A L E S *Brassica oleracea* Acephala Group

The kales are a diverse group of hardy, robust brassicas, mostly used during winter and spring. The mature leaves tend to be coarse, but some types are grown mainly for the tender, very palatable shoots produced in spring, notably during the Vegetable Gap. In recent years I have realized how valuable certain varieties of kale are as autumn-to-spring CCA crops, especially when grown under cover. They are used cooked or raw in salads. Kales are normally healthy and free of pests and diseases. I consider the following kales the most productive and worth growing, but there are many other interesting types and varieties, which can be obtained from heirloom seed libraries. (For further information, see Further Reading, page 372.)

CURLY KALE (Borecole, Scotch kale)
One of the hardiest brassicas, mostly with deeply crinkled green or blue-green leaves, but some forms have brilliant, deeply curled purple foliage. Curly kale is grown for both mature leaves and young spring shoots. Tall types grow up to 90cm/3ft high with similar spread. Compact dwarf types are often no more than 30cm/12in high and similar spread. Curly kales are also grown closely spaced as mini kale and CCA seedlings.

Site and soil
Less fussy than most brassicas, though does best in fairly rich, well-culti-vated soil. Needs good drainage. Lime soil if acid. Preferably manure previous autumn or for previous crop. Fairly resistant to clubroot. May succeed where other brassicas fail.

Cultivation and harvesting
Cultivation options:

1 For main winter/spring supply, sow mid-/late spring, thinly in seedbed, or in seed trays or modules for transplanting. Plant in permanent position early/mid-summer. Space plants 30–75cm/1–2½ft apart, depending on cv. Use the closer spacing for dwarf cvs.

   If necessary water in early stages to ensure plants are well estab-lished. Keep weed-free. Remove any lower rotting leaves. Dwarf plants can be covered with cloches/crop covers in autumn to make leaves more tender. You can give plants seaweed-based fertilizer the following spring to stimulate shoot production. Pick leaves for use from about late autumn onwards. Pick a few at a time to encourage fresh growth and prolong the season. Side shoots develop in early spring, typically from late winter until about mid-spring. Pick when young and tender, about 10–12cm/4–5in long. More develop over several weeks. Stop picking when flower buds form or stems become coarse.

2 For mini kales, use recommended cvs (see below). Sow early to late spring/early summer, *in situ*, in rows 15–20cm/6–8in apart, or in seedbed, in seed trays or in modules for transplanting. Grow plants at equidistant spacing, 15–20cm/6–8in apart each way. You can harvest whole plants when about 15cm/6in tall, about 14 weeks after sow-ing. For regular pickings over longer period, start picking a few leaves at a time, but do not denude whole plant, once plants reach 23cm/9in. Plants stand over many weeks. Occasional liquid feed beneficial to encourage continuous healthy growth. Where plants overwinter continue picking into following spring. Can be protected with cloches or crop covers in autumn to make leaves more tender.

3 A CCA seedling crop can be sown in succession throughout season, but growth is best in cooler months. Suggested sowings:
- ❧ under cover late winter
- ❧ outdoors early spring as soon as soil workable; can be covered with cloches or fleece initially
- ❧ mid-/late spring
- ❧ late summer outdoors (mild areas)
- ❧ early autumn under cover.

Sow thinly, *in situ* in single or wide drills about 15–20cm/6–8in apart. Kale grows fairly slowly, the rate of growth varying with variety and time of year. You can generally start cutting seedling leaves about 6 weeks after sowing when 5–7.5cm/2–3in high. Plants may resprout two or three times over many weeks. Alternatively you can thin out a little and cut as greens when 15–20cm/6–8in high.

Use

Kale has a fairly strong flavour. Use tender young curly kale leaves and shoots in salads. Otherwise steam, stir-fry or cook in minimum amount of water. Serve with butter or 'Glorious Garnish' sauce: 5:1 mix of vegetable oil and light soya sauce, plus crushed garlic – delicious and well worth trying! With its deep colour and attractive curly leaves, kale makes an excellent winter garnish.

Cultivars

Modern F1 hybrids stand longer than old cvs without 'yellowing'.
'Darkibor', 'Fribor', 'Showbor', 'Winterbor' – all F1 hybrids.
'Redbor' F1, 'Garna Red' – red-leaved.
'Dwarf Green Curled Afro' – older type.
'Showbor' F1, 'Starbor' F1– for mini kales.

VSR ★ single plants, ★★ CCA seedlings, ★★ mini kales; PP

BROAD-LEAVED KALE

Many vigorous varieties, often growing well over 90cm/3ft high. Leaves flat rather than curled. Mature plants grown primarily for abundant shoots in spring. Generally faster-growing than curly kale.

Cultivation

For main winter supply, grow as curly kale (1), above, spacing plants 60–75cm/2–2½ft apart.

Thin-leaved cvs excellent for CCA seedling crops, especially during the winter months.

Late autumn sowing under cover for late winter/early spring CCA supplies especially productive.

Cultivars

'Pentland Brig', 'Hungry Gap' – thin-leaved cvs suitable for mature plants and CCA seedlings.

VSR ★ CCA seedlings, ★★ single plants

RED RUSSIAN KALE

Very attractive kale with frilly edged, blue-green leaves that develop distinct purple and red tints as temperatures fall. Surprisingly mild-flavoured and smooth-textured. Plants will grow up to 70cm/27in tall, but most productive grown as CCA crop under cover or outside during winter. Smaller plants have pleasant, open habit.

Cultivation

For single plants, sow as curly kale (1), above, spacing plants about 60cm/2ft apart. You can pick individual leaves in early winter or shoots in late winter/spring.

For CCA seedlings, sow as curly kale (3), above. Make first sowings under cover late winter. (Sowings I made on 23 February 2001 under cover were cut for my niece's wedding on 5 May.) Make last outdoor sowing in mid-summer. Withstands moderate frost in good condition. Make last indoor sowings early autumn. These late sowings provide pickings over many months, until plants run to seed in hot spring weather. If plants are left in ground Russian kale will self-seed.

'Ragged Jack' is old variety of similar appearance, but dwarfer and less hardy. I have only grown it as a mature plant, spaced about 30cm/12in apart, but it may also be suitable for CCA seedlings.

VSR ★★ single plant, ★★★ CCA seedlings; PP

BLACK TUSCAN KALE

(Black kale/Black cabbage/Cavolo nero/Palm cabbage/Dinosaur kale)
Very distinctive kale producing handsome tuft of long, narrow, almost blue leaves with creped texture. Widely grown in Italy. Effectively a short-lived perennial growing well over 2m/4ft in second and third seasons, although by then very straggly. Reasonably hardy. Distinctly flavoured leaves, used cooked, often in soups, or picked young for salads.

Cultivation

For kitchen use, grow as annual. For large plants grow as curly kale (1), above, spacing plants 35–40cm/14–16in apart. For CCA seedlings, sow as Red Russian kale, above, making the autumn sowings a week or two earlier as growth is slower. Probably because of their perennial nature, black kale CCA seedlings overwintered under cover stand well into late spring the following season, after most other kales have bolted, making it particularly useful in the Vegetable Gap.

Cultivars
Little to choose between the various forms available.

VSR ★★

ORNAMENTAL KALES AND CABBAGES

Highly decorative, often brightly multicoloured plants, grown primarily for their ornamental qualities in winter. Can be used as garnish, and sparingly in salads. The kales have deeply serrated leaves and are hardiest; the cabbages are denser and more compact – but catalogue classification is often confused and misleading! Mainly grown for autumn and winter use, as colours deepen in cold weather. For cultivation, see *The Organic Salad Garden* and *Creative Vegetable Gardening*.

KOHL RABI *Brassica oleracea* Gongylodes Group

Kohl rabi is an odd but beautiful, fast-maturing brassica, which deserves to be more widely grown. The plants grow about 30cm/12in high, with the stem swelling, 'mid-stem', into a ball-like bulb roughly 5–7.5cm/2–3in diameter. There are purple- and green- or 'white'-skinned forms, the former with beautiful purplish leaves. Both types have creamy white flesh. Kohl rabi is an exceptionally nutritious vegetable with a delicate, sweet turnip flavour. Old cvs rapidly became fibrous on maturity; modern cvs are a huge improvement. The young leaves are edible. Compared with most brassicas, they are more drought-tolerant, heat-tolerant and resistant to pests and diseases, including clubroot, and may succeed where other brassicas fail.

Site and soil
Fertile, light sandy soil ideal, but tolerates heavier soil. Acid soils should be limed. Rotate in the brassica group.

Cultivation
Can mature within 8–10 weeks of sowing. Suitable for growing as catch crop, for intercropping, and as mini kohl rabi.

For continuous supply, make several sowings. Traditionally faster-maturing green cvs used for earliest sowings for main summer crop. Hardier purple cvs sown early summer onwards for winter use. Plants may bolt prematurely if sown at soil temperatures below 10°C/50°F.

Sowing programme:
1 For early summer crop, sow mid-winter/early spring in propagator. Preferably sow in modules, and plant about 6 weeks later; otherwise transplant seedlings when no more than 5cm/2in high to minimize bolting risk. Space plants 23–30cm/9–12in apart each way. You can protect with cloches or crop covers in early stages.
2 For main summer crop, sow in succession from early spring until late

summer. Sow in modules or *in situ* outdoors, in rows about 30cm/12in apart, station sowing 10cm/4in apart. Thin early as development is checked if seedlings become overcrowded. Plant or thin to spacing above.

3 If kohl rabi is popular in your household, for early winter crop, make late sowing under cover in late summer/early autumn.

Keep plants weed-free. Mulching is beneficial to retain soil moisture and encourage fast growth.

Mini kohl rabi

Very useful crop where space limited. Use recommended cvs (see below). For very early crop sow early spring under cover. Otherwise for supplies from early summer until mid-autumn sow *in situ* outside in succession from late spring until late summer. Sow in drills 15cm/6in apart. Thin plants to 2.5cm/1in apart.

Harvest at ping-pong ball size when very tender, normally within 9 weeks of sowing. Late sowings can be covered with cloches to prolong season.

Pests and diseases

Slugs, birds, flea beetle Most common problems.

Cabbage root fly Occasionally attacks.

Clubroot May affect plants, but they normally mature fast enough to avoid serious attack.

For control measures, see Cabbage, page 223.

Harvesting

With old cvs standard advice was to eat no larger than tennis-ball size as larger bulbs rapidly became 'woody'. Modern cvs remain tender when larger, and stand in good condition longer.

Moderately frost hardy. Can be left in the ground in early winter and mild weather, but quality deteriorates unless they are protected with cloches or fleece. In colder conditions lift and store in boxes of sand in frost-free shed. Remove outer leaves, but leave central tuft of leaves on bulb. Some flavour lost when stored.

Cook leaves and bulbs separately. Cook bulb unpeeled, as best flavour said to be just below the skin. Steaming recommended. Can be boiled/steamed then stuffed, served with sauces or grated raw in salads.

Cultivars

'Trero' F1, 'Rolano', 'Quickstar' F1, 'Cindy', 'Kongo' – green-/white-skinned.
'Roblau' F1, 'Blusta', 'Azur Star', 'Purple Danube' F1 – purple-skinned.
For mini kohl rabi: 'Logo', 'Rolano' – green-skinned.

VSR ★★; PP

KOMATSUNA (Mustard spinach) *Brassica rapa* Perviridis Group

The diverse 'Komatsuna' group of Japanese greens is derived by crossing various brassicas. They are characterized by large, usually glossy, bright green leaves and are notable for vigour, versatility, healthiness and tolerance of a wide range of temperatures. Some cvs are exceptionally hardy. Reputedly very nutritious, they are mainly grown for cooked greens, but young leaves and shredded mature leaves can be used in salads. Flavour varies with the cultivar, but it is generally in the cabbage spectrum with hints of mustard and spinach. Excellent value, especially in winter.

Site and soil
Open site; fertile, moisture-retentive soil. Like all oriental greens, needs to grow fast with plenty of moisture throughout growth.

Cultivation
Seems less prone to bolting from early sowings than many oriental greens. Although most cvs are very hardy, growing some plants under cover in winter is recommended. These will be exceptionally tender and more productive in mid-winter than outdoor plants.

Can be grown as single plants, harvested at any stage from small to fully mature, or as CCA seedlings. Responds well to CCA treatment at every stage.

To grow as single plants, sow *in situ* outdoors, or in seed trays or modules for transplanting. Space plants about 10cm/4in apart for small plants harvested young, or 30–35cm/12–14in apart for large plants harvested over a long period.

1 For the main late summer/autumn/winter crop outdoors, sow from early to late summer.
2 For top-quality winter-to-spring crop, sow late summer/early autumn for plants to be transplanted under cover.

To grow as CCA seedlings, sow thinly *in situ*, broadcast or sow in narrow or wide drills about 10cm/4in apart. Cut seedlings from about 10cm/4in high onwards. Several cuts can usually be made.

1 For early crop, sow mid-/late winter under cover.
2 For summer-to-autumn crop, sow outside early spring, as soon as soil workable, until late summer. Early and late sowings can be protected with cloches or crop covers to improve quality.
3 For winter/spring crop, sow early autumn under cover.

Pests and diseases
Theoretically susceptible to all brassica pests and diseases (see Cabbage, page 223), but generally a healthy crop. Growing under fine nets recom-

mended in summer months to protect against flying pests.

Harvesting and use

Average days from sowing to harvest varies with cv and sowing date: seedlings 20 to 35; small plants 35 (summer) to 60 (winter); large plants 55 (summer) to 80 (winter). Cut whole heads of young plants, or single leaves of larger plants when usable size. Leave plants to resprout; they normally remain productive over many months. Plants eventually run to seed in late spring.

The young flowering shoots are tasty raw or cooked. If eating raw, have trial taste first as some cvs are very peppery at flowering shoot stage. Use young leaves, young stems, flowering shoots and shredded older leaves raw in salads. Otherwise cook by any methods suitable for greens.

Cultivars

'Komatsuna', 'Tendergreen', 'Torason', 'Green Boy' F1.

Note: Excellent winter-hardy cvs 'Hiroshimana' and 'Shirona' (technically considered types of loose Chinese cabbage) perform like komatsuna. Seed currently rarely available. If obtained, grow like komatsuna and use for winter greens.

VSR **** CCA seedlings, *** single plants

LAMB'S LETTUCE see Corn salad

LAND CRESS (American land cress, Upland cress) *Barbarea verna*

The flavour of this very hardy, low-growing, glossy-leaved biennial is almost identical to watercress, though the leaves are coarser. Leaves remain green all winter. It is an easily grown watercress substitute, available all year round if sown regularly.

Site and soil

Requires moist, humus-rich soil. Succeeds in damp, semi-shaded positions unsuitable for many vegetables. Can be grown in borders and corners that receive little sun. Suitable for intercropping between taller vegetables, such as winter brassicas. Avoid exposed, dry situations, especially in mid-summer.

Cultivation

Can be grown as single plants or CCA seedlings.

Sowing programme:

1 For summer use, sow early spring to early summer.
2 For winter/spring use (probably the most useful crop), sow mid-summer to early autumn. You can plant late sowings under cover for top-quality winter crop.

For single plants sow by broadcasting, or in drills 23cm/9in apart.

Water drills thoroughly beforehand in dry weather. Alternatively sow in seed trays or modules and transplant. Thin or transplant to about 15cm/ 6in apart. For CCA seedlings, broadcast or sow in narrow or wide drills about 15cm/6in apart.

Young seedlings may be attacked by flea beetle, especially in hot weather. Keep well watered or take protective measures.

Harvesting and use

First leaves can normally be picked within about 8 weeks of sowing. May run to seed prematurely in hot weather/dry conditions; keep plants well watered.

Pick leaves as required. Leave plants to resprout, though, in my experience, this is not very productive. Probably better to make successive sowings. Will stand outside all winter, but quality much improved by protection with cloches or crop covers, or even with light covering of straw or bracken.

Plants run to seed early following spring. Will often conveniently seed themselves if left undisturbed in dampish soil. If dense crop of seedlings results, treat as CCA seedling crop. Otherwise thin out or transplant seedlings if necessary.

Mainly used as salad plant. Can be cooked as a substitute for watercress.

VSR★

LEEKS *Allium porrum*

A culinary staple, leeks are hardy winter vegetables in the onion family, grown for the long white shaft at the base of the stem. The natural blanching of the stem is enhanced by deep planting.

Site and soil

Open site. Leeks thrive in fertile, well-cultivated soil. Work in plenty of compost or well-rotted manure before planting, preferably during the previous autumn. The ideal pH is 6.5–7.5, so very acid soils should be limed. Avoid compacted soil. Rotate with the onion group. Some evidence that including leeks in a rotation may reduce clubroot infection in brassicas. Their fibrous root system seems to improve soil structure.

Types

Leeks are classified roughly according to main season of maturity; in practice groups overlap.

- ✿ Early – late summer/autumn
- ✿ Mid – winter
- ✿ Late – following spring.

Earlier cvs are generally taller, paler, longer white shaft, less hardy. Later cvs are shorter, broader, less white shaft, darker often blue-green leaves, hardier.

Cultivation

The key to growing large leeks is good soil, long growing season, large transplants, wide spacing. For mini leeks, see overleaf.

Leeks can be sown *in situ*, but it is preferable to use transplanting system, sowing in seedbed, seed trays or modules. This eliminates risk of weed competition in early stages and enables deep planting – necessary to produce long blanched shaft. Leeks grow well multisown in modules, with three to four seeds per module. Sow 1–2cm/½–¾in deep. Sow indoors at 10–15°C/50–60°F. Leeks germinate poorly at soil temperatures below 7°C/45°F.

For continuous supply, make several sowings, starting with earliest cvs:
1 Indoors in propagator late winter/early spring. Harden off well before planting out. Mainly early cvs.
2 Indoors, or outdoors provided soil workable and warm, early/mid-spring. Can be sown under cloches. Mainly mid-season cvs.
3 Indoors or outdoors late spring. Late cvs.

Plant leeks 10–15 weeks after sowing, ideally when about 20cm/8in tall (see Planting system, below). Plant in sequence from early to late summer.

Leek size is influenced by spacing. For reasonable yield of large leeks, space plants about 23cm/9in apart each way, or grow them 15cm/6in apart in rows 30cm/12in apart. (This enables intercropping with small lettuce, CCA seedlings, or winter salads such as corn salad, land cress, winter purslane.) Closer spacing, 10–15cm/4–6in apart in rows 30cm/12in apart, will give a high yield of slimmer leeks. Plant multisown leeks 23cm/9in apart each way.

Water in when planting. If dry weather follows, water gently every day until plants are established, at rate of about 70ml/⅛ pint per plant. Further watering is not normally necessary unless conditions very dry or exceptionally large leeks required. Occasional liquid feeds during the growing season are beneficial.

Planting system

Leeks can be planted on the flat, but are normally planted in holes to get blanched stem (right).

Make 15–20cm/6–8in deep hole with dibber. Drop leek in hole. Water gently with fine spout. Allow earth to fall into hole naturally in due course around the stem, so that it becomes blanched.

Alternatively plant in shallow trench, or V-shaped drill about 10cm/4in deep and wide. Gradually fill this with soil as plant grows, to blanch it. Try to prevent soil from falling between the leaves. The stems can also be earthed up above ground level to increase blanching.

Note: Belgian research has indicated that, contrary to popular belief, the traditional practice of trimming leaf tips and root ends before planting probably lowers yields. Leaf tips can be trimmed if trailing on soil.

Check leeks for several days after planting as worms often push them out. Replant if necessary.

Harvesting

Leeks ready from late summer onwards. Lift as required. Early varieties stand in good condition for at least 3 months. Mid-season varieties stand into winter, late-season varieties until spring.

If ground required for other crops or cultivation in spring, uproot leeks and 'heel in' to keep them fresh (see below).

Heeling in leeks in a shallow angled trench to preserve them at the end of the season. Cover the stems with soil.

Potager enthusiasts can leave a few stems to flower: they look beautiful. Use tiny individual flowers for garnish and seasoning. Dry stems and heads for dried-flower arrangements.

Mini leeks

Small, delicately flavoured leeks. Less demanding crop recommended for small gardens. Use suitable cvs (see below).

Sow early spring to mid-summer *in situ,* either in shallow wide drills, spacing seeds 0.5–1cm/¼–½in apart, or in rows 15cm/6in apart, spacing seeds 1cm/½in apart.

Pencil-thin leeks ready for pulling after about 13 weeks when 15–20cm/6–8in tall.

In my experience mini leeks can be left standing for many weeks without loss of quality; in mild winters they are still usable and tender the following spring, even after overwintering. Cook or use raw in salads.

Pests and diseases

Leeks relatively trouble-free – and generally surmount most problems.

Slugs Relish leaves but effect not as devastating as might be expected.

Cutworm Grubs can attack roots of young plants. Watering heavily when grubs are young is by far the best remedy.

Rust Leaves develop rust-coloured postules. Most serious in hot weather; seems to be on the increase. Lowers yields. No remedy, though cvs with considerable resistance are becoming available. Preventive measures include burning infected plants, destroying plant debris and practising rotation. In practice leeks normally usable though unsightly.

Leek moth Increasing in southern parts of UK. Tiny caterpillars tunnel into leaves and eventually deep into plant. If serious, grow under insect-proof nets.

Thrips Seen as silver dots on leaves. If serious, control by spraying.

White tip Fungal disease affecting leaf tips. Seems to be increasing in some areas, but no organic remedies.

Cultivars
Early: 'Carlton' F1 (very early), ^'King Richard', 'Poncho', 'Zermatt', 'Jolant'.
Mid: 'Newton' F1, 'Upton' F1, ^'Poristo', ^'Autumn Mammoth 2-Hannibal', 'Neptune'.
Late: ^'Musselburgh' (reliable old favourite), 'Bandit', 'Farinto', 'Porbella'.
Good rust resistance: 'Bandit', 'Porbella', ^'Poristo'.
Mini leeks: 'King Richard', 'Lancelot', ^'Jolant' and any early varieties.

VSR ★★; PP

LETTUCE *Lactuca sativa*

Lettuce is the most widely grown salad plant of all, and is ideally suited to temperate cool climates. While the standard lettuce today is green, there are also beautiful red- and bronze-leaved varieties in virtually every type.

Types
Divided broadly into hearting and non-hearting or loose-leaf types; also a few intermediate semi-hearting forms.

Hearting types
- ❀ Butterhead/roundhead/cabbagehead – flattish, gently rounded heads with soft, buttery-textured leaves. Mostly well flavoured, but the leaves wilt soon after picking. Fast-growing: summer butterheads mature about 12 weeks after sowing. Tendency to run to seed once mature, especially in warm weather.
- ❀ Crispheads – compact hearts of crisp leaves. Generally slower-maturing and slower-bolting than butterheads, standing about a week longer when mature. Include:
  - ❀ Iceberg type – name given to very crisp types sold with outer leaves stripped off. Many find Icebergs poorly flavoured, though more recently introduced reddish cvs have much more flavour.
  - ❀ Batavian type – traditional European group with crisp texture. Leaves thicker than butterheads, thinner than standard crispheads; some cvs green, some red tinted. Tend to be relatively hardy. Widely considered to have notable flavour.

∾ Cos/romaine – large, tall, upright, somewhat loose-hearted lettuces. Thick, slightly bubbled leaves with sweet 'real' flavour. Slower to mature than the cabbageheads. Many cvs relatively hardy.

   ∾ Semi-cos group – small-framed, crisp-hearted, exceptionally sweet cos lettuces typified by the well-known cv 'Little Gem'. One of the best cvs for small gardens.

Non-hearting loose-leaved types Plants form loose tuft of leaves and occasionally small, loose heart. Much slower bolting than headed lettuces; ideal for CCA harvesting over many weeks or months. Very productive where space limited. Generally vigorous and healthy. Very versatile in use. Distinct types include:

∾ Salad Bowl cvs – spreading habit. Characterized by indented leaves, in some cvs shaped like oak leaves. Soft, mild-flavoured leaves wilt rapidly once picked. Name 'Salad Bowl' loosely used for all non-hearting types.

∾ Lollo types – ground-hugging, very deeply curled leaves. Deep red and green cvs. Highly decorative so often grown in flower beds. Rated more highly for appearance than flavour. Exceptionally dark-coloured and near black cvs known as 'Double Red' and 'Triple Red'.

∾ Catalogna type – taller, narrow, indented leaves, arrow-shaped, often reddish hues. Generally distinctive flavour and seem to be amongst hardiest.

∾ Cutting lettuces – group of traditional continental cvs used for CCA seedling crops. Give very quick returns throughout growing season. Smooth and crisp-leaved cvs available.

∾ Stem lettuce (Asparagus lettuce, Celtuce) – Asiatic type grown primarily for the stem rather than the leaves. Stem can be up to 7.5cm/3in thick and 30cm/12in long. For cultivation, see page 279.

Site and soil
Does best on light, well-drained, fertile soil, slightly acid to slightly alkaline. Dig in plenty of well-rotted organic matter beforehand to make soil moisture-retentive. Avoid very dry soils. Rotate around garden to prevent build-up of the soil pest root aphid. Open site normally preferable, but summer lettuce tolerates light shade. Small cvs like 'Little Gem', 'Blush' and 'Tom Thumb' and CCA seedlings useful for intercropping.

Cultivation
With successive sowing, choice of appropriate cv and use of protected cropping, you can have lettuce almost all year round in the UK. For hearted crop in mid-winter, a heated greenhouse is normally necessary. (In my view it is more rewarding to grow endives, Sugar Loaf chicory and oriental greens for this period.)

Sowing options:
1 *In situ*, for
   ∾ CCA seedlings and leaf lettuce (see pages 278–9)
   ∾ summer sowings in hot weather, as lettuce transplants badly in hot dry conditions; the alternative is to sow in modules
   ∾ some overwintering sowings.
2 In modules, preferably, or seed trays for transplanting. These methods produce good plants.
3 In a seedbed to transplant. Only advisable where no facilities for raising plants. Germination often erratic on account of weather or soil conditions; seedlings vulnerable to soil pests.

Lettuce germinates well at low temperatures, but some types fail to germinate or germination is erratic, if soil temperature rises above 25°C/77°F during the critical period within a few hours of sowing. Potentially a problem from around late spring onwards. Butterhead types and overwintered lettuce sown in late summer most vulnerable. This can be overcome by:

∾ sowing between 2.00 and 4.00 p.m., so that critical period occurs in the evening or at night
∾ keeping seed in a fridge for a week or two before sowing to break the dormancy
∾ sowing in seed trays or modules, and then putting them in a cool place to germinate, or covering with damp newspaper until germination
∾ sowing on outdoor seedbed, watering soil before sowing to lower its temperature
∾ using crisphead cvs which germinate at soil temperatures up to 29°C/85°F.

When sowing *in situ*, start thinning when seedlings about 5cm/2in high. In cool conditions thinnings can be transplanted to give a succession, normally maturing about 10 days later. Transplant at four-to-five-leaf stage, so that the lowest leaves are just above soil level. Equidistant spacing strongly recommended, as lettuces blanket soil well when mature. Spacing varies with type and cv:

∾ small cvs: 15–20cm/6–8in apart each way
∾ standard butterheads: 27cm/11in apart each way
∾ crispheads: 33–38cm/13–15in apart each way
∾ large cos and Salad Bowl types: 35cm/14in apart each way.

If growing in rows adjust the spacing accordingly – see page 94. Planting through a mulch or mulching after planting is highly beneficial.

For continuous supply of hearted lettuce, it is advisable to sow 'little and often' in succession, roughly every 2 or 3 weeks. This will avoid the common problem of surplus bolting lettuce. Loose-headed types remain in good condition longer and can be cut over several months. Two sowings are normally sufficient for spring-to-autumn supply.

Sowing programme for hearted crop:

1 For early summer supplies, use cos types, butterheads (especially any recommended for early sowings) and Salad Bowl types. Make first sowing late winter (warm areas) or early spring (colder areas). Sow in seed trays or modules in gentle heat in propagator; or sow *in situ* in frames or under cloches. Thin out or transplant outside in early/mid-spring. You can protect with crop covers initially; remove them after 3–4 weeks, or earlier in very hot weather.

2 For main summer to mid-autumn supplies, use any types except butterheads recommended only for early sowings. Choose mildew-resistant cvs for late sowings. Sow in succession from spring to mid-summer. Use any methods for first and last sowings. Make mid-summer sowings *in situ* or sow in modules to transplant. Lettuce grows at different rates throughout the season. For continuous supply make 'next' sowing when the seedlings from previous sowing appear through the soil. In late autumn you can cover plants with cloches to prolong the season.

3 For winter and spring supplies (grown in unheated greenhouse or equivalent), use only butterhead or crisphead cvs recommended for winter greenhouse/protected production. Loose-leaved types sometimes successful. Sow late summer to mid-autumn, at optimum time specified for each cv. Sow in modules or seed trays. Transplant under cover late autumn onwards. Note: Success of these crops is dependent on weather, light levels and general plant health. Winter lettuce vulnerable to winter/spring fungal diseases. Avoid overcrowding and keep plants well ventilated to minimize risk.

4 For late spring/early summer supplies (overwintered outdoors), use cos and hardy butterhead cvs. Sow late summer or early autumn *in situ*. Thin to no more than 7.5cm/3in apart by late autumn. Thin to final spacing in spring. Although lettuces are hardy, cover with cloches or crop covers to improve quality and for earlier crop. Apply organic feed in spring to stimulate growth.

Sowing programme for CCA crop:

Use cutting lettuces, most loose-leaved types including Salad Bowl and Lollo, most cos and semi-cos types, purpose-made mixes of red and green cvs. Highly productive method of growing lettuce in limited space. Cut small leaves when 5–10cm/2–4in high. Normally ready 3–4 weeks after sowing; usually resprout to give a second, occasionally even a third cutting. Can be sown throughout growing season, but mid-summer sowings may bolt rapidly or quickly become coarse. The following sowings prove most productive:

ᴥ very early spring under cover
ᴥ spring outdoors
ᴥ late summer/early autumn outdoors
ᴥ early/mid-autumn under cover – this sowing may remain productive during winter until the following spring.

Sow in narrow or wide drills about 10cm/4in apart. Aim to space seeds about 1cm/½in apart.

For good-quality lettuce, fast growth and an adequate supply of moisture are essential. In dry weather weekly watering at rate of 22 litres per sq. m/4 gallons per sq. yd recommended. If regular watering not feasible, apply one heavy watering at 'critical period' 7–10 days before plants mature. Keep plants weed-free. Extra feeding normally unnecessary in fertile soil. Apply seaweed-based fertilizer if plants not growing well.

'Leaf lettuce' system
Very productive method of growing lettuce leaves developed at the Wellesbourne research station, to provide crisp cos lettuce leaves for catering trade without having to pull lettuce heads apart. The following formula was adapted from the technique. It aims to keep family of four in the UK supplied with lettuce from a small area from late spring to autumn, with successive sowings. Irregular sowing times suggested compensate for varying growth rates throughout season.

Sow approximately 1 sq. m/3 sq. ft at each sowing. Sow in fertile, weed-free ground. Sow in rows about 13cm/5in apart. Aim to space plants about 2.5cm/1in apart in row. Sow weekly from mid- to late spring. Cut each sowing twice, as with CCA seedlings above, cutting when leaves 8–13cm/3¼–5in high. Make the first cut 50 days or so later in early summer; second cut after another 50 days, i.e. from mid- to late summer. Sow weekly in late summer to maintain continuity. Make first cut about 24 days later in early autumn; second cut further 31 days later in mid-autumn. Unless you are experimentally inclined, only use tested cos cvs such as 'Lobjoits', 'Valmaine', 'Paris White Cos'. Others may become bitter under this system.

Stem lettuce
Grow like headed lettuce, making main sowing in late spring and early summer. Space plants 30cm/12in apart each way. Requires plenty of moisture throughout growth. Harvest stems at any stage once at least 2.5cm/1in diameter, roughly 14 weeks after sowing. Stems can be lifted in autumn, leaves trimmed off except for the top tuft, and stored for up to 2 months in cold frames at temperatures just above freezing. Slice stem into salads or stir-fry. Very pleasant lettuce flavour. Leaves only palatable raw when very young. (For further information, see *Oriental Vegetables*.)

Pests and diseases

Slugs, snails, cutworm, leatherjackets Attack below and above ground in early stages. Take standard control measures.

Birds Can be damaging. Protect with fine nets or black cotton.

Leaf aphids Take standard control methods as soon as noticed. Some cvs resistant to some aphid species, e.g. 'Barcelona', 'Sylvesta', 'Smile'.

Root aphids White, soil-inhabiting aphids colonize roots and cause sudden wilting (see illustration, page 133). No remedy. Practise rotation. Use cvs with some resistance, e.g. 'Musette', 'Libusa', 'Robinsons', 'Roxette'.

Fungal diseases Most common in early spring and autumn.

Damping off Occurs at seedling stage.

Downy mildew (**Bremia lactuca**) Angular patches on leaves, white spores on leaf undersides, leaves eventually turn brown and plants die. Transplanted crops less susceptible than direct sown. Grow resistant cvs.

Grey mould (**Botrytis cinerea**) Plants rot at base of stem. No resistant cvs at present. General preventive measures: grow plants well, thin seedlings early, avoid overcrowding, water soil not foliage, keep greenhouses well ventilated, remove and burn infected leaves.

Lettuce mosaic virus Seed-borne disease spread by aphids, causing stunted growth, yellow mottled leaves. Burn infected plants, control aphids if possible.

Harvesting and use

Hearting types Normally pull up when required. Heads maturing in early spring can be cut across stump, which may resprout to give secondary (very useful, but less than perfect-looking) head in about 5 weeks' time. Later in season secondary leaves tend to be bitter.

Non-hearting types Cut across head or pick individual leaves as required.

Lettuce is normally used raw in salads, but can be cooked and used in soup – a good way of utilizing bolted plants.

Cultivars
Enormous choice!

Butterhead
General use: 'Clarion', 'Libusa', ^'Diana', ^'Nancy', 'Sylvesta', 'Musette', 'Plenty' (all mildew-resistant); 'Marvel of Four Seasons' (reddish), 'Tom Thumb'.

Winter under cover: 'Novita', 'Columbus', 'Oscar', 'Troubadour'.
Hardy overwintering: 'Valdor', 'Arctic King'.

Crisphead
General use: 'Roxette', 'Barcelona', 'Court', ^'Challenge' (all mildew-resistant); ^'Robinson', 'Saladin'.
General use Batavian type: 'Rouge Grenobloise', 'Regina Ghiacci'/'Queen of the Ice', 'Nevada', 'Pierre Benite', 'Carmen', 'Magenta', 'Kendo' ('Little Gem' × Batavian).
Summer use Iceberg type: 'Saladin'; 'Blush' and 'Sioux' (reddish).
Winter under cover: 'Kellys', 'Olympus'.
Cos: 'Lobjoits Green Cos', 'Valmaine', 'Corsair', 'Paris White', ^'Remus', 'Cosmic', ^'Pinokkio'.
Semi-cos: ^'Little Gem', 'Jewel', 'Sherwood', 'Winter Density', 'Pearl', 'Rosny' (pink blush).

Loose leaf
Salad Bowl type: red and red-flecked – 'Valdai', 'Gaillarde', ^'Cerize', 'Freckles'; green – 'Smile', ^'Frisby', 'Frillice'.
Lollo: red – 'Lollo Rossa', 'Valeria', 'Mascara', 'Ibis', ^'Revolution' and ^'Malibu' (double red); green – 'Lobi'.
Catalogna types: 'Carnival', 'Catalogna', 'Cocarde', 'Devil's Tongue'.

VSR ★★★ summer, CCA and leaf lettuce; PP loose-leaved types

MARROWS (Vegetable marrow, Summer squash) *Cucurbita pepo*

There is much debate about the dividing line between marrows, or summer squash, and winter squash and pumpkins. For practical purposes marrows can be classed as those gourds which are normally used fresh, and those (sometimes called 'autumn' or 'intermediate' squash) which can be stored for one or two months; the latter merge and overlap with winter squash and pumpkins (see page 330), which develop harder skins on maturity and can be stored for longer periods. For courgettes, which are marrows picked at an immature stage, see page 250.

Marrows are tender annuals. They can be bush, semi-bush or trailing in habit. Trailing cvs may spread 1.5–1.9m/5–6ft or more, and can be trained to climb upwards. The fruits are very diverse in colour and shape. Flowers and shoot tips of trailing forms are edible.

Main types

Classic English 'vegetable marrow' Mature fruits about 30cm/12in long and up to 13cm/5in diameter. Mostly trailing or climbing but some bush forms. Skin colour ranges from creamy white, to yellow to all shades of green; often striped. Widely considered 'watery' and poor flavour. 'Spaghetti marrow' type has flesh of spaghetti-like texture and appearance when cooked. (My personal view – still no flavour!) Short storage.

Custard marrow/patty pan/scallop Fruits 'pie-like'; flattish with raised centre and scalloped edges. Skin colour from white, to emerald green, to yellow. Mostly statuesque bushes up to 90cm/3ft diameter and 60cm/2ft high. Generally best flavoured if harvested small, about 4–7.5cm/1½–3in; but most cvs also good stuffed and baked when about 13cm/5in diameter.

Crookneck Name from narrow, curved neck; slightly bulbous fruit, sometimes smooth, sometimes bumpy skin. Good eating quality. Bush habit. Best harvested 10–15cm/4–6in long.

Round-fruited Bush types can be harvested young as courgettes or up to 13cm/5in diameter for stuffing (for round trailing types, see Winter squash/Pumpkins, page 330).

Miscellaneous 'Tromboncino' – vigorous, climbing Italian variety; narrow fruits up to 1m/3½ft long while still retaining flavour.

Site and soil
Sunny, sheltered site. Soil as Cucumber, page 254.

Cultivation
Raise plants as Cucumber, page 254. Require soil temperature of 13–15°C/56–59°F to germinate. Plant bush types about 90cm/3ft apart; trailing types 45cm/18in apart if you are encouraging them to climb; 1.2m/4ft apart if trailing on ground. (For supports, see Winter squash, page 332).

Keep mulched and well watered; don't water in full sun or else plant may get leaf scorch. You can liquid feed from mid-summer if growth appears to be slowing.

Pick when they reach size required.

Pests and disease
As Cucumber, page 256.

Cultivars
Vegetable marrows: 'Long Green Trailing', 'Table Dainty', 'Hasta La Pasta' F1 (Spaghetti marrow). See also Courgettes, page 252.
Custard marrows: 'Custard White', 'Custard Yellow' (in my experience 'White' has better mildew resistance than 'Yellow'), 'Green Patty', 'Scallop Scallopini', 'Sunburst' F1, 'Peter Pan' F1, 'Yellow Bird' F1.
Crookneck: 'Yellow Crookneck', 'Sundance' F1.

VSR ★★; PP

MELONS see Further Reading, page 372.

MIBUNA GREENS *Brassica rapa* var. *nipposinica*

This fast-growing Japanese brassica forms a dense architectural clump with a spread of 25–30cm/10–12in or more. The narrow strap-like leaves are 30–45cm/12–18in long, and have a pleasant mild mustard flavour. It is moderately hardy, surviving about –6°C/21°F in the open. Rarely troubled by pests or diseases, it tolerates a wide range of temperatures but is most useful as late summer to winter greens. It is closely related to mizuna greens and used the same way (see below).

Cultivation
As Mizuna greens, below. Mibuna is inclined to bolt prematurely from spring sowing. Grow as single plants or as CCA seedlings; not quite as productive as mizuna.

Cultivars
'Green Spray' F1 only named cv currently available.

VSR **; PP

MIZUNA GREENS (Kyona, Potherb mustard)
Brassica rapa var. *nipposinica*

This is a beautiful Japanese brassica with glossy, serrated, dark green leaves with narrow white stalks. Mature plants form clumps up to 28cm/11in high, often over 30cm/12in across. It is a very adaptable, vigorous, easily grown plant, tolerating high and low temperatures. If kept cropped it will survive about –10°C/14°F in the open. It has a refreshing, mild mustard flavour.

Site and soil
Does best in fertile soil, but tolerates wide range of soils and conditions. Mid-summer crop requires plenty of moisture or may bolt prematurely. Normally grown in open situation, but tolerates light shade mid-summer. Very decorative; can be grown in flower beds in patches or as edging.

Cultivation
Very versatile plant. Grow as single plants or as CCA seedlings. Responds to CCA treatment at every stage. Excellent for undercropping and inter-cropping both as single plants kept compact by constant cutting or as CCA seedlings.

Sowing methods and times, as Komatsuna, page 270. In addition late spring to early summer sowings may succeed, as mizuna has more resistance to bolting prematurely from spring sowings than many oriental greens. Still some risk of bolting in very dry conditions.

Space plants 10cm/4in apart for small plants, 20–23cm/8–9in apart for medium plants, 30cm/12in apart for large plants. Thinnings can be transplanted or used in salads.

Excessive rainfall or snow can cause winter crop to rot. Protect out-door crops with cloches or low polytunnels if these are likely to occur.

Pests and diseases
Theoretically, mizuna greens are subject to common brassica pests (see Cabbage, page 223), but in practice flea beetle on young plants is most serious problem. Take standard measures, or grow under fine nets to protect from flying pests.

Harvesting and use
In good growing conditions you may be able to cut CCA seedlings within about 3 weeks of sowing; larger plants within 6–8 weeks. Pick single leaves or cut across whole plant about 5cm/2in above ground level, leaving to resprout. Can be cut frequently – sometimes up to five times over many months before running to seed. May even resprout after cutting back flowering shoots in spring.

Use whole young leaves or shredded mature leaves in salads. Can be steamed, stir-fried or used in soup. Popular pickling vegetable in Japan.

Cultivars
'Mizuna' (deeply serrated leaves); 'Tokyo Beau' F1, 'Tokyo Belle' F1 (broader leaved, hardier).

VSR *** single plants, **** CCA seedlings; PP

MUSTARD *Sinapsis alba*, SALAD RAPE *Brassica napus* var. *napus*, GARDEN CRESS *Lepidium sativum*

All these seedlings are commonly grown for use in salads and sandwiches all year round. Salad rape is milder flavoured and often used as a mustard substitute in 'mustard and cress' packs. Cress has both finely curled and broader flat-leaved types, which tend to be slower-growing. All can be grown indoors or in the garden.

Cultivation indoors
Sow in shallow boxes, seed trays or other shallow containers on thin layer of well-sifted soil, soil-less compost, bulb fibre or sifted leaf mould, or on dishes on damp flannel or moist paper towelling. Alternatively, use a patented 'raft' sprouter, in which seeds are sown in a fine mesh screen, suspended over water (see illustration, opposite). If you use soil or similar base, seedlings should give a second crop. Water sowing medium gently before sowing.

Sow seeds fairly thickly and evenly on surface; press in gently with board; do not cover with soil. Cover container or put in dark to encourage rapid growth. Move into light when seedlings 2.5cm/1in high, to become green.

*Mustard seed
sprouting on a base.*

Kitchen towel

Moisture-retaining material

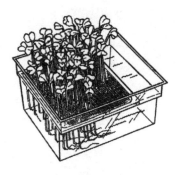

*Patented raft sprouter. Seeds are
sown on the screen, which fits
on to a ledge in the container.
After germination, roots dangle
in the water, so the seedlings
make a dense upright mat.
Change the water every 2 days.*

Mustard and rape normally germinate faster than cress, so if wanted together, sow 3 days after cress, in same or separate container. New cvs of cress are much faster-growing and can be sown at same time. In practice germination rates of different cvs of mustard, cress and rape are variable. Worth doing small trials to test, then sow slowest-germinating first. Flavour also varies; some cress cvs more pungent than others.

Cut for eating when 4–5cm/1½–2in high. At day temperature of 15–18°C/59–64°F older cress cvs ready for cutting 10 days after sowing; mustard and rape after 7 days.

Sow for succession at weekly or 10-day intervals all year round.

Quick method of resowing: scrape off cut stalks, sprinkle soil on top and resow.

Cultivation outdoors
Light soil; open site spring and autumn; shaded site in summer. Spring and autumn sowings best value; summer sowings run to seed fast. Broadcast seed in small patches, or intersow, e.g. between newly planted brassicas or on ground above newly planted potatoes.

Useful late sowing: early/mid-autumn under cover in unheated greenhouse, frame, etc. after tomatoes or summer crops cleared. Make one or two cuts in early winter. Growth normally ceases in mid-winter, but restarts very early in spring. Continue cutting until plants run to seed in spring. Very early sowings under cover also recommended.

In cool weather and moist soil four or five cuts can be made in succession. Rape is slowest to run to seed. Can be left to grow 20–25cm/ 8–10in high for use as greens. Provides pickings over many months, whereas cress and mustard become too coarse and peppery at later stages. Main drawback is that rape attracts slugs.

Relatively easy to save your own seed from all three.

Cultivars

Cress
Fast-growing curled: 'Victoria', 'Sprint', 'Polycress'.
Plain-leaved: 'Super Salad', 'Broad-Leaved', 'Greek' (distinctive flavour).

Mustard
'Tilney', 'Albatross'.

Rape
'Broad-leaved Essex', 'Hot Stuff' (forage rape).

VSR ★★★★

MUSTARDS, ORIENTAL *Brassica juncea*

This large group of rugged oriental vegetables is gradually being introduced to the West. Most are hardy and at their best during the winter. The leaves are somewhat coarse, but have a gutsy flavour, and are superb steamed or stir-fried with milder oriental greens. In some types the stems are thickened and exceptionally well flavoured. Really worth growing for 'something different' in winter.

Below are a selection of the many types in existence. Be prepared for considerable confusion over names in seed catalogues! For more information, see *Oriental Vegetables*.

Site and soil
Not as fussy as many brassicas, but do best in fertile, moisture-retentive, well-drained soil, on open site.

General cultivation
Fast-growing like most oriental greens; generally mature within 2–3 months of sowing. Have tendency to bolt from spring and early summer sowings.

Sowing programme:
1 For autumn-to-spring crops, make main sowing mid- to late summer.

2 For more productive, top-quality, winter crop, you can transplant under cover in early autumn.

Best sown in seed trays or modules and transplanted, but can be sown *in situ*. Outdoor plants can be covered with cloches/row covers in winter to improve quality, but this is not essential.

Generally healthy plants free of pests and diseases. Slugs and flea beetle in early stages most likely problems. Take standard control measures.

Mustards run to seed in following spring, becoming very hot-flavoured.

LARGE-LEAVED PURPLE MUSTARDS

Handsome large-leaved mustards. Crepe-like leaves with varying degrees of purple tints. Colours intensify at low temperatures. Easily grow 28cm/11in high with similar spread. Reasonably hardy. Very decorative in winter. Currently available cvs: 'Red Giant', 'Osaka Purple', 'Miike Giant'

Cultivation

For large plants, as General cultivation, above. Space plants about 30cm/12in apart. Cut whole plant or individual leaves as required. Will resprout over many weeks, especially where grown under cover, though not as vigorous as some types.

For CCA seedlings, sow from spring (first sowing under cover) to summer. Sow frequently as will run to seed fairly fast. For winter seedlings, make late sowing early autumn under cover. Seedlings make colourful, spicy addition to salads.

VSR ★★; PP

GREEN-IN-THE-SNOW (Serifong, Xue-li-hong – pronounced 'Shirley Hoong' – and many related spellings)

Very vigorous, extremely hardy plants, generally 25cm/10in high and similar spread. Invaluable winter vegetable. Strong-flavoured, serrated leaves.

Cultivation

As General cultivation, above. Can be grown at various spacings for harvesting at different size:

- as CCA seedlings
- spaced 10cm/4in apart to harvest as small plants
- spaced 20cm/8in apart for medium-sized plants
- 30cm/12in apart for large plants.

Responds well to CCA treatment at every stage.

VSR ★★★

LARGE-LEAVED MUSTARD 'AMSOI'
(sometimes listed as Indian mustard)
Large-leaved, thick-stemmed plant. Easily grows 30cm/12in high with similar spread; grows considerably larger and is generally more productive under cover. Moderately hardy. Traditional oriental pickling mustard with excellent flavour, notably in the stems, even when starting to run to seed.

Cultivation
As General cultivation, above. Space plants about 38cm/15in apart, or grow more closely for smaller plants.

Cut whole plant or individual leaves as required. Resprouts over many weeks.

VSR **

COMMON OR LEAF MUSTARDS (Gai choy)
Medium-sized leaves, often with serrated edges. Can grow up to about 30cm/12in high, depending on cv. Reasonably hardy. Quite strong flavour. Strong tendency to bolt from spring sowings.

Cultivation
As above. Can be grown:

- as CCA seedlings
- spaced 10–15cm/4–6in apart, for harvesting young when leaves 15–20cm/6–8in high
- spaced 23cm/9in apart for larger plants.

VSR **

ONIONS *Allium* spp.

Onions are a large family of strongly flavoured biennial and perennial plants. Different types are grown for their bulbs and for their leaves. With careful choice of types and cvs it is possible to have home-grown onions almost all year round.

Types

Bulb onions Main source of culinary onion, used fresh or stored. Tiny pickling onions can be obtained by growing selected cvs at close spacing. Egyptian or tree onion (*Allium cepa* Proliferum Group) is a curious-looking plant producing tiny aerial bulbs which can be harvested mid-winter; for cultivation, see *The Organic Salad Garden*. For shallots, see page 324.

Green onions All types grown primarily for their leaves. Include 'salad' or 'spring' onion, Welsh onion and Japanese bunching onion.

BULB ONIONS *Allium cepa* Cepa Group
Skin colour yellow, brown or white with creamy to white flesh; also red-skinned type with hints of red in flesh. Only certain cvs suitable for storage. Inherent flavour varies from strong to mild; can be affected by soil and growing conditions.

Site and soil
Open site; fertile, thoroughly dug, well-prepared soil. Ideally manure soil several months before sowing or planting as growth too lush if soil is freshly manured. Good drainage essential. Onions (especially spring onions) sensitive to acidity, so lime if soil is acid. In spite of permanent 'onion patch' tradition, it is advisable to rotate over minimum 4-year cycle if possible to prevent build-up of eelworm (nematodes) and soil-borne diseases.

Cultivation
Long growing season essential; bulb formation initiated when certain day length reached, and onions never 'catch up' if sown late. Must grow correct cvs for your climatic zone, or onions will fail to develop bulbs.

Onions are raised either from seed or from tiny bulbs known as sets. Each has pros and cons:

- ∾ Seed: advantages – available for all cultivars, less prone to bolting, more flexible sowing times, cheaper; disadvantages – more labour-intensive, longer growing season, more susceptible to disease and pests, especially onion fly.
- ∾ Sets: advantages – easier to grow, less prone to disease, usually avoid onion fly attacks, may give reasonable crop in poor soil, onion has 'head start' so ready earlier and better chance of maturing where growing season short; disadvantages – only available for some cvs, more prone to bolting, sowing date critical for heat treated sets (see below), more expensive.

For almost continuous supply, sow or plant as follows:
 1 For main summer supply of fresh onions ready mid-summer onwards and for storage onions lifted in late summer/early autumn, sow or plant early spring. Will keep until mid-spring the following year.
 2 For overwintering onions maturing early to mid-summer following year, sow or plant late summer/autumn. Use autumn-planting sets or Japanese overwintering types. These are only suitable for short-term storage but help fill gap before spring-sown/planted onions usable.

Grow shallots (see page 324) to bridge gap between last stored onions and first fresh onions.

To grow main summer supply of fresh onions and storage onions, use any of these methods:

Multisown bulb onions. Left: when planted. Right: nearing maturity.

1 For early start, especially in cold areas, sow seed indoors late winter in seed trays or modules, at temperature of 10–16°C/50–61°F. Once seeds have germinated, don't expose to temperatures above about 13°C/55°F before planting out. Prick out at 'crookneck' stage, when seedlings about 1cm/½in clear of soil but still bent over. Space seedlings about 5cm/2in apart. If sowing in modules you can multisow up to about six seeds per module, planting out 'as one' (see above). Harden off well before planting out mid-/late spring at two-to-three-leaf stage. Eventual size of onions is determined by spacing. For maximum yield of medium-sized onions, space 15cm/6in apart each way, or grow in rows 25cm/10in apart, spacing 5cm/2in apart. For larger bulbs, increase the spacing in the rows to 10cm/4in, or space them 18cm/7in apart each way. Space multisown modules 25–30cm/10–12in apart each way. Note: Onions can be started even earlier, in early winter, but this is inadvisable unless you have good greenhouse conditions.

2 Sow seed *in situ* outdoors as soon as the soil is workable in spring. Never sow in cold or wet soil. If necessary warm with cloches/films beforehand, or sow under cloches. Rake seedbed to very fine tilth. Sowing in stale seedbed is good practice to deter bean seed fly, which may attack onion seedlings. Sow thinly in rows about 30cm/12in apart. Thin in stages. Use thinnings as spring onions. Space as (1) above.

3 Grow from sets. Only plant firm, small to medium-sized sets. Optimum size about 2cm/¾in circumference. Large sets most prone to bolting. (Beware cheap offers of large sets!) Some sets are 'heat treated' to destroy flower embryo and prevent premature bolting. Must not be planted too early: follow instructions when purchased. Plant untreated sets, provided the soil is workable, from autumn to mid-spring. Alternatively, pot up individually in 5cm/2in modules or pots and plant out when soil conditions allow. Plant heat-treated sets late spring or when recommended. Push sets gently into soil so that tips at or just below surface level; otherwise birds pull them out. Space as (1) above.

Protect onions grown from sets with black cotton where birds a problem (see illustration, page 150). If birds disturb planted sets, carefully dig up and replant. Pushing them back into soil damages developing roots. Water in early stages until crop established. Normally no need to water in later stages of growth. Overwatering can be damaging. Keep weed-free, especially in the 6–8 weeks after seedlings have appeared, as onions compete poorly with weeds. Where onion fly is serious, grow under fine nets. Note: surplus sets can be planted very close together, almost touching, and young green leaves cut as spring onion.

To grow overwintered onions for early crop following summer, use either of the following options:
1 Use autumn sets. First introduced in 1980s. Have proved excellent method of raising earliest onions, with good record of surviving cold winters. Plant early to late autumn 18–20cm/7–8in apart each way, or 7.5–10cm/3–4in apart in rows 30cm/12in apart. Ready for use about mid-summer. Can lift and store for a few months.
2 Use short-day autumn-sown onions (also known as Japanese onions). Probably becoming less popular as more cvs of overwintering sets introduced. Sowing date critical. Onions must be 15–20cm/6–8in high by mid-autumn to survive winter conditions. If too far advanced, there is risk of bolting in spring and onions are more vulnerable to severe weather. Recommended sowing times in UK: north of England and Scotland, early August; the south-west and south Wales, end August; rest of England, second and third week August. Sow *in situ* as for spring-sown onions. Water drills well if weather dry. Sow in rows 25–30cm/10–12in apart. Space seed 2.5cm/1in apart to allow for losses during the winter. Thin to 5cm/2in apart in spring. You can apply seaweed-based feed in spring to boost growth. Note: In some areas local hardy cultivars recommended for late summer/autumn sowings.

Pests and diseases

Onion fly Small maggots attack seedlings, which turn yellow and die. Sow in stale seedbed; grow under fine nets.

Mildews, rots Attacks worse in damp seasons. No organic remedies. Prevent by rotating over as many years as possible. (For onion white rot, see page 175.) Harvest onions carefully to minimize the risk of storage rots.

Harvesting and storage
For fresh use, lift onions when they reach a usable size.

For storage, wait until foliage starts to die down and tops bend over naturally. *Don't* bend tops over artificially: although a traditional and much illustrated practice, it greatly increases the risk of storage rots. Ease bulbs gently from ground. If weather good, spread on upturned wooden boxes outdoors to dry for 10 days or so. Ready when skins are paper dry. If weather turns wet, finish drying indoors or in greenhouses. Handle gently; storage rots start with tiny cuts and bruises. Store in well-ventilated, frost-free shed or cellar, at low humidity and temperatures of 0–10°C/32–50°F. Suspend bulbs in bunches or plaits; or knot individually in nylon stockings; or spread on trays. To prolong storage life of onions, cut off any fresh roots which develop in late winter.

Cultivars

Spring-planted sets: ^'Centurion' F1, ^'Sturon', 'Setton', 'Red Baron'.

Spring-sown: 'Marco' F1, 'Rijnsburger Robusta', 'Hygro' F1, 'New Fen Globe', 'Red Baron', 'Mammoth Red', ^'Hysam' F1, 'Hystar' F1, 'Albion' (white).

Autumn–planted sets: 'Unwin's First Early', 'Radar', 'Swift', 'Senshyu', 'Shakespeare', 'Electric' (red), 'Bianco' (white).

Autumn-sown (Japanese type): 'Senshyu', 'Tough Ball' F1, 'Buffalo' F1, 'Keepwell' F1.

VSR ★★ from sets, ★ from seed

PICKLING ONIONS *Allium cepa* Cepa Group

Cultivation

Can be grown on fairly poor, dry soil, though do best in fertile soil. Sow in spring *in situ*. To get small, thumb-sized onions of pickling size, aim for about 30 plants per 30cm sq./1ft sq. Sow in rows 30cm/12in apart, thinning to 0.5cm/¼in apart; or sow in wide drills, allowing about 1cm/½in between plants. Generally no need to thin; competition keeps the bulbs small. Normally sown about 1cm/½in deep, but in Holland commercial pickling onions are sown 4–5cm/1½–2in deep to keep them white.

Allow foliage to die down, and harvest as for bulb onions. Don't leave too long in soil or they may resprout. If not pickled immediately, they can be stored until required for pickling.

Cultivars

'Paris Silver Skin', 'Barletta', 'Vera Prima', 'North Holland Flat', 'Yellow Plastro', 'Purplette' (purple).

VSR ★

SALAD OR SPRING ONION *Allium cepa*

Grown for young green leaves and small, rudimentary bulbs. Used mainly for salads and seasoning. They are selected cvs of bulb onions. The hardier cvs used for late sowings can be sown earlier, but tend to form bulbs quickly and have less healthy leaves. Useful hybrids of *Allium cepa* × *A. fistulosum* (Japanese bunching onion type) are being developed with increased hardiness and vigour.

Site and soil
As Bulb onions, page 290 (2).

Cultivation
Prepare seedbed as for maincrop onions *in situ* (see page 289).

Sowing programme:
1 For summer/autumn supply, sow in succession, every 2–3 weeks, from early spring to early summer.
2 For overwintered crop for use following spring, sow from mid-summer to early autumn. In cold areas use very hardy cultivars, or sow under cover. You can protect with cloches in winter.

Sow thinly in 7.5–10cm/3–4in wide drills, or narrow drills as close as 10cm/4in apart. Space seeds 2–3cm/¾–1¼in apart, for reasonable-sized spring onions.

No further thinning is necessary. Water in dry conditions. Pull as soon as they reach a usable size, normally within about 12 weeks from sowing.

Cultivars
Winter hardy: 'White Lisbon', 'Winter White Bunching', 'Winter Hardy White', 'Ramrod', 'Guardsman' (*Allium fistulosum* × *A. cepa* hybrid).
Mainly for summer use: 'White Lisbon', 'Guardsman', 'Ramrod'.
(See also Japanese bunching onion, below.)

VSR ★★

WELSH ONION *Allium fistulosum*
Robust hardy perennial growing in clumps 50cm/20in tall. Leaves hollow, round, rather coarse, generally thickened at base. Fairly strong-flavoured. Used for green onion all year; remains green all winter. Long cultivated in Europe. Useful permanent edging for vegetable beds.

Cultivation
To raise plants initially, sow in seed trays in spring and plant about 23cm/9in apart; or sow *in situ* in spring, thinning to same distance; or divide established clumps in spring, gently teasing them apart, and replant young outer pieces 23cm/9in apart.

Pick green leaves as required. To keep plants healthy, divide every two or three years, replanting in new site.

JAPANESE BUNCHING ONION *Allium fistulosum*
Refined, versatile and diverse form of Welsh onion, developed over centuries in Asia. Range from small dainty-leaved green onions to thick-

shafted forms grown and blanched like leeks. Generally milder-flavoured than Welsh onion. Increasingly popular in West for use as 'spring onion', as easier to grow and has longer season. Leaves are stronger, healthier and remain deep green longer. (For large-leaved types, see *Oriental Vegetables*.)

Cultivation

Although Japanese bunching onions are naturally perennial, cvs available in West are grown as annuals.

For tender young salad leaves, sow *in situ* outdoors throughout the growing season, as for spring onions, above, though fewer sowings are necessary as they stand in good condition for longer. You can make early and late sowings under cover; or multisow in modules, about six seeds per module, planting 7.5/3in apart. Pull for use at any stage from 5–15cm/2–6in tall, normally within about 6 weeks of sowing.

For larger plants with slightly thickened stems, thin to 4cm/1½in apart. Pull these, or cut single leaves as required, when 30cm/12in high, usually within 3 months of sowing.

In mild winters plants may stand for many months, still providing useful leaves even when flower heads are forming. If not pulled up they will virtually become perennial. Leaves can be cooked or sliced into salads.

Cultivars

'Kyoto Market', 'Laser', 'Long White Tokyo', 'Summer Isle', 'Savel', 'Sentry', 'Ishikura', 'White Spear' F1, 'Hikari Bunching'.

VSR ★★

ORACHE (Mountain spinach) *Atriplex hortensis*

There are red- and yellow-leaved forms of orache, the red forms being very decorative. Mature plants will grow 2m/6½ft high, but for culinary purposes it is best harvested young. The leaves have a mild, near-spinach flavour, are cooked like spinach and can be blended with spinach, the red forms retaining a pinkish colour when cooked. Very young leaves can be used raw in salads.

Soil and cultivation

Soil and general cultivation as *Chenopodium giganteum* 'Magentaspreen', page 238. In most respects orache exhibits similar growth patterns and characteristics. Unless wanted as a decorative plant, best grown as CCA seedlings or single plants harvested young.

Essential to pick constantly once plants about 10cm/4in high. Nip off the tip of plant to encourage bushiness. Unlike 'Magentaspreen', leaves picked off the maturing stem are not palatable. If leaving red forms to self-seed, select plants with deep red, rather than murky brown-coloured leaves.

VSR ★★; PP red forms

ORIENTAL SALADINI *Brassica* spp.

Oriental saladini is a mixture of oriental greens, which I originally devised in 1991, in conjunction with Suffolk Herbs seed company, to give a 'taster' of recently introduced oriental greens. It is primarily used for CCA seedlings both under cover and in the open, but has proved very versatile. With successive sowings you can provide greens for salads and cooking for much of the year. The original UK mixture included pak choi, loose-headed Chinese cabbage, purple mustard, mibuna, mizuna and komatsuna. It looks pretty growing, on account of the variation of leaf colours and textures.

Various other 'stir-fry' and 'spicy green' mixtures on the market, often including kales and mustards, can be used in much the same way as oriental saladini. Be guided by the supplier's instructions. See also Saladini, page 321.

Cultivation

Requires reasonably fertile soil, with plenty of moisture if several cuts being made over long period. Sow as for CCA seedlings. Make successive sowings, by broadcasting, or sowing in narrow or 7.5–10cm/3–4in wide drills. Sow in weed-free soil. Sow thinly, aiming for seeds about 1cm/½in apart.

Sowing options:
1 Late winter/early spring under cover.
2 Mid-/late spring outdoors.
3 Late summer/early autumn outdoors.
4 Autumn under cover.

In addition mid-summer sowings may be successful in cool districts. Normally there is risk of seedlings bolting rapidly, and growth being coarser, in hot weather.

Keep well watered. If growth seems to be flagging, feed with seaweed-based fertilizer. Although oriental saladini are subject to the common brassica pests (see page 223), most likely pests are flea beetle in the early stages and slugs. Take appropriate measures. Growing under fine nets is beneficial to protect against flying pests.

Harvesting and use

As salad seedlings Cut seedlings when about 5–10cm/2–4in high, about 1cm/½in above soil level, normally within 3–4 weeks of sowing. Leave to resprout. Depending on the season, they will resprout two or three times. Use raw in salads. Lovely bright colour and refreshing flavour.

For larger 'stir-fry' leaves Either thin the seedlings to 2.5–5cm/1–2in apart from outset, or thin after a couple of cuts have been made, so that remaining plants grow larger. Cut when about 15cm/6in high for cooking as greens.

For larger plants From late summer sowings you can prick out individual seedlings to grow into large individual plants. Seedlings of different types can be distinguished fairly early by variations in leaf form and colour. Plant 20–30cm/8–12in apart, outdoors or under cover. Allow to develop to full size. (For further cultivation, see individual plants.) They may remain productive over winter and into following spring.

Mature and flowering shoots In some cases oriental seedlings more or less thin themselves out, with some plants developing at the expense of others. Eventually, often in following spring after overwintering, flowering shoots develop (see Choy sum group, page 246). Cut them in bud stage. If tender enough, use raw; otherwise best lightly steamed or stir-fried. Most prove very sweet-flavoured.

Windowsill/window box saladini Oriental saladini can be grown in a seed tray on a windowsill, or in any shallow container, using good potting compost. If started indoors, move to good, even light as soon as germinated. Normally only one cut can be made.

VSR ★★★★; PP

PAK CHOI (Celery mustard) *Brassica rapa* Chinensis Group

This is a large group of smooth-leaved, very attractive, fast-growing oriental greens. Leaves typically have broad white (sometimes green) midribs, widening at the base to give mature plants a characteristic rounded butt. They are closely related to Chinese cabbage. Leaves, stems and flowering shoots are all excellent raw and cooked, being mild-flavoured, often refreshingly juicy and crisp-textured.

Types
Huge range available in China (see *Oriental Vegetables*). The following are the main types currently available in West:

Standard pak choi Smooth-leaved, characteristic wide midribs. Height ranges from small stocky cvs 8–10cm/3–4in high, to tall types up to 45cm/18in high. Most cvs only moderately hardy, but very useful under cover during winter. Green-stemmed cvs considered better flavoured than white.

Soup Spoon type Mostly tall elegantly 'waisted' plants with slightly cupped leaves and long leaf stalks (petioles). Delicately flavoured. Sadly not widely available.

Rosette pak choi Distinct, hardy type with dark crêped leaves and outstanding flavour. (See page 298.)

Site and soil
As Chinese cabbage, page 245.

Cultivation of standard and Soup Spoon type
General cultivation as Chinese cabbage, page 245. Very versatile: can be used at any stage from small seedlings to flowering shoots. Responds well to CCA treatment as seedlings, semi-mature and mature plants. Like Chinese cabbage, has tendency to bolt from early sowings, unless grown as CCA crop. Some cvs have reasonable bolting resistance.

Cultivation options:
1 For CCA seedlings, grow as Chinese cabbage, page 245. For spring and early summer sowings, use bolt-resistant cultivars where available, though you can usually get at least one cut from standard cultivars before plants run to seed.
2 For mature and semi-mature plants, grow as Chinese cabbage, headed crop, page 246. Make last sowing about 6 weeks before first frost expected. Sow *in situ,* or in seed trays or modules to transplant. Spacing depends on cultivar and stage being harvested:
   ∾ small plants and squat types: 13–15cm/5–6in apart
   ∾ medium-sized plants: 18–23cm/7–9in apart
   ∾ large plants: 35–40cm/14–16in apart.

Use thinnings in salads, or, in cool conditions, transplant elsewhere.

Pests and diseases
As Cabbage, page 223.

Harvesting and use

CCA seedlings Cut at any stage from 4–13cm/1½–5in high. Depending on season, first cut may be made within 3 weeks of sowing. Two or three further successive cuts often possible.

Mature and semi-mature plants Cut individual leaves as needed; or cut across head about 2.5cm/1in above ground level leaving it to resprout; or pull up entire plant. Often ready within 6 weeks of sowing. With CCA treatment semi-mature and mature heads may remain productive over several weeks or months. Especially useful for plants under cover in autumn/early winter, as cut-back plants have more resistance to frost. Plants eventually run to seed.

Young and mature flowering shoots are mild-flavoured; use before buds open. All parts can be used raw in salads when young, or cooked lightly when mature, e.g. by steaming or stir-frying.

Cultivars
White-stemmed: 'Joi Choi' F1 (large), 'Canton Dwarf' (squat type for small heads).

Green-stemmed (all small): 'Choko' F1 (slow-bolting for summer); 'Shuko' F1(good heat and cold tolerance);'Mei Qing Choi', 'Chingensai', 'Riko' F1.
Soup Spoon type:'Tai-Sai'.

VSR ★★★ single plants, ★★★★ CCA seedlings

ROSETTE PAK CHOI (Tatsoi, Tah tsai and assorted spellings)
Brassica rapa var. *rosularis*
This is a distinct, eye-catching type of pak choi with rounded, dark green, crêpe-like leaves. They are upright in hot weather, but later form flat, very symmetrical rosettes. Leaves are small in older cvs, but larger in improved cvs. The flavour is excellent and more pronounced than in most types of pak choi.

Soil, cultivation and harvesting
Grows best in cool weather. Hardier than other types of pak choi. Soil as Pak choi, above. In well-drained soil may survive -10°C/14°F, but may not survive in prolonged wet winter weather unless protected. Grow either as CCA seedlings or as single plants, as Pak choi, above. Strong tendency to bolt from early sowings; most productive sowings mid- to late summer for autumn/winter crop. For top-quality plants, can be transplanted under cover in autumn. Space 15cm/6in apart for small plants; 30–40cm/12–16in apart for larger plants.

Slightly slower-growing and less productive than standard pak choi. Either cut individual leaves as required, or cut across plants leaving them to resprout. (For more information, see *Oriental Vegetables*.)

Improved cultivars
'Ryokusai' F1, 'Yukina Savoy'.

VSR ★★; PP

PARSNIP *Pastinaca sativa*

Parsnip is a very hardy vegetable, grown for its well-flavoured root. Roots vary from fairly stocky broad-shouldered bulbous and wedge-shaped types to longer, 'bayonet' types 25cm/10in long.

Site and soil
Open site. Grows best on deep, light, stone-free, well-drained soil. High level of fertility unnecessary. Soil preferably manured for previous crop. Lime if acid. On very shallow and very heavy soils grow shorter-rooted cvs. There was a long-held belief that growing on recently manured ground led to fanged roots, but experiments have demonstrated that this is not necessarily true. Rotate in the same group as carrots.

Cultivation

Long growing season necessary to develop good-sized roots. Use fresh seed, as viability falls off rapidly.

Normally sown *in situ*, but can be sown in modules and transplanted, provided planted out before tap root starts to develop. Theoretically can be sown from late winter until late spring. However, germination slow, and in practice early sowings have very high failure rate. In cold areas, or cold heavy soils, better to delay sowing until mid- or late spring. If necessary warm the soil before sowing by covering it with cloches/films, or sow under cloches. Prepare seedbed with fine tilth. As germination slow, it is advisable to station sow, sowing radish between stations to mark rows. (You can use small lettuces if stations at least 18cm/7in apart.) Grow small types in rows 20cm/8in apart and thin to 5–10cm/2–4in apart. Grow large types in rows 30cm/12in apart and thin to 13–20cm/5–8in apart. Alternatively can be grown at equidistant spacing. After final thinning hoe or hand weed carefully to avoid damaging crowns, and mulch between rows.

Parsnip seed can be mixed with annual flowers and sown together, to save space and deter carrot fly.

Extra watering is not normally necessary, unless soil is drying out completely, in which case water every 2–3 weeks, giving roughly 11 litres per sq. m/2 gallons per sq. yd each time.

Mini parsnips

Sow appropriate bayonet-type cvs *in situ* in suitable conditions from early spring to early summer. Sow in rows 15cm/6in apart, thinning to 2–4cm/1–1½in apart. Pull for use about 14 weeks after sowing when roots 10–15cm/4–6in long and finger-thick with no central core. They are exceptionally tender. Plants can be left to develop to full size if required.

Pests and diseases

Canker Crowns crack or are damaged by pests, then invaded by fungi. Most likely to occur in drought and highly fertile soil. Small roots less vulnerable. Where canker common, use resistant cultivars or make later sowings, i.e. mid-/late spring.

Celery fly Blisters leaves. Pick off and destroy diseased leaves.

Carrot fly Generally less serious than on carrots, but can be a problem. See page 229.

Harvesting and use

Roots available early autumn to following mid-spring. Best left in soil all winter, though can be stored in boxes of sand in shed. Frost improves flavour. Foliage dies down almost completely, so mark position of rows with canes so that they can be found, especially in snow. They can be covered with straw or bracken to prevent ground freezing and make lifting easier in frost. If ground required for cultivation in spring, lift and heel in like leeks (see illustration, page 274). For decorative and ecological purposes, leave one or two plants to run to seed in spring. They grow into exceptionally handsome umbelliferous plants, often 2m/6½ft high. Masses of beneficial hoverflies are attracted to flowers.

Eat parsnips boiled, mashed, fried, roasted under joint, or baked with brown sugar.

Cultivars

Good canker resistance: ^'Avonresister' (short-rooted), ^'Cobham Improved Marrow', ^'Gladiator' F1, ^'White Gem', ^'Arrow', ^'Javelin' F1, ^'New White Skin', ^'Archer' F1, ^'Panache' F1.

For mini parsnips: ^'Arrow', ^'Lancer', 'Dagger' F1 (more recent so not included in organic trials) – all with good canker resistance.

VSR *

PEAS *Pisum sativum*

Peas are moderately hardy annuals in the legume family. Height can range from less than 45cm/18in to over 1.8m/6ft; their tendrils cling naturally to supports. Shelled peas are eaten fresh or dried. Mangetout types are eaten as immature pods, while the tendrils of semi-leafless types are a delicacy raw or lightly cooked. Pea seeds are excellent sprouted (see *The Organic Salad Garden*). The quality of home-grown peas is so superior to shop-bought ones that they deserve a place in every garden.

Types

Shelling peas

∾ Standard – grown for peas within pods, normally eaten fresh as green peas. Round-seeded cvs hardier but starchy. Wrinkle-seeded cvs sweet-flavoured but generally less hardy. Some cvs pink-podded. Peas can be dried for winter use. Some heirloom cvs (often with pink or bicoloured flowers), naturally starchy and most suitable for drying.

∾ 'Petit pois' – tiny, exceptionally sweet peas.

Mangetout (sugar peas/snow peas/edible podded peas)

∾ Flat-podded type – pods from 5–12cm/2–4½in long, flat, often sickle-shaped with slightly bloated look. Immature pods edible because virtually free of parchment. Very good, sweetish flavour. Mature pods can be shelled and peas used normally.

∾ Sugar Snap type – pods rounded, smooth, peas almost 'welded' to pod walls. Crunchy texture and superb sweet flavour when fully mature.

Semi-leafless types, in which many leaves are converted into tendrils, making plants almost self-supporting, have been developed for mechanical harvesting but excellent for gardens as little staking required. Also compact, healthy (the lack of foliage makes them well ventilated) and decorative. Very young tendrils can be picked without jeopardizing pea crop. All types can occur in semi-leafless forms.

Peas are classified according to approximate time taken to mature. 'Earlies': 11–12 weeks; 'second earlies': 12–13 weeks; 'maincrop': 13–14 weeks. Earlier types dwarfer in habit so require less staking, but tend to be lower-yielding. Later cvs taller, higher overall yields, staking more difficult. With a few exceptions most types can be sown any time.

Site and soil

Open site; light shade tolerated in summer. Good drainage essential. Soil must be fertile, deeply worked, preferably manured previous autumn. High levels of nitrogen unnecessary, as nodules on pea roots start fixing nitrogen about 5 weeks after sowing, meeting plant's needs for nitrogen. Rotation advisable to avoid soil-borne diseases.

Cultivation

Sow in weed-free soil; peas awkward to weed when growing.

Main sowings:
1 For early summer crop, sow dwarf early cvs outdoors, from late winter in mild areas, in early or mid-spring in colder areas. Don't sow until soil temperature at least 7°C/45°F (see also sowing methods for early crop, below). For early sowings you can warm soil by covering with cloches/clear film for a week or so beforehand and cover with cloches/films after sowing.
2 For main summer crop, continue sowing until early summer. The earlier peas are in the soil the better; growth much less vigorous in hot weather. Use mildew-resistant cvs for later sowings. For a succession of peas throughout summer you can sow every 2–3 weeks from mid-spring to early summer using any cv; or sow three cvs, one from each group, on the same dates in mid- to late spring.
3 For autumn crop, sow dwarf early cvs in mid-summer. Something of a gamble, as growth will be poor in hot summers. Very welcome late crop when it succeeds.
4 For late spring crop following year, in mild areas sow hardy overwintering types in a sheltered place outside from mid- to late autumn. You can protect with cloches, but give ventilation on warm days.

Where space available, you can sow late/mid-winter in unheated greenhouses, polytunnels or frames. Use dwarf cvs of ordinary or mangetout types.

Peas sown outdoors *in situ* early in year are very vulnerable in early stages and often fail to germinate. Following methods help get early crop established. Fairly labour-intensive: probably only worth doing with relatively small quantities.

∾ Germinate seed indoors on moist paper towelling. Sow individual seeds carefully outdoors when tiny radicle emerging from seed.
∾ Sow indoors, preferably in modules. Transplant the young plants after hardening off.
∾ Block the ends of a length of guttering; fill with sieved soil or potting compost; sow pea seeds in it. Keep in cool greenhouse or sheltered place outdoors. When seedlings well established, gently push the soil/compost out of the guttering into a shallow trench of similar dimensions, made in the ground.

Sow 2.5–4cm/1–1½in deep. Not necessary to rake seedbed to fine tilth, as seeds relatively large. For main sowings, space dwarf and semi-leafless cvs about 5cm/2in apart, taller cvs about 7.5cm/3in apart. For autumn/early spring sowings, sow as close as 2.5cm/1in apart to compensate for higher seed losses.

Research has shown that peas sown/planted as much as 12cm/4½in apart each way crop over a much longer period because they have less competition. For this system, grow peas in bands of three rows, each row 12cm/4½in apart. Thin to correct spacing after germination. Allow 45cm/18in between bands.

Many sowing patterns are feasible. Choice will be influenced by support system. Typical systems are:

∾ Single rows with supports behind.
∾ Double rows 23cm/9in apart with supports down centre.
∾ Flat-bottomed drills 15–23cm/6–9in wide with supports behind. Space seeds evenly across drill or sow in parallel rows.
∾ Evenly spaced patches or circles, up to 90–120cm/3–4ft diameter, with main support system, e.g. wire net held upright with long canes, around the periphery. In this case it is easiest to sow by making holes with small dibber across area. Drop peas in hole, making sure they touch the bottom and are not suspended in air.

Traditionally space between adjacent wide drills/pairs of rows is roughly that of height of peas. In practice peas are often grown closer with no ill effect, though access is more awkward.

Set mouse traps for all sowings. During winter pull a little soil up around stems to give them extra support and protection. Protect from birds after sowing with black cotton or wire pea guards. Mulch heavily as soon as seedlings established to keep down weeds. Only water in early stages if conditions exceptionally dry; overwatering can result in leafy growth at expense of pods. If weather dry, once peas start to flower water weekly to increase yields at rate of 22 litres per sq. m/4 gallons per sq. yd.

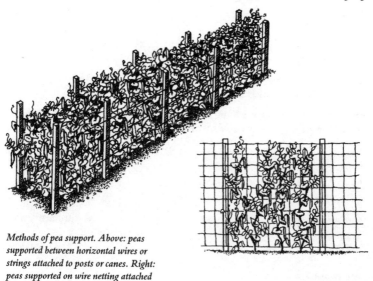

Methods of pea support. Above: peas supported between horizontal wires or strings attached to posts or canes. Right: peas supported on wire netting attached to posts, canes or piping.

Methods of support

Support peas as soon as the first tendrils appear – usually when plants are 7.5–10cm/3–4in high. Plants never yield as highly once they flop on the ground.

Dwarf and semi-leafless cvs can be grown without supports, but benefit from some twigs/brushwood pushed among them to keep stems and lower leaves off the ground. Same applies to peas grown in patches with mainly peripheral support (see above).

Supports must be reasonably strong as mature crop can become weighty and top heavy. Use:

- ∞ Criss-crossed brushwood or pea sticks where available. The more branched they are the better. They should be at least 1.5m/5ft high for tall cvs.
- ∞ Parallel wires or strings attached to wire or posts (see illustration, above) on either side of crop.
- ∞ Wire netting, or nylon or string net, of 5–10cm/2–4in mesh. Height of 1.2–1.5m/4–5ft normally sufficient. Attach firmly to upright posts or piping to keep taut (see illustration, above). You can anchor wire netting with bamboo canes pushed in and out of wire and into ground.
- ∞ Patented pea support systems, such as netting on tent-shaped metal frame placed over pea rows after sowing.

Pests and diseases

Mice Can devastate early and winter sowings, burrowing down for seeds. Set mousetraps.

Birds Most serious in early stages but may attack throughout growth. Protect with nets if necessary.

Pea moth Attacks in summer; maggots found in peas. Spray with derris when flowering, or grow under fine nets to deter adult fly.

Pea weevil Nibbles leaf margins in spring, retarding seedlings. Spray with derris when you notice it.

Pea thrips/thunderflies Most serious in a hot summer. Pods become silvered and distorted. Spray with derris.

*Various mildews, wilts and rotting disease*s Attack at different stages depending on the weather. Practise rotation, burn unhealthy and diseased leaves; use disease-resistant cvs if the problems are encountered regularly.

Harvesting and use

Shelling peas Pick while pods bright green. Cook shelled or, to conserve flavour, cook pods whole and shell afterwards.

Dried peas Leave pods on plants till they turn brown towards end of season. Pull up plants. Hang by roots in airy place, e.g. well-ventilated greenhouse, to finish drying. When pods crackly dry, split open, remove peas and store in airtight jars.

Mangetout – flat-podded types Pick when outline of peas just visible through skin and pods snap cleanly in half. In their prime for fairly short season. Some cvs need strings removed from pods. Good sliced raw in salads as well as cooked lightly, e.g. steamed or stir-fried. If left to mature can eventually be shelled like ordinary peas.

Mangetout – Sugar Snap type Pick while green, plump and easily snapped in half. Use like flat mangetout. Later can be treated as shelled peas.

At end of season cut off plants at soil level and dig in roots to return nitrogen to soil from root nodules.

Cultivars

Shelling peas

Early: 'Douce Provence', 'Meteor', 'Feltham First' – all round-seeded; 'Holiday' (wrinkle-seeded).

Second early: 'Jaguar' (mildew-resistant), 'Early Onward', 'Kelvedon Wonder', 'Waverex' (petit pois).

Maincrop: 'Cavalier' (mildew-resistant), 'Onward', 'Ambassador', 'Hurst Green Shaft', 'Rondo'.
Semi-leafless: 'Canoe', 'Markana'.

Mangetout
Second early: 'Dwarf Sweet Green', 'Delicata' (mildew-resistant); 'Sugar Bon', 'Sugar Ann', 'Edula', 'Honeypod' – Sugar Snap types.
Maincrop: 'Oregon Sugar Pod', 'Carouby de Maussane';'Zucolla' (mildew-resistant); 'Sugar Snap', 'Cascadia', 'Delikett' – Sugar Snap types.
Semi-leafless: 'Sugar Crystal' (mildew-resistant)

VSR * earlies, ** maincrop, *** mangetout – Sugar Snap types; PP semi-leafless

PEPPER, SWEET (Capsicum) *Capsicum annuum* Grossum Group
PEPPER, CHILLI *C. annuum* Longum Group, *C. frutescens*

There has been a huge surge of interest in this tropical family of vegetables. Both sweet peppers and the much hotter chilli peppers can be used immature or mature.

Types

Sweet peppers Annual plants, ranging in size from dwarf bush cvs 25cm/10cm tall, to cvs growing 60–105cm/2–3½ft tall. Fruits display tremendous variation in shape, being upright, pendulous, square, round, rectangular, tomato (bonnet-shaped) or long. Commonest cultivars in Europe are green when immature, turning red, yellow, orange or purple on maturity. Cvs with thick walls can be stuffed. Thinner-walled cvs bred in Europe are adapted to lower temperatures and lower light levels. Early-maturing F1 hybrid cvs recommended for cold climates. European cvs grow best at temperatures of 18–21°C/65–70°F.

Chilli peppers Naturally short-lived perennials. Display similar range in plant size, from very compact dwarf cvs to large bushy plants. Some purple-leaved and variegated-leaved types very decorative; can be grown as house plants. Fruits generally smaller and thinner than sweet peppers, but there is astonishing diversity in fruit size, shape, colour, flavour and piquancy. Some cvs (e.g. Cayenne type) suitable for drying. Fleshy Hungarian Wax and Anaheim types sweeter, used fresh. (For more on chillies, see Further Reading, page 372.) Grow suitable cvs in the same way as sweet peppers.

Site and soil
In cool climates grow peppers under cover in unheated greenhouse or polytunnel for best results. As a rough guide, where tomatoes succeed, peppers will succeed, though they require slightly higher temperatures to

thrive. When growing outside choose sheltered, sunny situation, or grow under cloches.

Need reasonably fertile but not over-rich soil. Lush growth adversely affects fruit production, especially with chillies. Avoid using fresh manure; work in well-rotted compost beforehand. Need high light intensity to flourish.

Cultivation

Can be planted directly in ground, or grown in 13–23cm/5–9in pots, or planted three per standard growing bag, outdoors or under cover. Dwarf cvs can be grown successfully in pots on windowsills. Advisable to use fresh seed as viability falls after a year or so. Sow indoors in early spring in seed trays or modules. Germination best at about 21°C/ 70°F. Sow 8–10 weeks before last frost if planting outside, 2 weeks earlier if growing under cover. Lower temperature gradually after germination. Give extra protection with fleece if weather cold. Normally ready for planting about 8 weeks after sowing.

If sown in seed trays prick out at about the three-leaf stage into 5–7.5cm/2–3in pots. You can pot on again into 10cm/4in pots to obtain good sturdy plants. Plant in permanent position – indoors, outdoors or in a container – when the plants are about 10cm/4in high and first flowers are showing. Space standard cvs 38–45cm/15–18in apart, dwarf cvs 30cm/12in apart. Harden off well before planting outside. Delay planting until all risk of frost is past.

Planting through black and white mulching film recommended. Protect with cloches or crop covers at least in early stages.

Aim is to produce sturdy plants. Typically plant grows on single stem initially, then branches out naturally, with a 'crown' fruit developing at the central point. If plant is growing well, leave crown fruit to mature. If growth is slow, remove it to encourage plant to bush out. If branches weak and spindly when plant is 30–38cm/12–15in high, nip out tips of branches.

Peppers don't normally require supports, but they can be brittle. If necessary tie to canes, or prop up branches with twigs or split canes. If plants are growing and fruiting well, supplementary feeding is unnecessary. Otherwise feed every 10 days once fruits start to form. Use high-potash feed, such as seaweed-based fertilizer formulated for tomatoes. Water sufficiently to prevent soil and roots from drying out, but don't overwater. Keep plants mulched.

Where plants are grown under cover, keep well ventilated. Indoor plants require high humidity. In warm weather damp down or spray/syringe plants frequently with water. This helps fruit to set and discourages greenhouse pests.

Plants often continue growing well into autumn. If frost is likely, protect plants at night with cloches or fleece.

Pests and diseases

Outdoors poor weather is the most significant problem.

Aphids, red spider mite, whitefly All potential problems under cover. Use biological controls. In my experience interplanting with French marigolds (*Tagetes* spp.) helps deter whitefly.

Harvesting

Sweet peppers Start picking green peppers when smooth, glossy and usable size. Picking early fruits encourages further cropping. Mature fruits, most notably red-skinned ones, are sweeter, with enhanced flavour. Can take 3–6 weeks to turn from immature green stage to fully ripe: may never happen in cool summers!

Chilli peppers Start picking chilli peppers when immature to encourage a long cropping season.

Towards end of season uproot remaining plants before frosted. Hang by roots in frost-free shed or greenhouse. Sweet peppers (and fleshy chillies) continue to colour and may keep firm for many weeks. Only dry fully mature chillies of appropriate type (e.g. Cayenne types). To retain flavour, store in airtight jars in dark cupboard. May keep for 2 or more years.

Cultivars

Sweet peppers

'Ace', 'Bell Boy', 'Canape', 'Gypsy', 'Unicorn', 'Banana Supreme', 'Redskin' (dwarf) – F1 hybrids.
'Californian Wonder' – blocky fruits.

Chilli peppers

Cayenne type:'Apache' F1 (dwarf), 'Cayenne'.
Decorative (and edible) cayenne: 'Firecracker', 'Pretty in Purple', 'Medusa'.
Moderate heat, good flavour: 'Hungarian Wax' ('Hot Banana'), 'Anaheim', 'Hero'.
Hot:'Jalapeno', 'Habanero' (very hot).

VSR **; PP some chilli peppers

POTATOES *Solanum tuberosum*

Recent years have seen a remarkable revival of interest in potatoes. Seedsmen have responded by offering a wide range of new and heirloom cvs, many notable for flavour and other qualities. Skin colour usually white, russet, pink or occasionally blue; flesh can be white, creamy, yellow, occasionally highly coloured. Potatoes are frost tender, requiring a long growing season and a fair amount of space.

Maturity groups

Potatoes are roughly grouped according to average number of growing days to reach maturity.

Earlies Lower yields, planted closer, primarily used fresh as 'new' potatoes.

Maincrop Used fresh or stored.

They are normally planted in sequence, but potatoes from any group can be planted at any time, i.e. earlies can be planted late and maincrops early.

Days to maturity:

- ∾ very early earlies – 75 days
- ∾ earlies – 90 days
- ∾ second earlies – 110 days
- ∾ early to late maincrop – 135–160 days

Where space is limited, earlies are most worth growing: they give quickest returns, require least space, escape most maincrop diseases, are ready when prices high and taste delicious home-grown.

Culinary purposes

Texture of potato and hence its suitability for different methods of cooking is related to inherent dry matter:

- ∾ cvs with low dry matter are waxier and remain intact when cooked – most suitable for boiling and salads.
- ∾ cvs with high dry matter become floury when cooked – suitable for baking, roasting, chips.

Many cvs have intermediary qualities. Evaluating flavour is highly subjective. (See Cultivars, page 313.)

Site and soil

Open site; avoid frost pocket. Potatoes grow on wide range of soils and tolerate acid conditions. Deep, fertile, well-drained, medium loam ideal. Manure previous autumn. Often planted in new gardens to improve and 'clean' soil; wireworms invading the tubers are removed when crop lifted. Rotate early potatoes over minimum 3-year cycle, maincrop over 5 years if possible to prevent build-up of eelworm. If rows orientated from north to south, sun falls more evenly on ridges, helping growth.

Cultivation

Crop is raised from specially grown tubers known as 'seed potatoes'. Always buy certified healthy seed. Unwise to save your own as easily becomes diseased. Buy seed mid-winter (mild areas) to late winter. For early cvs 2kg/4½lb sufficient for 10m/33ft row planted 30cm/12in apart.

Large tubers generally better for early crops than small/medium-sized tubers, but not necessarily the case with maincrop potatoes.

Chitting is the process of starting tubers into growth indoors to get crop up to 3 or 4 weeks earlier – though may be at expense of maximum overall yield. Some merchants sell pre-chitted seed. You can start chitting mid-/late winter.

Chitting seed potatoes in an egg tray.

Chitting method (developed by champion potato grower Charlie Maisey):

1 Place tubers 'rose end' (end with most 'eyes') upwards in seed trays, shallow boxes or containers such as empty egg trays (see illustration, above).
2 Put in frost-free shed or cool room, in the light but away from direct sunlight. Leave for the shoots to develop. For extra sturdy growth and early root development, line tray with thick layer of newspaper.
3 Spray potatoes lightly with seaweed-based fertilizer every 10 days or so once sprouting starts.

Theoretically potatoes should be planted when sprouts are about 2.5cm/1in long. In practice they can be planted successfully when very much longer – but great care needed to avoid snapping them off when planting. Reject unsprouted and diseased tubers.

The longer the growing season, the higher the yields will be. Start planting early/mid-spring, provided soil warm. Soil temperature at 10cm/4in depth should have reached 6°C/43°F for 3 consecutive days before planting. Delay planting if soil very dry, very wet or sticky, or if heavy frost forecast.

Make 10–15cm/4–6in deep drill, or make individual holes with trowel. Plant tubers 5cm/2in below soil surface, rose end upwards. Cover them with soil.

Various depths can be used. On average early potatoes covered by 5cm/2in of soil, maincrops by 10cm/4in soil. Make shallow V-shaped trench 10–15cm/4–6in deep, or make individual holes with trowel. Plant tubers upright with rose end upwards. Cover carefully with soil so that sprouts are not damaged.

Potatoes grow successfully at different spacing. Spacing can be adjusted according to method of cultivation and cv. Cvs with spreading habit require more space. Small tubers can be planted more closely; larger tubers further apart. Average spacing:

ᦇ earlies 30–38cm/12–15in apart in rows 38–50cm/15–20in apart
ᦇ maincrop 38cm/15in apart in rows 75cm/2½ft apart.

After planting, covering with 15cm/6in compost, straw or well-rotted manure is beneficial – gives extra protection against frost and helps conserve soil moisture. Also excellent way of building up soil fertility for following crop. (Drawback is risk of encouraging slugs.) If necessary, protect young leafy growth from frost with cloches, or by covering with newspaper at night if frost forecast or seems likely. Plants usually recover from light frost damage, but will have suffered a setback. You can grow them under perforated polythene film or fleece to obtain earlier, heavier crops. Remove film 3–4 weeks after potatoes have emerged.

Potatoes are a thirsty crop. Adequate water influences quality, yield and maturity.

ᦇ Earlies – for optimum yield, in dry weather water throughout grow-ing period every 10–14 days, at rate of 16–22 litres per sq. m/3–4 gallons per sq. yd. Delay lifting until foliage has started to die back. For very early crop, delay watering until tubers size of marbles. (Gen-tly pull away soil to ascertain size.) Then apply one heavy watering at rate of 22 litres per sq. m/4 gallons per sq. yd.
ᦇ Maincrop – on average soils generally unnecessary to water until tubers starting to form and reaching marble size. (This stage often coincides with plants flowering.) Apply one heavy watering at rate of 22–27 litres per sq. m/4–5 gallons per sq. yd. On very light soils in dry conditions may need to give heavy watering weekly.

Ways to prevent greening
Tubers near surface get pushed upwards as plants grow, and become green and poisonous. Covering with earth prevents greening and gives protection from tuber blight. Earthing up also suppresses weeds and may increase yields. When plants roughly 15–23cm/6–9in high, pull soil up around stems, covering lower leaves and leaving only tops exposed. Can be done in one operation or several stages.

Alternatively, grow under black film, which saves earthing up as light excluded by film. More suitable for earlies than maincrop, as watering throughout summer laborious, and temperatures tend to rise too high under film. After planting, cover potatoes with black polythene film. Anchor edges in the soil on either side of potatoes. When tips of plants start pushing up film from below, cut slits or crosses in the film and ease young growths through. Water carefully through the slits when necessary. Tubers form very near surface, and are easily lifted by pulling back film.

Growing in barrels or tubs

Choose cvs with compact growth (see Cultivars, page 313). Use wooden or plastic barrels about 75cm/2½ft deep and 60cm/2ft diameter. Purpose-made barrels are available.

1 Use multipurpose potting compost; or mix well-rotted manure, leaf mould and/or garden compost with fresh or spent potting compost to make friable mixture. Water with seaweed-based fertilizer.
2 Put 10cm/4in-layer compost mix in barrel.
3 Place four sprouted tubers on top. Cover with 10cm/4in compost mix. Firm down and water.
4 When stems about 15cm/6in high, add another 10cm/4in layer.
5 Repeat until plants are about 5cm/2in below rim of barrel. Add final layer of soil or compost.
6 Keep well watered. Apply weekly foliar feed of seaweed-based fertilizer.
7 Harvest when plants flower. Carefully poke inside barrel to check when tubers reasonable size to use.

Heavy-duty black polythene rubbish sacks can also be used. Make a few drainage holes in the bottom. Roll down the sides when planting, and roll them up gradually as the potatoes develop and sack is filled.

'Second cropping' potatoes (late crop of 'new' potatoes)

Technique depends on seedsmen keeping certain cvs dormant at low temperatures until mid-summer. Despatched to customers when starting to sprout. Worth trying for late-season treat. Main snag is susceptibility to late blight. Plant as earlies, mid-summer in ground; or plant singly in pots of at least 30 × 30cm/12 × 12in. Keep well watered. You can start lifting mid-October. For Christmas 'new' potatoes, best to leave in ground until required. They can be protected with cloches/fleece/light layer of straw early/mid-autumn.

Pests and diseases

Potato cyst eelworm (golden and white forms) Cause 'potato sickness'. Widespread in soils where potatoes previously grown. Plants stunted, leaves turn yellow and die, yields drastically reduced as tubers small. If suspected, lift roots and plunge into bucket of water; pinhead-sized white, yellow or brown cysts rise to surface if present. Remedy/prevention:

∾ Grow resistant cvs. Many cvs resistant to golden form; a few have double resistance, including 'Sante' and 'Lady Balfour'.
∾ Concentrate on earlies, which may mature before seriously affected.
∾ Be resigned to lower yields or give up potato growing for at least 6 years, ideally 10 years!
∾ Prevent by using certified seed so not introduced; rotate over at least 4 years, incorporate plenty of compost.

Potato blight Worst in warm, moist conditions from mid-summer onwards, so early potatoes less affected, though not immune. Brownish black spots appear on leaves and stems. Eventually spores washed into soil and affect tubers. Reduce risk/damage by wide spacing and deep earthing up to make soil barrier for spores and reduce tuber infection. If crop affected seriously towards end of summer (or earlier if necessary), cut back plants to within 5cm/2in of ground. Remove and burn leaves and stems. Leave plants in ground for 3 weeks before lifting so that spores on surface die. Watch for promising blight-resistant cvs under development.

Virus diseases Potatoes susceptible to several aphid-borne virus diseases. Leaves become mottled; plants stunted. Lift and burn diseased plants. Try to control aphids. Important preventive measures:

∾ Do not save your own seed.
∾ Remove overwintered tubers ('volunteers' or ' keepers') before they produce leaves in spring.
∾ Burn or bin, rather than compost, old whole tubers (peelings can be composted).

Potato blackleg Worse when potatoes thickly mulched. Leaves become pale, margins roll inwards, stems rot at base. Dig up and destroy seriously affected plants. Don't store tubers, as rots will develop in store.

Common scab Corky scabby areas develop on tubers. Essentially a cosmetic disease. Worst in light and chalky soils. Don't lime before planting; work in plenty of organic matter. To prevent in dry conditions, water lightly but regularly once potatoes have emerged. Grow resistant cvs.

Slugs Take normal control measures. If very serious, try to lift crop by early autumn. Some cvs, e.g. 'Cara', more susceptible than others.

Harvesting

Earlies In many cvs flowers being open indicates tubers reaching edible size, generally early/mid-summer. Dig as required. Remove even tiny tubers in soil as they may carry over disease.

Maincrop For use fresh, lift as required. For storage, if plants healthy and growing well, leave in ground to bulk up until early autumn. If becoming diseased, cut back haulm late summer/early autumn. Leave plants further 2 weeks before lifting so that tuber skins harden. Preferably lift for storage on dry sunny day. Leave tubers exposed for several hours to dry off, but not much longer or they will start to become green. Store in hessian or double-thickness paper sacks tied at neck, never in plastic sacks. Store in dark (hessian sacks not light-proof) in cool, frost-proof conditions, at 4–10°C/39–50°F. If severe frost likely, cover with old carpeting etc. Store in mouse- and rat-proof buildings or containers. Will keep until following spring.

Cultivars
Performance and flavour of potato cvs varies considerably with soil and climatic conditions. Worth trying several cvs, then settling for those that perform best under your conditions. Every cv unique in characteristics – e.g. resistance to particular pests, diseases or adverse conditions. Consult current seed catalogues for details. The following cvs have been chosen primarily because they are generally agreed to have good flavour.

Very early/earlies 'Orla', 'Red Duke of York', 'Sharpes Express', 'Lady Christl', 'Dunluce', 'Accent', 'Winston'.

Second earlies/mid-season 'Nadine', 'Celine', 'Nicola', 'Kestrel' , 'Saxon', 'British Queen', 'Charlotte', 'Carlingford'.

Maincrop 'Rooster', 'Maris Piper', 'King Edward', 'Valor', 'Casanova', 'Picasso', 'Ratte'/'Asparges'.

Compact cvs suitable for tubs 'Foremost', 'Dunluce', 'Swift'.

Recommended for specific purposes
Salad – 'Belle de Fontenay', 'Cherie', 'Red Duke of York', 'Swift', 'Carlingford', 'Anya', 'Charlotte', 'Juliette', 'Nicola', 'Roseval', 'Pink Fir Apple', 'Ratte'.
Baking – 'Picasso', 'Golden Wonder', 'Marfona', 'Winston', 'Valor', 'Red Duke of York', 'Swift', 'Nicola', 'Valor'.
Roasting – 'Accent', 'Nicola', 'King Edward', 'Kestrel', 'Maxine', 'Lady Balfour', 'Maris Piper', 'Valor'.
Chips – 'Maris Piper', 'Pink Fir Apple', 'Kestrel', 'Celine', 'Golden Wonder', 'Valor'.
Boiling – 'Kestrel', 'Lady Balfour', 'Picasso', 'Maris Peer', 'Estima', 'Nadine', 'Maxine', 'Nicola', 'Pink Fir Apple'.
Mashing – 'Accent', 'Winston', 'Kestrel', 'Nadine', 'Edzell Blue', 'Avalanche', 'Picasso'.

VSR ★★★ earlies, ★★ main

PUMPKINS see Squash, Winter

PURSLANE, SUMMER *Portulaca oleracea*

Summer purslane is a small plant with very pretty, succulent, rounded or oval leaves and fleshy stems. It is tender, thriving in warm weather but miserable in cold wet conditions. The leaves and young stems are mainly used raw in salads. Its cool, refreshing quality compensates for a rather bland flavour. There are green- and yellow- or gold-leaved forms.

Types

Green-leaved Thinner, narrower leaves, probably hardier and more prolific. Reputedly better-flavoured.

Yellow-leaved Leaves thicker, more succulent, glossier and more decorative.

Site and soil
Light, well-drained soil. Open site in full sun, but sheltered from wind.

Cultivation
Grow either as single plants spaced 15cm/6in apart, or as CCA seedlings, sown by broadcasting or in narrow or wide drills. Seeds are tiny and seedlings damp off easily, so there is no advantage in sowing prematurely.

Cultivation options:
1 For very useful early crop, sow *in situ* under cover early/mid-spring as CCA seedlings.
2 Sow in gentle heat in propagator in seed trays mid-spring/early summer. Prick out (can be pricked out into modules) when seedlings large enough to handle. Harden off well and plant outside after all risk of frost has past. They can be protected with cloches/films in the early stages. Alternatively plant under cover.
3 For follow-on crop outdoors, sow in seed trays in late spring or in early summer.
4 Sow *in situ* outdoors late spring/early to mid-summer as CCA seedlings, as long as no risk of frost.
5 For useful autumn crop, sow *in situ* under cover late summer.

Require little attention other than regular picking. Gold-leaved forms are said to retain their colour better if watered in full sun.

Harvesting
In favourable conditions CCA seedlings ready within 4–5 weeks of sowing; single plants within 8 weeks. Start cutting CCA seedlings when about 5cm/2in high. Pick young leaves, shoot tips and stems of single plants as soon as usable size. Pick regularly to encourage further growth, as plants rapidly become coarse. Remove any seed heads that appear: they are knobbly and unpleasant to eat, and inhibit the production of more tender shoots.

When plants start to run to seed towards the end of the cropping period, cut stems right back to within about 4cm/1½in of ground. They will often regenerate. Covering with cloches or fleece in autumn prolongs their useful life.

VSR ★★★ indoor seedlings, ★★ single plants

PURSLANE, WINTER (Claytonia, Miner's lettuce, Spring beauty)
Montia perfoliata (previously *Claytonia perfoliata*)

One of the most useful spring salads, winter purslane is an exceptionally pretty, dainty little plant with white flowers. It forms clumps rarely more than 20cm/8in across, with stems up to 20cm/8in high when flowering. The first triangular leaves on short stalks are superseded by larger, semi-circular leaves 'wrapped' around the flowering stalks. Leaves, stems and flowers are all edible when young. All are mild-flavoured with a succulent texture. While it can be available all year round, it is most useful in autumn, spring and early summer. It grows astonishingly fast early in the year. A salad plant children love.

Site and soil
Not fussy, but does best on light sandy soil. Good drainage essential. Tolerates light shade. Be warned: it seeds itself and can become invasive.

Cultivation
Sowing options:

1　For summer use, sow early to late spring.
2　For autumn harvest, sow mid- to late summer. Plant later sowings under cover.
3　For spring crop, sow late summer/early autumn. Plant under cover.

Either sow *in situ* and thin to required spacing, or sow in seed trays or modules. Sow shallowly, as seeds are tiny. Space plants 10–13cm/4–5in apart each way. Can also be broadcast in patches for seedling CCA crop. Start cutting as soon as leaves large enough to handle.

Reasonably hardy, surviving most winters outdoors if soil well drained, but looks poorly and 'blue' in cold weather.

For valuable spring crop, have some plants under cover during winter: they will be more luxuriant and ready well ahead of outdoor plants.

Once winter purslane is established, seedlings appear all over the garden (and in greenhouses if left to seed in previous years) in autumn and spring. Transplant them carefully to where you want them, or dig them in as gratis green manure. They are easily uprooted if not required.

Note: in my experience the pink-flowered species, *Montia sibirica*, has an acrid aftertaste and should be avoided.

VSR ★★★; PP

RADISH *Raphanus sativus*

Radishes are a range of annual and biennial plants of varying hardiness, grown mainly for their roots, though the seedling leaves, young leaves and seed pods of various cvs are edible. The roots have a characteristic sharp flavour. The same sharpness is often, but not invariably, found in leaves and pods. (For cultivation of leaf radish and radish seed pods, see *The Organic Salad Garden*.)

Types

Standard Small roots, rarely more than 2.5cm/1in diameter and on average up to 5cm/2in long, though some longer. Flesh is white but skin colour can be white, red, pink, yellow, purplish or red and white. Round or cylindrical in shape. Can be grown for much of year outside and under cover. Must be used fresh.

Storage and winter-hardy radish Moderately large radishes; somewhat coarse. Round forms 5–10cm/2–4in diameter; long types up to about 20cm/8in long. White flesh, but skin colour pink, or black to violet. Traditional cvs known as 'Chinese' or 'Spanish'. Hardy to -8 to -10°C/ 17.5–14°F. Used fresh or stored in winter. Can be grated or sliced and eaten raw or cooked like turnips. Excellent in stews.

Asian radish Diverse group of large radishes including some gigantic types and remarkable red-fleshed, green-skinned, sweet-flavoured Chinese Beauty Heart radish. Mooli/Daikon type best known in West: typically large roots, from 10–60cm/4–24in long, weighing up to 500g/1lb. Skin smooth, usually white but sometimes partly green. In standard types flesh is white. Mainly used fresh, raw or cooked. Flavour ranges from mild to hot. (For other Asian types, see *Oriental Vegetables*).

Site and soil

Rich light soil, good drainage and plenty of moisture are the secret of success with radishes. Soil should be humus-rich but not freshly manured. Open site for spring and autumn sowings; light shade for summer sowings of ordinary radish or they run to seed rapidly.

Cultivation of standard radish

Fast-maturing, ready 20–30 days after sowing. Useful for intercropping or marking rows of slow-germinating seeds. Failures are usually caused by sowing in dry position, failing to thin early or poor tilth on seedbed. Never let seedlings become lanky through overcrowding.

Sowing programme:
1 For main spring-to-autumn supplies outdoors, sow outdoors spring to early autumn.

Make first outdoor sowing early spring in sheltered situation as soon as soil is warm and workable. You can protect it with cloches or fleece. For continuous supply, sow in succession at 10–14 day intervals. Radishes generally mature together, so only sow short rows each time. Mid-summer sowings best in semi-shade, ideally between other crops. Try to sow at even depth of about 1cm/½in, slightly deeper for long varieties. If sowing is uneven, first seedlings to germinate overshadow and swamp those that germinate later. Essential to sow thinly in narrow or wide drills 10–15cm/4–6in apart. Equally important to thin early to 2–2.5cm/¾–1in apart. Can also be broadcast thinly.

Dust with derris if seedlings nibbled by flea beetle. In dry weather water weekly at rate of 11 litres per sq. m/2 gallons per sq. yd. Pull radishes as soon as ready, as most run to seed rapidly when mature. Some cvs have good bolting resistance; especially useful for mid-summer sowings.

2 For very early spring crop, sow late winter/early spring in unheated greenhouse or frame as above. If sown very thinly, further thinning is often unnecessary. Give plenty of ventilation; keep well watered.

3 For autumn-to-early-winter crop, sow early autumn in unheated greenhouse or frame as (2) above.

4 For mid-winter/early spring radishes under cover, sow appropriate cvs from mid-autumn to late winter. Use small-leaved, slower-maturing cvs developed for winter use in unheated polytunnels and greenhouses. For them to grow well, night temperatures should not drop below about 5°C/41°F. Give extra protection with cloches, film or fleece if low temperatures are forecast. Thin to 5cm/2in apart. Don't overwater. Leaves turning very dark green indicates watering necessary.

Cultivation of Asian radish

With standard cvs delay sowing until early/mid-summer as they have tendency to bolt prematurely from earlier sowings, as do many Asian vegetables. Some bolt-resistant cvs can be sown late spring – even so may bolt if there is sudden fall in temperature.

Sow *in situ* 1–2cm/½–¾in deep. You can sow them in sunken drills 4cm/1½in deep, pulling soil around stems as they grow to give extra support. Very fast-growing. Spacing depends on cv. Average spacing 10–13cm/4–5in apart in rows 23–25cm/9–10in apart. Can also be sown in modules and transplanted, provided planted before tap root starts to develop. Sow Beauty Heart cvs mid- to late summer. Can be sown or transplanted under cover for early winter crop. (For more information on Beauty Heart radish, see *The Organic Salad Garden*.)

Most oriental cvs mature in 7–8 weeks; normally stand for several weeks once mature without deteriorating.

Cultivation of winter radish (large type)

Sow thinly *in situ* outdoors, mid-/late summer, in moist soil. Sow in drills 30cm/12in apart; thin to 13–15cm/5–6in apart. Roots can grow over 50cm/20in long.

Flavour best if left in the soil during winter. You can protect from elements with light covering of bracken, straw or fleece. May keep in good condition until mid-spring. Advisable to lift and store if soil is heavy or wet, if there is high risk of slug or mouse damage, or if temperatures are liable to fall much below –8°C/17°F. Store somewhere cool under cover, laid horizontally in boxes of sand or clamp like carrots (see page 230).

In their second season these big radishes produce a huge crop of large, very succulent seed pods. Worth leaving a plant in the ground in spring to run to seed. Pick seed pods regularly when crisp and supple. As long as they can be snapped in half, they will be tender.

Radish seedlings

Wonderful fresh, spicy flavour; very productive. Grow as Mustard, page 284. For suitable cvs, see below.

Pests and disease

Plants are in ground for relatively long time, so subject to same pests as brassicas (see page 223). The outdoor summer crop can be grown under fine nets to protect from cabbage root fly and other flying insect pests.

Cultivars

Standard radish: 'Crystal Ball', 'French Breakfast', 'Long White Icicle', 'Pink Beauty', 'Sparkler', 'Cherry Belle'.

Good bolting resistance: 'Pontvil', 'Red Prince'/'Prinz Rotin', 'White Breakfast'.

For mid-winter sowing under cover: 'Helro', 'Robino', 'Saxa', 'Marabelle'.

Mooli radish (slow-bolting cvs): 'April Cross' F1, 'Minowase Summer Cross'.

Winter radish: 'Cherokee' F1, 'Black Spanish Round', 'Violet de Gournay', 'China Rose'.

Seedling radish: 'Bisai', 'Jaba', 'Early 40 Day'.

VSR **** seedling radish, *** ordinary radish, ** winter radish

RHUBARB *Rheum × hybridum*

Although eaten as a fruit, rhubarb is so entrenched in kitchen gardens that it earns its place in vegetable books. It is a large deep-rooting perennial plant often up to 90cm/3ft high, spreading to 1.2–1.5m/4–5ft. The stems are normally eaten in spring and early summer, though some cvs are autumn-cropping. Exceptionally early and sweet stems are obtained by forcing and blanching.

Site and soil

Grows in wide range of soil types, provided fertile and well-drained. Tolerates acid soil. Must be grown in open site; does not tolerate shade. Established plants are reasonably drought-tolerant, probably on account of deep roots.

Cultivation

Plants often remain productive for 10 years or more, so prepare site well, eliminating all perennial weeds. Dig in plenty of well-rotted manure or compost. Well-grown plants very prolific: three or four sufficient for most households.

Rhubarb established by purchasing young plants, by planting sets (crowns) or from seed.

Sets (offsets) best planted in early/mid-winter, though can be planted early spring. Sets are pieces of root with at least one dormant bud. Must be taken from healthy, vigorous plants. (Old rhubarb plants often become virused, seen in yellowing, mottled leaves and declining yields: offsets taken from them would be infected.) Lift 'mother plant' after leaves have died right back. Using sharp spade, slice off sections of root and bud from outside edges, roughly 10cm/4in diameter. Replant the original root if still wanted. Plant offsets at least 90cm/3ft apart. On light soil plant with buds just below ground; on heavy soil, or where buds very large, plant with buds just above ground to prevent rotting.

Plants raised from seed are of very variable quality. In long term propagate from best plants and jettison poorest. Sow seed about 2.5cm/1in deep in spring in outdoor seedbed, thinning initially to 15cm/6in apart, finally to about 30cm/12in apart. In autumn or the following spring select the strongest plants and plant in permanent situation. Alternatively sow indoors in spring, prick out into small pots and plant in permanent position early summer.

Plants respond well to being kept heavily mulched to retain moisture, throughout the growing season. To maintain fertility, apply heavy dressing of manure in winter or spring. Cut off flowering seed heads when young or rots may start in the hollow stems. If plants not growing well, apply liquid feed in spring. To maintain a good plantation, it is advisable to replant in sequence: proliferation of very thin stalks sign of declining vigour.

Forcing

Various methods used to obtain very early blanched crop:

1 Lift well-established plant in early winter, when dormant but after exposure to frost, which breaks their natural dormancy. Plant in ordinary soil in tub, ashcan or similar container. Trim back roots if necessary to fit in. Exclude light either by putting in dark cellar or by covering with upturned ashcan, or frame covered with black plastic.

Rhubarb can even be forced in a black polythene rubbish sack. In all cases allow headroom of about 45cm/18in for stems to develop. Temperature of 7.5–16°C/45–60°F sufficient; higher temperatures unnecessary. Make sure roots don't dry out. Normally ready within about 5 weeks. Roots generally exhausted by forcing and unsuitable for further cropping, though sets taken from them can be replanted.

2 Lift roots and replant in soil under greenhouse staging or similar situation. (See Witloof chicory, page 244). Treat as (1) above. Roots will normally take a little longer to develop.

3 Cover dormant crowns *in situ*. Any time from mid-winter to early spring cover with about 10cm/4in dry light material such as dried leaves or straw. Then exclude light with ashcan or purpose-made clay rhubarb pot. Tender shoots ready within 3–5 weeks.

Pests and diseases

Honey fungus, crown rot and virus diseases May eventually weaken plants. Dig up and start new plantation in fresh site.

Harvesting

Don't pull any rhubarb in first season; pull lightly second season. Be guided by appearance of plant; if not vigorous leave unpulled so that crown can build up. Afterwards pull as much as required, as long as stems firm. Stems usually start to soften mid-summer, except in autumn-cropping cvs. Harvest by grasping stem low on plant and pulling, rather than cutting.

Cultivars

Available as crowns: 'Timperley Early', 'Champagne', 'Livingstone' (autumn cropping)
Available from seed: 'Victoria', 'Glaskin's Perpetual'.

VSR ★★

ROCKET (Mediterranean rocket/cress, salad rocket, Italian cress)
Eruca sativa, E. versicaria

A spicy-leaved annual of Mediterranean origin, rocket is one of the most popular salad plants. It is a small plant with straight-edged or indented leaves. It withstands several degrees of frost but runs to seed rapidly in hot dry conditions, becoming very pungent. It is very fast-growing and highly productive. The flowers are edible, pleasantly flavoured and decorative in salads. Wild rocket is a closely related perennial with smaller, more pungent leaves. It is slower growing and much less productive.

Site and soil

Tolerant of most soils. Slightly shaded site preferable in summer.

Cultivation

Year-round supplies feasible by growing outside from spring to summer and under cover in winter. Can also be grown in seed trays or dishes indoors for use as small seedlings (see Mustard, page 284). Grow as single plants or as CCA seedlings. Responds well to CCA treatment at every stage.

For CCA seedlings, sow *in situ* by broadcasting or in narrow or wide drills about 13cm/5in apart. Ideal for intercropping and undercropping; often sown in bands between and around slow-maturing brassicas.

For single plants, sow *in situ*, thinning to 15cm/6in apart, or sow in seed boxes or modules, planting out when young.

Make first sowings in cold greenhouse or frame mid-/late winter. (This is one of my first polytunnel sowings every year.) Sow in succession outdoors from early spring until early autumn. Summer sowings in hot weather may bolt very rapidly. For winter and spring supplies, sow in early/mid-autumn under cover (see Mustard, page 286).

Flea beetle frequently attacks seedlings. Spray with derris or grow under fine nets. Keep well watered, especially in summer.

Pick leaves from single plants as required. Start cutting seedling crops when about 5cm/2in high, often within 3–4 weeks of sowing. In cool seasons up to four more cuts may be made before plants coarsen or run to seed.

Note: Turkish rocket (*Bunias orientalis*) is a hardy perennial resembling dandelion. Strains of salad rocket are sometimes misleadingly sold as Turkish rocket.

VSR ★★★★

RUBY CHARD see Spinach group (Swiss chard)

SALADINI (Saladisi)

This name, which my husband and I coined in the 1970s to describe the bags of mixed salad we were then selling, is now frequently applied to mixtures of salad seed. These are based on the traditional European mixtures known as *misticanza* in Italy and *mesclun* in France. Popular ingredients in the typical modern mixture are various types of lettuce and chicory, endive, rocket, chervil and corn salad, but there are many possible alternatives. Saladini mixtures look colourful both growing and when cut for salads. They are a great 'short cut' to attractive salads for the household.

For mixtures based on oriental greens, see Oriental saladini, page 295.

Cultivation

Grow as CCA seedling crops. Sow as for lettuce CCA seedlings (see page 276).

Inevitably the fastest germinating plants (usually rocket) emerge first. Cut when ready, leaving other plants to mature in due course. Patches may remain productive over several months. Dig them in when starting to coarsen or run to seed.

VSR ★★★★; PP

SALSIFY (Oyster plant, salsafy, vegetable oyster) *Tragopogon porrifolius*

A hardy biennial growing 90cm/3ft high, salsify produces beautiful purple flowers in its second season. Although cultivated primarily for its light-skinned, long, thinnish, delicately flavoured roots which are mainly used in winter, it is also grown for the edible flower buds, petals and chards (blanched young shoots) which develop in spring. All are subtly flavoured. Salsify takes little space but has a fairly long growing season.

Site and soil
Open site; moderately fertile, light, stone-free sandy soil is best. Roots rarely develop to a good size in heavy soils. In heavy soil, it is worth making shallow trench 25–30cm/10–12in deep, filled with spent potting compost or sandy soil, to encourage root penetration. Avoid freshly manured soil.

Cultivation for roots
Use fresh seed, as viability deteriorates fairly fast. Sow *in situ* outdoors in spring in ground raked to a fine tilth. Station sowing advisable as germination slow. Succeeds at various spacing. Spacing rows 30cm/12in apart, thinning to 10–15cm/4–6in apart, is satisfactory.

Little attention required. Rarely troubled by pests or diseases. Water in dry weather; mulch after watering.

Harvesting and use of roots
Roots ready mid-autumn to following mid-/late spring. Lift as required. Best flavour if left in soil in winter; if necessary cover with bracken or straw for extra protection. Alternatively lift and store in sand in shed.

To prepare, scrub clean, cook unpeeled, squeeze skin off after cooking. Can be boiled, baked, fried, served in sauces, parboiled and finished in pan with margarine or butter and brown sugar.

Cultivation for flower buds/flowers
Sow as above, but seeds can be spaced more closely. Leave roots in soil for second season. Flowering normally starts late spring/early summer but may continue all summer.

Harvest and use of flowers
Pick flower buds when plump, just before they open, with about 10cm/4in of stem attached. (Stems have excellent flavour.) Lightly steam

or boil buds and stems; eat hot, or cooled and served with vinaigrette. For petals, pick when flowers open in morning; they usually close later. Sprinkle petals on salads. Leave a few flowering plants to self-seed.

Cultivation for chards
Sow as for roots above. Forcing/blanching can be done in autumn or spring.

Autumn method:
 1 Cut off old leaves about 2.5cm/1in above ground in autumn.
 2 Cover the stems with up to 15cm/6in of light soil. Shoots push their way through in spring, becoming naturally blanched in the process.
 3 Emerging shoots can be covered with upturned buckets or flower pots with drainage holes blocked to increase blanching effect (see illustration, page 243.)

Spring method: when growth starts in spring, cover with about 10cm/4in of straw or dry leaves. Chards will be less well blanched but very clean. You can increase blanching with pots as above. Probably best method if soil wet or heavy.

Harvesting and use of chards
Cut chards when about 10–13cm/4–5in long. The roots may resprout. Use cooked or raw like Witloof chicory, page 243.

Cultivars
'Mammoth', 'Sandwich Island'.

VSR ★; PP when flowering

SCORZONERA (Viper's grass) *Scorzonera hispanica*

Scorzonera is always twinned with salsify, but differs in being a hardy perennial with long, black-skinned, white-fleshed roots and yellow flowers in its second season. These form plumper, more substantial buds than salsify.

Site and soil, cultivation, use and VSR
As Salsify, above. Being perennial, roots can be left in the soil for second season to grow larger. Lift one or two roots in autumn. If they are only finger thickness, leave rest in ground until following autumn; they will thicken without toughening. Can also be sown in late summer for use following autumn.

Cultivars
'Maxima', 'Habil', 'Russian Giant'.

VSR ★; PP when flowering

SENPOSAI HYBRIDS *Brassica* hybrids

These excellent Japanese-bred vegetables result from cabbage and komat-suna crosses. They are characterized by their vigour, healthiness, and tolerance of heat and cold. They eventually grow into large, loose cabbage-like plants, but their flavour (cabbage with a hint of spinach) is best when they are picked young for cooked greens, or used raw in salads. Seeds can be sprouted and grown as seedling sprouts (see *The Organic Salad Garden.*)

Soil, cultivation, harvesting and use

As Komatsuna, page 270. Can be sown throughout growing season. For maximum returns, sow in wide drills and cut when 5–10cm/2–4in high for use as CCA seedlings. After one or possibly two cuts, thin to 5–7.5cm/2–3in apart; cut for use as young greens when 15–20cm/6–8in high. Depending on time of year, CCA stage may be reached 4–5 weeks after sowing, young greens stage 6–8 weeks after sowing. For very early crop, make last sowing early autumn outdoors, late/mid-autumn under cover.

Excellent lightly steamed or stir-fried.

Cultivars

'Senposai No. 2' – excellent. Unfortunately seed currently not easily available; I hope it will be reintroduced in future.

VSR ★★★

SHALLOTS (Multiplier onion) *Allium cepa* Aggregatum Group

Shallots are valued members of the onion family on account of their distinct, fresh flavour and ability of the bulbs to store for up to nine months. In the UK this enables them to bridge the gap between the last stored onions and the first fresh onions. European cvs are moderately hardy and withstand high temperatures much better than bulb onions. They can be planted close for use as 'green onions' or scallions.

Main groups

Yellow Flask-shaped, outer skin straw or bronze-coloured, white flesh, largest type.

Red Flask-shaped, outer skin red, flesh rose tinted in varying degrees, smaller, some cvs very strong-flavoured.

French 'Jersey' Long, thin, popular in France, excellent flavour; some cvs short-term storage only.

Site and soil
As Bulb onions, page 289. Compacted soils unsuitable as shallots pushed out of the soil by growing roots.

Cultivation
Cultivation options:

1 Raising from sets. Most widely used method as very simple. Each individual set or small bulb develops into cluster of eight to ten bulbs. Drawback is tendency to bolt prematurely; some stocks virused and low-yielding. Always buy certified stock from reputable seedsmen. Beware of cheap offers!

2 Raising from seed. More labour-intensive, requires longer growing season. Each seed normally produces one set, occasionally divided into two or three. Good bolting resistance, healthy, said to be stronger-flavoured than set-raised.

Growing from sets: ideal size for planting about 1cm/½in circumference. Sets over 1.5cm/⅝in more likely to bolt prematurely. Remove dry loose outer scales. 0.5kg/1lb normally sufficient for 3m/10ft row planted 18cm/7in apart. Generally plant as early as possible: early/mid-winter in mild areas, otherwise late winter/early spring. Some cvs, e.g. 'Sante', only suitable for late spring planting. (Follow supplier's directions for appropriate planting time.) Plant in reasonably firm but not compacted soil. For highest yields, space 18cm/7in apart each way. Alternative spacing 15cm/6in apart in rows 23cm/9in apart. Push set into soil to half its depth, or plant in shallow drill, so that only tips are protruding. Firm soil around set after planting. Protect against birds with strong black cotton above row. If bulbs uprooted by birds, replant carefully. Keep weed-free; you can mulch between rows, but take care not to cover developing sets. No further attention necessary.

To grow from seed, sow indoors early spring as for Bulb onions, page 289, or sow *in situ* outdoors as soon as soil workable. To obtain single shallot from each seed, sow in rows 10–13cm/4–5in apart, thinning seedlings to 2.5–5cm/1–2in apart. Alternatively space seedlings 5cm/2in apart each way. At wider spacing than this more multiple bulbs likely to develop. Seed-raised sets unsuitable for saving to plant following season.

For green shallot shoots/scallions, plant small sets or seedlings 2.5cm/1in apart each way in spring, under cover for early crop, or outdoors as soon as soil workable. Cut when 7.5–10cm/3–4in high to use as green onion substitute.

Harvesting, storage and use
Shallots normally ready mid-summer onwards. Lift clumps whole; no need to split them up. Harvest and store as for Bulb onions, page 291. Provided sets look healthy, keep small ones to plant following season.

Use in cooking, raw or for pickling.

Cultivars

Yellow from sets: 'Atlantic', 'Topper', 'Golden Gourmet'.
Yellow from seed: 'Creation' F1.
Red from sets: 'Pikant', 'Delicato', 'Red Sun', 'Sante', 'Success'.
Red from seed: 'Atlas' F1, 'Ambition' F1.
French Jersey type: 'Longor', 'Jermor', 'Mikor'.

VSR ★★

SPINACH GROUP

Several different plants are popularly termed spinach:

- ∾ True or ordinary spinach *Spinacia oleracea*.
- ∾ Leaf beet *Beta vulgaris* subsp. *cicla*. This includes perpetual spinach, also known as spinach beet, silver beet and Swiss chard, also known as seakale beet and silver chard.
- ∾ New Zealand spinach *Tetragonia expansa*.
- ∾ Mountain spinach *Atriplex hortensis* – see Orache, page 294.

TRUE OR ORDINARY SPINACH *Spinacia oleracea*

Fast-growing, moderately hardy, cool weather annual, generally 15–20cm/6–8in high. Tends to run to seed rapidly in hot weather but new cvs much improved. Most types round-leaved; some have pointed leaves. Leaf texture varies from thin, smooth-leaved types to thicker, pucker-leaved types. These are more robust and used in supermarket salad packs. Ordinary spinach now widely grown as a 'baby leaf' CCA crop. Probably most nutritious and delicately flavoured of spinach group.

Site and soil

Requires very fertile, moisture-retentive soil, rich in organic matter. Avoid poor, dry soils. Preferred pH neutral to slightly acid; very acid soils should be limed. Rotate to avoid build-up of downy mildew; its resting spores remain in the soil. Don't grow near cucumbers, as spinach blight is caused by cucumber mosaic virus. Open site for most sowings, but tolerates light shade in mid-summer provided it has adequate moisture. Summer crops can be intercropped between beans, peas or sweet corn.

Cultivation and harvesting

Traditional distinctions between more heat-tolerant 'round-seeded' types used for summer crops, and 'prickly-seeded' types used for autumn/winter crops being eroded. Modern cvs more versatile; mostly round-seeded. Divided into slow-growing, 'long-day' varieties with good bolting resistance and faster-growing, 'short-day' varieties. For year-round supply, sow appropriate cvs for each season where possible, though in practice there is considerable flexibility. Still some risk of premature bolting with very early sowings.

Main sowings:

1 For summer supplies, sow late spring to early summer. Protect spring sowings with cloches/films in early stages if necessary. Use slow-growing, long-day cvs with good bolting resistance.

2 For autumn, winter and spring supplies, use faster growing, short-day cvs

ⓦ Sow mid- to late summer outside. In autumn protect outside crops with cloches/films if weather poor. May continue cropping well into winter.

ⓦ Sow early to mid-autumn under cover. Plants from this sowing may stop growing in mid-winter, but will start again in early spring.

ⓦ Sow under cover late winter/early spring.

Grow as single plants or CCA seedlings. For single plants, sow *in situ* in drills 28–30cm/11–12in apart, thinning to 15cm/6in apart. Or sow in seed trays or modules and transplant. For CCA seedlings, sow thinly in single or broad drills 10cm/4in apart. For continuous supply, make successive sowings at 3–4 week intervals throughout growing season, but spring and late-summer sowings generally most successful.

Leaves can be cut at any stage once they reach a usable size.

Cultivars
For summer supplies (slower growing long-day cvs): 'Medania', 'Tetona' F1, 'Bloomsdale', 'Spokane' F1, 'Trinidad' F1, 'Palco' F1 (also winter under cover).

For autumn, late winter and spring supplies (fast-growing short-day cvs): 'Galaxy' F1, 'Giant Winter', 'Samish' F1, 'Triathlon' F1.

VSR ★★ single plants, ★★★ CCA

PERPETUAL SPINACH/SPINACH BEET *Beta vulgaris* subsp. *cicla*
Both perpetual spinach and Swiss chard (see page 328) are vigorous, productive biennials in the beetroot family. Naturally healthy plants. Hardier and more heat-tolerant than spinach. Leaves coarser and less subtly flavoured. Respond well to CCA treatment at every stage.

Perpetual spinach is thin-stemmed, with moderately thick, fairly smooth leaves. Grows 30–38cm/12–15in high with similar spread when mature. When grown as CCA seedlings it is one of most productive vegetables for small gardens.

Site and soil
As Spinach, above. Tolerates drier conditions.

Cultivation and harvesting
Grow as single plants or as CCA seedlings. For single plants, sow in drills about 38cm/15in apart. Thin in stages to 25–30cm/10–12in apart. For

CCA seedling crop, grow in rows or wide drills 10cm/4in apart, or broadcast. Can be sown thinly, so no further thinning necessary; or thin to about 5cm/2in apart. Spacing not critical.

For continuous supply, make several sowings:

1 For late spring/early summer crop, early sowing late winter/early spring under cover.
2 Main sowing early to late spring outdoors. Will crop during summer and autumn, and frequently through winter into late spring/early summer following year.
3 Mid- to late summer outdoors. Usually less productive crop, but may crop through winter and well into following summer.
4 For good-quality winter crop, final late sowing CCA seedlings under cover, late summer/early autumn.

Protect young seedlings from birds. Keep weed-free. Water in dry weather; mulching beneficial. In winter protect outdoor crop with cloches or dried bracken to improve leaf quality.

Harvesting

Pick/cut leaves as soon as useful size – when leaves are 5–10cm/2–4in high – leaving plants to resprout. First cut normally within 6 weeks of sowing. Several cuts possible if kept well watered.

Plants naturally perennial, and often continue cropping in second season, though tend to be less vigorous. Pick off any flowering shoots/seed heads to prolong cropping. If left to seed they will self-sow, virtually perpetuating themselves. Seedlings can be transplanted to new site.

Cultivars

'Perpetual spinach', 'Popeye'.

VSR ★★★

SWISS CHARD (Seakale beet, silver chard, silver beet)
Beta vulgaris subsp. *cicla*
Strong, upright plants, growing 45cm/18in high with similar spread. Leaves thick, glossy, crêped texture, with prominent white or coloured mid-ribs and stems. Remarkable range of colour in stems: pink, rose, yellow, orange, red, white with same colouring echoed in leaf veins. Leaf colour ranges from dark to very light green, to varying shades of reddish green. Stems and leaves cooked as separate vegetables. 'Baby leaves' used in supermarket salad packs. White-stemmed cvs probably most productive. Older red-stemmed cvs, e.g. 'Rhubarb Chard' and 'Ruby Chard', prone to bolting prematurely.

Site and soil
As Spinach, page 326. Succeeds on most soils, but best on heavy well-manured soil. Its deep roots enable plants to tolerate drought.

Cultivation and harvesting
Ideal vegetable for beginners and absentee gardeners, as withstands neglect and maltreatment well. Rarely attacked by pests, though in some gardens snails eat holes in leaves.

Mainly grown as single plants; coloured-stem cvs can be sown as CCA seedlings for use in salads.

Single plants can be sown *in situ* and thinned to final spacing, but best sown in seed trays or modules and transplanted, as 'seeds' are technically 'fruits' containing several seedlings and germinate thickly. Eventually space plants about 38cm/15in apart each way.

For all-year-round supply, make two sowings:
1 Sow late spring. (Earlier sowings may bolt prematurely.) These crop through summer and autumn, and frequently through winter until late spring/early summer the following year, when they run to seed. Cut leaves individually, leaving plant to resprout.
2 Sow mid- to late summer. Use as successional crop from autumn until mid-summer the following year. Depending on the season, these may remain productive all winter.

Transplant some under cover in late summer/early autumn, for a highly productive, very useful early/late spring crop under cover.

Although moderately hardy, plants grown outdoors in winter may develop rots and deteriorate in quality. Protection with cloches/fleece/low polytunnels beneficial. Cut back flowering shoots to encourage further cropping.

For CCA seedlings, sow thinly as seedling clusters difficult to thin.

Sowing programme for CCA seedlings:
1 For main summer supply, sow spring to late summer outdoors. (Early sowings may bolt prematurely.)
2 For winter and spring supply, sow early autumn and early spring under cover.

Cultivars
'Fordhook Giant', 'Lucullus' – green-leaved, white-stemmed.
'Feurio', 'Charlotte' – improved, red-stemmed, with good bolting resistance.
'Bright Lights' – coloured stems mixture.
(Single yellow-stemmed selection is becoming available.)

VSR ★★★

NEW ZEALAND SPINACH *Tetragonia expansa*
Tender, sprawling perennial, grown as annual in cool climates. Small triangular leaves. Has good drought resistance. Milder flavoured than ordinary spinach.

Site and soil
Open site. Does best in well-drained, reasonably fertile soil, but tolerates poorer soil than spinach and leaf beet. Does not require high levels of nitrogen. Very useful as a ground-cover plant in fairly dry, sunny corners. Can look attractive in flower beds or as path edging.

Cultivation and harvesting
Germination sometimes difficult. If so, soak seeds in water overnight before sowing.

Sow indoors mid- to late spring in seed trays or modules. Harden off before planting outside after all risk of frost is over. Space plants 45–75cm/1½–2½ft apart each way. Alternatively sow *in situ*, after all risk of frost past. Station sow in groups, about 15cm/6in apart, thinning to one seedling after germination.

Keep picking tips and young leaves to encourage further growth. In mild areas may self-sow and reappear following year.

VSR ★★; PP

SQUASH, WINTER, and PUMPKINS
Cucurbita pepo, C. maxima, C. moschata

This extraordinarily diverse group of gourds ranges from the relatively small 'acorn' squash, weighing roughly 1kg/2lb, to giant pumpkins well over 22.5kg/50lb. Skin colour ranges from grey to green to deep orange with many intermediate colours. They can be round, oval, squat, long, or turban or onion-shaped, with ridged, smooth or warted skin. The majority are vigorous trailing plants; some are moderately vigorous and a few grow as bushes. They vary in flavour and culinary quality. For culinary use my advice is to opt for those that feel heavy for their size, which indicates dense dry flesh that cooks well. Depending on variety, they store 2–6 months or more. For the related summer squash or marrows, see Marrows, page 281, and Courgettes, page 250.

Main culinary types of winter squash

Acorn Small, ribbed, slightly oval fruits, typically cream- or dark-green-skinned. Up to about 1kg/2lb in weight. Bush and semi-bush. Short storage but can be stored without curing (see below) Good cvs: 'Cream of the Crop', 'Table Ace' F1.

Buttercup/Kabocha Green-skinned, slightly flattened, round fruits, Butternut types (see below) with 'button' on base. Medium-sized, weighing up to about 2.2kg/5lb. Trailing. Good storage. Excellent cooking quality. Good cvs: 'Buttercup', 'Kabocha', 'Sweet Mama'.

Butternut Typically cylindrical with bulbous end, 'waisted' pear shape, but some cvs flat cylindrical shape. Buff-coloured skin. Weight ranges from ½–2.2kg/1–5lb. Trailing. Very long storage. Good culinary quality. Good cvs: 'Ponca', 'Sprinter' F1.

Round 'Little Gem' Round fruit, tennis-ball size. Green skin ripening to orange. Moderately vigorous climbers; suitable for arches, tepees. Short storage. Good cvs: 'Little Gem', 'Rolet' (longer keeping)

'Delicata'/'Sweet Dumpling' type Small fruits distinguished by green stripes on cream skin. 'Delicata' at least 18cm/7in long, 'Sweet Dumpling' squat shape, up to 10cm/4in diameter. Semi-trailing. More numerous fruits than most winter squash. Medium storage with no need for curing. Sweet flesh. Good cvs: 'Delicata', 'Sweet Dumpling'.

Hubbard Characteristically spinning top or teardrop shape with tapered ends. Some onion-shaped. Often slightly warted skin. Skin colour ranges from blue to dark green to orange. Mostly vigorous trailers. Potentially large, weighing from 3–9kg/7–20lb depending on cv. Good storage. Excellent culinary qualities. Good cvs: 'Red Kuri'/'Uchiki Kuri', 'Blue Hubbard'.

'Crown Prince' F1 Flattened round shape, grey/metallic blue skin, lightly ridged fruits, typically 20–23cm/8–9in diameter. Weigh up to 5kg/10lb. Long storage. Excellent culinary quality.

Types of culinary pumpkin
The term 'pumpkin' generally embraces winter squashes which have deep orange skin when mature. Many are grown primarily for carving and painting and have no particular culinary merit. The following are recommended for culinary use. Some types have 'semi-naked' seeds suitable for roasting as snacks.

Small-fruited Ridged or smooth fruits up to about 10cm/4in diameter and 0.75–1kg/1½–2lb in weight. Trailing habit. Medium storage. Convenient for baking whole; reasonable culinary quality. Some small ornamental gourds edible young. Group merges into slightly larger New England pie pumpkins. Good cvs: 'Baby Bear' (edible seeds), 'Jack be Little', 'Munchkin', 'Baby Boo' (creamy-skinned ornamental); slightly larger type 'Becky', 'Triple Treat' (edible seeds).

French Best known is large, ribbed, slightly flattened, deep orange 'Rouge Vif d'Etampes'. Easily 45cm/18in diameter; can weigh up to 12.5kg/25lb. Vigorous trailer. Medium storage. Good eating quality.

Cultivation

Sunny, sheltered site. Soil as for cucumbers. Raise plants as Cucumbers, page 254. (Semi-naked seed types need slightly higher temperatures to germinate; it is inadvisable to sow *in situ*.) Seedlings normally ready for planting 4–6 weeks after sowing. Plant bush types about 1.5m/5ft apart, trailing types at least 2–2.5m/6–8ft apart. To mature, they require 3–4 months' warm weather after planting, depending on cv.

Training methods to save space:

- ✿ Train less vigorous climbers on strong wooden or metal structures. In early stages tie in if necessary. 'Little Gem', 'Rolet' can be trained up strings.
- ✿ Train in neat circle (see illustration, page 165). Guide or pin down main shoot as it grows with sticks on either side of stem, or tent pegs or wire pins holding it down. Move them on daily if necessary. Plants usually produce useful secondary roots on stem. Mark the centre point with a cane for watering.
- ✿ Allow trailing types to trail through sweet corn.

'Stopping' plants

For earlier yields and larger fruits of large-fruiting types on trailing plants, it is advisable to limit production to two or three per plant by 'stopping' plants. Once sufficient fruits have developed, remove surplus flowers or small fruits. When remaining fruits are developing well, trim off trailing stems several leaves beyond the fruit to concentrate energy into fruits.

Harvesting, curing, storage and use

Cut away shading leaves at end of season to help fruits mature. For use fresh, pick early-maturing types when required size. For winter storage, leave on plant as long as possible so that skins can harden naturally. Signs of maturity are cracks appearing in skin and on stem. Must be lifted for storage before frost. Cut fruit with long piece of stem attached. This helps to delay rotting and the stem can be used as handle.

Most types need curing to harden skin completely. Preferably expose to sun for about 10 days in sunny sheltered position – e.g. against a wall. Cover or bring indoors if frost threatens. In poor weather bring indoors and keep at temperature of 27–32°C/80–90°F for 4 days.

Store in airy conditions, ideally at temperature of 7–10°C/45–50°F.

Squashes and pumpkins are still underutilized. Bake, roast or stir-fry as vegetable, use in soups or sweet pies, or to make sweet pickle.

VSR ★

SWEDE *Brassica napus* Napobrassica Group

Swede is a relatively hardy brassica, grown for its turnip-like root which is normally yellow-fleshed. It is sweeter and milder-flavoured than turnips. The purple-skinned or 'purple-top' cvs are considered best-flavoured. The roots are generally round, but are sometimes misshapen or long, probably because of seed quality. Swedes can also be grown as spring greens, while the roots can be forced for young shoots in spring. Swedes often succeed where turnips fail, but are slower-maturing. They are regaining popularity on account of their flavour. They divide roughly into cvs with low dry matter and superior culinary qualities, which stand little frost, and 'harder' cvs with high dry matter, which keep better in the post-Christmas period.

Site and soil
As Turnip, page 347. Rotate in brassica group, to avoid the build-up of root rotting diseases.

Cultivation
Sow in well-prepared, firm seedbed, raked to fine tilth. Sow *in situ* late spring (in cold regions), early summer (warmer regions). Never rush to sow early: early sowings are prone to mildew. Sow in rows 38–45cm/15–18in apart. Sow very thinly or station sow with stations 11cm/4½in apart. Thin in stages to 23cm/9in apart. Alternatively grow spaced about 30cm/12in apart each way. Early thinning essential; seedlings grow very rapidly and deteriorate if they become overcrowded.

Water in dry periods or else growth will be checked (see Turnip, page 348).

For spring greens, sow as Turnip, page 348.

Harvesting
Roots ready 20–26 weeks after sowing. Can be left in ground in most areas until mid-winter/Christmas. Quality then deteriorates, roots becoming coarse and woody, so advisable to lift and store in boxes of sand under cover. Except in very cold areas, 15cm/6in layer of straw over roots is sufficient.

Forcing roots
1 Lift roots mid-winter, trim off tops.
2 Replant in the ground under greenhouse staging in a darkened area (see illustration, page 244), or plant in box of soil, covered with thick layer of straw or upturned box to exclude light.
3 Put in cool shed or sheltered spot outdoors.

The resulting young semi-blanched growths develop in about 3–4 weeks, depending on temperature. Very pleasant flavour. Eat raw in salads or lightly cooked.

Pests and diseases
As Turnip, page 349. Mildew the most common problem. Grow cvs with good resistance.

Cultivars
Good mildew resistance: 'Marian', 'Invitation' (longer keeping) – both also good clubroot resistance); 'Ruby', 'Acme', 'Brora', 'Joan', 'Lizzy', 'Magres' (longer keeping).

VSR★★

SWEET CORN *Zea mays*

Sweet corn is a half-hardy plant developed from the traditional maize grown for corn flour. Cobs are borne on plants growing up to about 1.8m/6ft tall. They are normally yellow, white or bicoloured but there are colourful blue, red and multicoloured forms, used ornamentally, for maize flour or for popcorn. Sweet corn requires a fairly long warm season to mature, so success is variable in cool climates. Recent years have seen the introduction of new types with improved quality. Most types are eaten 'on the cob', but popcorn is shelled and 'popped' (see below).

Types

Normal 'sugary' Traditional sweet corn. Sweetness lost very soon after picking as sugars rapidly convert to starch. Many believe has special 'traditional flavour'. Relatively robust and easy to grow, though in cool climates only faster-maturing early and mid-season cvs likely to mature in normal season. Quality superseded by new types.

Sugary enhanced Cobs with genes (not genetically engineered) which bestow increased tenderness and sweetness, the degree of sweetness depending on cv. Once cobs are picked the sugars convert to starch more slowly than with 'normal' varieties. No need to grow isolated from normal varieties, as with sugarsweet cvs. No germination problems.

Supersweet/shrunken gene Dried kernels shrunken – hence the name. Notably sweeter than other types and sugars much slower to convert to starches after harvest. Ideally should be grown in isolation as cross-pollination with other types can result in starchy kernels both in the supersweet cv and those involved in cross-pollination. Scarcely noticeable with freshly picked cobs eaten young. Seeds smaller, more delicate, harder to germinate in cool conditions. Must be kept moist when sown, as seeds require more moisture and higher soil temperature than above types to germinate.

Tendersweet Recently developed. Dried kernels shrunken but combine kernel quality of normal sugary with sweetness of sugarsweet. Very slow to go starchy. Very thin-skinned tender grains with superb flavour. No need to isolate from supersweet and normal sugary types. Require warm conditions to perform well. Grow through clear polythene mulch.

Popcorn Types with small cobs and small kernels suitable for popping. Easily grown; cultivated like sweet corn.

Baby corn/mini corn Miniature immature cobs eaten about 10cm/4in long. Used raw, stir-fried, pickled, etc. (In my view immaturity equates with lack of flavour!) Sweet corn, popcorn and maize cvs can all be used.

Bicoloured cvs Occur in all types; usually mixed white and yellow kernels. Best grown in isolation to avoid cross-pollination.

Site and soil
Open site, sheltered from strong winds. Moderately fertile, well-drained, moisture-retentive soil. Sweet corn performs poorly in dry conditions. Excellent plant for intercropping and undercropping.

Cultivation
Key facts:

- Requires long, frost-free growing season. Fastest-maturing UK cvs ready about 90 days after sowing in south of country; others can take several weeks longer.
- Seed slow to germinate at soil temperatures below about 13°C/55°F – a temperature not normally reached until late spring in southern England. Best to delay sowing until soil temperature about 18°C/65°F. Never sow in wet soil.
- Does not transplant well unless raised in modules and planted quite small.
- Male tassels (at top of plant) and female cobs (with attached 'silks') borne on same plant. Must be wind-pollinated to form full cobs. To assist pollination, grow in groups or blocks at least four rows deep, rather than in single straight rows.
- Use fresh seed as viability can fall off fairly rapidly.
- For best quality, isolation of supersweet and bicoloured cvs is advisable. This is difficult in home gardens as pollen can travel far. (Commercial crops are separated by 60m/200ft!) The greater the distance separating cvs, the less the cross-pollination: 9m/30ft is a reasonable compromise. In small gardens easiest solution is just to grow one cultivar. Alternatively stagger sowing so that pollination occurs at different times. Start first cv indoors in modules, and plant out under fleece or perforated polythene film. Then sow second cv, either indoors and plant in open ground or *in situ*. This will separate pollination times by about 3–4 weeks.

Sowing options (sow 2.5–4cm/1–1½in deep):

1 Sow in modules indoors mid-spring at about 18°C/65°F. Only sow one seed per module, as tap roots easily damaged if become inter-twined. Harden off carefully and plant outside after all risk of frost. Plant before plants get too big or growth stunted. You can protect with cloches/crop covers in early stages.

2 Sow *in situ* outside with protection, once soil temperature over 13°C/55°F, in late spring, using any of the following methods:

   ∾ Sow seeds under cloches or individually under jam jars. Once seeds are germinated remove covers during day to harden off gradually.

   ∾ Sow under clear polythene film. Cut slits and pull seedlings through when seen beneath film. Watch carefully to ensure plants not flattened.

   ∾ Sow under fleece. Remove once plants reach about five-leaf stage. Watch carefully as above. In good conditions these plants may catch up with pot-raised plants.

3 Sow *in situ* in open, early summer. Station sow, thinning to one per station after germination.

Recommended spacing for optimum yields is 36cm/14in apart in rows 60cm/2ft apart (or roughly 45cm/18in apart each way). Plant very tall cvs up to 45cm/18in apart in similar rows. Wider spacing makes intercropping easier, results in heavier cobs and is recommended on light soils where there is more competition for moisture.

Protect seedlings from slugs and birds. Keep weed-free. Mulching in summer beneficial. Can be planted through black mulching film at outset.

Harvesting

Ready mid-summer to late autumn depending on region. Normally only one or two cobs per plant; two more likely in good growing conditions with wide spacing. Important to pick cobs at peak, when sugar levels highest. They deteriorate rapidly once past maturity. Kernels ripe when pale yellow; overripe when dark yellow. When silks turning dark brown, test kernels for ripeness by pulling back sheath and pressing kernel with fingernail. If 'watery' unripe; if 'milky' ripe; if 'doughy' over-ripe.

Use as soon as possible. Surplus stocks best blanched and frozen. If cobs kept in fridge, remove leaves, as they draw moisture from them.

Mini corn

Various methods of growing mini corn. Can use most types at close spacing, or specially recommended cvs as per supplier's recommenda-tions. Unnecessary to grow in block formation; pollination not needed as once pollinated, grains start to swell. Tassels can be removed to prevent pollination. Grow in rows about 45cm/18in apart, spacing plants about

15cm/6in apart. Harvest when cobs tiny, when silks just emerging or slightly earlier. Normally only get two or three cobs per stem.

Popcorn
Grow as sweet corn. Harvest cobs at end of season when fully mature and becoming hard. Exposure to light frost beneficial. Pull off husks and dry for several weeks in dry, airy place. From time to time strip off corn and do trial popping. Must be dried to correct moisture level to pop successfully.

To pop, put oil in bottom of heavy pan, cover with kernels, replace lid, turn up heat. Should pop in minute or two if ready. If not, dry a little longer, then test again. Once right moisture level is reached, strip kernels from cobs and store in airtight jars.

Pests and diseases

Frit fly Maggots attack base of very young seedlings, eating growing point below ground. Plants not attacked after five-or-six-leaf stage. Avoid by raising plants in modules and/or grow under fine nets in early stage.

Cultivars
The following are all F1 hybrids, listed in each group in approximate order of maturity.
Standard cvs: 'Earliking', 'Earlibelle', 'Sundance', 'Northern Belle', 'Jubilee'.
Sugary enhanced: 'Champ', 'Incredible'.
Supersweet: 'Dickson', 'Earlibird', 'Conquest', 'Prelude', 'Golden Giant', 'Ovation', 'Sweet Nugget', 'Herald', 'Challenger', 'Dynasty'.
Supersweet (white): 'Sugarburst'.
Tendersweet: 'Swift', 'Lark', 'Swallow'.
Bicolour: 'Honey Bantam', 'Ambrosia', 'Honey and Cream'.
Popcorn: 'Red Strawberry'.
Mini corn: 'Minipop'.

VSR ★

SWISS CHARD see Spinach group

TEXSEL/TEXEL GREENS *Brassica carinata*

Texsel greens was developed in the late twentieth century from an Ethiopian mustard, so it is a rare 'new' vegetable. It has smallish glossy leaves with a refreshingly pleasant spinach/cabbage flavour, with a hint of garlic. It is very nutritious and rich in Vitamin C. Texsel is reasonably hardy (to at least −7°C/25°F in my experience) and very fast-growing. It can be grown even where clubroot is a problem, as it is harvested before it would become seriously affected.

Site and soil

Open position, but tolerates light shade in mid-summer. Grows best in fertile, well-drained, moisture-retentive soil. Useful for intercropping and catch cropping.

Cultivation

Essentially a cool-season crop. May bolt prematurely in hot, dry conditions. Spring and late summer sowings probably the best value in small gardens.

Best sown *in situ*. Can be grown as CCA seedlings, or as 'greens' harvested as small plants 20–30cm/8–10in high. Also suitable for seedling sprouts (see Mustard, page 284).

Sowing options:

1 For first spring crop, sow late winter/early spring under cover.
2 For continuous supply from early summer to autumn, sow outdoors in succession every 3 weeks or so, as soon as soil workable in spring until early autumn. Mid-summer sowings may not prove worthwhile in warm, dry areas.
3 For good-quality autumn/winter/spring supply, sow under cover in early/mid-autumn.

For CCA seedlings, sow by broadcasting or in narrow or wide drills about 13cm/5in apart. For small plants, various spacings have proved satisfactory. For highest yield of small plants, sow in rows 15cm/6in apart, thinning to 5cm/2in apart; or in rows 30cm/12in apart, thinning to 2.5cm/1in apart. You can also space plants 8–10cm/3–4in apart each way for small plants; 15cm/6in apart each way for medium-sized plants; or 25–30cm/10–12in apart for large plants.

In soils that are infected by clubroot, successive sowings can be made if plants are pulled up by their roots when harvested and a 3-week gap left before resowing. Protect winter crop with cloches/crop covers to improve quality.

Pests and diseases

Normally very healthy, though may be affected by common brassica pests (see page 223.)

Flea beetle Attacks plants in early stages. Take standard control measures. Grow under fine nets if necessary.

Harvesting and use

CCA seedlings ready 3–4 weeks after sowing, depending on season. Spring and late summer sowings generally fastest growing. Cut about 2cm/¾in above ground. They usually resprout, though may develop bitterness with second cut. Young plants ready on average 7 weeks after sowing. Either pull whole plant when 20–30cm/8–12in high, or pick off individual leaves as required, leaving to resprout. Will run to seed after few weeks, but small leaves on seeding stems quite palatable.

Cook as greens or use young leaves in salads.

VSR ★★★

TOMATO *Lycopersicon esculentum*

Tomatoes are among the most rewarding crops to grow, not least because the flavour when picked at their peak is far superior to that of any bought tomato. Tomatoes are tender annuals from South America, so in cool climates require protection at some stage. The fruits display enormous diversity in shape, size and colour. They can be red, pink, orange, yellow, golden, red and orange striped, black, purple, green, dark and light green striped, and even white. Many interesting heirloom cvs are now available. Some have excellent flavour, but they tend to have poor disease resistance and most are late maturing. (For specialist suppliers, see page 275.) Tomatoes are classified by fruit shape and growth habit.

Main fruit types

Standard Medium-sized, smooth, round, tomatoes, mainly red- or yellow-skinned. Variable flavour. Typically 2.5–4cm/1–1½in diameter. Several 'long-keeping' cvs retain their flavour well, both on plant when mature and for couple of months after picked.

Beefsteak Very large, smooth, fleshy, mostly well-flavoured fruits. Fruits 'multilocular', i.e. display several compartments when sliced horizontally. Red- and yellow-skinned. Often weigh over 225g/8oz. Rarely perform well outdoors in cool climates.

Marmande Large, irregular shape, often ribbed; fleshy, multilocular fruits. Generally well-flavoured, but maybe some of the rounder, smoother 'improved' modern cvs have less flavour than older cvs. Mostly red-skinned. Often 5–6cm/2–2½in diameter.

Oxheart Medium to large, conical, fleshy, fruits; variable colours in skin and flesh. Some exceptionally well flavoured.

Plum Small to medium-sized, rectangular, solid, traditional Italian canning tomato. Tend to freeze well. Variable flavour, mainly red-skinned. Mostly late maturing.

Cherry plum Small, firm distinctly flavoured plum type for eating raw, typified by red-skinned 'Santa'.

Cherry Small, round fruits usually less than 2.5cm/1in diameter; often (not invariably) sweet or distinctly flavoured. Red- and yellow-skinned. Most reliable type for outdoor crops in cool climates.

Growth habit groups

Tall or 'indeterminate' Main shoot naturally grows several metres/yards high in warm climate. Side shoots can develop into long branches. When cultivated, they are usually grown as vertical cordons tied to supports, in greenhouses twisted up overhead strings. Side shoots and growing point nipped out to restrict growth and ensure fruits mature in cool climates. In 'semi-determinate' sub-group main shoot naturally stops growing when about 1m/3ft high. Most Marmande cultivars are in this sub-group.

Bush or 'determinate' Side branches develop instead of main shoot. Essentially a 'self-stopping' plant that sprawls on ground as a bush of 60–90cm/2–3ft spread – or more. Requires no side shooting or stopping. Often early maturing. Useful for culture outdoors as no supports required. Good where space limited; can be grown under cloches/low tunnels, or even in hanging baskets.

Dwarf Very small, compact types, often no more than 20cm/8in high. No pruning or support required. Ideal for container growing or edging beds.

Growing options
Tomatoes grow poorly at temperatures below 10°C/50°F; most cvs need at least 8 frost-free weeks after planting to mature properly. Also need high light intensity. So difficult crop in cold areas, and/or where light levels poor. In UK growing tomatoes under cover gives guarantee of better crop, but in good summers/warm areas you can grow very satisfactory crops outside. New gardeners should be guided by practice in their area.

Growing system options (treat harvesting dates as approximations, as there is considerable variation from one area to another):
1 Heated greenhouses. For very early summer crops. (Not covered here.)
2 Unheated greenhouses/polytunnels. Crops ready mid-summer onwards. Can be grown in the soil or in containers. All types can be grown in greenhouses/polytunnels, but tall indeterminate cvs grown as cordons make optimum use of space. Indoor tomatoes more susceptible to disease and eelworm. Use resistant cvs where available.
3 Outdoors in frames, under cloches, or protected with crop covers in the early stages (see page 343). Ready late summer. Use bush cvs. Can grow in soil or containers.
4 Outside without protection. Grow in the ground or in containers. Ready late summer/early autumn.

Except for cultivars bred for heated greenhouses, beefsteaks and late-maturing heirloom cvs, in practice most 'indoor' cvs can be grown successfully outdoors and *vice versa*.

Note on flavour

Tomato flavour is essentially a balance between acidity and sweetness. Inherent flavour affected by many interacting factors; can vary from plant to plant, even from fruit to fruit on plant. First trusses generally best-flavoured. My hunch is that flavour highest where watering and feeding are minimal, albeit sufficient. If flavour is your priority, I suggest growing cv recommended for flavour, and not overwatering or overfeeding, even if potential yields lowered. Flavour is very subjective. Try a range of cvs to find what you like.

Soil sickness

Where tomatoes are grown for several consecutive years (probably starting after 3–4 years) in the same soil, yields progressively decline through the build-up of soil pests and diseases, until results very poor. Most evident in greenhouses and polytunnels; also occurs outdoors.

Outdoors, prevent by rotating over 4- or 5-year cycle if possible. Rotate in potato group (but see Tomato/potato blight, page 344).

If growing in polytunnel, move to fresh site every 4 years or so. If space allows, you can rotate tomatoes within tunnel/greenhouse, say from one side to another, to delay build-up of soil sickness. (Peppers and aubergines are in same family, so rotate with crops like cucumbers or basil.)

In permanent greenhouse, you normally have to adopt one of the following options after growing tomatoes for 3–4 years:

∾ Grow in containers or growing bags in uncontaminated soil or potting compost.

∾ Graft required tomato cv on to resistant rootstock such as 'KNVF'. Rootstocks are easily raised from seed (listed in seed catalogues), though grafting requires some skill. Follow supplier's instructions.

∾ Use soil-less 'ring culture' system. (Not suitable for organic gardening but for further information see *Gardening under Plastic*, Further Reading, page 372.)

Growing outdoors – site and soil

Sunny site, shelter from wind essential. In cold areas grow against wall or fence, but avoid hedges, as ground too dry. Tomatoes require fertile, well-drained soil, limed if acid. You can prepare ground by digging 30cm/12in deep trench, 30–45cm/12–18in wide. Work in well-rotted manure, compost and/or wilted comfrey before planting (high level of potash in comfrey is beneficial).

Although tomatoes are rotated within potato family, in areas affected by tomato/potato blight try to avoid growing *alongside* potatoes to avoid cross-infection from air-borne blight spores. Obviously not easy in practice. Infection may start with early potatoes, but increasingly severe with maincrop potatoes. Erecting physical barrier such as polythene sheeting around tomatoes will help delay infection. (Tomatoes in poly-tunnels/greenhouses escape infection much longer than outdoor crops.)

Growing outdoors – cultivation
(See also Growing in containers, page 346.) Sow indoors mid-spring, roughly 7–8 weeks before last frost expected. Best to sow singly 2cm/¾in deep in modules. (Alternatively sow in seed tray and prick out.) Ideal germination temperature 20°C/68°F; sow in propagator if necessary. Outdoor bush cvs germinate at slightly lower temperature. Germinated seedlings can withstand lower temperatures of about 16°C/60°F once established, but must be kept above 10°C/50°F. (Beefsteaks need slightly higher temperatures at this stage.)

Pot seedlings on into about 9cm/3½in pots of good potting compost at the three-leaf stage. Keep in good light so that plants remain sturdy and don't become elongated and 'drawn'. Keep them well spaced out so that adjacent plants are not touching. Harden off well before planting outside. Delay planting if soil temperature below 10°C/50°F, or further frost expected. Generally plant early summer.

If plants are purchased ready to plant, choose short sturdy plants, grown in individual pots rather than boxes or seed trays.

With indeterminate/tall types, plant when 18–20cm/7–8in high, with first flowers showing. Plant 38–45cm/15–18in apart, either in single rows or in double rows of staggered plants. Plant firmly with the lowest leaves just above soil level. Can be interplanted with French marigolds to deter whitefly. Can be planted through polythene film mulches to keep weeds down and conserve moisture. Use either black mulch, or black/white mulch with white surface uppermost to reflect light up towards ripening fruit. Alternatively mulch with organic mulch such as straw or compost once plants established.

Where possible protect with cloches in early stages. When cloches outgrown protect with cloches turned sideways (see illustration, page 112) or with side panels of polythene film battened or stapled to wooden frame.

Erect supports as soon as possible. Use:

- ∾ strong individual canes or posts at least 1.5m/5ft high
- ∾ 1.2–1.5m/4–5ft-high posts at either end of rows, with two or three parallel wires between them.
- ∾ individual metal spiral supports.

Training:
1 As plants grow, tie the main stem to canes or wires, allowing for the stems to thicken.
2 Remove side shoots and any basal growths as they develop. (If extra plants required, you can pot up side shoots – they root easily.)

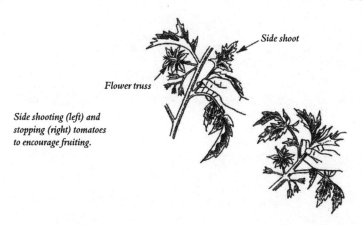

Side shoot

Flower truss

Side shooting (left) and stopping (right) tomatoes to encourage fruiting.

3 In mid- to late summer 'stop' the plants, to give time for remaining fruits to mature and ripen. In cold areas this will normally be when three trusses have set; in warmer areas after four or five trusses have set. Remove growing point a couple of leaves above topmost flower truss (see above).

With bush and dwarf types, planting outdoor bush cvs when first flower truss *just visible* gives best combination of earliness and high yield. Planting when first flower truss *fully open* gives earlier fruit, but lower yields overall. Plant dwarf types 25–30cm/10–12in apart; plant bush types 45–60cm/18–24in apart. They can be planted through polythene film mulches as for indeterminate types, above; this helps to keep fruit clean. Can be mulched with straw for same reason, but this may attract slugs, which are potentially more damaging on bush and dwarf cvs. Where feasible, plant under cloches or protect with row covers (see below). Let plants grow naturally. No side shooting or stopping is necessary.

Other than in exceptionally dry conditions outdoor tomatoes rarely need extra watering until they start to flower. If weather dry at this stage, give a heavy watering weekly of about 11 litres per sq. m/2 gallons per sq. yd. Growth will suffer if soil dries out completely, but see comments above on effect of overwatering on flavour. Outdoor tomatoes require far less supplementary feeding than indoor crop, especially if ground well prepared beforehand. If growth poor when second truss is setting, feed weekly with organic tomato feed or diluted liquid comfrey.

Growing bush cvs under perforated film or fleece

The following system was developed by researchers to get early crop outdoors in cool areas. Fruits ripen about 2 weeks ahead of other outdoor tomatoes.

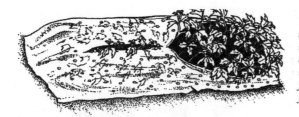

Weaning bush tomatoes growing under perforated film or fleece. Small initial slit (left); film flopping open when final cuts are made.

1 Raise plants indoors in normal way; plant out as soon as risk of frost is over. You can plant through mulching films as above.
2 When planted, either cover with perforated film or fleece laid directly over plants, or lay film/fleece over low hoops. (Unperforated films are unsuitable, as temperature and humidity become too high, resulting in disease and poor growth.) Anchor the edges of the films.
3 Leave film/fleece in place until flowers start to press against it. Then slit open to allow insects to pollinate. Do so gradually to 'wean' plants, i.e. acclimatize them to colder conditions. Initially make intermittent cuts in the film roughly 90cm/3ft long down the centre of the row (see illustration, above).
4 Around a week later cut remaining gaps so that film flops open. Leave in place on either side of plants as a low windbreak.
5 From then on grow as standard outdoor tomatoes.

Pests and diseases outdoors
Apart from potato/tomato blight, few problems arise with outdoor tomatoes: poor weather is worst enemy.

Tomato/potato blight Edges of leaves become browned, fruits develop blackened patches. Problem worst in wet humid summers, usually appearing mid-summer, but tending to appear earlier with increasingly severe potato blight attacks. No effective organic remedy once plants attacked. Growing within an enclosing barrier of clear plastic, 1.2m/4ft high, can delay infection. New cvs, such as 'Ferline' F1, have some resistance. Remove and burn diseased leaves as soon as noticed.

Harvesting and use of outdoor tomatoes
Pick fruits as they ripen. Fruit quality ruined by even light frost. If chances of ripening in open by end of season seem slender, cut indeterminate/cordon plants free of supports in late summer, leaving roots in ground. Mulch ground with straw or plastic film and carefully bend plants down so that they can be covered with cloches. Cover bush cvs in same way so that ripening will continue. Alternatively pull plants up by roots and hang in greenhouse or indoors; green fruits gradually ripen on plant. Immature individual fruits also ripen slowly in darkness, wrapped or covered in paper – though much flavour lost.

Unripened green fruits can be cooked or used to make tomato chutney.

Cultivation in unheated greenhouses/polytunnels

Grow in the soil or in containers (see Soil sickness, pages 151 and 341). For growing in containers, see overleaf.

To grow in soil, for double row of tomatoes, prepare ground by making trench 30cm/12in deep and 30–45cm/12–18in wide. Trench can be narrower for single rows. Allow at least 90cm/3ft between trenches of double rows. Line base of trench with wilted comfrey and work in well-rotted compost.

Raise plants as for outdoor tomatoes, above. Sow early spring. Plant in permanent position mid- to late spring. Plant 45cm/18in apart in single rows and in double rows at same spacing but staggering plants. I always interplant with French marigolds, *Tagetes* spp., as they seem to deter whitefly. Either plant through mulching film (as above) or mulch with organic mulch. Wilted comfrey and wilted lawn mowings can be used; gradually build up to layer 7.5cm/3in deep or more as plants grow.

To make optimum use of vertical space, allow vigorous indeterminate plants to grow to ridge of greenhouse. Simplest support method is suspending heavy-duty string or twine from overhead bar or taut horizontal wire running length of structure. Have one string per plant; tie loosely below lowest leaves on plant, allowing enough slack for stem thickening and for twisting top of plant around string as it grows.

Alternatively support with individual canes or post-and-wire system as for outdoor tomatoes, above. Attach strings to top of support, tied to overhead bar or wire, in later stages when supports outgrown.

Train as for outdoor tomatoes, but growth is much faster and more lush, so side shooting must be done regularly. Allow up to seven or eight trusses if growth healthy; otherwise stop at five or six trusses. Once tomatoes have reached top of greenhouse, train leading shoot horizontally along overhead wire.

Remove and burn withered and diseased leaves. Leaves below first truss can be removed to improve air circulation.

Water well when planting, then water lightly until fruit starts to set. Once fruit is setting, water more heavily, at least weekly at the rate of 11 litres/2 gallons per plant. Water more frequently if it seems necessary. Allowing soil to almost dry out between waterings, rather than being continually moist, may lead to improved flavour.

Once fruits starting to set, feed weekly with high potash tomato fertilizer, such as liquid comfrey or seaweed-based fertilizer formulated for tomatoes. Fruit may be slow to set in spring/early summer. If so, tap canes or wires around midday to encourage spread of pollen.

Keep greenhouse/polytunnel well ventilated. In hot weather 'damp down' regularly, both to help fruit setting and to prevent the build-up of greenhouse pests.

Harvesting indoor tomatoes

As outdoor tomatoes, above. Towards end of season plants can be draped with fleece to protect against night frosts and encourage further ripening.

Pests and diseases indoors

Greenhouse pests Plants can be attacked by aphids, whitefly and red spider mite. Use biological controls.

Diseases Tomatoes are susceptible to a range of diseases, for which there are no remedies. Use disease-resistant cvs where available. Remove and burn diseased foliage, and if a plant dies dig it out carefully by the roots with attached soil and burn. See also Soil sickness, pages 151 and 341.

Growing in containers

Tomatoes can be grown successfully in all types of container, including growing bags and hanging baskets. For good results, the larger the container the better: 23cm/9in pot minimum satisfactory size. Three plants can be fitted into standard growing bag, but two plants per bag preferable. To minimize evaporation in growing bags, cut small squares in top surface, rather than cutting it out completely (see illustrations, pages 170 and 172).

Fill container with good-quality potting compost, leaving 5–7.5cm/ 2–3in headroom to allow for top dressing with fresh compost in later stages.

Raise plants in normal way. Where feasible at least partially sink pots into soil to conserve moisture. Support with single canes, or train up strings if appropriate. Manufactured support frames can be purchased for growing bags. In early stages water carefully so that soil neither dries out nor becomes waterlogged. Once first truss sets, feed weekly as indoor plants, above. If roots get pushed up to the surface, top dress with good potting soil or compost.

Restrict growth to four or five trusses depending on vigour of plants.

Cultivars

Enormous choice today. Cvs on this shortlist widely considered well flavoured.

Standard: 'Ailsa Craig', 'Harbinger', 'Shirley' F1, 'Alicante', 'Typhoon' F1, 'Counter' F1, 'Cristal' F1, 'Burpee Long Keeper', 'Ferline' F1.

Beefsteak: 'Big Boy' F1, 'Dombello' F1, 'Buffalo' F1.

Marmande: 'Marmande', 'Supermarmande'.

Tall cherry (red): 'Cherry Belle' F1, 'Gardener's Delight', 'Sweet 100', 'Sweet Million', 'Supersweet', 'Sungold' F1 (gold), 'Yellow Debut' F1 (yellow), 'Sugar Lump'.

Tall plum-shaped: 'Britain's Breakfast', 'Brigade' F1 (both recommended for freezing), 'Santa' F1, 'Sun Belle' (golden teardrop).

Bush: 'Red Alert', 'Tornado' F1, 'Gold Nugget' (yellow).

Dwarf bush, suitable for hanging baskets: 'Phyra' (small fruit), 'Pixie' F1, 'Tiny Tim', 'Tumbler' F1, 'Balconi Red', 'Balconi Yellow', 'Tumbling Tom Red', 'Tumbling Tom Yellow', 'Whippersnapper' (tiny boxy fruit).

Heirloom: most 'Oxheart'/'Cuor di Bue' cvs; 'Green Grape', 'Green Zebra', 'Nepal', ' Brandywine', 'Yellow Brandywine'.

VSR ★★

TURNIP *Brassica napus* Rapifera Group

Turnips are fast-growing brassicas, cultivated mainly for the roots, which can be flat or round, with white or yellow flesh. They can be grown to be available for most of the year. The fast-maturing early types are used fresh, while the slower-maturing, hardier types are used fresh or stored for winter.

The small, white Japanese types are a more recent introduction. They are exceptionally sweet and fast-growing, sometimes ready within 35 days of sowing. Some cvs (e.g. 'Tokyo Cross' F1) bolt prematurely from early spring sowings and sowing should be delayed until early summer. Others have good bolting resistance. Very young leaves can be used in salad.

Turnips can also be grown as leafy spring greens and turnip 'tops'.

Site and soil

Open site. Light, humus-rich soils best. Require higher fertility than swedes. Ground preferably manured for previous crop; limed if acid. Avoid dry situations. Moisture throughout growth essential, or turnips become woody. Rotate in brassica group. Early types very useful for intercropping/catch cropping (see below).

Cultivation for roots

For regular supply for most of the year, sow *in situ* in succession every 3–4 weeks, from early spring until mid-summer, using appropriate cvs for each season.

Sowing programme:

1 For earliest crop of fresh turnips in late spring/early summer, sow under cover (e.g. in cold greenhouses, under cloches) in early spring. Use early types. Sow in rows 23cm/9in apart. Thin in stages to 10cm/4in apart. If spaced slightly further apart roots will develop faster.

2 For main supply of fresh turnips from mid-summer to mid-October, sow outdoors from early spring (if soil workable) until mid-summer. Use early types. Sow at spacing for (1) above. If necessary protect early sowings with cloches/crop covers.

3 For use fresh or for storage from late autumn to winter, sow mid-summer. Use maincrop cvs. Sow in rows 30cm/12in apart. Thin to 15cm/6in apart.

Sow in well-prepared, firm seedbed, raked to fine tilth. Turnips are so fast-growing that it is essential to start thinning early, so that adjacent seedlings don't touch; otherwise they become overcrowded and good roots never develop. Thinnings can be eaten as greens.

Keep weed-free. Growth becomes checked if soil dries out. In dry weather water at the rate of 11 litres per sq. m/2 gallons per sq. yd.

Harvesting

Spring/summer turnips Some cvs ready within 6 weeks of sowing. Sweetest and most tender if pulled young when no more than 2.5–4cm/1–1½in diameter. Tend to deteriorate and coarsen rapidly.

Maincrop and storage turnips Ready 10–12 weeks after sowing. Pull when roots reach a usable size. These hardier cvs stand in condition longer without deterioration.

In most areas can be left in soil in winter, provided soil well drained. Where winters severe or soil heavy, either protect with good covering of bracken or straw, or lift before end of year and store indoors in boxes, or outdoors in clamps, as for carrots (see page 230).

Cultivation and harvesting for greens and tops
Sowing programme:
1 For greens early/mid-spring following year, sow late summer/early autumn. Very useful crop in the Vegetable Gap.
2 Sow mid-autumn, outdoors in mild areas, otherwise under cover. May provide pickings during winter or very early following year.
3 For follow-on crop in spring/early summer, sow late winter, very early spring under cover or outdoors if soil conditions suitable.

Use maincrop cvs for autumn sowings; early cvs for late winter/very early spring sowings. Sow thinly, by broadcasting or sowing in single or broad drills about 10cm/4in apart. Subsequent thinning normally unnecessary.

Start harvesting when 10–15cm/4–6in high. Tend to toughen quickly if not harvested young. Cut frequently 2.5cm/1in or so above ground level, and leave to resprout. Even a small patch can give excellent returns. Often resprout over many weeks before running to seed. Young flower heads edible as 'tops' like broccoli raab (see page 215). Finally remaining plants can be dug in as green manure.

Pests and diseases
Subject to same pests as all brassicas (see page 223), but so fast-growing that in practice often trouble free.

Flea beetle Most likely problem on seedlings. Use standard remedies, or grow under nets, at least in early stages.

Clubroot Yellow-fleshed cvs reputedly less susceptible to clubroot.

Powdery mildew Most serious in dry weather and on light dry soils. Avoid overcrowding; keep plants watered in dry weather.

Cultivars
Early: 'Atlantic', 'Snowball', 'Purple Top Milan', 'Ivory', 'Arcoat'.
White Japanese early: 'Tokyo Cross' F1, 'Tokyo Top' F1 (good bolting resistance), 'Market Express' F1.
Main crop/storage: 'Golden Ball'/'Orange Jelly' (yellow flesh), 'Green Top Stone', 'Green Globe', 'Veitch's Red Globe'.

VSR ★★★

SEASONAL GUIDE TO MAIN GARDEN JOBS

GENERAL NOTE

The term 'under cover' includes cloches, frames, low and walk-in poly-tunnels, and unheated greenhouses. Timings are based on 'average' UK conditions. In cold districts, make spring sowings and plantings slightly later and autumn sowings earlier. The reverse applies in milder districts.

Only a few perennial and minor vegetables are included in this guide.

CCA = cut-and-come-again seedlings.

MID-WINTER (January)

Sow in heat Early summer cauliflower.

Sow under cover (mild areas only) Broad beans, lettuce, peas, radish. CCA: cress, komatsuna, oriental saladini, salad rape, salad rocket, senposai, Sugar Loaf chicory, Texsel greens.

Plant Mid-autumn-sown lettuce (under cover), garlic (on light soils), rhubarb (sets).

Jobs Digging and manuring when soil not frozen.
Sort through stored crops; remove any rotting vegetables.
Weed crops under cover.
Start chitting seed potatoes.
Blanch endive and force Witloof chicory.
Start forcing *in situ* rhubarb crowns by excluding light.
Place seed order.

LATE WINTER (February)

Sow in heat Globe artichoke, asparagus, hybrid broccolis, mini cauliflower, celeriac, celery, leeks, onions.

Sow under cover Beetroot, broad beans, broccoli raab, Brussels sprouts, summer and autumn cabbage, carrots, chrysanthemum greens, red Russian kale, leeks, lettuce, Japanese bunching, main crop and spring onions, orache, peas (warm areas only), radish.
CCA: as mid-winter, plus cress, curly endive, cutting lettuce, kales, komatsuna, mizuna greens, orache, oriental saladini, pak choi.
Sow outdoors in favourable conditions Broad beans, kohl rabi, onions, parsnip, peas, radish, spinach.

Plant Jerusalem artichokes, spring cabbage, garlic, onion sets, rhubarb (sets), shallots.

Jobs Digging and manuring light soils unless ground frozen.
Start preparing seedbeds.
Chit seed potatoes.
Force Witloof chicory and rhubarb.
Lift parsnips and heel in if sprouting.
Thin overwintered onions.

EARLY SPRING (March)

Sow in heat Aubergines, peppers, tomatoes.

Sow under cover Dwarf beans (warm areas), beetroot, hybrid broccolis, Brussels sprouts, carrots, mini, summer and autumn cauliflowers, celery, celeriac, endive, kales, leeks, lettuce, orache, winter purslane, rhubarb, tree spinach; CCA seedlings (see late winter) plus summer purslane, saladini.

Sow in open Broad beans, broccoli raab, summer, autumn and winter cabbage, calabrese, mini, summer and autumn cauliflowers, corn salad, chrysanthemum greens, endive (curled), kales, land cress, lettuce, spring, Japanese bunching and main crop onions, parsley, parsnip, peas, radish, shallots, spinach beet, spinach, peas, turnips.
CCA: *Chenopodium giganteum*, kales, komatsuna, lettuce, oriental saladini, pak choi, salad rocket, saladini, senposai, spinach, Texsel greens.

Plant Chinese artichokes, Jerusalem artichokes, early summer and mini cauliflowers, garlic, lettuce, autumn-sown onion seedlings, onion sets, early and maincrop potatoes, rhubarb (sets), shallots.

Prick out Tomatoes, and other seedlings germinated in heat.

Jobs Continue preparing ground for sowing.
Weed overwintered crops in open and under cloches.
Feed overwintered spring cabbage, kale and onions with seaweed-based fertilizer if looking 'jaded'.
Lift, divide and replant chives and Welsh onions.
Lift and heel in remaining leeks, parsnips and celeriac.
Prepare ground for tomatoes.

MID SPRING (April)

Sow in heat Aubergines, courgettes, cucumbers, iceplant, peppers, pumpkins, summer purslane, New Zealand spinach, winter squash, tomatoes.

Sow under cover Hybrid broccolis, dwarf beans, late summer, autumn and mini cauliflowers, celeriac, celery; and slightly later: runner beans, chicory (early red), courgettes, cucumber, kales, marrows, summer and winter purslane, rhubarb, sweet corn, tomatoes.

Sow in open Globe artichokes, asparagus pea, beetroot, broad beans, broccoli raab, sprouting broccoli, Brussels sprouts, autumn and winter cabbage, calabrese, carrots, mini cauliflowers, *Chenopodium giganteum*, Witloof chicory, chrysanthemum greens, corn salad, endive, Hamburg parsley, kales, kohl rabi, land cress, leeks, lettuce, spring, Japanese bunching and pickling onions, orache, parsley, parsnip, peas, radish, rhubarb, salad rape, salad rocket, salsify, scorzonera, spinach beet, summer spinach, Texsel greens, turnips, CCA seedlings as early spring.

Prick out Aubergine, celery, celeriac, peppers, tomatoes.

Plant Asparagus (crowns, module-raised), Brussels sprouts (sown under cover), spring cabbage, early summer cauliflowers, lettuce, onion sets, early and maincrop potatoes.

Jobs Keep weeding, especially among seedlings.
Remove old brassica stumps.
Earth up early potatoes.
Take offsets of best globe artichoke plants.
Support peas.
Prepare ground for tomatoes if not already done.
Remove protection from globe artichokes if not already done.
Watch out for flea beetle attacks on brassica seedlings.
Harden off seedlings started under glass.
Feed overwintered vegetables (see early spring).
Start mulching if soil is warm.

LATE SPRING (May)

Sow under cover Amaranthus (leaf), hybrid broccolis, mini, autumn and winter (spring heading) cauliflowers, chicory (early red), courgettes, cucumbers, iceplant, kales, marrows and sweet corn.

Sow in open Broad, French and runner beans, beetroot, broccoli raab, sprouting broccoli, summer, autumn and winter cabbage, calabrese, carrots, mini, autumn and winter/spring heading cauliflowers, all chicories, corn salad, endive, fennel, iceplant, kales, kohl rabi, land cress, lettuce, Japanese bunching, spring and pickling onions, Hamburg parsley, peas, summer and winter purslane, radish, salad rocket, salsify, scorzonera, spinach beet, summer and New Zealand spinach, swedes, Swiss chard, turnips.
CCA: *Chenopodium giganteum*, kales, komatsuna, lettuce, orache, oriental saladini, pak choi, saladini, senposai, Texsel greens.

Sow in open When nearing early summer: cucumbers, marrows, pumpkins, winter squash, sweet corn.

Prick out or pot up Aubergines, celery, celeriac, cucumbers, marrows, peppers, tomatoes.

Thin out Beet, carrots, lettuce, parsnip, radish, spinach, turnip.

Plant Globe artichokes (seed-raised), asparagus (module-raised), French and runner beans (raised under cover), hybrid broccolis, Brussels sprouts, summer, autumn and winter cabbage, mini, summer and autumn cauliflowers, celery, celeriac, leeks, lettuce; maincrop potatoes.

Plant out under cloches initially Aubergines, courgettes, cucumbers, marrows, peppers, pumpkins, winter squash, sweet corn, tomatoes.

Jobs Harden off seedlings under cloches/crop covers.
    Protect seedbed against birds.
    Watch out for asparagus beetle, blackfly, carrot fly, cabbage root fly, flea beetle and onion fly, and take protective measures.
    Continue weeding; start mulching.
    Earth up early potatoes; protect with soil/newspaper/fleece if frost threatens.
    Support peas.
    Start side shooting tomatoes.
    Mulch all established vegetables when conditions are suitable.

EARLY SUMMER (June)

Sow in open Amaranthus (leaf), French and runner beans, beetroot, broccoli raab, calabrese, carrots, mini cauliflowers, all chicories, Chinese cabbage, chrysanthemum greens, corn salad, courgettes, cucumbers, endive, iceplant, mini kale, kohl rabi, komatsuna, land cress (light shade), lettuce, marrows, mibuna and mizuna greens, Japanese bunching and spring onions, pak choi, peas, pumpkins, summer purslane, summer and oriental radish, salad rocket, spinach beet, summer and New Zealand spinach, winter squash, swedes, sweet corn, turnips.
CCA: amaranthus (leaf), *Chenopodium giganteum*, orache.

Thin Direct-sown vegetables such as beans, beetroot, carrots, lettuce and parsnip.

Plant Asparagus (from seed, module-raised), hybrid broccolis, sprouting broccoli, Brussels sprouts, autumn, summer and winter cabbages, mini, late summer and autumn cauliflowers, celery, celeriac, courgettes, fennel, iceplant, kale, leeks, marrows, peppers, pumpkins, summer purslane, winter squash, sweet corn, tomatoes.

Jobs Pinch out broad bean tops.
Hoeing, weeding, mulching.
Stake and earth up brassicas, when planted out.
Side shoot, stake and tie tomatoes.
Watch out for pests as in late spring.

MID-SUMMER (July)

Sow in seed boxes or modules to transplant under cover, mainly for winter Celery (leaf), red and Sugar Loaf chicories, corn salad, endive, fennel, land cress, lettuce, oriental mustard, salad rocket, Swiss chard, winter purslane.

Sow in open Leaf amaranthus, dwarf French beans (to cloche later), beetroot, broccoli raab, spring cabbage (in cold areas only), cabbage for spring greens (towards the onset of late summer), carrots, autumn and mini cauliflowers, red and Sugar Loaf chicories, Chinese broccoli, Chinese cabbage, choy sum, endive (curled and broad), kales, kohl rabi, komatsuna, land cress (in light shade), winter lettuce, mibuna and mizuna greens, Japanese bunching and spring onions, pak choi, oriental mustards, peas (dwarf), summer, oriental and winter radish, senposai, spinach, spinach beet, Swiss chard, turnips (for storage), winter purslane.
CCA: *Chenopodium giganteum*, orache, oriental saladini, salad rape, salad rocket, spinach.

Thin Beetroot, carrots, lettuce, oriental greens, swedes.

Plant Hybrid broccolis, sprouting broccoli, Brussels sprouts, summer, autumn and winter cabbage, calabrese, mini, autumn and winter/spring-heading cauliflowers, kale, leeks, oriental greens, 'second cropping' potatoes.

Jobs Keep weeding, hoeing, mulching.
Tie, stake, side shoot and 'stop' cordon tomatoes.
Tie climbing cucumbers, feed, water if dry, top dress roots with compost if necessary.
Watch out for cabbage caterpillars.
Water and feed celeriac, celery, cucumbers, leeks, marrows, potatoes in barrels; water French and runner beans where necessary.
Earth up and stake Brussels sprouts and other greens in exposed sites.
Blanch trench celery with collars.
Pinch out cucumber and climbing bean tops when they reach the top of their supports.
Start harvesting garlic and shallots.

LATE SUMMER (August)

Sow in seed boxes or modules, to transplant under cover As mid-summer, plus hybrid broccolis (some), calabrese (toward the onset of early autumn), celery (leaf), Chinese cabbage, Chinese broccoli, choy sum, fennel, komatsuna, mibuna and mizuna greens, pak choi, senposai.

Sow *in situ* indoors Summer purslane. CCA: orache, tree spinach.

Sow in open Broccoli raab, spring cabbage (beginning of late summer), Chinese broccoli, Chinese cabbage, Chinese leaf mustard, chrysanthemum greens, corn salad, red Russian kale, land cress, winter lettuce, Japanese bunching and spring onions, Japanese and traditional over-wintering onions, summer, oriental and winter radish, spinach beet, Swiss chard, winter spinach, Texsel greens, turnips (to eat small and for tops). CCA: kales, saladini.

Sow to cover later Beetroot, carrots, endive, winter lettuce, winter purslane, Texsel greens.

Thin Beetroot, carrots, Chinese greens, spinach, turnips, etc.

Plant outside Mini cauliflowers, leeks.

Plant under cover Crops sown mid-to late summer for winter cropping.

Jobs 'Stop' cordon tomatoes, feed if necessary.
    Cut down blight-infected potato haulms.
    Earth up and stake winter greens; watch out for caterpillars.
    Cut away old leaves of squashes and pumpkins to help fruits ripen.
    Water and feed as in mid-summer.
    Harvest Chinese artichokes, garlic, shallots and onions.

EARLY AUTUMN (September)

Sow under cover Broccoli raab, calabrese, mini cauliflowers, Japanese bunching onions, radish.
CCA: chrysanthemum greens, corn salad, cress, endive, Sugar Loaf chicory, several types kale, komatsuna, lettuce, mibuna and mizuna greens, ordinary and oriental mustard, orache, pak choi, oriental saladini, salad rape, salad rocket, saladini, senposai, spinach, Texsel greens, winter purslane.

Sow outside Spring cabbage, endive, kohl rabi, saladini, winter lettuce, and last sowings of ordinary radish, winter spinach, turnips for tops.

Thin Outdoor winter radish, spinach, Swiss chard, turnips for storing.

Plant Spring cabbage, garlic, autumn onion sets, winter lettuce. Under cover: crops sown mid-to late summer for transplanting under cover.

Jobs Ensure greens are earthed up and staked; watch out for caterpillars. Finish harvesting onions.

Cut down tomatoes to ripen off indoors or under cloches.

Put marrows, winter squashes and pumpkins in sun to ripen.

Continue feeding celeriac and leeks.

Cover late sowings of dwarf beans, carrots, endive, lettuce, oriental greens, 'second cropping' potatoes, radish, salad crops, with cloches or low polytunnels.

MID-AUTUMN (October)

Sow under cover Early summer cauliflowers, winter lettuce.
CCA: cress, oriental saladini, salad rape, salad rocket, saladini, Texsel greens.

Sow outside Broad beans, hardy peas.

Plant Spring cabbage, garlic, autumn onion sets, winter lettuce. Under cover: endive, remaining salad and oriental greens from late-summer sowing.

Thin Corn salad, winter lettuce, autumn onion sets, swedes.

Jobs Lift and store carrots, beetroot (cold areas).

Protect Chinese artichokes from frost with fleece, straw or cloches.

Start blanching endive.

Transplant strongest seed-raised rhubarb plants.

Cut down Jerusalem artichokes.

Earth up leeks.

Lift chicory for indoor forcing; cut back and earth up chicory for outdoor forcing.

Lift storage cabbage before heavy frost.

Bring in marrows, pumpkins and winter squashes before frosts.

Clear away pea sticks and bean poles.

Start digging and manuring on heavy soil.

Mulch celeriac and parsnips with straw.

Earth up and protect globe artichoke crowns with leaves/fleece.

Protect red chicories, other salad plants and oriental greens with cloches, low tunnels or straw to improve quality.

LATE AUTUMN AND EARLY WINTER
(November and December)

Sow outside Broad beans, hardy peas, field bean green manure (by early winter).

Plant Garlic, rhubarb (sets, in early winter).

Jobs Digging and manuring on heavy soil.
Force Witloof chicory; blanch endive.
Protect celeriac from frost with bracken.
Move early summer and mini cauliflowers to cold frames.
Occasionally weed crops under cloches and overwintering crops.
Check stored vegetables; remove any rotting ones.
Mark positions of overwintering root crops in case of snow.
Lift rhubarb crowns for forcing indoors.
Remove yellowing leaves from brassicas.
Thin or transplant protected overwintered lettuce 5cm/2in apart in late autumn.
Lift and store late-sown beetroot, carrots, turnips, swedes.

APPENDIX

Many are suitable for intercropping and for catch crops (see pages 159 and 165).

Sprouted seeds
The following are the most commonly sprouted, but there are many others – see *The Organic Salad Garden*:

Alfalfa (lucerne)
Beans (azuki, mung and soya)
Brassicas (all can be sprouted)
Fenugreek
Lentils
Radish

Cut-and-come-again seedlings
See chart opposite.

Maturing under eight weeks
To mature within this time the vegetables must have good growing conditions and be sown in the correct season.

Amaranthus, leaf
Broccoli raab
Chenopodium giganteum 'Magentaspreen'
Chinese cabbage (loose-headed)
Chrysanthemum greens
Flowering rape 'Bouquet'
Komatsuna
Land cress
Pak choi
Radish
Summer purslane
Texsel greens
Turnips (early types and greens)

Maturing under twelve weeks
Asparagus pea
Beans (dwarf French)
Beetroot (to harvest young)
Cabbage (Chinese)

CUT-AND-COME-AGAIN (CCA) SEEDLINGS CHART

Use the chart to plan for a continuous supply of young salad leaves, and to plan intercropping.
For more information on CCA seedling crops, see page 156.

	Germination time	Cuts	Lasts (months)	When to sow
Amaranthus spp. Leaf amaranthus	√	2	2–3	W
Atriplex hortensis Orache	√√	3	3	★
Beta vulgaris Cicla Gp Perpetual spinach	√√	3+	6+	★
Brassica carinata Texsel greens	√√	2	2–3	C
B. juncea Red mustard	√	2	2–3	★
B. napus Salad rape	√	3–4	3–4	★
B. oleracea Acephala Gp Curly kale	√√	2–3	6–8+	★
B. oleracea Acephala Gp Fine-leaved kale ♦	√–√√	3–4	6–8+	★
B. rapa Chinensis Gp Pak choi	√	2–3	2–4	C
— Rosette pak choi	√	2	2–4	C
— var. *nipposinica* Mibuna greens	√√	2	3+	C
— — Mizuna greens	√√	3–4	4+	C
— var. *perviridis* Komatsuna	√–√√	3–4	4+	★
Cichorium endivia Curled endive	√√	2–3	3–4	★
C. intybus Sugar Loaf chicory	√√	2–3	3–4	★
Eruca sativa Salad rocket	√	3–5	2–3	C
Lactuca sativa 'Salad Bowl' and cutting lettuce	√√	2–3	3–4	★
Lepidium sativum Garden cress	√	2–5	1–2	C
Medicago sativa Alfalfa (Lucerne) ■	√	2–4	●12+	★
Montia perfoliata Winter purslane	√–√√	2–3	2–3	C
Plantago coronopus Buck's horn plantain ■	√	2	6–8	★
Portulaca oleracea Summer purslane	√√	2–3	2	W
Raphanus sativus Leaf and seedling radish	√	2	1–2	★
Spinacia oleracea Spinach	√√	3–4	2–5	★
Valerianella locusta Corn salad	√	2–3	3+	C
MIXES: #				
Oriental saladini	√	3–4	2–5	C
Saladini/Mesclun	√√	2–3	3–4	★

KEY

Germination time √ = less than a week;
√√ = 2–3 weeks; √√√ = 3 weeks
This is the average time (under favourable
conditions) before the seedling appears above
ground. Most are then large enough to eat
within 2–3 weeks.
Cuts The average number of cuts from one
sowing. This will vary according to the season.
Most CCA crops run to seed rapidly in hot

weather, and grow more slowly in cold weather,
limiting the number of cuts
Lasts The average period in months during which
the crop can provide tender leaves
When to sow
★ = can be sown throughout the growing season
C = best sown in cool conditions
W = requires warm conditions
# = Performance will depend on the actual seed
mixture

NOTES

♦ *Brassica oleracea* Acephala Gp Fine-leaved kale: e.g. 'Pentland Brig', 'Hungry Gap', 'Red Russian'
■ See *The Organic Salad Garden*
● Alfalfa is perennial, but leaves become coarse unless plants are cut back regularly
Other seedling crops
Brassica campestris Rapifera Gp Turnip. See *B. napus* Salad rape
B. oleracea Acephala Gp Tuscan kale. See Fine-leaved kale, though it can be cut as CCA leaves
for 7–8 months
B. rapa Pekinensis Gp Loose-headed Chinese cabbage. See *B. r.* Chinensis Gp Pak choi
Chenopodium giganteum 'Magentaspreen' Tree spinach. See *Atriplex hortensis* Orache

Calabrese
Carrots (early)
Chinese broccoli
Choy sum
Corn salad
Courgettes
Cucumbers
Endive
Fennel, Florence
Hybrid broccolis
Iceplant
Japanese bunching onions
Kohl rabi
Lettuce (summer)
Mibuna greens
Mizuna greens
Oriental mustard Green-in-the-snow
Turnips

VEGETABLES FOR SUCCESSIONAL SOWING

These can be sown at two-to-three-week intervals throughout the growing season.

Beetroot
Broccoli raab
Carrots
Kohl rabi
Lettuce
Radishes
Spinach
Spring onions
Texsel greens

VEGETABLES IN THE GROUND ALL WINTER

These normally survive temperatures of –5°C/23°F provided they are on reasonably well-drained soil.

Brassicas
Broccoli, purple sprouting
Brussels sprouts
Cabbage (spring, savoy and hardy winter types)
Kale (green, purple, 'Red Russian' and 'Black Tuscan')
Komatsuna
Mizuna greens
Oriental mustards (e.g. Green-in-the-snow, purple)
Pak choi, rosette

Radish (winter and hardy oriental types)
Texsel greens
Turnips (for tops)

Root vegetables
Artichokes, Jerusalem
Kohl rabi
Parsley, Hamburg
Parsnips
Radish (see above)
Salsify
Scorzonera

Miscellaneous
Beans, broad (autumn-sown)
Celeriac (if well mulched)
Celery (leaf types)
Chrysanthemum greens
Leeks
Onions (Welsh, hardy autumn-sown bulb onions and some cvs Japanese
    bunching onions)
Peas (autumn-sown)
Spinach
Swiss chard

Salad crops
Survival outdoors and quality will depend upon the severity of the
winter, on choosing the hardiest and most suitable cultivars and, in some
cases, on crops being grown as CCA rather than mature crops (see page
156). Protection with cloches, fleece, etc. is recommended (see page
107). ★ = the more vulnerable plants.

Chicories (Grumolo, red Treviso and ★Sugar Loaf)
Corn salad
★Endive
Land cress
★Lettuce
★Mibuna greens
Mizuna greens
Onions (as above)
Oriental mustards (hardy cvs above)
★Purslane winter
Radish (hardy oriental types)
Salad rape
Salad rocket
Senposai
Texsel greens

FRESH VEGETABLES FOR THE VEGETABLE GAP

This is roughly late winter to mid-spring in the British Isles. Choose suitable cultivars for this period. ★ = better results if cloched at some stage.

Vegetables in the ground all winter, above, plus:

Broccoli raab
Calabrese (under cover)
★Carrots (early)
Chicory, Witloof (forced)
Good King Henry
★Lettuce (overwintered)
Sorrel
Turnip tops
Turnips

VEGETABLES SUITABLE FOR FREEZING

Some vegetables, such as aubergines, peppers, tomatoes and red cabbage, are best precooked or frozen in mixtures such as ratatouille. Consult current seed catalogues for most suitable varieties for freezing.

Asparagus, aubergines, beans (all types), beetroot (young), broccoli (purple sprouting), Brussels sprouts, cabbage (red, previously cooked), calabrese, carrots (young), cauliflower, kale (curly), peas, peppers, spinach, sweet corn, Texsel greens, tomatoes.

VEGETABLES FOR PARTICULAR SITUATIONS

Tolerant of light shade (provided there is some moisture)

Artichokes, Jerusalem
Chicories (Grumolo, red Italian and Sugar Loaf)
Chinese cabbage
Chinese chives
Chrysanthemum greens
Cresses
Endive (spring-sown)
Parsley (Hamburg and herb)
Land cress
Mizuna greens
Purslane, winter
Spinach
Sorrel
Herbs: angelica, chervil, comfrey, Good King Henry, lovage, mint

Tolerant of light shade in mid-summer
These can be used for undercropping.

Chicories (Sugar Loaf and red)
Corn salad
Cucumbers
Lettuce
Land cress
Pak choi
Parsley, herb
Peas
Radish, winter
Spinach

Tolerant of fairly dry conditions in mid-summer
There must be enough moisture to get the plants established. Initially seedlings will need to be watered regularly, and some further watering may be necessary for the plants to thrive.

Amaranthus, leaf
Chard, Swiss
Chenopodium giganteum 'Magentaspreen'
Chicory, Sugar Loaf
Iceplant
Onions, pickling
Purslane, summer
Purslane, winter
Rhubarb
Spinach, New Zealand
Herbs: Good King Henry, hyssop, rosemary, thyme, savory

Fairly damp (provided not waterlogged)

Artichokes, Chinese
Celeriac
Celery
Chicory, red
Chinese cabbage
Corn salad
Fennel, Florence
Land cress
Leeks
Lettuce, stem
Mizuna greens
Sorrel

VEGETABLES FOR FLOWER BEDS

Choose appropriate varieties – see *Creative Vegetable Gardening*.

Taller vegetables and climbers for the back of the border

Artichokes, globe
Beans, climbing
Cardoon
Chenopodium giganteum 'Magentaspreen'
Chicories (when in flower)
Cucumbers (outdoor varieties)
Marrows and squashes (climbing forms)
Orach, red
Sweet corn

Medium-height, mid-border vegetables

Amaranthus, leaf (red-leaved forms)
Asparagus
Asparagus pea
Beans, dwarf French
Kales (Cavolo nero, Red Russian, green and red curled)
Leeks
Mibuna greens
Ornamental cabbages and kales
Pak choi, flowering
Salsify
Scorzonera
Swiss chard
Tomatoes

Lower-growing vegetables for the front of beds, or as edges

Beetroot
Carrots intersown with annuals
Chrysanthemum greens
Endive, curly
Iceplant (*Mesembryanthemum*)
Lettuce (Salad Bowl types)
Mizuna greens
Pak choi, rosette
Parsley (Hamburg and herb)
Purslane, summer
Purslane, winter
Decorative herbs: chervil, chives, basil, fennel, thymes, marjoram, sage,
    Chinese chives
Edible flowers: Anchusa, *Bellis perennis* daisies, borage, calendula, Chinese
    chives, nasturtiums, pansies, roses, *Tagetes signata,* violas

VEGETABLE GROUPS FOR STRIP CROPPING WITH CLOCHES

(see Protection, Chapter 6)

Group 1 Winter/spring

Hardy vegetables cropping spring onwards; under cloches mid-winter to mid-spring. Some are cloched the previous autumn.

a)   Crops normally cleared from the ground towards late spring, allowing others to be sown or planted:

- spring cabbages (planted mid-autumn; cloched in cold districts only)
- lettuce (sown mid-autumn, mid- or late winter)
- radish (sown early spring)
- carrots (sown mid-winter in mild districts)
- corn salad, land cress, winter purslane (sown previous summer or autumn), hardy chicories, hardy oriental greens (planted late summer/autumn).

b)   Crops which will not be cleared from the ground until early summer or later, though cloches are removed in mid-spring. For example:

- broad beans (sown late autumn or mid-winter)
- beetroot (sown early spring, ready early summer)
- calabrese (sown early to late spring)
- carrots (sown late winter)
- cauliflower (planted mid-autumn)
- peas (sown late winter or spring-sown)
- spinach (sown autumn)
- early potatoes (planted early to late spring).

c)   spring sowings

- CCA salads (see pages 156 and 359)
- fast-growing broccoli raab, young kale greens, radishes, turnips.

d)   to raise seedlings of hardy vegetables for planting out later. For example: Brussels sprouts, cabbage (summer and winter), calabrese, cauliflower (summer and autumn), chicory (Sugar Loaf), lettuce (summer), leeks, onions (bulb and oriental bunching).

Group 2 Late spring crops

Half-hardy vegetables started two to three weeks earlier, by sowing *in situ* under cloches in mid- or late spring or raising indoors and planting under cloches in mid- or late spring. Cloches normally removed later. For example: aubergines, beans (French and runner), cucumbers, marrows/courgettes, New Zealand spinach, sweet corn, tomatoes.

Group 3 Summer crops

Tender crops which can be grown under cloches all through the summer season. For example: aubergines, cucumbers (bush types), peppers, tomatoes (bush types, or cordon types trained horizontally).

Group 4 Autumn crops

a) late-maturing and/or second sowings which benefit from protection:

- ∾ dwarf French and runner beans (sown early summer; will be killed by the first frost if not under cloches – normally cleared by late autumn)
- ∾ broccoli raab, carrots, chicories (red and Sugar Loaf), endive, lettuce, oriental greens (such as Chinese cabbage, pak choi, mizuna, mibuna, komatsuna), peas (early types, late sowing), radish, CCA seedling salads (see page 156), spinach/spinach beet/Swiss chard (all mainly sown late summer, cloched during early autumn/mid-autumn for use in late autumn/early winter)
- ∾ potatoes – early cultivars planted mid-summer, cloched early/mid-autumn (will need extra protection against frost).

b) hardy overwintering:

- ∾ dwarf early peas (sown mid-summer)
- ∾ corn salad, land cress, winter purslane, hardy winter lettuce, oriental greens (rosette pak choi, mizuna, mibuna, komatsuna), spring onions, winter radish, spinach/spinach beet/Swiss chard (mainly sown late summer, cloched during early/mid-autumn for use in late autumn/early spring)
- ∾ spring cabbage (sown mid-/late summer; cloche protection necessary in cold areas)
- ∾ red cabbage seedlings
- ∾ broad beans (dwarf forms, autumn-sown).

MIND THE GAP

This article was originally published in The Kitchen Garden Magazine *in August 2001. It won the 2001 Garden Writers' Guild 'Practical Journalist of the Year' award. It is included here because it covers the subject of the Vegetable Gap in more detail than the main text and may be useful in planning (see Chapter 9).*

Back in May my daughter Kirsten rang me. 'Mum . . .' Then there was that slight pause that comes before asking a favour. 'Mum, do you think you could *post* us a salad?' Well, the answer was yes and we did, but it made me realize that the oft-mentioned Vegetable Gap is not a figment of garden writers' imaginations. If your garden is not yet established and you live in a small country town there is only a very limited choice of fresh vegetables early in the year. Of course there are cabbages and leeks and root crops and rather soulless imported lettuces – but if you yearn for really tasty leafy greens . . . you'll have to go on yearning.

Just which months are covered by the term 'Vegetable Gap' is debatable, and varies from one season to the next. Winter frosts slowly knock back everything but the hardiest crops in the ground – so from the turn of the year onwards things are getting leaner. It falls on those worthy brassicas – Brussels sprouts, winter- and spring-heading cauliflowers, kales and hardy cabbages – to supply the bulk of our fresh vegetables. With luck purple sprouting broccoli starts to come in as the sprouts and savoys end in March or April. We long for the first overwintered broad beans or peas, and the fresh lettuces and salad from the spring sowings – but in the wet conditions most of us experienced earlier this year, there were few spring sowings. May was a very bare month. And I don't doubt that the 'fresh greens' famine extended well into June in some parts of the country.

So I thought it would be a good exercise to analyse what we do, not just to fill that spring gap (in case you're asked to post a salad in May), but to have interesting greens and salad all through the winter. Immediately two facts hit me in the face: how much we depend on our polytunnel, and how long in advance you have to start. Just about now [August/midsummer] in fact.

As regular readers may have gathered, our East Anglian garden is next to a wartime airfield, and when we moved in thirty years ago there was a hideous, rusting Nissen hut in what was to become the kitchen garden. Over the years it was stripped of corrugated iron, covered with increasingly robust film and home-made ventilation panels, and converted into a polytunnel. It is nearly 3.5m/11ft high at the ridge – a lovable, permanently anchored monster! A smaller conventional polytunnel rotates around the plot in its shadow. In summer these tunnels are used for tomatoes, early French beans, cucumbers, basil and so on. In winter they are verdant with salads and leafy greens. They are never heated, and temperatures at night can be as low as outside. Their value lies in their sheltering effect, essentially in keeping off the wind. For it is the combination of low temperature and cold wind that is potentially lethal and invariably damaging for plants, especially salad plants. Who wants to eat wind-toughened salads? A second benefit is that whenever the sun does shine during winter days, temperatures soar. And once the temperature rises above 6°C/43°F, plants start growing again. Indeed on sunny early spring days they grow extraordinarily fast. If you have neither a greenhouse nor a polytunnel, cloches and frames can be used instead for winter crops, though they offer less protection and are more awkward to work.

We have four distinct groups of plants in our polytunnels in winter:

- traditional hardy to semi-hardy European salads
- oriental greens
- cut-and-come-again seedlings
- 'ordinary' vegetables like peas and calabrese, grown indoors for an extra early crop.

The traditional salads are mainly endives and chicory. I'm always impressed with the way endives remain bright green and vigorous looking in winter, unlike lettuce, which struggles with the low light levels and the humid atmosphere. I grow broad-leaved endives like the old 'Cornet de Bordeaux' and the newer 'Golda', and curly-leaved 'frisée' types such as 'Minerva' and 'Frisela'. They are sown at the end of July and in early August, invariably in some kind of module (seed trays divided into individual cells) and planted in the tunnel in August. After the first heads are cut the plants are left to resprout, so providing more cuttings until spring. Then, as temperatures rise, the leaves become too bitter to use raw. All endives have a slightly bitter edge but earlier in the season the curly-leaved forms are easily blanched and made more tender by covering them with a dinner plate for a few days. By the way, bitterness in most salad leaves can be modified by shredding the leaves.

Two other traditional standbys are the red Italian chicory, often called 'radicchio', and Sugar Loaf chicory. Both are raised like endives. Grow modern varieties of red chicory such as 'Indigo', 'Cesare', 'Versuvio' and 'Augusto', which produce dense, deep red to pink heads, rather than the old variegated varieties. The glorious colour of the leaves lifts a salad – and the spirits – in winter. Plants often deteriorate in the early months of the year, with the outer leaves developing moulds. Remove infected leaves gently and you may find crisp pink leaves beneath. The red chicories produce some secondary leaves after the main heads are cut.

The bulkiest source of green salad in winter is undoubtedly Sugar Loaf chicory. Resembling a rather solid cos lettuce, the tight head means the inner leaves are to some extent naturally blanched, making it, though distinctly flavoured and crisp, less sharp than most chicories. It is very vigorous, regrowing rapidly after the initial head is cut, often lasting into late April. Improved modern varieties such as 'Jupiter', though not always easy to come by, are exceptional value.

Red chicories should be sown by mid-July, Sugar Loaf by early August. Marshalls Seeds now supply plants of these, and oriental greens, for planting in August for winter crops – a useful short cut. As far as possible, I plant all winter salads and oriental greens through the soft, dark, permeable mulching film Permealay (available from Agralan). Not only does it keep down weeds, conserve moisture, and keep the plants clean but it keeps the soil in a nice condition.

Our second polytunnel group, oriental greens, have had a special place in our garden since I started experimenting with them many years ago. Familiarity could breed contempt, but every winter I'm struck again by their versatility, their sheer beauty and the gorgeous range of flavours, from the fresh mildness of pak choi to the sweetness of Chinese broccoli to the spiciness of the purple and Green-in-the-snow mustards. While these last two and komatsuna are very hardy and would survive winter outside, they, and all the others, are amazingly productive under cover.

Oriental greens are much faster-growing than Western brassicas, but tend to bolt if sown early in the year. So I make the winter polytunnel sowings, again in modules, between late July and mid-August, planting in August and into early September. When grown under cover these greens are mostly tender enough to use in salads, but I feel their flavours are brought out best by quickly stir-frying them, mixing several types together, with a touch of ginger and garlic. The richness of their combined flavours is beyond description: it makes 'January King' seem awfully mundane.

The natural vigour of oriental greens and their ability to resprout is phenomenal. After the early heads or leaves are cut they continue sprouting until they start to run to seed in spring; in most cases these flowering shoots are edible raw and are very sweet. The exception is the mustards. They are just too hot for comfort by then. Just today (4 June), I picked a shoot from the last of the Chinese broccoli – and it was still chunky, tender and delicious.

Last year's oriental plantings included the mustards mentioned above, green-stemmed and rosette pak choi (its rosetted form is spectacular), the shiny, jagged-leaved mizuna and the narrow-leaved mibuna, loose-headed Chinese cabbage 'Ruffles', and a group grown specifically for their flowering shoots rather like our sprouting broccoli – Chinese broccoli (misleadingly also called Chinese kale), the purple-flowering choy sum or pak choi (there's a lot of doubling up with names) and the flowering rape 'Bouquet'.

Cut-and-come-again (CCA) seedlings are the third group in the winter polytunnel. Sow the seeds and push them gently into the damp soil, then cover them with dry soil, pressing them down finally with the palm of the hand. This dry soil acts as a mulch, preventing the soil moisture from evaporating until the seeds have germinated.

CCA seedlings are the most flexible of crops for these late sowings. As the soil is still warm, they germinate and grow fast. They can be fitted in as soon as something is harvested. Even a 60cm/2ft-long drill can be worth doing. Last year I lifted the last of the basil in November, and, as the soil was still warm, made a sowing of Texsel greens – one of the tastiest of winter brassicas. They were still being picked in mid-April this year.

I tend to make three main CCA sowings.

In the first ten days of September I sow oriental greens, kales and some traditional salads.

The oriental greens that are suitable for CCA seedlings include mibuna, mizuna, ordinary and rosette pak choi, purple and Green-in-the-snow mustard, komatsuna and an honorary 'oriental' (its origins were in Ethiopia), Texsel greens. There are also several seed mixtures, 'oriental saladini' and 'spicy greens' for example, which are largely oriental greens.

The most suitable kales, and I've only realized this recently, are thin-leaved kales like 'Pentland Brig', 'Hungry Gap' and the very pretty 'Red Russian' kale. All these are tender enough to use raw in salads and can be cut right through until May. Equally successful, though slightly coarser, is the decorative, blue, savoy-leaved Tuscan or black kale. Outdoors it grows into a large handsome plant but under cover it produces endless flushes of smallish leaves right through into June.

Among traditional salads are corn salad (again, perfectly hardy, but much lusher under cover), chervil, which will be a rare and welcome green herb in the early months of the year until it runs to seed in April, and Salad Bowl types of lettuce. Spinach is hardly a traditional salad with us Brits – it is much more prized in the US – but an August sowing under cover pays handsome dividends. The young leaves are delicious raw and can be allowed to grow larger for cooking. The variety 'Triathlon' was excellent last year.

In early October, as the last tomatoes and cucumbers are cleared, I'll sow the really fast growing things such as rocket, cress, mustard and salad rape. It might also be worth trying a second sowing of some of the oriental greens.

The final sowing aimed directly at closing the Vegetable Gap is made as early in the year as possible. This year I was trying to produce some 'salading' for a family wedding in early May. The most successful sowings (made in the tunnel on 23 February) were rocket, Red Russian kale, spinach 'Vivat' (eventually providing wonderful 'Gap' leaves for cooking in late May/early June), rosette pak choi (which bolted rapidly after the first cut) and lettuce mixtures. These were augmented by swathes of succulent winter purslane, which, having been sown in previous years in the tunnel, providentially reappears every year in March, April and May.

Needless to say, any of these seedling sowings can be made in containers, flower pots, or even window boxes. They lend themselves to small spaces.

The final use of our polytunnels is for what would be considered 'ordinary vegetables'. With extra protection, they come in that much earlier, and are better quality than they would be if grown outdoors. The star is Swiss chard. Sowings made in July were transplanted into the tunnel on 30 August last year and supplied wonderful pickings in early spring when the outdoor crop had become far too battered and tattered to use. Other early pickings from the polytunnel are spring cabbage, sown at the end of August in modules and in this case not planted until mid-February, calabrese sown at the end of August and planted in early November (ready in the leanest of times in May), mangetout peas sown *in situ* at the end of January and broad beans (which we had failed to sow outdoors in autumn), sown in modules on 12 November, planted under cover in early February, to give the first pickings on 5 June. Last, but not least lettuce: 'Little Gem', 'Wonder of Winter', 'Catalogna' and 'Nevada' were sown at the end of August, planted mainly in November, to give us welcome pickings in April. So one way and another, we've kept the pot boiling.

WHEN TO SOW TO BRIDGE THE 'GAP'

Traditional salads

end July/early August	endives
mid-July	red chicory
early August	Sugar Loaf chicory

Oriental greens

late July to mid-August	oriental greens

Cut-and-come-again

first 10 days of September	* oriental greens, kales, traditional salads
August	* corn salad, chervil, 'Salad Bowl' lettuces, spinach
early October	* quick-growing crops: rocket, cress, mustard, salad rape
late February	* rocket, kale, spinach, rosette pak choi, lettuce

Ordinary vegetables

July	Swiss chard
end August	spring cabbage, calabrese, lettuce
November or January	* mangetout peas
early to mid-November	broad beans

* sown *in situ* under cover

FURTHER READING

Other books by Joy Larkcom

The Organic Salad Garden, Frances Lincoln, revised hardback 2001,
ISBN 0 7112 1716 5

Creative Vegetable Gardening, Mitchell Beazley, revised paperback 2004,
ISBN 1 84000 898 9

Oriental Vegetables: the complete guide for the gardening cook, John Murray,
revised paperback 1997, ISBN 0 7195 5597 3

Salads for Small Gardens, Hamlyn, revised paperback 1995,
ISBN 0 600 58509 3 (available from Eco-logic Books)

The Vegetable Garden Displayed, Royal Horticultural Society, completely
revised edition 1992, ISBN 0 906603 87 0 (out of print)

Grow Your Greens, Channel 4 Television, 1993, ISBN 1 85144 059 3
(out of print)

Other books on vegetables

Aaron, Chester, *The Great Garlic Book,* Ten Speed Press, 1997,
ISBN 0 89815 919 9

Bleasdale, J.K.A., and others, ed., *The Complete Know and Grow Vegetables,*
Oxford University Press, revised edition 1991, ISBN 0 19 286114 X
(the scientific basis of vegetable growing)

Boisset, Caroline, *Pumpkins and Squash,* Mitchell Beazley, 1997,
ISBN 1 85732 954 6

Brennan, Georgeanne, and Glenn, Charlotte, *Peppers Hot and Chile,*
Aris Books, 1988, ISBN 0 201 17019 1

Caplan, Basil, ed., *The Complete Manual of Organic Gardening,* Headline
Book Publishing, 1992, ISBN 0 7472 0515 9, paperback 1994,
ISBN 07472 7830 X (organic techniques including greenhouse
crops)

Goldman, Amy, *Melons: a Passionate Grower's Guide,* Artisan (division
of Workman Publishing Company), 2002, ISBN 1 57965 213 1

Hickmott, Simon, *Growing Unusual Vegetables,* Eco-logic Books, 2003,
ISBN 1 899233 11 3

Maiden, Joe, *Success with Exhibition Vegetables,* 2001 (booklet available
from Marshalls Seeds)

Marshall, Terry, *Organic Tomatoes: the Inside Story,* Harris Associates, 1999

McFadden, Christine, and Michaud, Michael, *Cool Green Leaves and
Red Hot Peppers,* Frances Lincoln, 1998, ISBN 0 7112 1223 6
(inspirational on growing and cooking for flavour)

Miller, Mark, *The Great Chile Book,* Ten Speed Press, 1991,
ISBN 0 89815 428 6

Phillips, Roger, and Rix, Martyn, *Vegetables,* Pan Books, 1993,
    ISBN 0 330 31594 3 (650 vegetables photographed in colour)
Stickland, Sue, *Heritage Vegetables,* Gaia, 1998, ISBN 1 85675033 7
    (beautifully illustrated guide)
Vilmorin-Andrieux, *The Vegetable Garden,* English edition ed. William
    Robinson, published 1885, Ten Speed Press facsimile, 1993
    (out of print; superb classic)
Wilson, Alan, *The Story of the Potato,* Alan Wilson, 1993,
    ISBN 0 9520973 11

Technical
Appelhof, Mary, *Worms Eat My Garbage: how to set up and maintain
    a worm composting system,* Flower Press, 1982, ISBN 0 942256 03 4
Buczacki, Stefan, and Harris, Keith, *Collins Guide to the Pests, Diseases
    and Disorders of Garden Plants,* Collins, 2nd edition 1998,
    ISBN 000220063 5
Coleman, Eliot, *New Organic Grower,* Cassell Publishers, 1989,
    ISBN 0 304 34013 8 (directed towards market gardening)
McVicar, Jekka, *New Book of Herbs,* Dorling Kindersley, 2004,
    ISBN 1 4053 0579 7
NIAB Organic Vegetable Handbook, 2003, National Institute of
    Agricultural Botany (guide to cultivars of most widely grown
    vegetables for organic gardeners)
Rose, Francis, *The Wild Flower Key (British Isles–NW Europe),*
    Frederick Warne, 1981, ISBN 0 7232 2419 6
Salt, Bernard, *Gardening under Plastic,* B.T. Batsford/Chrysalis Books,
    reprinted 2001 (use of fleeces, films, polytunnels)
Stickland, Sue, *Back Garden Seed Saving,* Eco-logic Books, 2001,
    ISBN 1 899233 09 1 (heritage varieties and seed saving)

Other sources of information
Henry Doubleday Research Association (HDRA), Ryton Organic
    Gardens, Coventry CV8 3LG UK. HDRA is a research and
    advisory organic gardening association, and operates the Heritage
    Seed Library. Publications include *Encyclopaedia of Organic Gardening
    2001, Beds – labour saving, space saving, more productive gardening.*
    Booklets in the HDRA Step-by-step series include: *Worm
    Composting, Organic Pest and Disease Management, Comfrey for
    Gardeners, Green Manures for Organic Gardening.* Informative fact
    sheets on many subjects such as soil analysis.
Eco-logic Books, 19 Maple Grove, Bath BA2 3AF, UK (suppliers of
    organic and related gardening books)
Kitchen Garden Magazine, 12 Orchard Lane, Woodnewton,
    Peterborough, PE8 5EE (comprehensive monthly magazine)
Royal Horticultural Society, 80 Vincent Square, London SW1P 2PE.
    Offers members wide range of publications and advisory services

SEED SUPPLIERS

The mail-order companies below are among those that currently offer a wide or unusual range of seed. Addresses change frequently, so check before ordering.

Association Kokopelli (formerly Terre de Semences), Ripple Farm, Crundale, Canterbury, Kent CT4 7EB, UK and 131 Impasse des Palmiers, 30100, Alès, France

D. T. Brown, Bury Road, Newmarket, Suffolk CB8 7PR, UK

Cook's Garden Seeds, PO Box 535, Londonderry, Vermont 05148, USA

De Nieuwe Tuin, Trompwegel 27, 3170 De Klinge, Belgium

Diggers Garden Company, PO Box 300, Dromana, Victoria 3936, Australia

Dobies Seeds, Long Road, Paignton, Devon TQ4 7SX, UK

Ferme de Sainte Marthe, Export Service Harry Kramer, BP 77, F-78490, Montfort L'Amaury, France (for UK see Organic Gardening Catalogue)

★ Future Foods, Luckleigh Cottage, Hockworthy, Wellington, Somerset TA21 0NN, UK

Graines Baumaux, BP 100, 54062, Nancy Cedex, France

Home Garden Seeds, Pymoor, Ely, Cambridgeshire CB6 2ED, UK

Johnny's Seeds, Foss Hill Rd, Albion, RR no. 1, Box 2580, Maine 04910, USA

E. W. King, Monks Farm, Coggeshall Road, Kelvedon, Colchester, Essex CO5 9PG, UK

King's Seeds (NZ) Ltd, PO Box 283 Katikati, Bay of Plenty, New Zealand

Marshalls Seeds, Wisbech, Cambridgeshire PE13 2RF, UK

Mr Fothergill's Seeds, Kentford, Newmarket, Suffolk CB8 7QB, UK

Nichol's Garden Nursery, 1190 N. Pacific Highway, Albany, Oregon 97321, USA

Organic Gardening Catalogue, Riverdene Business Park, Molesey Road, Hersham, Surrey KT12 4RG, UK

★ Real Seeds (previously Vida Verde Seed Collection), 14 Southdown Avenue, Lewes, East Sussex BN7 1EL, UK

★ W. Robinson & Sons, Sunny Bank, Forton, near Preston, Lancashire PR3 0BB, UK

★ Seeds of Italy, 260 West Hendon Broadway, London NW9 6BE, UK

Shepherd's Garden Seeds, 30 Irene St, Torrington, Connecticut
06790-6658, USA
★ Simpson's Seeds, The Walled Garden Nursery, Horningsham,
Warminster, Wiltshire BA12 7NQ, UK
Suffolk Herbs, Pantlings Lane, Coggeshall Road, Kelvedon,
Essex CO5 9PG, UK
Suttons Seeds, Woodview Road, Paignton, Devon TQ4 7NG, UK
Tamar Organics, Gulworthy, Tavistock, Devon PL19 8JE, UK
Thompson & Morgan, London Road, Ipswich, Suffolk IP2 OBA, UK
Tucker's Seeds, Brewery Meadow, Stonepark, Ashburton, Newton
Abbot, Devon TQ13 7DG, UK
Unwins Seeds, Freepost ANG 1015, Wisbech, Cambridgeshire
PE13 2BR, UK
Xotus Delft, Middelweg 1, 2616 LV Delft, The Netherlands

★ = specialist suppliers

ACKNOWLEDGMENTS

Please take as read my thanks to all those whose help I acknowledged in the original edition of *Vegetables from Small Gardens* in 1976, and the reprints in 1986 and 1995.

I have several people to thank for their help in this revised and enlarged edition, retitled *Grow Your Own Vegetables*.

First Colin Randel of Thompson & Morgan seeds, for working through the text and suggesting changes to bring it completely up to date. Second, Mike Day of the National Institute of Agricultural Botany (NIAB) who volunteered, and may have lived to regret his generous offer, to check the varieties. With his help we have been able to suggest the best of modern varieties and, drawing on government-financed trials run by NIAB in conjunction with the Henry Doubleday Research Association (HDRA), include those that have performed well in organic trials. Thank you to James Trounce, also of NIAB, for advice on the potato section.

I would like to renew thanks to those companies and organizations who carry out seed trials, an invaluable source of information for gardeners: Elsoms Seeds, Suttons Seeds, Thompson & Morgan, Tozers Seeds, Unwins Seeds and the Royal Horticultural Society at Wisley Gardens, and the magazine *Gardening Which?* for the trials carried out for their members.

I am constantly pestering seedsmen for information. Special thanks to Richard Massey at Marshalls Seeds, Peter Crisp of Crisp Innovar, at Tozer Seeds Dr Peter Dawson, Steven Winterbottom, Angus Duguid, Nick Forsyth and other members of staff, Andrew Tokely of Thompson & Morgan, Trevor Shaw at Clause Tézier and Colin Simpson at Simpson Seeds. For technical advice, thank you to staff at Horticulture Research International and the HDRA members' advisory service, and to Dr Jonathan Pickering, for earlier advice on soils. A big thank you to gardening friends and colleagues who are always willing to share knowledge and give encouragement – Sue Stickland, Michael and Joy Michaud, Ulrike Paradine, Frances Smith, Sarah Wain, John Walker (especially for last-minute help in checking tables); and to Andrew Blackford and Pamela Deschamps, founders of *The Kitchen Garden Magazine*, which has filled such a need for vegetable lovers.

On the equipment side I would like to thank the following for samples and/or advice. For a wide range of horticultural products for organic gardeners, Alan Frost at Agralan (agralan@cybermail.uk.com) and Peter Groeneveld at P. G. Horticulture (pghorticulture@limited2. freeserve.co.uk); for biological controls, Defenders Ltd (www. defenders.co.uk) and John and Annie Manners at Green Gardener (www.greengardener.co.uk); for seaweed extracts, Maxicrop Ltd (info@maxicrop.com); for root trainers, Ronash Ltd (sales@ rootrainers.co.uk/www.rootrainers.co.uk); for coir Jiffy 7s, Unwins Seeds (www.unwins.mailorder.co.uk); and for the Ibis hoe, Gundaroo Tillers (59 South Hill Park, London NW3 2SS, tel.: 020 7794 3181).

For the new illustrations, a warm thank you to Elizabeth Douglass for getting out her pencils and pens once again: a happy working partnership began over twenty-five years ago with the first edition in 1976. Thank you to Basil Caplan for allowing us to use a drawing from *The Complete Manual of Organic Gardening*, ed. Basil Caplan; to John Murray for permission to use illustrations from *Oriental Vegetables*; to HDRA and the artist John Beaman for permission to use the drawing of the worm compost box; and to Ivy Salt for permission to use as reference the photograph of applying biological control in *Gardening under Plastic*, taken by her late husband, Bernard.

At the publishers Frances Lincoln, a special thank you to the editor, Anne Askwith, who has been wonderfully sane and supportive – besides improving the text enormously; to Michael Brunström for being so patient at the computer end; to Jane Havell, for all her work on the design; to Jo Christian and Anne Fraser, for their warm enthusiasm and encouragement; and to John Nicoll, for enabling this book to remain in print in the twenty-first century.

The last, and biggest, thank you is to my husband Don Pollard. I could never have written any of my books, or had so much fun in gathering information and experimenting, without you.

If I have overlooked anybody, forgive me.

Joy Larkcom
2002

INDEX

Main entries are indexed in **bold**, illustrations in *italics*.

alfalfa 64, 61
Allium ampeloprasum
see garlic, elephant
Allium cepa
Aggregatum Group
see shallots
Allium cepa see
onions, salad/spring
Allium cepa Cepa
Group see onions,
bulb and pickling
Allium fistulosum see
onions, Japanese
bunching and Welsh
Allium porrum see
leeks
Allium sativum see
garlic
Allium tuberosus see
garlic chives
amaranthus, leaf 155,
164, **192–3**
Amaranthus spp. see
amaranthus
Amblyseus cucumeris
145
American cress see
land cress
angelica 156
animal pests 109, 135,
149–50
annual plants
(definition) 15
Aphidoletes aphidomyza
145
aphids 109, 133, 137,
143, 145, 148
Apium graveolens var.
dulce see celery
arches and pergolas
154
artichokes
Chinese 39, **193–4**
globe 75, **194–5**
Jerusalem 20, 38,
155, 156, **195–6**

asparagus 11, 155,
178, 179, **196–8**
asparagus beetle 132
Asparagus officinalis see
asparagus
asparagus pea 198–9
Atriplex hortensis see
orache
aubergines 22, 123,
128, 154, 164, 174,
199–201
Awards of Merit 84,
191

baby leaves see cut-
and-come-again
(CCA)
Bacillus thuringiensis
143, 144, 145
Barbarea verna see
cress, land
bacterial diseases 136
bare-root transplants
93, 94
basil 95, 128, 154, 173
bay 173
bean seed fly 88, 138
bean sprouts 208–10
beans 79, 87, 89, 91,
153, 155, 174
see also broad beans,
dwarf beans, field
beans, French beans,
mung beans, runner
beans
beds 22–5, 176–7
edgings 24–5, *25*
intensive deep beds
69
narrow 22, 23, 36,
164
raised 23–4, *24*, 35,
69, 165
shape 23
width 23
beet, leaf see spinach

beet, spinach see
spinach
beetroot 85, 93, 131,
163, 164, **210–13**
Bellis perennis 137
Beta vulgaris see
beetroot
Beta vulgaris subsp.
cicla see spinach,
perpetual/beet,
Swiss chard
biennial plants 15
bindweed 76
bird pests 135, 150–1
bird and rabbit
manures 43, 53
Black Jack 49, *49*
blackfly 139, 143
blood, dried 48
blood, fish and
bonemeal 47
bobby beans 203
bonemeal 47
Brassica carinata see
Texsel greens
Brassica juncea see
mustards, oriental
Brassica napus
Rapifera Group see
turnips
Brassica napus var.
napus see salad rape
Brassica oleracea
Acephala Group see
kales
Brassica oleracea
Botrytis Group see
cauliflower
Brassica oleracea
Capitata Group see
cabbage
Brassica oleracea
Gemmifera Group
see Brussels sprouts
Brassica oleracea
Gongylodes Group
see kohl rabi

Brassica oleracea Italica
Group see sprouting
broccoli and calabrese
Brassica oleracea var.
algoglabra see Chinese
broccoli
Brassica rapa Chinensis
Group see pak choi
Brassica rapa Pekinensis
Group see Chinese
cabbage
Brassica rapa Perviridis
Group see komatsuna
Brassica rapa Ruvo
Group see broccoli
raab
Brassica rapa var.
nipposinica see mizuna
greens and mibuna
greens
Brassica rapa var. *oleifera*
see rape, hybrid
flowering
Brassica rapa var.
purpurea see purple-
flowered pak choi
Brassica rapa var.
rosularis see pak choi,
rosette
brassicas 88, 93, 120,
132, 136, 137, 139,
160, 163
pests see cabbage
see also individual
vegetables
broad bean blackfly
137
broad beans 38, 65,
84, 119, 139, 163,
179, **201–3**
broccoli
Chinese 213–14
hybrids 214–16
sprouting 160, 179,
216–17
Brussels sprouts 12,
160, 163, **217–19**
buckwheat 64

cabbage mealy aphids 143

cabbage root fly *133*, 137, 141, 147, 148–9, 223

cabbages 9, 12, 78, 131, 158, 163, 164, 179, **219–25**
autumn cabbage 219, 222, 224
ornamental cabbage 220, 268
pests and diseases 223–4
red cabbage 220, 222
spring cabbage 46, 119, 131, 219, 221–2, 224
summer cabbage 219, 222, 224
winter cabbage 220, 222, 224–5
see also Chinese cabbage

calabrese 128, 166, **225–6**

calaloo see amaranthus

calcium 26, 31

Capsicum annuum Grossum Group see peppers, sweet

Capsicum annuum Longum Group see peppers, chilli

Capsicum frutescens see peppers, chilli

carabid beetles 140

carrot fly 49, *132*, 137, 139, 147, 149, 229

carrots 40, 83, 85, 91, 93, 120, 128, 131, 139, 161–2, 163, 165, 173, 178, 179, **226–30**
earlies 227–8
intersowing with annual flowers 162
maincrop 227, 228
pests 229

catch cropping 13, 61, 165–6

caterpillars 132, 143, 145, 147

cats 150

cauliflowers 12, 119, 131, 160, 179, **231–4**
perennial broccoli 233–4

celeriac 95, 160, 178, **234–5**

celery 79, 131, 179, **235–8**

celery fly 49

celery leaf spot 136

chafer grubs 12, 133, 134, 145

chalk soils 37, 42

Chenopodium giganteum
'Magentaspreen' 10, 155, **238–9**

chervil 84, 173

chickweed 75

chicory 81, 118, 119, **239–45**
forcing 242–4, *243, 244*
red 131, 159, 161, 163, 164, **239–41**
Sugar Loaf 156, 157, 159, 161, **241–2**
Witloof 128, 179, **242**

chilli peppers 173, **305, 307**

Chinese artichokes 39, **193–4**

Chinese broccoli 213–14

Chinese cabbage 97, 158, **245–6**

Chinese chives 156, **261**

Chinese kale see Chinese broccoli

Chinese spinach see amaranthus

chitting 309, *310*

chives 156, 173

choy sum 246–7

chrysanthemum greens 159, 163, 164, **248–9**

Cichorium endiva see endive

Cichorium intybus see chicory

clay soil 28, 31, 33, 36

claytonia see purslane, winter

click beetle 133, 134

climate 14
see also frost; wind

climbing vegetables see vertical growing

cloches 109, 111–15, *111, 112, 113*, 117–20, 170
anchoring 114, *114*
glass 109, 111, *111*
home-made 111–12, *112*
intercropping under 119–20
plastic and other materials 111
side shelters 112, 115
size 114
strength and stability 113
strip cropping 119, 120
ventilation 113, *113*, 115
watering 116
year-round uses 117–20

clover 61, 64, 139
Alsike clover 65
crimson clover 61, 65
Essex red clover 65

clubroot 31, 61, 95, 136, *136*, 137, 138, 140, 175, 178

cockchafer beetle 134

Colorado beetle 132, 143

comfrey 47, 48, 56–7
liquid 48, 56–7, *57*
potting compost 101

compost 49–55
aerobic composting 50, 51
anaerobic composting 50, 51
building the heap 53
carbon/nitrogen ratio 53
compost bins 51–2, *52, 55*
ingredients 52
leaf compost 55
moisture 54
readiness 54
siting the compost heap 51
sowing and potting compost 100–1
trench composting 54
turning 54
worm composting 57–60, 101

container gardening 13, 166–73
compost 168–9
container size 167–8
container types 167
drainage 168
feeding 171
growing bags *170*, 171–2, *172*
siting containers 170–1
suitable vegetables 173
vertical polytubes 172–3
watering 169–70
windowsill gardening 173

contaminated soils 38

corn salad 84, 131, 160, 161, 163, 173, **249–50**

couch grass 76

courgettes 74, 79, 131, 156, 173, 176, 178, **250–3**

cranefly 134

cress
garden cress 39, 84, 91, 120, 157, 161, 163, **284–6**
land cress 161, 163, 173, **271–2**

crop covers 128–31
fleeces 13, 129–30, 131, 147–8
managing 130–1
perforated films 129
removing 131

cucumber mosaic virus 136, 256

cucumbers 74, 79, 91, 95, 123, 135, 140, 152, 155, 164, 173, **252–6**

cucumbers (cont.)
  greenhouse/indoor
    252–3, 255
  pests and diseases
    256
  ridge/outdoor 253,
    256
Cucumis sativus see
  cucumber
Cucurbita maxima see
  squash
Cucurbita moschata see
  squash
Cucurbita pepo see
  courgettes, marrows
  and squash
cultivator 18
cut-and-come-again
  (CCA) systems 9, 10,
  156–9
  CCA chart 359
  mature CCA 158–9
  seedlings 13, 85, 91,
    118, 128, 157, 157,
    160–1, 164, 165,
    173, 178, 179
  semi-mature CCA
    159
  sowing 157
cutworms 133, 134,
  140, 143, 145, 146,
  147
Cynara scolymus
  Scolymus Group see
  globe artichoke

damp situations 156
damping-off diseases
  136
dandelions 76
Daucus carota see
  carrots
decorative qualities
  of plants 11
derris 143
devil's coach horse
  beetle 140
dibber 18
digging 66–9
  double digging 67–8
  forking 66–7, 68
  no-digging system
    69–70
  single digging 67,
    67, 68

tips 68
  winter ridging 36, 69
diseased plant
  material 137–8
  diseases 136–7
  see also pests and
    diseases
dock 76, 77
dolomite 32
double-cropping 164,
  221
downy mildew 135,
  137, 140
drainage 27, 28, 33–5
  in containers 168
  improving 34–5, 37,
    40
  poor drainage 33–4
  trench drains 34–5,
    34
dry situations 156
dwarf beans 40, 118,
  120, 163, 173
dwarf cultivars 164

earthworms see
  worms
edible flowers 156
eelworm 133, 175,
  178, 311
Encarsia formosa 145
endives 9, 79, 81, 118,
  119, 131, 157, 159,
  173, 257–9
  blanching 258–9
  broad-leaved/
    Batavian 257, 259
  curled 257, 259
Eruca sativa see rocket
Eruca versicaria see
  rocket

F1 hybrids 83–4
Fagopyrum esculentum
  see buckwheat
farmyard manure 43
fat hen 75
fava beans 65
fennel 140
fenugreek 61, 65
  Florence fennel
    259–60
fertilizers 139
  application 46–7
  artificial 40, 41

foliar feeding 46, 47,
  63
  organic 41–2, 46–9
  top dressings 46, 171
  see also manures
field beans 61, 62, 65
flageolets see French
  beans
flea beetles 132, 137,
  138–9, 143, 147
fleece 13, 129–30,
  131, 147–8
Foeniculum vulgare var.
  dulce see fennel,
  Florence
forcing vegetables 179
forking 66–7, 68
forks 16, 17
frames 121–3, 121
freezing vegetables
  174
French beans 83, 118,
  120, 131, 154, 163,
  164, 203–5
frost
  action on soil 36, 68
  frost pockets 19
  protection from 108
  resistance 159
fungal diseases 135–6,
  138
fungicides 141

galls 136
gap filling 166
garden cress 284
garden hygiene 137–8
garden lines 18
garlic 118, 128, 139,
  175, 261–3
  elephant garlic 262
garlic chives 156, 263
germination 79, 88,
  95, 101–2
  post-germination
    treatment 104
globe artichokes 75,
  194–5
grass cuttings 44, 71
green manures 36, 41,
  60–2, 63, 64, 91
greenfly 143
greenhouse pests 135,
  144, 145
greenhouses 123–4

grey mould 135
ground cover,
  vegetables as 155
ground elder 76, 77
groundsel 75, 137
growing bags 153,
  170, 171–2, 172
growing season 107
growing under cover
  see protected
  cropping

half-hardy plants
  (definition) 15
Hamburg parsley 160,
  263
hard pan 33–4
hardening off 96, 106
hardiness 191
hardy plants
  (definition) 15
haricot beans see
  French beans
hay 44
heeling in 94–5
Helianthus tuberosus
  see Jerusalem
  artichoke
herbs 13, 173, 178
heritage varieties 9
Heterohabditis megidis
  145
hoes 16, 17, 17, 18
hoof and horn 47
hoops 154–5
hoverfly 140
humus 27, 29, 49

iceplant 128, 263–4
insecticides 141
intercropping 13,
  159–64, 161
  around individual
    plants 160–1
  between rows 162–3
  climbing plants 161
  double-cropping
    164, 221
  mixed sowings
    161–2
  under cloches
    119–20
  undercropping 160,
    161, 163–4
  within rows 160

interplanting 139
irrigation systems 80
Italian cress see rocket

Japanese knotweed 76
Jerusalem artichokes
20, 38, 155, 156,
195–6
Jiffy 7s *98*, 99

kales 178, **264–8**
black Tuscan 267
broad-leaved 266–7
curly 159, 265–6
ornamental 11, 268
red Russian 267
kidney beans see
French beans
kohl rabi 163, 178,
268–9
komatsuna 119,
270–1

lacewings 140
Lactuca sativa see
lettuce
ladybirds 140
lamb's lettuce see
corn salad
land cress 161, 163,
173, **271–2**
lawns
digging up 39
grass cuttings 44, 71
leaf miners 147
leaf mould 55
leatherjackets 12, 133,
134, 140, 145, 146
leek rust 136
leeks 12, 81, 85, 88,
120, 162, 163, 173,
178, 179, **272–5**
Lepidium sativum see
cress, garden
lettuce mosaic virus
136, 140
lettuce root aphid
133, 140
lettuce 13, 40, 78, 79,
81, 86, 88, 93, 95,
118, 119, 120, 131,
135, 160, 163, 164,
165, 170, 173, 176,
11, 159, 179, **275–81**
hearting 275–6,
280–1

'leaf lettuce' system
279
loose-leaved 276,
281
pest-resistant
varieties 140
pests and diseases
135, 280
stem lettuce 279
liming 32–3, 39, 40
loam soils 28, 35
long-season
vegetables 179
Lotus purpureus see
asparagus pea
lovage 156
lucerne see alfalfa
lupin, bitter blue 61, 64
Lupinus angustifolius see
lupin
Lycopersicon esculentum
see tomato

mache see corn salad
magnesium 26, 31
mangetout peas
300–1, 304
manures 40–6
bulky organic
manures 41, 42–6,
63
comfrey manure/tea
46, 56–7, *57*
digging in 45
green manures 36,
41, 60–62, 63, 64–5,
91
mulching with 45–6
nettle manure 57
see also compost;
fertilizers
marestail 76
marjoram 173
marrows 91, 152, 155,
163, 164, **281–2**
Medicago lupulina see
trefoil
Medicago sativa see
alfalfa
*Mesembryanthemum
crystallinum* see
iceplant
mibuna greens 159,
164, **283**
mice 149

millipedes 134, 140
mint 173
mizuna greens 119,
120, 157, 159, 164,
283–4
modules 97–9, *98*,
103, *103*
moles 149
Montia perfoliata see
purslane, winter
mosaic virus 136,
140, 256
mountain spinach see
orache
mulching 36, 63, 69,
70–4, 87
benefits 36, 70–1
films 71, 72–4, *73*,
75
inorganic mulches
70, 72–3
mats 76
organic mulches
45–6, 70, 71, 76
timing 74
for weed control 38,
39, 75–6, 77
mung beans 208–10
mushroom compost,
spent 43–4, 76
mustards 39, 61, 64,
91, 163, 164, 166,
284–8
large-leaved 287–8
oriental 286–7

nasturtiums 154, 156
neglected gardens
38–9, 77
nematodes 12, 133,
145, 175
nettles 76
manure 57
new gardens 39, 40
nitrogen 26, 27, 30,
42, 43, 45, 47, 60, 61,
175
nutrients, plant 26–7,
31, 40, 41

onion fly 88, 138,
139, 147
onion hoe 17, *18*
onion rots 136, 175

onions 14, 46, 78, 81,
83, 95, 118, 119, 120,
128, 139, 175, 179,
288–94
bulb onions 288–92
harvesting and
storage 291–2
Japanese bunching
onion 293–4
onion sets 290
pests and diseases
136, 175, 291
pickling onions 292
salad/spring 40, 120,
162, 163, 173, 178,
292–3
shallots 163, **324–6**
Welsh onion 293
orache 294
red orache 155
organic gardening
11–12, 41, 140
organic matter 30,
35–6, 38, 40, 41,
43–6, 63, 71, 78
oriental greens 9, 10,
12, 95, 118, 119, 128,
131, 139, 157, 159,
166, 179
oriental mustards
286–7
oriental saladini *162*,
295–6

pak choi 120, 157,
159, 160, 162, 163,
296–8
rosette pak choi **298**
parasitic wasps 145
parsley 83, 131, 160,
162, 164, 173
parsnips 14, 81, 85,
90, 93, 140, 160, 162,
179, **298–300**
Pastinaca sativa see
parsnips
paths 22, 25, 165
pea moth 147, 303
pea weevil 49, 132,
303
peas 79, 87, 89, 91,
118, 119, 120, 152,
163, 164, 170, 174,
179, **300–5**
asparagus pea 198–9

peas (cont.)
mangetout 300–1, 304
pests and diseases 303
shelling peas 300
support 303, *304*
peat soils 31, 37, 42
peat substitutes 71
peppers
chilli 173, **305, 307**
sweet 22, 95, 118, 123, 128, 129, 131, 139, 154, 164, 173, 174, 178, **305–7**
perennial plants (definition) 15
perilla 128
pesticides 140, 141–2, 143
pests and diseases 12, 31, 49, 108–9, 132–51, 178
alternative control methods 145–51
animal pests 109, 135, 149–50
beneficial predators 140
biological control 12, 142, 144–5
chemical controls 141–2
diseases 135–6
insect pests 132–3, 134, 147–8
plant disorders 136
prevention 137–41, 175
resistant varieties 139–40
soil pests 133, 135, 146
soil sickness 123, 151, 175, 341
see also individual vegetables (main page references)
Petroselinum crispum var. *tuberosum* see Hamburg parsley
pH 30–2, 40, 137
analysis 32, 39
correcting 32, 42
Phacelia tanacetifolia 61, 62, 64, 140, 166

Phaseolus aureus see bean sprouts
Phaseolus coccineus see runner beans
Phaesolus vulgaris see French beans
Phasmarhabditis hermaphrodita 145
phosphate 31
phosphorus 26, 42, 47, 48
Phytoseiulus persimilis 145
pickling onions 292
Pisum sativum see peas
planning 174–83
for continuity 179
drawing up the plan 180
family preferences 174
Feed the Family Plan 180, 182
Gourmet Plan 180, 183
grouping for convenience 178
Planning Information chart 180
priorities 174
rotation 175–8
value for space rating (VSR) 181
the Vegetable Gap 179
plug plants 97
pollen beetles 143, 147
pollution 41
polythene film 110–11
perforated 129
polytunnels 13, 115–17, *116*, 124–8, *124, 126, 127*
pond mud 44
Portulaca oleracea see purslane, summer
pot marigolds 140
potagers 11, 23
potash 26, 42, 46, 47, 48, 49
potassium 31
potato blight 139, 178, 312

potato scab 31, 137, 312
potatoes 38, 46, 86, 131, 139, 173, 175, 179, 180, **307–13**
in barrels or tubs 311
chitting 309, *310*
double-cropping 164
earlies 308, 312
maincrop 308, 313
pests and diseases 311–12
potting on 96, 105–6
powdery mildew 135, 143
pricking out 96, 104–5, *105*
propagators 101–2, *102*
protected cropping 107–31, 165
benefits 107–9
cloches 111–15, *111, 112, 113,* 117–20, 170
crop covers 128–31
garden frames 121–3, *121*
greenhouses 123–4
materials 109–11
polytunnels 13, 115–17, *116,* 124–8, *124, 126, 127*
pumpkins see squash
purple-flowered pak choi **287**
purple sprouting broccoli 160, 179, **216–17**
purslane 159, 173
summer 128, **314–15**
winter 119, 163, **315**
pyrethrum 143

rabbits 150
radicchio (red chicory) 131, 159, 161, 163, 164, **239–41**
radish 13, 40, 78, 84, 85, 89–90, 120, 130, 131, 139, 160, 162, 164, 165, 173, 179, **316–18**

Asian radish 316, 317
fodder radish 61, 62, 64
seedlings 318, 359
standard radish 316–17
winter radish 316, 318
rakes 17, *17*
rape
hybrid flowering 247
salad rape 39, 120, 157, **284–6**
rape seed oil 143
Raphanus sativus see radish
red cabbage 220, 222
red orache 155
red spider mite 109, 135, 143, 145
Rheum × hybridum see rhubarb
rhubarb 156, 178, 179, **318–20**
forcing 319–20
rhubarb spray 142
rock phosphate 48
rocket 39, 84, 91, 120, 157, 159, 170, **320–1**
root flies 132
root trainers 99, *99*
rosemary 154, 173
rotation 138, 175–8
bed system 176–7
groups 176
pest and disease control 175
in small gardens 177, 178
soil fertility 175
time scale 177
weed control 175
runner beans 84, 120, 154, 163, **205–8**
supports 206, *207*
rye, grazing 61, 62, 65

salad rape 39, 120, 157, **284–6**
salad rocket see rocket
salad/spring onions 40, 120, 162, 163, 173, 178, **292–3**
saladini 162, *162*, **321–2**
salsify 81, 160, **322–3**

sandy soil 28, 32, 36, 42
savory 173
scarecrows 151
scorzonera 81, 160, **323–4**
Scorzonera hispanica see scorzonera
seakale beet see Swiss chard
season and month conversion chart 15
seaweed 42, 44, 46
calcified seaweed 32, 37
extracts 48
meal 47–8
seed 81–105
buying 191
chitted 83
deterioration 81
dressed and treated 83
Fl hybrid seed 83–4
genetically modified 84
large 103
naked 82
organic 84
pelleted 82
pills and split pellets 82
primed 83
quality 81
saving 84–5
storage 82
tapes and sheets 83
viability 81–2
see also sowing seed; sowing under cover
seed drills 88–90, *89, 90*
seed raising kits 100
seed trays 97, *98*
seedbeds 85, 86–8, 138
preparation 87
siting 86
soil temperature 88
stale seedbed 88, 138
tilth 86–7
seedlings
compost 100–1
germination 79, 88, 95, 101–2

hardening off 96, 106
post-germination treatment 104
potting on 96, 105–6
pricking out 96, 104–5, *105*
thinning 92–3, *92*
senposai hybrids 324
sewage sludge and municipal waste 44
shaded areas 155–6, 170
shallots 163, **324–6**
shelter 20–2
shepherd's purse 137
silver beet see spinach
Sinapsis alba see mustard
site 19–25
bed system 22–5
paths 25
shelter 20–2
see also drainage; soil fertility
slugs and snails 49, 133, 137, 145–6, 175
traps 145–6
snow peas see peas, mangetout 300–301
soap sprays 143, 144
soil acidity and alkalinity 30–3, 40
see also pH
soil, alkaline 31, 33
soil blocks 99–100
soil conditioners 36–7
soil erosion 19
soil fertility 11, 22, 26–7, 35–7, 137, 175
improving and maintaining 35–7, 40, 63
pockets of fertility 40
see also compost; fertilizers; manures
soil pests 133, 135, 146
soil sickness 123, 151, 175, 341
soil structure 27–30
humus 27, 29, 49
topsoil and subsoil 29, 33, 34, 39

soil temperature 88, 107
soil types 28
assessing 29
chalk soils 37, 42
clay soil 28, 31, 33, 36
loams 28, 35
peat soils 31, 37, 42
sandy soil 28, 32, 36, 42
silts 28
soil-testing kits 32, 42
Solanum melongena see aubergine
Solanum tuberosum see potatoes
soot 48–9
sowing seed 85–92, 138–9
in adverse conditions 91–2
broadcasting 91, *91*
cut-and-come-again (CCA) crops 157
indoor sowing 85, 95–106
large seeds 91
in narrow drills 88–90, *89*
seedbeds 85, 86–8
in situ 85
sowing evenly 89, *89*
station sowing 89, *89*
successional sowing 165
thinning seedlings 92–3, *92*
transplanting 79, 93–4, *94*
in wide drills 90, *90*
sowing under cover 85, 95–106, 138
brushing 106, *106*
compost 100–101
equipment 97–101, *98, 99*
hardening off 96, 106
large seeds 103
modules 97–8, *98, 103, 103*
multisowing 104
post-germination treatment 104

potting on 96, 105–6
pricking out 96, 104–5, *105*
propagators 101–2, *102*
in standard containers 102–3, *103*
space saving 152–73
bush forms 164
catch cropping 13, 61, 165–6
container gardening 166–73
cut-and-come-again (CCA) systems 156–9
difficult situations 155–6
double-cropping 164, 221
dwarf cultivars 164
gap filling 166
intercropping 159–64, *161*
narrow beds 164
paths 165
planting in flower beds 156
protected cropping 107–31, 165
raised beds and mounds 23–4, *24*, 55, 69, 165
seed sprouting 166
successional sowing 165
undercropping 160, *161*, 163–4
vertical growing 152–5
spacing plants 75, 94, 139
spades 16, *17*
spinach 79, 119, 131, 157, 161, 163, 170, 176, 179, **326–30**
leaf beet 326
New Zealand spinach 39, **330**
perpetual spinach/spinach beet 119, 326, 327–8

Spinacia oleracea see spinach

Swiss chard 39, 119, 156, 176, **328–30**

spiral stakes 154

spring/salad onions 40, 120, 162, 163, 173, 178, **292–3**

sprouting seeds 166, 179

see also bean sprouts

squash 75, 91, 153, 164, 175, **330–2**

pumpkins 55, 153, 155, 163, 175, **331–2**

winter squash 330–2

Stachys affinis see Chinese artichoke

Steinernema feltiae 145

stem rot 135–6

stir-fry and braising mixes 162, 295–6

stone mulches 72

storage 139, 175, 179

storage rots 136

straw 44

strip cropping 119, 120

subsoil 29

successional sowing 165

sugar peas see peas, mangetout

sulphur 26, 143

summer purslane 128, **314–15**

sunflowers 20, 155

swede 140, **333–4**

sweet corn 20, 83, 91, 120, 155, 163, 164, 166, 176, 178, 179, **334–7**

popcorn 337

Swiss chard 39, 119, 156, 163, 173, 176, **328–30**

tares, winter 61, 65

tender plants (definition) 15

Texsel greens 157, 159, **337–9**

thrips 109, 143, 145, 147

thyme 140, 173

tilth 86–7

tomato blight 108

tomatoes 13, 22, 46, 74, 79, 81, 95, 118, 120, 123, 128, 129, 131, 135, 136, 139, 154, 164, 166, 171, 178, **339–47**

in containers 346

cultivation 341–7

flavour 341

growth habit 340

main types 339

pests and diseases 108, 344, 346

tools and equipment 16–18, *17*

topsoil 29, 33, 39

improving 34

trace elements 26–7, 42

deficiencies 42, 47

Tragopogon porrifolius see salsify

transplanting 79, 93–4, *94*

trefoil 64

trench composting 55

trench drains 34–5, *34*

Trifolium hybridum see clover, Alsike

Trifolium incarnatum see clover, crimson

Trifolium pratense see clover, Essex red

Trigonella foenum-graecum see fenugreek

turnip fly 143

turnip moth 134

turnips 13, 39, 85, 91, 120, 139, 162, 163, **347–9**

undercropping 160, *161*, 163–4

value for space rating (VSR) 181

varieties/cultivars 191

vertical growing 152–5

fencing 152, *153*

intercropping 161

low hedges 155

screens 155

structures 154–5

walls 152–4, *153*

vertical polytubes 172–3

Valerianella locusta see corn salad

vetch see tares

Vicia faba see broad beans, field beans

Vicia sativa see tares

vine weevil 95

virus diseases 136

walled gardens 21–2

water tanks 138

watering 77–80, 139

cloches 115

containers 169–70

critical times 79–80, 139

equipment 80

general advice 78–9

moisture-absorbing wicks 170, *170*

overwatering 78

underwatering 79

water conservation 78

watering cans 18

weeds 38, 40, 74–7

annual weeds 75–6

controlling 22, 75–7, 137, 175

on neglected sites 77

perennial weeds 76–7

weed-supressing mulches 38, 39, 75–6, 77

weevils 143

Welsh onion 293

whitefly 109, 135, 139, 145, 147

wigwams and tepees 154

wind 108

funnelling 21

shelter from 20–1

windbreaks 20–1, *21*, *112*

windowsill gardening 173

winter purslane 119, 163, **315**

winter ridging 36, 69

wireworm 133, 134, 175

wood ash 49

worms 30, 31, 45, 59, 171

casts 30, 60

compost 57–60, 101

wormeries 58–9, *58*

Xanthophthalmum coronarium see chrysanthemum greens

Zea mays see sweet corn